Guide to Graphics Software Tools

Springer
New York
Berlin
Heidelberg
Hong Kong
London
Milan
Paris
Tokyo

Jim X. Chen

Guide to
Graphics Software Tools

With 49 Illustrations

INCLUDES
CD-ROM

 Springer

Jim X. Chen
Department of Computer Science
George Mason University
Fairfax, VA 22030
jchen@cs.gmu.edu

Library of Congress Cataloging-in-Publication Data
Chen, Jim X.
    Guide to graphics software tools / Jim X. Chen.
        p. cm.
    Includes bibliographical references and index.
    ISBN 0-387-95049-4 (alk. paper)
        1. Computer graphics.   2. Computer software.   I. Title.
    T385 .C473 2002
    006.6′6—dc21   2002070738

ISBN 0-387-95049-4   Printed on acid-free paper.

Printed in the United States of America.

9 8 7 6 5 4 3 2 1   SPIN 10768692

Typesetting: Pages created by the author using a Springer TeX macro package.

www.springer-ny.com

Springer-Verlag   New York Berlin Heidelberg
A member of BertelsmannSpringer Science+Business Media GmbH

Preface

Many scientists in different disciplines realize the power of graphics, but are also bewildered by the complex implementations of a graphics system and numerous graphics tools. More often than not, they choose the wrong software tools and end up with unsatisfactory results. Hopefully, if we know how a graphics system works and what basic functions many graphics tools provide, we can understand and employ some graphics tools without spending much precious time on learning all the details that may not be applicable, and we can become graphics experts through such a shortcut.

Overview

This book aims to be a shortcut to graphics theory, programming, tools, and applications. It covers all graphics basics and several advanced topics without including some implementation details that are not necessary in graphics applications. It categorizes current graphics tools according to their applications and provides many weblinks to important resources on the Internet. The purpose is to provide an exhaustive list of graphics tools with their major applications and functions. The reference list may contain some inaccuracies, since new tools are constantly emerging and old tools become obsolete. Through explaining and categorizing these graphics tools and their primary applications, we hope to provide learners and researchers with different means and application areas in computer graphics, and help them understand and use visualization, modeling, animation, simulation, virtual reality, and many online resources.

Organization and Features

The book is divided into two independent parts. Part I concisely introduces graphics theory and programming. It serves as a basis for better understanding the components in Part II of the book. Part II categorizes popular 3D graphics tools and explains their applications and functions. We have compiled a list of 266 different 3D graphics tools.

In Part I, both graphics theory and OpenGL programming are covered succinctly in 90 pages. A top-down approach is used to lead the audience into programming and applications up front. The theory provides a high-level understanding of all basic graphics principles without some detailed low-level implementations. The emphasis is on understanding graphics and using OpenGL instead of implementing a graphics system like OpenGL. The contents of the book are integrated with the sample programs, which are specifically designed for learning and accompanying this book. Chapter 1 introduces OpenGL and basic graphics concepts including object, model, image, framebuffer, scan-conversion, clipping, and anti-aliasing. Chapter 2 discusses transformation theory, viewing theory, and OpenGL programming in detail. 3D models, hidden-surface removal, and collision detection are also covered. Chapter 3 overviews color in hardware, eye characteristics, gamma correction, interpolation, OpenGL lighting, and surface shading models. The emphasis is on OpenGL lighting. Chapter 4 surveys OpenGL blending, image rendering, and texture mapping. Chapter 5 wraps up basic computer graphics principles and programming with some advanced concepts and methods for advanced courses.

In Part II, 266 different graphics tools are listed in the Appendix with Chapters 6 to 12 introducing the basic concepts and categories of the tools. Low-level graphics libraries, visualization, modeling and rendering, animation and simulation, virtual reality, Web3D tools and networked environments, and finally 3D file format converters are covered in respective chapters. Chapter 12 contains an extensive survey of different 3D graphics file formats. For each tool listed in the Appendix, we include information on its platforms, prices, vendor or supplier, applications, examples, functions, and Web resources. The list of tools is a reference for scientific researchers as well as advanced computer graphics learners and programmers. The tools are indexed according to their alphabetic order in the Table of Contents and their application categories in the Appendix. The tools are interactively available on the CD provided with the text.

CD-ROM and Web Resources

All the graphics tools, OpenGL sample programs (their sources and executables), and figures in the book are provided on the CD featuring convenient access to extra information and online resources. Again, the tools are indexed both according to their alphabetic order and their application categories. More graphical samples, examples, web resources, and companies associated with the tools are available in the Weblinks on the CD.

The following Web address contains all the updates and additional information, including setting up the OpenGL programming environment, sample program sources, and accompanying Microsoft PowerPoint course notes for learners and instructors as well:

> http://www.cs.gmu.edu/~jchen/graphics/

Audience

The book is intended for a very wide range of readers, including scientists in different disciplines, undergraduates in Computer Science, and Ph.D. students and advanced researchers who are interested in learning and using computer graphics.

Chapters 1 through 4 in Part I of are suitable for a one-semester graphics course or self-learning. These chapters should be covered in order. Prerequisites for this part are good C programming skills and basic knowledge of linear algebra and trigonometry. Chapters 5 to 12 are independent introductions suitable for additional advanced graphics courses. They can be studied together with the individual graphics tools provided in the Appendix.

Part II of the book, especially the list of tools in the Appendix, is mainly a reference or informational toolkit for computational engineers, computer programmers, and graphics researchers. No prerequisite knowledge is needed for this part.

Acknowledgments

Mr. Wayne Yuhasz of Springer Verlag conceived and initiated the idea of this book. Emily Xu helped organize the software reviews and contact the vendors for corrections and permission to use online materials. Some of my former students in CS 451, CS 652, CS 752, and INFT 852 at George Mason University contributed to the graphics software reviews.

Special thanks to the following friends who spent extra time and effort reviewing this book, they are (in alphabetical order): Jayfus Doswell, Trent Duewer, Randy Latimer, Matt Parker, Duncan MacPherson, Shuangbao Wang, Xusheng Wang, and Yonggao Yang. Thanks to my wife Susan and my kids Mike, Jack, and Iris. Their love, patience, and understanding have made this book possible.

I acknowledge the anonymous reviewers and the whole production team at Springer Verlag. Their precious comments, editings, and help have significantly improved the quality and value of the book.

Jim Xiong Chen
August 2002

Contents

Part I: A Shortcut to Computer Graphics Principles

Chapter 1   *Objects and Models*

Part II: Computer Graphics Software Tools

Chapter 6   *Low-Level Graphics Libraries*

Chapter 7   *Visualization*

Chapter 8   *Modeling and Rendering*

Chapter 9   *Animation and Simulation*

Chapter 10   *Virtual Reality*

Chapter 11   *Web3D Tools and Networked Environments*

Chapter 12   *3D File Formats*

Appendix: Graphics Software Tools

2,3

A

1
Objects and Models

Chapter Objectives:

- Introduce basic graphics concepts — object, model, image, graphics library, frame buffer, scan-conversion, clipping, and anti-aliasing

- Set up an OpenGL programming environment

- Understand simple OpenGL programs

1.1 Graphics Models and Libraries

A graphics *display* is a drawing area comprised of an array of fine points called pixels. At the heart of a graphics system there is a magic pen, which can move at lightning speed to a specific pixel and draw the pixel with a specific color — a red, green, and blue (RGB) vector value. This pen can be controlled directly by hand through an input device (mouse or keyboard) like a simple paintbrush. In this case, we can draw whatever we imagine, but it takes a real artist to come up with a good painting. Computer graphics, however, is about using this pen automatically through programming.

A real or imaginary *object* is represented in a computer as a model, and is displayed as an image. A *model* is an abstract description of the object's shape (vertices) and attributes (colors), which can be used to find all the points on the object corresponding to the pixels in the drawing area. Given a model, the application program will control the pen through a graphics library to generate the corresponding image. An *image* is simply a 2D array of pixels.

A *graphics library* provides a set of graphics commands or functions. These commands can be bound in *C*, *Java*, or other programming languages on different platforms. Graphics commands can specify primitive 2D and 3D geometric models to be digitized and displayed. Here *primitive* means that only certain simple shapes (such as points, lines, and polygons) can be accepted by a graphics library. To draw a complex shape, we need an application program to dissect it into pieces of simple shapes (primitives). We have the magic pen that draws a pixel. If we can draw a pixel, we can draw a line, a polygon, a curve, a block, a building, an airplane, and so forth. A general application program can be included into a graphics library as a command to draw a complex shape. Since our pen is magically fast, we can draw a complex object, clear the drawing area, draw the object at a slightly different location, and repeat the above processes — the object is now *animated*.

OpenGL is a graphics library, which we will integrate with the *C programming language* to introduce graphics theory, programming, and applications.

1.2 OpenGL Programming

OpenGL is the most widely used graphics library (GL) or application programming interface (API), which is supported across all popular desktop and workstation platforms, ensuring wide application deployment. First, let's spend some time to set up our working environment, compile Example 1.1.point.c, and run the program. The following file contains links to all the example programs in this book, and detailed information for setting up working environments on different platforms:

> **http://www.cs.gmu.edu/~jchen/graphics/**

/* Example 1.1.point.c: draw randomly generated points */

```
#include <stdlib.h>
#include <GL/glut.h>

#define Height 400
#define Width 400


void display(void)
{
    int x, y;

    //a. generate a random point
    x = rand() % Width;
    y = rand() % Height;
```

```
    //b. specify a drawing color: red
    glColor3f(1, 0, 0);

    //c. specify to draw a point
    glBegin(GL_POINTS);
        glVertex2i (x,y);
    glEnd();

    //d. start drawing
    glFlush();
}


static void reshape(int w, int h)
{
    //e. specify the window's coordinates
    glMatrixMode (GL_PROJECTION);
    glLoadIdentity ();
    glOrtho(0, Width, 0, Height, -1.0, 1.0);
}


int main(int argc, char **argv)
{
    //f. initialize a drawing area
    glutInit(&argc, argv);
    glutInitDisplayMode(GLUT_SINGLE);
    glutInitWindowSize(Width, Height);
    glutCreateWindow("Example 1.1.point.c");

    //g. specify event callback functions
    glutReshapeFunc(reshape);
    glutDisplayFunc(display);
    glutIdleFunc(display);
    glutMainLoop();
}
```

1.2.1 Understanding Example 1.1

Example 1.1 is complex to us at this point of time. We only need to understand the following:

1. The OpenGL Utility Toolkit (GLUT) helps set up a drawing area and handle user interactions for OpenGL. Since it is intended to be system independent, our program can be compiled and run on a PC, SGI workstation, or other platforms. All GLUT commands have the prefix "glut":

```
//f. initialize a drawing area
glutInit(&argc, argv);
glutInitDisplayMode(GLUT_SINGLE);
glutInitWindowSize(Width, Height);
glutCreateWindow("Example 1.1.point.c");
```

The above functions set up a single drawing area of $Width \times Height$ pixels. A corresponding window titled *Example 1.1.point.c* will appear after *glutMainLoop()* is called.

2. An *event* is often a user input (or a system state change), which is queued with other earlier events. GLUT will check out each event from the queue and take actions until the queue is empty. Our program is event-driven: GLUT waits for an event to appear in the event queue and then calls the appropriate function to handle the event. We can set up the event handling functions (namely *callback* functions) through GLUT so that when GLUT detects a specific event, it can call its corresponding callback function.

```
//g. event callback functions
glutReshapeFunc(reshape);
glutDisplayFunc(display);
glutIdleFunc(display);
glutMainLoop();
```

The above commands set up three callback functions each corresponding to a different event: Reshape, Display, and Idle. The last command puts our program into an infinite loop: checking out an event and calling its callback function. The Reshape and Display events are generated when the display area appears on the screen the first time. In other words, *reshape()* and *display()* will be called once early in the event loop, and the system passes the width (w) and height (h) of the current display area to the Reshape callback function. When the event queue is empty, GLUT will detect an Idle event, and call its corresponding callback function, which is *display()* here. Therefore, *display()* will be called many times whenever there are no other events in the event queue.

3. If we move or stretch the window display area using the mouse, a Reshape event is generated. Soon GLUT will check out this event and call its callback function *reshape()*.

```
//e. specify the window coordinates
glMatrixMode (GL_PROJECTION);
glLoadIdentity ();
glOrtho(0, Width, 0, Height, -1.0, 1.0);
```

The above lines set up the window coordinates, which are specified as $0 \leq x \leq$ *Width* from the left to the right side of the window, $0 \leq y \leq$ *Height* from the bottom to the top side of the window, and $-1 \leq z \leq 1$ in the direction perpendicular to the window. The z direction is ignored in 2D applications.

4. All OpenGL commands are prefixed with "gl".

5. *glFlush()* tells the graphics system to execute the drawing.

In summary, *main()* creates a window of drawing area, sets up callback functions, and waits for events in the *glutMainLoop()*. It calls *reshape()* and *display()* once to set up the coordinates of the window and draw a randomly generated pixel. After that, whenever the event loop is idle, it calls *display()* again. In *display()*, a random point in the window is generated and a red pixel is drawn.

1.3 Frame Buffer, Scan-conversion, and Clipping

The graphics system digitizes a specific model into a frame of discrete color points saved in a piece of memory called a *frame buffer*. This digitization process is called *scan-conversion*. Sometimes *drawing* or *rendering* is used to mean scan-conversion. However, drawing and rendering are more general terms that do not focus on the digitization process. The color points in the frame buffer will be sent to the corresponding pixels in the display device by a piece of hardware called the *video controller*. Therefore, whatever is in the frame buffer corresponds to the image on the screen. The application program accepts user input, manipulates the models (creates, stores, retrieves, and modifies the descriptions), and produces an image through the graphics system. The display is also a window for us to manipulate the model behind the image through the application program. A change on the display corresponds to a change in the model. A programmer's tasks concern mostly creating the model, changing the model, and handling user interaction. OpenGL, GLUT and C functions are the interfaces between the application program and the graphics hardware (Fig. 1.1).

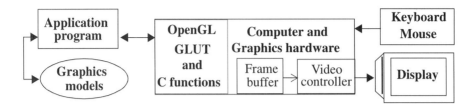

Fig. 1.1 A conceptual graphics system

Before using OpenGL primitive drawing functions directly, let's look at how these functions are implemented. Graphics libraries may be implemented quite differently, and many functions can be implemented in both software and hardware.

1.3.1 Scan-converting Lines

A line object is described as an abstract model with two end points (x_0, y_0) and (x_n, y_n). It is scan-converted into the frame buffer by a graphics library function. The line equation is $y = mx + B$, where the slope $m = (y_n-y_0)/(x_n-x_0)$ and B is a constant. Let's assume $-1 \leq m \leq 1$. For the pixels on the line, $x_{i+1} = x_i + 1$ and $y_{i+1} = mx_{i+1} + B = m(x_i + 1) + B = (mx_i + B) + m = y_i + m$. To scan-convert the line, we need only to draw all the pixels at $(x_i, \text{Round}(y_i))$ for $i=0$ to n.

/* Example 1.2.line.c: draw random generated lines */

```
void line(int x0,int y0,int xn,int yn)
{
    int x; float m, y;

    m = (float) (yn-y0)/(xn-x0);
    x=x0; y=y0;

    while (x<xn+1) {
        // write a pixel into the framebuffer
        glBegin(GL_POINTS);
            glVertex2i (x, (int) (y+0.5));
        glEnd();

        x++; y+=m;/* next pixel's position */
    }
}
```

Bresenham[1] developed a line scan-conversion algorithm using only integer operations, which can be implemented very efficiently in hardware. Let's assume pixel (x_p, y_p) is on the line and $0 \le m \le 1$ (Fig. 1.2). Which pixel should we choose next: E or NE? The line equation is $y = mx + B$, i.e. $F(x, y) = ax + by + c = 0$, where $a = dy = (y_n - y_0)$, $b = -dx = -(x_n - x_0) < 0$, and $c = B*dx$. Because $b < 0$, if y increases, $F(x, y)$ decreases, and vice versa. Therefore, if

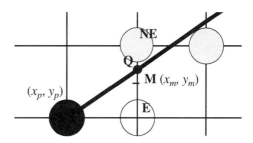

Fig. 1.2 Finding the next pixel: E or NE

the midpoint $M(x_m, y_m)$ between pixels NE and E is on the line, $F(x_m, y_m) = 0$; if $M(x_m, y_m)$ is below the line, $F(x_m, y_m) > 0$; and if $M(x_m, y_m)$ is above the line, $F(x_m, y_m) < 0$.

If $F(x_m, y_m) > 0$, Q is above $M(x_m, y_m)$, we choose NE; otherwise we choose E. Therefore, $F(x_m, y_m)$ is a *decision factor:* d_{old}. From d_{old}, we can derive the decision factor d_{new} for the next pixel. We can see that $x_m = x_p + 1$ and $y_m = y_p + 1/2$. Therefore we have:

$$d_{old} = F(x_m, y_m) = F(x_p+1, y_p+1/2) = F(x_p, y_p) + a + b/2 = a + b/2. \qquad \text{(EQ 1)}$$

If $d_{old} \le 0$, E is chosen, the next middle point is at $(x_p+2, y_p+1/2)$:

$$d_{new} = F(x_p+2, y_p+1/2) = d_{old} + a. \qquad \text{(EQ 2)}$$

If $d_{old} > 0$, NE is chosen, the next middle point is at $(x_p+2, y_p+3/2)$:

$$d_{new} = F(x_p+2, y_p+3/2) = d_{old} + a + b. \qquad \text{(EQ 3)}$$

We can see that only the initial d_{old} is not an integer. If we multiply by 2 on both sides of Equation 1, 2, and 3, all decision factors are integers. Note that if a decision factor is greater/smaller than zero, multiplying it by 2 does not change the fact that it is still

---

1. Bresenham, J. E., "Algorithm for Computer Control of Digital Plotter," *IBM Systems Journal*, 4 (1), 1965, 25–30.

greater/smaller than zero. So the decision remains the same. Let $dE = 2dy$, $dNE = 2(dy - dx)$, and $d_{old} = 2dy - dx$:

$$\textit{If E is chosen, } d_{new} = d_{old} + dE; \qquad \text{(EQ 4)}$$

$$\textit{If NE is chosen, } d_{new} = d_{old} + dNE. \qquad \text{(EQ 5)}$$

Therefore, in the line scan-conversion algorithm, the arithmetic needed to evaluate d_{new} for any step is a simple integer addition.

```
//Bresenham's Middle point Line algorithm (for 0≤m≤1)

void line(int x0, int y0, int xn, int yn)
{
    int dx, dy, incrE, incrNE, d, x, y;

    dy=yn-y0; dx=xn-x0; x=x0; y=y0;
    d=2*dy-dx; incrE=2*dy; incrNE=2*(dy-dx);

    while (x<xn+1) {
        writepixel(x,y); /* write framebuffer */
        x++; /* consider next pixel */
        if (d<=0) d+=incrE;
        else { y++; d+=incrNE; };
    }
}
```

We need to consider the cases in which the line's slope is in an arbitrary orientation. Fortunately, an arbitrary line can be mapped into the case above through a mirror around x axis, y axis, or the diagonal line ($m=1$). The following is an implementation of Bresenham's algorithm that handles all these cases. In this program, we can reshape the display window (i.e., the viewport) by dragging the window's corner. Function *main()* is omitted because it is the same as the one in Example 1.1. In the rest of this book, most of the examples are only segments. The complete source code can be downloaded online or from the provided CD.

/* Example 1.3.line.c: draw random lines (Bresenham's Alg.)*/

```
#include <stdlib.h>
#include <math.h>
```

```
#include <GL/glut.h>
int Height=400, Width=400;


void swapd(int *a, int *b)
{// swap the numbers
   int tmp;

   tmp=*a; *a=*b; *b=tmp;
}


void writepixel(int x, int y, int flag)
{ // write the pixel into the framebuffer

   glBegin(GL_POINTS); // flag for different slope cases
      if (flag==0) glVertex2i (x,y);
      else if (flag==1) glVertex2i (y,x);
      else if (flag==10) glVertex2i (x,-y);
      else if (flag==11) glVertex2i (y,-x);
   glEnd();
}


void line(int x0,int y0,int xn,int yn)
{ // Bresenham's midpoint line algorithm
   int dx, dy, incrE, incrNE, d, x, y, flag = 0;

   if (xn<x0) { swapd(&x0,&xn); swapd(&y0,&yn); }
   if (yn<y0) { y0 = -y0; yn = -yn; flag=10; }

   dy=yn-y0; dx=xn-x0;

   if (dx<dy) {
      swapd(&x0,&y0);swapd(&xn,&yn); swapd(&dy,&dx);
      flag++;
   }

   x=x0; y=y0; d=2*dy-dx;
   incrE=2*dy; incrNE=2*(dy-dx);

   while (x<xn+1) {
      writepixel(x,y,flag);

      x++; // next pixel
      if (d<=0) d+=incrE;
      else { y++; d+=incrNE; };
   }
}
```

```
void display(void)
{ // generate a random line
   int x0, y0, xn, yn;

   x0 = (rand() % Width) - Width/2;
   y0 = (rand() % Height) - Height/2;
   xn = (rand() % Width) - Width/2;
   yn = (rand() % Height) - Height/2;

   glColor3f(1, 1, 1); // white color

   // draw the generated line
   line(x0, y0, xn, yn);

   glFlush();
}


static void Reshape(int w, int h)
{
   // clear the framebuffer to black color (background color)
   glClearColor (0.0, 0.0, 0.0, 1.0);
   glClear(GL_COLOR_BUFFER_BIT);

   //Reshape() receives adjusted window size (w, h) from GLUT
   Width = w; Height = h;

   //adjust the size of the drawing area
   glViewport (0, 0, w, h);

   glMatrixMode (GL_PROJECTION);
   glLoadIdentity ();

   //adjust the coordinates accordingly
   glOrtho(-w/2, w/2, -h/2, h/2, -1.0, 1.0);
}
```

Of course, OpenGL has a line scan-conversion function. To draw a line, we can simply call

```
glBegin(GL_LINES);

   glVertex2i(x0,y0);
   glVertex2i(xn,yn);

glEnd();
```

1.3.2 Scan-converting Curves, Triangles, and Polygons

Although the above example (Example 1.3) is really a simulation, because the program does not directly manipulate the frame buffer, it does help us understand the scan-conversion process. Given a line equation, we can scan-convert the line by calculating and drawing all the pixels corresponding to the equation in the frame buffer. Similarly, given a circle equation, we can calculate and draw all the pixels of the circle into the frame buffer. This applies to all different types of curves. To speed up the scan-conversion process, we often use short lines to approximate short curve segments. Therefore, a curve can be approximated by a sequence of short lines.

A wireframe object is an object composed of only lines and curves without filled surfaces. Since a wireframe polygon is composed of line segments, we only discuss scan-converting filled triangles and polygons. Given three vertices corresponding to a triangle, we have three lines (edges). Since we can find all the pixels on the lines, we can scan-convert the triangle by drawing all pixels between the pixel pairs on different edges that have the same y coordinates. In other words, we can find the intersections of each horizontal line (called a scan-line) with the edges of the triangle, and fill the pixels between the intersections that lie in the interior of the triangle. If we can scan-convert a triangle, we can scan-convert a polygon because a polygon can be divided into triangles. The emphasis of this book is more on using the implemented scan-conversion functions through programming.

A graphics library provides basic primitive functions. For example, OpenGL draws a convex polygon with the following commands:

```
glBegin(GL_POLYGON);
    // a list of vertices
    ...
glEnd();
```

A *convex* polygon means that all the angles inside the polygon formed by the edges are smaller than 180 degrees. If a polygon is not convex, it is *concave*. Convex polygons can be scan-converted faster than concave polygons.

In summary, different scan-conversion algorithms for a graphics primitive (line, polygon, etc.) have their own merits. If a primitive scan-conversion function is not provided in a graphics library, we know now that we can create one or implement an existing one.

1.3.3 Scan-converting Characters

Characters are polygons. However, they are used so often that we prefer saving the polygon shapes in a library called the *font library*. The polygons in the font library are not represented by vertices. Instead, they are represented by *bitmap font* images — each character is saved in a rectangular binary array of pixels. The shape of small bitmaps do not scale well. Therefore, more than one bitmap must be defined for a given character for different sizes and type faces. Bitmap fonts are loaded into a font cache (fast memory) to allow quick retrieval. Displaying a character is simply copying its image from the font cache into the frame buffer at the desired position. During the copying process, colors may be used to draw into the frame buffer replacing the 1s and 0s in the bitmap font images.

Another method of describing character shapes is using straight lines and curve sections. These fonts are called *outline font*s. Outline fonts require less storage since each variation does not require a distinct font cache. However, the scaled shapes for different font sizes may not be pleasing to our eyes, and it takes more time to scan-convert the characters into the frame buffer.

Although the idea is simple, accessing fonts is often platform-dependent. GLUT provides a simple platform-independent subset of font functions. If you need more flexibility, you may look into a specific platform/environment in the future. On the Unix platform, GLX provides font functions and interfaces between OpenGL and the X window system. WGL is the equivalent of GLX on the Microsoft Windows platform.

1.3.4 Clipping

When a graphics system scan-converts a model, the model may be much larger than the display area. The display is a window used to look at a portion of a large model. Clipping algorithms are necessary to clip the model and display only the portion that fits the window. For example, if a line's two endpoints are inside the clipping window, then the clipping is trivially done. Otherwise, we can cut the line into sections at the edges of the clipping window, and keep only the section that lies inside the window. Clipping algorithms for lines, polygons, and other 2D primitives have been developed. In addition to primitive 2D rectangular clipping, clipping algorithms have also been developed to cut models in other 2D shapes or 3D volumes. We will further discuss clipping against 3D volumes in Chapter 2.

1.4 Attributes and Antialiasing

In general, any parameter that affects the way a primitive is to be displayed is referred to as an attribute parameter. For example, a line's attributes include color, intensity (or brightness), type (solid, dashed, dotted), width, cap (shape of the end points: butt, round, etc.), join (miter, round, etc.), and so forth.

The display and the corresponding frame buffer are discrete. Therefore, a line, curve, or an edge of a polygon is often like a zigzag staircase. This is called *aliasing*. We can display the pixels at different intensities to relieve the aliasing problem. Methods to relieve aliasing are called *antialiasing* methods, and we introduce several below. In order to simplify the discussion, we only consider line antialiasing.

1.4.1 Area Sampling

A displayed line has a width. Here we simply consider a line as a rectangular area overlapping with the pixels (Fig. 1.3(a)). We may display the pixels with different intensities or colors to achieve the effect of antialiasing. For example, if we display those pixels that are partially inside the rectangular line area with colors between the line color and the background color, the line looks less jaggy. Fig. 1.3(b) shows parallel lines that are drawn with or without antialiasing. Area sampling determines a pixel intensity by calculating the overlap area of the pixel with the line.

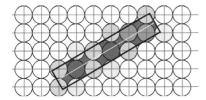 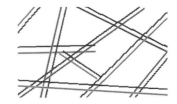

a) A line is a rectangular area   *b) Parallel lines with or without antialiasing*

Fig. 1.3 Antialiasing: area sampling

Unweighted area sampling determines the pixel intensity by the overlap area only. For unweighted area sampling, if a pixel is not completely inside or outside the line, it is cut into two or more areas by the boundaries of the rectangular line area. The portion inside the line determines the pixel intensity.

Weighted area sampling allows equal areas within a pixel to contribute unequally: an area closer to the pixel's center has greater influence on the pixel's intensity than an equal area further away from the pixel's center. For weighted area sampling, we assume each pixel is occupied by a 3D solid cone (called a *cone filter*) or a bun-shaped volume (*Gaussian filter*) with the flat bottom sitting on the pixel. The bottom of the cone may even be bigger than the pixel itself. The boundaries of the rectangular line area cut through the cone in the direction perpendicular to the display, and the portion (volume) of the cone inside the line area determines the corresponding pixel's intensity. The center area in the pixel is thicker (higher) than the boundary area of the pixel, and thus has more influence on the pixel's intensity. Also, you can see that if the bottom of the cone is bigger than the pixel, the pixel's intensity is affected even though the line only passes by without touching the pixel.

1.4.2 Antialiasing a Line with Weighted Area Sampling

For weighted area sampling, calculating a pixel's intensity according to the cone filter or Gaussian filter takes time. Instead, we can build up an intensity table, and use the distance from the center of the pixel to the center of the line as an index to find the intensity for the pixel directly from the table. The intensities in the table are precalculated according to the filter we use and the width of the line. The following is an implementation of scan-converting an antialiased line.

If we assume the distance from the current pixel to the line is D, then the distances from the E, S, N, and NE pixels can be calculated, respectively. The distances are shown in Fig. 1.4. (The distances from the pixels above the line are negatively labeled, which are useful for polygon edge antialiasing.) We can modify Bresenham's algorithm to scan-convert an antialiased line. The distances from the pixels closest to the line are calculated iteratively.

Given a point (x, y), the function *IntensifyPixel(x, y, D)* will look up the intensity level of the point according to the index D and draw the pixel (x, y) at its intensity into the frame buffer. In our example, instead of building up a filter table, we use a simple equation to calculate the intensity. Here we implement a three-pixel wide antialiased line algorithm as an example.

In Bresenham's algorithm, the distance from the center of the pixel to the center of the line is $|D| \leq 0.5$. Therefore, the distance from N (the pixel above the current pixel) is $|D - \cos\alpha| \leq 1.5$, and the distance from S is $|D + \cos\alpha| \leq 1.5$. Given the current pixel's color *(r, g, b)*, we can modify the intensity by: *(r, g, b)*(1-D/1.5)*. When a pixel is exactly on the line *(D=0)*, the pixel's intensity is not changed. When a pixel is far away from the center of the line *(D=1.5)*, the pixel's intensity is modified to *(0, 0, 0)*. Therefore, the pixels have different intensity levels depending on their distances from the center of the line. The following example (Example 1.4) is simplified without considering all different slopes, which we discussed in Example 1.3.

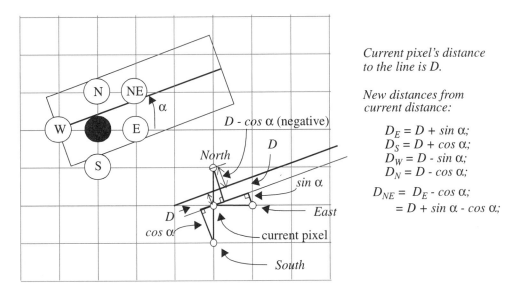

Current pixel's distance to the line is D.

New distances from current distance:

$$D_E = D + sin\ \alpha;$$
$$D_S = D + cos\ \alpha;$$
$$D_W = D - sin\ \alpha;$$
$$D_N = D - cos\ \alpha;$$

$$D_{NE} = D_E - cos\ \alpha;$$
$$= D + sin\ \alpha - cos\ \alpha;$$

Fig. 1.4 Iteratively calculating the distances from the pixels to the line

/* Example 1.4.line.c: scan-convert 3 pixel wide lines with antialiasing */

```
void IntensifyPixel(int x,int y, double D)
{
    float d, r1, g1, b1;

    if (D<0) d = -D;
    else d = D;

    r1=r*(1-d/1.5); g1=g*(1-d/1.5); b1=b*(1-d/1.5);
    glColor3f(r1, g1, b1);
    writepixel(x,y);
}
```

```
void antialiasedLine(int x0,int y0,int xn,int yn)
{
    int dx, dy, incrE, incrNE, d, x, y;
    float D=0, sin_a, cos_a, smc_a, Denom;

    dy=yn-y0; dx=xn-x0; x=x0; y=y0; d=2*dy-dx;
    incrE=2*dy; incrNE=2*(dy-dx);

    Denom = sqrt(dx*dx + dy*dy);
    sin_a = dy / Denom; cos_a = dx / Denom;
    smc_a = sin_a - cos_a;

    while (x<xn+1) {
        IntensifyPixel(x,y,D); // current pixel
        IntensifyPixel(x,y+1,D-cos_a); // North
        IntensifyPixel(x,y-1,D+cos_a); // South

        x++;
        if (d<=0) { D+=sin_a; d+=incrE; }
        else { D+=smc_a; y++; d+=incrNE; };
    }
} /* AntiAliased Midpoint Algorithm */
```

1.5 Double-buffering for Animation

A motion picture effect can be achieved by projecting images at 24 frames per second on a screen. Animation on a computer can be achieved by drawing or refreshing frames of different images. Here, the display *refresh rate* is the speed of reading from the frame buffer and sending the pixels to the display by the video controller. A refresh rate at 60 (frames per second) is smoother than one at 30, and 120 is marginally better than 60. Refresh rates faster than 120 frames per second are not necessary, since the human eye cannot tell the difference. Let's assume that the refresh rate is 60 frames per second. We can then build an animation program as follows:

```
open_window_with_single_buffer_mode();

for (i = 0; i < 100; i++) {
    clear_buffer();
    draw_frame(i);
    wait_until_1/60_of_a_second_is_over();
}
```

Items drawn first are visible for the full 1/60 second; items drawn toward the end are instantly cleared as the program starts on the next frame. This causes the display to present a blurred or jittered animation.

To solve this problem, we can have two frame buffers instead of one, which is known as double-buffering. One frame buffer named the *front buffer* is being displayed while the other, named the *back buffer,* is being drawn for scan-converting models. When the drawing of a frame is complete, the two buffers are swapped. That is, the back buffer becomes the front buffer for display, and the front buffer becomes the back buffer for scan-conversion. The animation program looks as follows:

```
open_window_with_double_buffer_mode();

for (i = 0; i < 100; i++) {
    clear_back_buffer();
    draw_frame_into_back_buffer(i);
    wait_until_1/60_of_a_second_is_over();
    swap_buffers();
}
```

What often happens is that a frame is too complicated to draw in 1/60 second. If this happens, each frame in the front buffer is displayed more than once and the display refresh rate is still 1/60. However, the image frame rate is much lower, and the animation could be jittering. The image frame rate depends on how fast frames of images are scan-converted, which corresponds to the rate of swapping the buffers. To achieve smooth animation, we need high performance algorithms as well as graphics hardware to carry out many graphics functions efficiently.

Example 1.5 demonstrates animation: drawing a circle with a radius that is changing every frame. It also helps us review vector operations. The circle is approximated by a set of triangles, as shown in Fig. 1.5. At the beginning, *v1, v2, v3, v4,* and the center of the coordinate *v0* are provided. When the variable *depth=0*, we draw four triangles, and the circle is approximated by a square. When

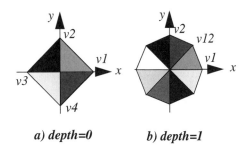

a) depth=0   b) depth=1

Fig. 1.5 Drawing a circle by subdivision

depth=1, each triangle is subdivided into two and we draw eight triangles. Given *v1* and *v2*, how do we find *v12*? Let's consider *v1*, *v2*, and *v12* as vectors. Then, *v12* is in the direction of $(v1 + v2)=(v1_x+v2_x, v1_y+v2_y, v1_z+v2_z)$ and the lengths of the vectors are equal: $|v1| = |v2| = |v12|$. If the radius of the circle is one, then *v12 = normalize(v1 + v2)*. Normalizing a vector is equivalent to scaling the vector to a unit vector. In general, *v12 = circleRadius*normalize(v1 + v2)*, and for every frame the program changes the value of *circleRadius* to achieve animation. We can find all other unknown vertices in Fig. 1.5(b) similarly through vector additions and normalizations. This subdivision process goes on depending on the value of the *depth*. Given a triangle with two vertices and the coordinate center, *subdivideCircle()* recursively subdivides the triangle *depth* times and draws 2^{depth} triangles.

/* Example 1.5.circle.c: animation and cycle by subdivision */

```
#include <stdio.h>
#include <stdlib.h>
#include <math.h>
#include <GL/glut.h>

int Height=400, Width=400;
int depth=0, circleRadius=2, cnt=1;


static float vdata[4][3] = {
// four vertices on the circle

    {1.0, 0.0, 0.0}, {0.0, 1.0, 0.0},
    {-1.0, 0.0, 0.0}, {0.0, -1.0, 0.0}
};


void normalize(float v[3]) {
// normalize vector v, so |v|=1

    float d = sqrt(v[0]*v[0]+v[1]*v[1]+v[2]*v[2]);

    if (d == 0) {
       printf("zero length vector");
       return;
    }

    v[0] /= d;
    v[1] /= d;
    v[2] /= d;
}
```

```
void drawtriangle(float *v1, float *v2, float *v3)
{
    glBegin(GL_TRIANGLES);
        glVertex3fv(v1);
        glVertex3fv(v2);
        glVertex3fv(v3);
    glEnd();
}


void subdivideCircle(int radius,
                float *v1, float *v2, int depth)
{// subdivide the circle according to the depth

    float v11[3], v22[3], v00[3] = {0, 0, 0}, v12[3];
    int i;

    if (depth == 0) {

        // the triangle color depends on its vertices:
        // different triangles have different colors
        glColor3f(v1[0]*v1[0], v1[1]*v1[1], v1[2]*v1[2]);

        for (i=0; i<3; i++) {
            v11[i] = v1[i]*radius;
            v22[i] = v2[i]*radius;
        }

        drawtriangle(v11, v22, v00);
        return;
    }

    v12[0] = v1[0]+v2[0];
    v12[1] = v1[1]+v2[1];
    v12[2] = v1[2]+v2[2];

    normalize(v12);
    subdivideCircle(radius, v1, v12, depth - 1);
    subdivideCircle(radius, v12, v2, depth - 1);
}


void drawcircle(int circleRadius)
{
    subdivideCircle(circleRadius, vdata[0], vdata[1], depth);
    subdivideCircle(circleRadius, vdata[1], vdata[2], depth);
    subdivideCircle(circleRadius, vdata[2], vdata[3], depth);
    subdivideCircle(circleRadius, vdata[3], vdata[0], depth);
}
```

```
void display(void)
{
   if (circleRadius>Width/2 || circleRadius<2) {
      cnt=-cnt; depth++;
      depth = depth % 5;
   }

   // the radius of the circle changes every frame
   circleRadius+=cnt;

   glClear(GL_COLOR_BUFFER_BIT);
   drawcircle(circleRadius);

   // for double-buffering:swap back and front buffers;
   // It replaces glFlush() to tell the system start drawing.
   glutSwapBuffers();
}


static void Reshape(int w, int h)
{
   glClearColor (0.0, 0.0, 0.0, 1.0);
   glClear(GL_COLOR_BUFFER_BIT);

   Width = w; Height = h;
   glViewport (0, 0, Width, Height);

   glMatrixMode (GL_PROJECTION);
   glLoadIdentity ();
   glOrtho(-Width/2, Width/2, -Height/2, Height/2, -1.0, 1.0);
}


int main(int argc, char **argv)
{
   glutInit(&argc, argv);

   // here we specify double-buffering for the display window
   glutInitDisplayMode(GLUT_DOUBLE);

   glutInitWindowSize(Width, Height);
   glutCreateWindow("Example 1.5. circle.c");

   glutReshapeFunc(Reshape);
   glutDisplayFunc(display);
   glutIdleFunc(display);

   glutMainLoop();
}
```

2
Transformation and Viewing

Chapter objectives:

- Understand basic transformation and viewing methods

- Understand 3D hidden-surface removal and collision detection

- Design and implement 3D models (cone, cylinder, and sphere) and their animations in OpenGL

2.1 Geometric Transformation

In Chapter 1, we discussed creating and scan-converting primitive models. After a computer-based model is generated, it can be moved around or even transformed into a completely different shape. To do this, we need to specify the rotation axis and angle, translation vector, scaling vector, or other manipulations to the model. The ordinary *geometric transformation* is a process of mathematical manipulations of all the vertices of the model through matrix multiplications, where the graphics system then displays the final transformed model. The transformation can be predefined, such as moving along a planned trajectory; or interactive, depending on the user input. The transformation can be permanent — the coordinates of the vertices are changed and we have a new model replacing the original one; or just temporary — the vertices return to their original coordinates. In many cases a model is transformed in order to be displayed at a different position or orientation, and the graphics system discards the transformed model after scan-conversion. Sometimes all the vertices of a model go through the same transformation and the shape of the model is preserved; sometimes different vertices go through different transformations, and the shape is dynamic.

A model can be displayed repetitively with each frame going through a small transformation step. This causes the model to be animated on display.

2.2 2D Transformation

Translation, *rotation*, and *scaling* are the basic and essential transformations. They can be combined to achieve most transformations in many applications. To simplify the discussion, we will first introduce 2D transformation, and then generalize it into 3D.

2.2.1 2D Translation

A point (x, y) is translated to (x', y') by a distance vector (d_x, d_y):

$$x' = x + d_x,$$
(EQ 6)

$$y' = y + d_y.$$
(EQ 7)

In the homogeneous coordinates, we represent a point (x, y) by a column vector

$P = \begin{bmatrix} x \\ y \\ 1 \end{bmatrix}$. Similarly, $P' = \begin{bmatrix} x' \\ y' \\ 1 \end{bmatrix}$. Then, translation can be achieved by matrix

multiplication:

$$\begin{bmatrix} x' \\ y' \\ 1 \end{bmatrix} = \begin{bmatrix} 1 & 0 & d_x \\ 0 & 1 & d_y \\ 0 & 0 & 1 \end{bmatrix} \begin{bmatrix} x \\ y \\ 1 \end{bmatrix}.$$
(EQ 8)

Let's assume $T(d_x, d_y) = \begin{bmatrix} 1 & 0 & d_x \\ 0 & 1 & d_y \\ 0 & 0 & 1 \end{bmatrix}$. We can denote the translation matrix equation as:

$$P' = T(d_x, d_y)P.$$
(EQ 9)

If a model is a set of vertices, all vertices of the model can be translated as points by the same translation vector (Fig. 2.1). Note that translation moves a model through a distance without changing its orientation.

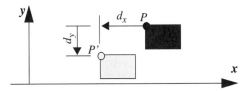

Fig. 2.1 Basic transformation: translation

2.2.2 2D Rotation

A point $P(x, y)$ is rotated counter-clockwise to $P'(x', y')$ by an angle θ around the origin $(0,0)$. If the rotation is clockwise, the rotation angle θ is then negative. The rotation axis is perpendicular to the 2D plane at the origin:

$$x' = x\cos\theta - y\sin\theta,$$ (EQ 10)

$$y' = x\sin\theta + y\cos\theta.$$ (EQ 11)

In the homogeneous coordinates, rotation can be achieved by matrix multiplication:

$$\begin{bmatrix} x' \\ y' \\ 1 \end{bmatrix} = \begin{bmatrix} \cos\theta & -\sin\theta & 0 \\ \sin\theta & \cos\theta & 0 \\ 0 & 0 & 1 \end{bmatrix} \begin{bmatrix} x \\ y \\ 1 \end{bmatrix}.$$ (EQ 12)

Let's assume $R(\theta) = \begin{bmatrix} \cos\theta & -\sin\theta & 0 \\ \sin\theta & \cos\theta & 0 \\ 0 & 0 & 1 \end{bmatrix}$. The simplified rotation matrix equation is:

$$P' = R(\theta)P.$$ (EQ 13)

If a model is a set of vertices, all vertices of
the model can be rotated as points by the
same angle around the same rotation axis
(Fig. 2.2). Rotation moves a model around
the origin of the coordinates. The distance
of each vertex to the origin is not changed
during rotation.

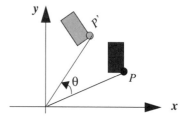

2.2.3 2D Scaling

Fig. 2.2 Basic transformation: rotatio

A point $P(x, y)$ is scaled to $P'(x', y')$ by a scaling vector (s_x, s_y):

$$x' = s_x x, \qquad \text{(EQ 14)}$$

$$y' = s_y y. \qquad \text{(EQ 15)}$$

In the homogeneous coordinates, again, scaling can be achieved by matrix
multiplication:

$$\begin{bmatrix} x' \\ y' \\ 1 \end{bmatrix} = \begin{bmatrix} s_x & 0 & 0 \\ 0 & s_y & 0 \\ 0 & 0 & 1 \end{bmatrix} \begin{bmatrix} x \\ y \\ 1 \end{bmatrix}. \qquad \text{(EQ 16)}$$

Let's assume $S(s_x, s_y) = \begin{bmatrix} s_x & 0 & 0 \\ 0 & s_y & 0 \\ 0 & 0 & 1 \end{bmatrix}$. We can denote the scaling matrix equation as:

$$P' = S(s_x, s_y)P. \qquad \text{(EQ 17)}$$

If a model is a set of vertices, all vertices of the model can be scaled as points by the
same scaling vector (Fig. 2.3). Scaling amplifies or shrinks a model around the origin
of the coordinates. Note that a scaled vertex will move unless it is at the origin.

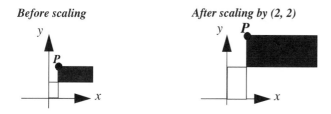

Fig. 2.3 Basic transformation: scaling

2.2.4 Composition of 2D Transformations

A complex transformation is often achieved by a series of simple transformation steps. The result is a composition of translations, rotations, and scalings. We will study this through the following three examples.

Example 2.1: finding the coordinates of a moving clock hand in 2D

Consider a single clock hand. The center of rotation is given at $c(x_0, y_0)$, and the end rotation point is at $h(x_1, y_1)$. If we know the rotation angle is θ, can we find the new end point h' after the rotation? As shown in Fig. 2.4, we can achieve this by a series of transformations.

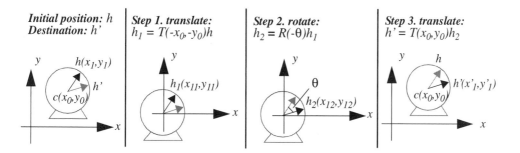

Fig. 2.4 Moving the clock hand by matrix multiplications

1. Translate the hand so that the center of rotation is at the origin. Note that we only need to find the new coordinates of the end point h:

$$
\begin{bmatrix} x_{11} \\ y_{11} \\ 1 \end{bmatrix} = \begin{bmatrix} 1 & 0 & -x_0 \\ 0 & 1 & -y_0 \\ 0 & 0 & 1 \end{bmatrix} \begin{bmatrix} x_1 \\ y_1 \\ 1 \end{bmatrix} . \tag{EQ 18}
$$

That is, $h_1 = T(-x_0, -y_0)h$. **(EQ 19)**

2. Rotate θ degrees around the origin. Note that the positive direction of rotation is counter-clockwise:

$$
h_2 = R(-\theta)h_1. \tag{EQ 20}
$$

3. After the rotation. We translate again to move the clock back to its original position:

$$
h' = T(x_0, y_0)h_2. \tag{EQ 21}
$$

Therefore, putting Equations 19 to 21 together, the combination of transformations to achieve the clock hand movement is:

$$
h' = T(x_0, y_0)R(-\theta)T(-x_0, -y_0)h. \tag{EQ 22}
$$

That is:
$$
\begin{bmatrix} x'_1 \\ y'_1 \\ 1 \end{bmatrix} = \begin{bmatrix} 1 & 0 & x_0 \\ 0 & 1 & y_0 \\ 0 & 0 & 1 \end{bmatrix} \begin{bmatrix} \cos\theta & \sin\theta & 0 \\ -\sin\theta & \cos\theta & 0 \\ 0 & 0 & 1 \end{bmatrix} \begin{bmatrix} 1 & 0 & -x_0 \\ 0 & 1 & -y_0 \\ 0 & 0 & 1 \end{bmatrix} \begin{bmatrix} x_1 \\ y_1 \\ 1 \end{bmatrix} . \tag{EQ 23}
$$

In the future, we will write matrix equations concisely using only symbol notations instead of full matrix expressions. However, we should always remember that the symbols represent the corresponding matrices.

Let's assume $M = T(x_0, y_0)R(-\theta)T(-x_0, -y_0)$. We can further simplify the equation:

$$
h' = Mh. \tag{EQ 24}
$$

The order of the matrices in a matrix expression matters. The sequence represents the order of the transformations. For example, although matrix M in Equation 24 can be calculated by multiplying the first two matrices first $[T(x_0,y_0)R(-\theta)]T(-x_0,-y_0)$ or by multiplying the last two matrices first $T(x_0,y_0)[R(-\theta)T(-x_0,-y_0)]$, the order of the matrices cannot be changed.

When we analyze a model's transformations, we should remember that, logically speaking, the order of transformation steps are from right to left in the matrix expression. In this example, the first logical step is: $T(-x_0,-y_0)h$; the second step is: $R(-\theta)[T(-x_0,-y_0)h]$; and the last step is: $T(x_0,y_0)[R(-\theta)[T(-x_0,-y_0)]]$.

Example 2.2: reshaping a rectangular area

In OpenGL, we can use the mouse to reshape the display area. In the Reshape callback function, we can use *glViewport()* to adjust the size of the drawing area accordingly. The system makes corresponding adjustments to the models through the same transformation matrix. Viewport transformation will be discussed later in Viewing.

Here, we discuss a similar problem: a transformation that allows reshaping a rectangular area directly. Let's assume the coordinate system of the screen is as in Fig. 2.5. After reshaping, the rectangular area (and all the vertices of the models) go through the following transformations: translate so that the lower-left corner of the area is at the origin, scale to the size of the new area, and then translate to the scaled area location. The corresponding matrix expression is:

$$T(P_2)S(s_x,s_y)T(-P_1). \hspace{2cm} \text{(EQ 25)}$$

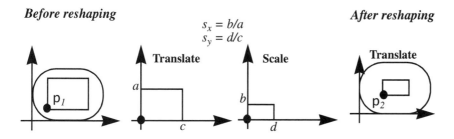

Fig. 2.5 **Scaling an arbitrary rectangular area**

Example 2.3: drawing a 2D robot arm with three moving segments

A 2D robot arm has 3 segments rotating at the joints in a 2D plane (Fig. 2.6). Given an arbitrary initial posture (A, B, C), let's find the transformation matrix expressions for another posture (A_f, B_f, C_f) with respective rotations (α, β, γ) around the joints. Here we specify (A, B, C) on the x axis, which is used to simplify the visualization. (A, B, C) can be initialized arbitrarily. There are many different methods to achieve the same goal. Here, we elaborate three methods to achieve the same goal.

Initial position: (A, B, C)   *Final position*

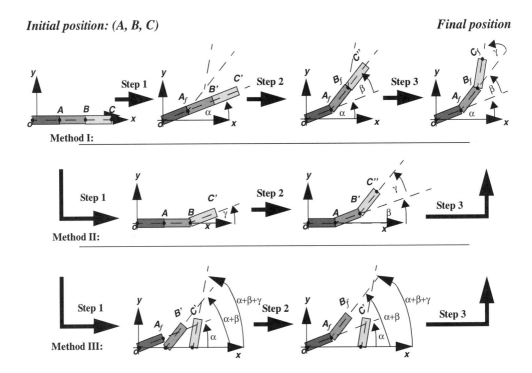

Fig. 2.6 A 2D robot arm rotates (α, β, γ) degrees at the 3 joints, respectively

Method I.

1. Rotate $oABC$ around the origin by α degrees:

$$A_f = R(\alpha)A; \ B' = R(\alpha)B; \ C' = R(\alpha)C. \qquad \text{(EQ 26)}$$

2. Consider $A_fB'C'$ to be a clock hand like the example in Fig. 2.4. Rotate $A_fB'C'$ around A_f by β degrees. This is achieved by first translating the hand to the origin, rotating, then translating back:

$$B_f = T(A_f)R(\beta)T(-A_f)B';\ C'' = T(A_f)R(\beta)T(-A_f)C'. \qquad \textbf{(EQ 27)}$$

3. Again, consider B_fC'' to be a clock hand. Rotate B_fC'' around B_f by γ degrees:

$$C_f = T(B_f)R(\gamma)T(-B_f)C''. \qquad \textbf{(EQ 28)}$$

Method II.

1. Consider BC to be a clock hand. Rotate BC around B by γ degrees:

$$C' = T(B)R(\gamma)T(-B)C. \qquad \textbf{(EQ 29)}$$

2. Consider ABC' to be a clock hand. Rotate ABC' around A by β degrees:

$$B' = T(A)R(\beta)T(-A)B;\ C'' = T(A)R(\beta)T(-A)C'. \qquad \textbf{(EQ 30)}$$

3. Again, consider $oAB'C''$ to be a clock hand. Rotate $oAB'C''$ around the origin by α degrees:

$$A_f = R(\alpha)A; \qquad \textbf{(EQ 31)}$$

$$B_f = R(\alpha)B' = R(\alpha)T(A)R(\beta)T(-A)B; \qquad \textbf{(EQ 32)}$$

$$C_f = R(\alpha)C'' = R(\alpha)T(A)R(\beta)T(-A)T(B)R(\gamma)T(-B)C. \qquad \textbf{(EQ 33)}$$

Method III.

1. Consider oA, AB, and BC as clock hands with the rotation axes at o, A, and B, respectively. Rotate oA by α degrees, AB by $(\alpha+\beta)$ degrees, and BC by $(\alpha+\beta+\gamma)$ degrees:

$$A_f = R(\alpha)A;\ B' = T(A)R(\alpha+\beta)T(-A)B;\ C' = T(B)R(\alpha+\beta+\gamma)T(-B)C. \qquad \textbf{(EQ 34)}$$

2. Translate AB' to A_fB_f:

$$B_f = T(A_f)T(-A)B' = T(A_f)R(\alpha+\beta)T(-A)B. \qquad \text{(EQ 35)}$$

Note that $T(-A)T(A) = I$, which is the identity matrix: $I = \begin{bmatrix} 1 & 0 & 0 \\ 0 & 1 & 0 \\ 0 & 0 & 1 \end{bmatrix}$. Any matrix

multiplied by the identity matrix does not change. The vertex is translated by vector A, and then reversed back to its original position by translation vector $-A$.

3. Translate BC' to B_fC_f:

$$C_f = T(B_f)T(-B)C' = T(B_f)R(\alpha+\beta+\gamma)T(-B)C. \qquad \text{(EQ 36)}$$

2.3 3D Transformation and Hidden-surface Removal

2D transformation is a special case of 3D transformation where $z=0$. For example, a 2D point (x, y) is $(x, y, 0)$ in 3D, and a 2D rotation around the origin $R(\theta)$ is a 3D rotation around the z axis $R_z(\theta)$ (Fig. 2.7). The z axis is perpendicular to the display with the arrow pointing towards the viewer. We can assume the display to be a view of a 3D drawing box, which is projected along the z axis direction onto the 2D drawing area at $z=0$.

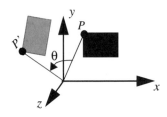

Fig. 2.7 A 3D rotation around z axi

2.3.1 3D Translation, Rotation, and Scaling

In 3D, for translation and scaling, we can translate or scale not only along the x and the y axis, but also along the z axis. For rotation, in addition to rotating around the z axis, we can also rotate around the x axis and the y axis. In the homogeneous coordinates, the 3D transformation matrices for translation, rotation, and scaling are as follows:

$$Translation:\ T(d_x, d_y, d_z) = \begin{bmatrix} 1 & 0 & 0 & d_x \\ 0 & 1 & 0 & d_y \\ 0 & 0 & 1 & d_z \\ 0 & 0 & 0 & 1 \end{bmatrix} ;$$

(EQ 37)

$$Scaling:\ S(s_x, s_y, s_z) = \begin{bmatrix} s_x & 0 & 0 & 0 \\ 0 & s_y & 0 & 0 \\ 0 & 0 & s_z & 0 \\ 0 & 0 & 0 & 1 \end{bmatrix} ;$$

(EQ 38)

$$Rotation\ around\ x\ axis:\ R_x(\theta) = \begin{bmatrix} 1 & 0 & 0 & 0 \\ 0 & \cos\theta & -\sin\theta & 0 \\ 0 & \sin\theta & \cos\theta & 0 \\ 0 & 0 & 0 & 1 \end{bmatrix} ;$$

(EQ 39)

$$Rotation\ around\ y\ axis:\ R_y(\theta) = \begin{bmatrix} \cos\theta & 0 & \sin\theta & 0 \\ 0 & 1 & 0 & 0 \\ -\sin\theta & 0 & \cos\theta & 0 \\ 0 & 0 & 0 & 1 \end{bmatrix} ;$$

(EQ 40)

$$Rotation\ around\ z\ axis:\ R_z(\theta) = \begin{bmatrix} \cos\theta & -\sin\theta & 0 & 0 \\ \sin\theta & \cos\theta & 0 & 0 \\ 0 & 0 & 1 & 0 \\ 0 & 0 & 0 & 1 \end{bmatrix} .$$

(EQ 41)

For example, the 2D transformation Equation 31 can be replaced by the corresponding 3D matrices:

$$A_f = R_z(\alpha)A,$$

(EQ 42)

$$\text{where } A = \begin{bmatrix} A_x \\ A_y \\ A_z \\ 1 \end{bmatrix}, A_f = \begin{bmatrix} A_{fx} \\ A_{fy} \\ A_{fz} \\ 1 \end{bmatrix}, \text{ and } A_z = 0. \text{ We can show that } A_{fz} = 0 \text{ as well.}$$

2.3.2 Transformation in OpenGL

As an example, we will implement in OpenGL the robot arm transformation *Method II* in Fig. 2.6. We consider the transformation to be a special case of 3D at $z=0$.

In OpenGL, all the vertices of a model are multiplied by the matrix on the top of the MODELVIEW matrix stack and then by the matrix on the top of the PROJECTION matrix stack before the model is scan-converted. Matrix multiplications are carried out on the top of the matrix stack automatically in the graphics system. The MODELVIEW matrix stack is used for geometric transformation. The PROJECTION matrix stack is used for viewing, which will be discussed later. Here, we explain how OpenGL handles the geometric transformations in the following example (Example 2.4, which implements *Method II* in Fig. 2.6.)

1. Specify that current matrix multiplications are carried out on the top of the MOD-ELVIEW matrix stack:

```
glMatrixMode (GL_MODELVIEW);
```

2. Load the current matrix on the matrix stack with the identity matrix:

```
glLoadIdentity ();
```

The identity matrix for 3D homogeneous coordinates is: $I = \begin{bmatrix} 1 & 0 & 0 & 0 \\ 0 & 1 & 0 & 0 \\ 0 & 0 & 1 & 0 \\ 0 & 0 & 0 & 1 \end{bmatrix}$.

3. Specify the rotation matrix $R_z(\alpha)$, which will be multiplied by whatever matrix is on the current matrix stack already. The result of the multiplication replaces the matrix currently on the top of the stack. If the identity matrix is on the stack, then $IR_z(\alpha)=R_z(\alpha)$:

```
glRotatef (alpha, 0.0, 0.0, 1.0);
```

4. Draw a robot arm — a line segment between point O and A. Before the model is scan-converted into the frame buffer, O and A will first be transformed by the matrix on the top of the MODELVIEW matrix stack, which is $R_z(\alpha)$. That is, $R_z(\alpha)O$ and $R_z(\alpha)A$ will be used to scan-convert the line (Equation 31):

```
drawArm (O, A);
```

5. In the following code section, we specify a series of transformation matrices, which in turn will be multiplied by whatever is already on the current matrix stack: I, $[I]R(\alpha)$, $[[I]R(\alpha)]T(A)$, $[[[I]R(\alpha)]T(A)]R(\beta)$, $[[[[I]R(\alpha)]T(A)]R(\beta)]T(-A)$. Before $drawArm\ (A,\ B)$, we have $M = R(\alpha)T(A)R(\beta)T(-A)$ on the matrix stack, which corresponds to Equation 32:

```
glPushMatrix();
    glLoadIdentity ();
    glRotatef (alpha, 0.0, 0.0, 1.0);
    drawArm (O, A);

    glTranslatef (A[0], A[1], 0.0);
    glRotatef (beta, 0.0, 0.0, 1.0);
    glTranslatef (-A[0], -A[1], 0.0);
    drawArm (A, B);
glPopMatrix();
```

The matrix multiplication is always carried out on the top of the matrix stack. *glPushMatrix()* will move the stack pointer up one slot, and duplicate the previous matrix so that the current matrix on the top of the stack is the same as the matrix immediately below it. *glPopMatrix()* will move the stack pointer down one slot. The obvious advantage of this mechanism is to separate the transformations of the current model between *glPushMatrix()* and *glPopMatrix()* from the transformations of models later.

Let's look at the function *drawRobot()* in Example 2.4 below. Fig. 2.8 shows what is on the top of the matrix stack, when *drawRobot()* is called once and then again. At *drawArm(B, C)* right before *glPopMatrix()*, the matrix on top of the stack is $M = R(\alpha)T(A)R(\beta)T(-A)T(B)R(\gamma)T(-B)$, which corresponds to Equation 33.

Status of the OpenGL MODELVIEW matrix stack

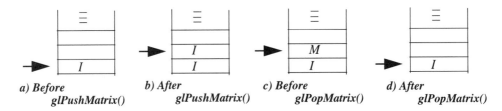

a) Before   b) After   c) Before   d) After
glPushMatrix()   glPushMatrix()   glPopMatrix()   glPopMatrix()

Fig. 2.8 Matrix stack manipulations with *glPushMatrix()* and *glPopMatrix()*

6. Suppose we remove *glPushMatrix()* and *glPopMatrix()* from *drawRobot()*, if we call *drawRobot()* once, it appears fine. If we call it again, you will see that the matrix on the matrix stack is not an identity matrix. It is the previous matrix on the stack already (Fig. 2.9).

Status of the OpenGL MODELVIEW matrix stack

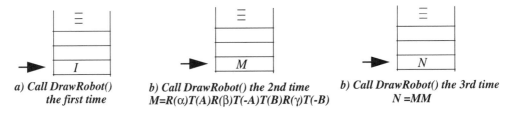

a) Call DrawRobot()   b) Call DrawRobot() the 2nd time   b) Call DrawRobot() the 3rd time
the first time   M=R(α)T(A)R(β)T(-A)T(B)R(γ)T(-B)   N =MM

Fig. 2.9 Matrix stack manipulations without using *glPushMatrix()* and *glPopMatrix()*

For beginners, it is a good idea to draw the state of the current matrix stack while you are reading the sample programs or writing your own programs. This will help you clearly understand what the transformation matrices are at different stages.

Methods I and III (Fig. 2.6) cannot be achieved using OpenGL transformations directly, since OpenGL provides matrix multiplications, but not the vertex coordinates after a vertex is transformed by the matrix. This means that all vertices are always fixed at their original locations. This method avoids floating point accumulation errors. We can use *glGetDoublev(GL_MODELVIEW_MATRIX, M[])* to get the current 16 values of the matrix on the top of the MODELVIEW stack, and multiply the coordinates by the matrix to achieve the transformations for Methods I and III. Of course, you may implement your own matrix multiplications to achieve all the different transformation methods.

/* Example 2.4.robot2d.c: 2D three segments arm transformation */

```
float O[3] = {0.0, 0.0, 0.0}, A[3] = {0.0, 0.0, 0.0},
      B[3] = {0.0, 0.0, 0.0}, C[3] = {0.0, 0.0, 0.0};

float alpha, beta, gama, aalpha=.1, abeta=.3, agama=0.7;

void drawArm(float *End1, float *End2)
{
   glBegin(GL_LINES);
      glVertex3fv(End1);
      glVertex3fv(End2);
   glEnd();
}


  void drawRobot(float *A, float *B, float*C,
                 float alpha, float beta, float gama)
{
   glPushMatrix();

      glColor3f(1, 0, 0);
      glRotatef (alpha, 0.0, 0.0, 1.0);

      // R_z(alpha) is on top of the matrix stack
      drawArm (O, A);

      glColor3f(0, 1, 0);
      glTranslatef (A[0], A[1], 0.0);
      glRotatef (beta, 0.0, 0.0, 1.0);
      glTranslatef (-A[0], -A[1], 0.0);

      // R_z(alpha)T(A)R_z(beta)T(-A) is on top of the stack
      drawArm (A, B);
```

```
        glColor3f(0, 0, 1);
        glTranslatef (B[0], B[1], 0.0);
        glRotatef (gama, 0.0, 0.0, 1.0);
        glTranslatef (-B[0], -B[1], 0.0);

        // R_z(alpha)T(A)R_z(beta)T(-A)T(B)R_z(gama)T(-B)
        drawArm (B, C);

    glPopMatrix();
}


void display(void)
{
    if (rand() % 10000 == 0) aalpha = -aalpha;

    // arm rotation angles
    alpha+= aalpha; beta+= abeta; gama+= agama;

    glClear(GL_COLOR_BUFFER_BIT);
    drawRobot(A, B, C, alpha, beta, gama);

    glutSwapBuffers();
}


void Reshape(int w, int h)
{
    glClearColor (0.0, 0.0, 0.0, 1.0);

    //initialize robot arm end positions
    A[0] = (float) w/7;
    B[0] = (float) w/5;
    C[0] = (float) w/4;

    Width = w; Height = h;
    glViewport (0, 0, Width, Height);

    // hardware set to use PROJECTION matrix stack
    glMatrixMode (GL_PROJECTION);
    // initialize the current top of matrix stack to identity
    glLoadIdentity ();
    glOrtho(-Width/2, Width/2, -Height/2, Height/2, -1.0, 1.0);

    // hardware set to use model transformation matrix stack
    glMatrixMode (GL_MODELVIEW);
    // initialize the current top of matrix stack to identity
    glLoadIdentity ();
}
```

2.3.3 Hidden-surface Removal

Bounding volumes. We first introduce a simple method, called *bounding volume* or *minmax testing*, to determine visible 3D models without using a time-consuming hidden-surface removal algorithm. Here we assume that the viewpoint of our eye is at the origin and the models are in the negative z axis. If we render the models in the order of their distances to the viewpoint of the eye along z axis from the farthest to the closest, we will have correct overlapping of the models. We can build up a rectangular box (bounding volume) with the faces perpendicular to the x, y, or z axis to bound a 3D model, and compare the minimum and maximum bounds in the z direction between boxes to decide which model should be rendered first. Using bounding volumes to decide the priority of rendering is also known as *minmax testing*.

The z-buffer (depth-buffer) algorithm. In OpenGL, to enable the hidden-surface removal (or visible-surface determination) mechanism, we need to enable the depth test once and then clear the depth buffer whenever we redraw a frame:

```
// enable zbuffer (depthbuffer) once
glEnable(GL_DEPTH_TEST);

// clear both framebuffer and zbuffer
 glClear(GL_COLOR_BUFFER_BIT | GL_DEPTH_BUFFER_BIT);
```

Corresponding to a frame buffer, the graphics system also has a z-buffer, or depth buffer, with the same number of entries. After *glClear()*, the z-buffer is initialized to the z value farthest from the view point of our eye, and the frame buffer is initialized to the background color. When scan-converting a model (such as a polygon), before writing a pixel color into the frame buffer, the graphics system (the z-buffer algorithm) compares the pixel's z value to the corresponding xy coordinates' z value in the z-buffer. If the pixel is closer to the view point, its z value is written into the z-buffer and its color is written into the frame buffer. Otherwise, the system moves on to considering the next pixel without writing into the buffers. The result is that, no matter what order the models are scan-converted, the image in the frame buffer only shows the pixels on the models that are not blocked by other pixels. In other words, the visible surfaces are saved in the frame buffer, and all the hidden surfaces are removed.

A pixel's z value is provided by the model at the corresponding xy coordinates. For example, given a polygon and the xy coordinates, we can calculate the z value according to the polygon's plane equation $z=f(x,y)$. Therefore, although scan-conversion is drawing in 2D, 3D calculations are needed to decide hidden-surface removal and others (as we will discuss in the future: lighting, texture mapping, etc.)

A plane equation in its general form is $ax + by + cz + 1 = 0$, where (a, b, c) corresponds to a vector perpendicular to the plane. A polygon is usually specified by a list of vertices. Given three vertices on the polygon, they all satisfy the plane equation and therefore we can find (a, b, c) and $z = -(ax + by + 1)/c$. By the way, because the cross-product of two edges of the polygon is perpendicular to the plane, it is proportional to (a, b, c) as well.

2.3.4 Collision Detection

In addition to visible-model determination, bounding volumes are also used for *collision detection*. To avoid two models in an animation penetrating each other, we can use their bounding volumes to decide their physical distances and collision. Of course, the bounding volume can be in a different shape other than a box, such as a sphere. If the distance between the centers of the two spheres is bigger than the summation of the two radii of the spheres, we know that the two models do not collide with each other. We may use multiple spheres with different radii to more accurately bound a model, but the collision detection would be more complex. Of course, we may also detect collisions directly without using bounding volumes, which is likely much more complex and time consuming.

2.3.5 3D Models: Cone, Cylinder, and Sphere

Approximating a cone. In Example 1.5, we approximated a circle with subdividing triangles. If we raise the center of the circle along the z axis, we approximate a cone, as shown in Fig. 2.10. We need to make sure that our model is contained within the defined coordinates (i.e., the viewing volume):

```
glOrtho(-Width/2, Width/2, -Height/2,
        Height/2, -Width/2, Width/2);
```

Fig. 2.10 A cone

/* Example 2.5.cone: draw a cone by subdivision */

```
int depth=5, circleRadius=200, cnt=1;
```

```
static float vdata[4][3] = {
    {1.0, 0.0, 0.0}, {0.0, 1.0, 0.0},
    {-1.0, 0.0, 0.0}, {0.0, -1.0, 0.0}
};


void subdivideCone(float *v1, float *v2, int depth)
{
    float v0[3] = {0, 0, 0}, v12[3];
    int i;

    if (depth == 0) {
        glColor3f(v1[0]*v1[0], v1[1]*v1[1], v1[2]*v1[2]);

        drawtriangle(v1, v2, v0); // bottom cover of the cone
        v0[2] = 1; // height of the cone, the tip on z axis
        drawtriangle(v1, v2, v0); // side cover of the cone
        return;
    }

    for (i=0; i<3; i++) v12[i] = v1[i]+v2[i];
    normalize(v12);
    subdivideCone(v1, v12, depth - 1);
    subdivideCone(v12, v2, depth - 1);
}


void drawCone(void)
// draw a unit cone: center at origin and bottom in xy plane
{
    subdivideCone(vdata[0], vdata[1], depth);
    subdivideCone(vdata[1], vdata[2], depth);
    subdivideCone(vdata[2], vdata[3], depth);
    subdivideCone(vdata[3], vdata[0], depth);
}


void display(void)
{
    // clear both framebuffer and zbuffer
    glClear(GL_COLOR_BUFFER_BIT | GL_DEPTH_BUFFER_BIT);

    glRotatef(1.1, 1., 0., 0.); // rotate 1.1 deg. alone x axis
    glPushMatrix();
        glScaled(circleRadius, circleRadius, circleRadius);
        drawCone();
    glPopMatrix();
    glutSwapBuffers();
}
```

```
static void Reshape(int w, int h)
{
    glClearColor (0.0, 0.0, 0.0, 1.0);

    // enable zbuffer (depthbuffer) for hidden-surface removal
    glEnable(GL_DEPTH_TEST);

    Width = w; Height = h;
    glViewport (0, 0, Width, Height);

    glMatrixMode (GL_PROJECTION);
    glLoadIdentity ();

    // make sure the cone is within the viewing volume
    glOrtho(-Width/2, Width/2 -Height/2,
            Height/2, -Width/2, Width/2);

    glMatrixMode (GL_MODELVIEW);
    glLoadIdentity ();
}
```

Approximating a cylinder. If we can draw a circle at $z=0$, then we can draw another circle at $z=1$. If we connect the rectangles of the same vertices on the edges of the two circles, we have a cylinder, as shown in Fig. 2.11.

Fig. 2.11 A cylinder

/* Example 2.6.cylinder.c: draw a cylinder by subdivision */

```
void subdivideCylinder(float *v1, float *v2, int depth)
{
    float v11[3], v22[3], v00[3] = {0, 0, 0}, v12[3];
    float v01[3], v02[3];
    int i;

    if (depth == 0) {
        glColor3f(v1[0]*v1[0], v1[1]*v1[1], v1[2]*v1[2]);

        for (i=0; i<3; i++) {
            v01[i] = v11[i] = v1[i];
            v02[i] = v22[i] = v2[i];
        }

        // the height of the cone along z axis
        v01[2] = v02[2] = 1;
```

```
        // draw the side rectangles of the cylinder
        glBegin(GL_POLYGON);
            glVertex3fv(v11);
            glVertex3fv(v22);
            glVertex3fv(v02);
            glVertex3fv(v01);
        glEnd();

        return;
    }

    for (i=0; i<3; i++)
            v12[i] = v1[i]+v2[i];
    normalize(v12);

    subdivideCylinder(v1, v12, depth - 1);
    subdivideCylinder(v12, v2, depth - 1);
}
```

Approximating a sphere. Let's assume that we have an equilateral triangle with its three vertices (v_1, v_2, v_3) on a sphere and $|v_1|=|v_2|=|v_3|=1$. That is, the three vertices are unit vectors from the origin. We can see that $v_{12} = normalize(v_1+v_2)$ is also on the sphere. We can further subdivide the triangle into four equilateral triangles, as shown in Fig. 2.12(a). Example 2.7 uses this method to subdivide an octahedron (Fig. 2.12(b)) into a sphere.

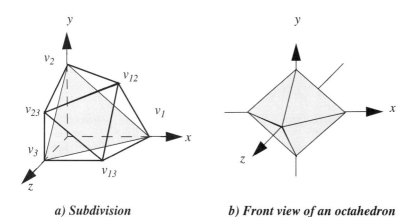

a) Subdivision   *b) Front view of an octahedron*

Fig. 2.12 Drawing a sphere through subdivision

/* Example 2.7.sphere.c: draw a sphere by subdivision */

```
static float vdata[6][3] = {
    {1.0, 0.0, 0.0}, {0.0, 1.0, 0.0}, {0.0, 0.0, 1.0},
    {-1.0, 0.0, 0.0}, {0.0, -1.0, 0.0}, {0.0, 0.0, -1.0}
};


void subdivideSphere(float *v1,
                float *v2, float *v3, long depth)
{
    float v12[3], v23[3], v31[3];
    int i;

    if (depth == 0) {
        glColor3f(v1[0]*v1[0], v2[1]*v2[1], v3[2]*v3[2]);
        drawtriangle(v1, v2, v3);
        return;
    }

    for (i = 0; i < 3; i++) {
        v12[i] = v1[i]+v2[i];
        v23[i] = v2[i]+v3[i];
        v31[i] = v3[i]+v1[i];
    }

    normalize(v12);
    normalize(v23);
    normalize(v31);
    subdivideSphere(v1, v12, v31, depth - 1);
    subdivideSphere(v2, v23, v12, depth - 1);
    subdivideSphere(v3, v31, v23, depth - 1);
    subdivideSphere(v12, v23, v31, depth - 1);
}


void drawSphere(void)
{
    // draw eight triangles to cover the octahedron
    subdivideSphere(vdata[0], vdata[1], vdata[2], depth);
    subdivideSphere(vdata[0], vdata[2], vdata[4], depth);
    subdivideSphere(vdata[0], vdata[4], vdata[5], depth);
    subdivideSphere(vdata[0], vdata[5], vdata[1], depth);

    subdivideSphere(vdata[3], vdata[1], vdata[5], depth);
    subdivideSphere(vdata[3], vdata[5], vdata[4], depth);
    subdivideSphere(vdata[3], vdata[4], vdata[2], depth);
    subdivideSphere(vdata[3], vdata[2], vdata[1], depth);
}
```

2.3.6 Composition of 3D Transformations

Example 2.8 implements the robot arm in Example 2.4 with 3D cylinders, as shown in Fig. 2.13. We also add one rotation around the y axis, so the robot arm moves in 3D.

Fig. 2.13 **A 3-segment robot arm**

/* Example 2.8.robot3d.c: 3D 3-segment arm transformation */

```
drawArm(float End1, float End2) {

    float scale;

    scale = End2-End1;

    glPushMatrix();

        // the cylinder lies in the z axis;
        // rotate it to lie in the x axis
        glRotatef(90.0, 0.0, 1.0, 0.0);
        glScalef(scale/5.0, scale/5.0, scale);

        drawCylinder();
    glPopMatrix();
}


static void drawRobot(float alpha, float beta, float gama)
{
    ...
    // the robot arm is rotating around the y axis
    glRotatef (1.0, 0.0, 1.0, 0.0);
    ...
}
```

Example 2.9 is a simplified solar system. The earth rotates around the sun and the moon rotates around the earth in the xz plane. Given the center of the earth at $E(x_e, y_e, z_e)$ and the center of the moon at $M(x_m, y_m, z_m)$, let's find the new centers after the earth rotates around the sun e degrees, and the moon rotates around the earth m degrees. The moon also revolves around the sun with the earth (Fig. 2.14).

This problem is exactly like the clock problem in Fig. 2.4, except that the center of the clock is revolving around y axis as well. We can consider the moon rotating around the earth first, and then the moon and the earth as one object rotating around the sun.

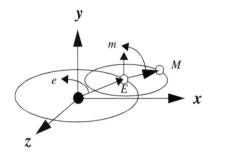

The moon rotates first:
$$M' = T(E)\, R_y(m)\, T(-E)\, M;$$
$$E_f = R_y(e)\, E;$$
$$M_f = R_y(e)\, M';$$

The earth-moon rotates first:
$$E_f = R_y(e)\, E;$$
$$M' = R_y(e)\, M;$$
$$M_f = T(E_f)\, R_y(m)\, T(-E_f)\, M'$$

Fig. 2.14 Simplified solar system: a 2D problem in 3D

In OpenGL, since we can draw a sphere at the center of the coordinates, the transformation would be simpler.

/* Example 2.9.solar.c: draw a simplified solar system */

```
void drawSolar(float E, float e, float M, float m)
{
    glPushMatrix();
        glRotatef(e, 0.0, 1.0, 0.0); // rotate around the "sun"
        glTranslatef(E, 0.0, 0.0);
        drawSphere(); // Ry(e)Tx(E)

        glRotatef(m, 0.0, 1.0,0.0); // rotate around the "earth"
        glTranslatef(M, 0.0, 0.0);
        drawSphere(); // Ry(e)Tx(E)R(m)Tx(M)
    glPopMatrix();
}
```

Next, we change the above solar system into a more complex system, which we call the generalized solar system. Now the earth is elevated along the y axis, and the moon is elevated along the axis from the origin towards the center of the earth, and the moon rotates around this axis as in Fig. 2.15. In other words, the moon rotates around the vector E. Given E and M and their rotation angles e and m respectively, can we find the new coordinates of E_f and M_f?

$r = sqrt(x^2+y^2+z^2);$
$\alpha = arc\ cos\ (y/r);\quad \beta = arc\ tg\ (z/x);$

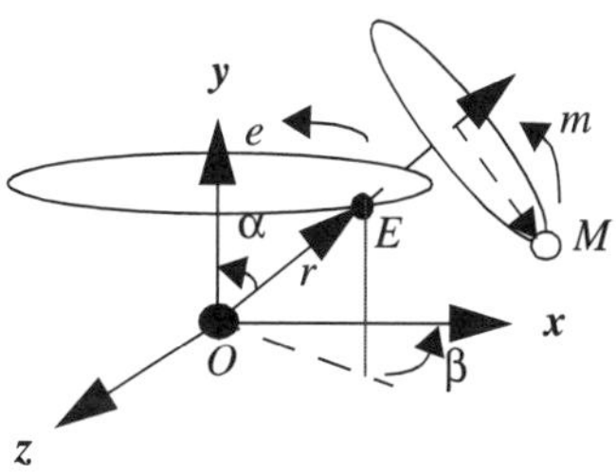

$E_f = R_y(e)\ E;$ // the earth rotate around the y axis

$M_1 = R_y(\beta)\ M;$ // the center of rotation OE is in the xy plane

$M_2 = R_z(\alpha)\ M_1$ // OE is along the y axis

$M_3 = R_y(m)\ M_2;$ // the moon rotates along the y axis

$M_4 = R_z(-\alpha)\ M_3;$ //OE returns to the xy plane

$M_5 = R_y(-\beta)\ M_4;$ // OE returns to its original orientation

$M_f = R_y(e)\ M_5;$ // the moon proceeds with the earth

$M_f = R_y(e)R_y(-\beta)\ R_z(-\alpha)\ R_y(m)\ R_z(\alpha)\ R_y(\beta)\ M;$

Fig. 2.15 Generalized solar system: a 3D problem

We cannot come up with the rotation matrix for the moon, M, immediately. However, we can consider E and M as one object and create the rotation matrix by several steps. Note that for M's rotation around E, we do not really need to rotate E, but we use it as a reference to explain the rotation.

1. As shown in Fig. 2.15, the angle between the y axis and E is $\alpha = arc\ cos\ (y/r)$; the angle between the projection of E on the xz plane and the x axis is $\beta = arc\ tg\ (z/x)$; $r = sqrt(x^2+y^2+z^2)$.

2. Rotate M around the y axis by β degrees so that the new center of rotation E_1 is in the xy plane:

$$M_1 = R_y(\beta)M;\ E_1 = R_y(\beta)E. \tag{EQ 43}$$

3. Rotate M_1 around the z axis by α degrees so that the new center of rotation E_2 is coincident with the y axis:

$$M_2 = R_z(\alpha)M_1; \; E_2 = R_z(\alpha)E_1.$$

(EQ 44)

4. Rotate M_2 around the y axis by m degree:

$$M_3 = R_y(m)M_2.$$

(EQ 45)

5. Rotate M_3 around the z axis by $-\alpha$ degree so that the center of rotation returns to the xz plane:

$$M_4 = R_z(-\alpha)M_3; \; E_1 = R_z(-\alpha)E_2.$$

(EQ 46)

6. Rotate M_4 around y axis by $-\beta$ degree so that the center of rotation returns to its original orientation:

$$M_5 = R_y(-\beta)M_4; \; E = R_y(-\beta)E_1.$$

(EQ 47)

7. Rotate M_5 around y axis e degree so that the moon proceeds with the earth around the y axis:

$$M_f = R_y(e)M_5; \; E_f = R_y(e)E.$$

(EQ 48)

8. Putting the transformation matrices together, we have

$$M_f = R_y(e)R_y(-\beta) \; R_z(-\alpha) \; R_y(m) \; R_z(\alpha) \; R_y(\beta) \; M$$

(EQ 49)

Again, in OpenGL, we start with the sphere at the origin. The transformation is simpler. The following code demonstrates the generalized solar system. The result is as shown in Fig. 2.16. Incidentally, *glRotatef(m, x, y, z)* specifies a single matrix that rotates a point along the vector *(x, y, z)* by m degrees. Now, we know that the matrix is equal to $R_y(-\beta)$ $R_z(-\alpha)$ $R_y(m)$ $R_z(\alpha)$ $R_y(\beta)$.

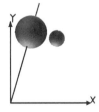

Fig. 2.16 Generalized solar system

/* Example 2.10.gensolar.c: draw a generalized solar system */

```
void drawSolar(float E, float e, float M, float m)
{
    float alpha=30;

    glPushMatrix();
        glRotatef(e, 0.0, 1.0, 0.0); // rotate around the "sun"
        glRotatef(alpha, 0.0, 0.0, 1.0); // tilt angle
        glTranslatef(0., E, 0.0);
        drawSphere(); // the earth

        glRotatef(m, 0.0, 1.0, 0.); // rotate around the "earth"
        glTranslatef(M, 0., 0.);
        drawSphere(); // the moon
    glPopMatrix();
}
```

The generalized solar system corresponds to a top that rotates and proceeds as shown in Fig. 2.17(b). The rotating angle is m and the proceeding angle is e. The earth E is a point along the center of the top and the moon M can be a point on the edge of the top. We learned to draw a cone in OpenGL. We can transform the cone to achieve the motion of a top. In the following example (Example 2.11), we have a top that rotates and proceeds, and a sphere that rotates around the top (Fig. 2.17(c)).

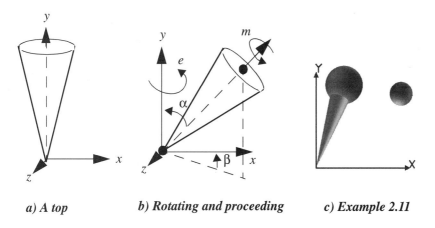

a) A top   b) Rotating and proceeding   c) Example 2.11

Fig. 2.17 Generalized solar system: a top rotates and proceeds

/* Example 2.11.conesolar.c: draw a cone solar system */

```
void drawSolar(float E, float e, float M, float m)
{
    float alpha=30;

    glPushMatrix();
        // rotating around the "sun"; proceed angle
        glRotatef(e, 0.0, 1.0, 0.0);
        glRotatef(alpha, 0.0, 0.0, 1.0); // tilt angle
        glTranslatef(0., E, 0.0);
        glPushMatrix();
            glScalef(E/8,E,E/8);
            glRotatef(90, 1.0, 0.0, 0.0); // orient the cone
            drawCone();
        glPopMatrix();

        glRotatef(m, 0.0, 1.0, 0.); // rotate around the "earth"
        glTranslatef(M, 0., 0.);
        glScalef(E/8,E/8,E/8);
        drawSphere();
    glPopMatrix();
}
```

2.4 Viewing

The display has its device coordinate system in pixels, and our model has its (virtual) modeling coordinate system in which we specify and transform our model. We need to consider the relationship between the modeling coordinates and the device coordinates so that our virtual model will appear as an image on the display. Therefore, we need a *viewing* transformation — the mapping of an area or volume in the modeling coordinates to an area in the display device coordinates.

2.4.1 2D Viewing

In 2D viewing, we specify a rectangular area called the *modeling window* in the modeling coordinates and a display rectangular area called the *viewport* in the device coordinates (Fig. 2.18). The modeling window defines what is to be viewed; the viewport defines where the image appears. Instead of transforming a model in the modeling window to a model in the display viewport directly, we can first transform the modeling window into a square with the lower left corner at (-1,-1) and the upper right corner at (1,1). The coordinates of the square are called the *normalized* coordinates. Clipping of the model is then calculated in the normalized coordinates against the square. After that, the normalized coordinates are scaled and translated to the device coordinates. We should understand that the matrix that transforms the modeling window to the square will also transform the models in the modeling coordinates to the corresponding models in the normalized coordinates. Similarly, the matrix that transforms the square to the viewport will also transform the models accordingly. The process (or pipeline) in 2D viewing is shown in Fig. 2.18. Through normalization, the clipping algorithm avoid dealing with the changing sizes of the modeling window and the device view port.

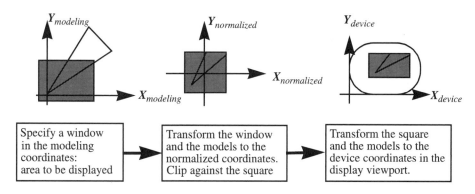

Fig. 2.18 **2D viewing pipeline**

2.4.2 3D Viewing

The display is a 2D viewport, and our model can be in 3D. In 3D viewing, we need to specify a viewing volume, which determines a projection method (*parallel* or *perspective*) — for how 3D models are projected into 2D. The projection lines go from the vertices in the 3D models to the projected vertices in the projection plane — a 2D *view plane* that corresponds to the viewport. A parallel projection has all the projection lines parallel. A perspective projection has all the projection lines converging to a point named the *center of projection*. The center of projection is also called the *view point*. You may consider that your eye is at the view point looking into the viewing volume. Viewing is analogous to taking a photograph with a camera. The object in the outside world has its own 3D coordinate system, the film in the camera has its own 2D coordinate system. We specify a viewing volume and a projection method by pointing and adjusting the zoom.

As shown in Fig. 2.19, the viewing volume for the parallel projection is like a box. The result of the parallel projection is a less realistic view, but can be used for exact measurements. The viewing volume for the perspective projection is like a truncated pyramid, and the result looks more realistic in many cases, but does not preserve sizes in the display — objects further away are smaller.

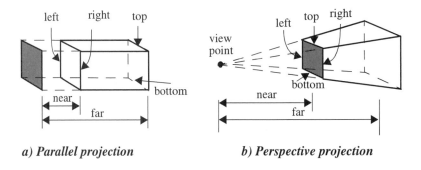

a) Parallel projection   *b) Perspective projection*

Fig. 2.19 **View volumes and projection methods**

In the following, we use the OpenGL system as an example to demonstrate how 3D viewing is achieved. The OpenGL viewing pipeline includes normalization, clipping, perspective division, and viewport transformation (Fig. 2.20). Except for clipping, all other transformation steps can be achieved by matrix multiplications. Therefore, viewing is mostly achieved by geometric transformation. In the OpenGL system, these transformations are achieved by matrix multiplications on the PROJECTION matrix stack.

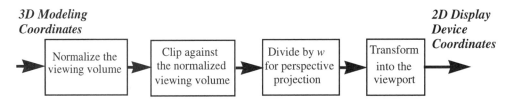

Fig. 2.20 **3D viewing pipeline**

Specifying a viewing volume. A parallel projection is called an *orthographic projection* if the projection lines are all perpendicular to the view plane. *glOrtho*(left, right, bottom, top, near, far) specifies an orthographic projection as shown in Fig. 2.19(a). *glOrtho()* also defines six plane equations that cover the orthographic viewing volume: x=left, x=right, y=bottom, y=top, z=-near, and z=-far. We can see that (left, bottom, -near) and (right, top, -near) specify the (x, y, z) coordinates of the lower-left and upper-right corners of the near clipping plane. Similarly, (left, bottom, -far) and (right, top, -far) specify the (x, y, z) coordinates of the lower-left and upper-right corners of the far clipping plane.

glFrustum(left, right, bottom, top, near, far) specifies a perspective projection as shown in Fig. 2.19(b). *glFrustum()* also defines six planes that cover the perspective viewing volume. We can see that (left, bottom, -near) and (right, top, -near) specify the (x, y, z) coordinates of the lower-left and upper-right corners of the near clipping plane. The far clipping plane is a cross section at z=-far with the projection lines converging to the view point, which is fixed at the origin looking down the negative z axis.

Normalization. Normalization transformation is achieved by matrix multiplication on the PROJECTION matrix stack. In the following code section, we first load the identity matrix onto the top of the matrix stack. Then, we multiply the identity matrix by a matrix specified by *glOrtho()*.

```
// hardware set to use projection matrix stack
  glMatrixMode (GL_PROJECTION);
  glLoadIdentity ();
  glOrtho(-Width/2, Width/2, -Height/2, Height/2,-1.0, 1.0);
```

In OpenGL, *glOrtho()* actually specifies a matrix that transforms the specified viewing volume into a *normalized* viewing volume, which is a cube with six clipping planes as shown in Fig. 2.21 (x=1, x=-1, y=1, y=-1, z=1, and z=-1). Therefore, instead of calculating the clipping and projection directly, the normalization transformation is carried out first to simplify the clipping and the projection.

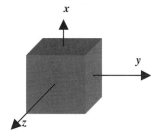

Fig. 2.21 Normalized viewing volume — a cube with (*-1* to *1*) along each axis

Similarly, *glFrustum( )* also specifies a matrix that transforms the perspective viewing volume into a normalized viewing volume as in Fig. 2.21. Here a division is needed to map the homogeneous coordinates into 3D coordinates. In OpenGL, a 3D vertex is represented by (x, y, z, w) and transformation matrices are 4×4 matrices. When $w=1$, (x, y, z) represents the 3D coordinates of the vertex. If $w=0$, (x, y, z) represents a direction. Otherwise, $(x/w, y/w, z/w)$ represents the 3D coordinates. A perspective division is needed simply because after the *glFrustum( )* matrix transformation, $w \neq 1$. In OpenGL, the perspective division is carried out after clipping.

Clipping. Since *glOrtho( )* and *glFrustum( )* both transform their viewing volumes into a normalized viewing volume, we only need to develop one clipping algorithm. Clipping is carried out in homogeneous coordinates to accomodate certain curves. Therefore, all vertices of the models are first transformed into the normalized viewing coordinates, clipped against the planes of the normalized viewing volume ($x=-w$, $x=w$, $y=-w$, $y=w$, $z=-w$, $z=w$), and then transformed and projected into the 2D viewport.

Perspective Division. The perspective normalization transformation *glFrustum( )* results in homogenous coordinates with $w \neq 1$. Clipping is carried out in homogeneous coordinates. However, a division for all the coordinates of the model (x/w, y/w, z/w) is needed to transform homogeneous coordinates into 3D coordinates.

Viewport transformation. All vertices are kept in 3D. We need the z values to calculate hidden-surface removal. From the normalized viewing volume after dividing by w, the viewport transformation calculates each vertex's (x, y, z) corresponding to the pixels in the viewport, and invokes scan-conversion algorithms to draw the model into the viewport. Projecting into 2D is nothing more than ignoring the z values when scan-converting the model's pixels into the frame buffer. It is not necessary but we may consider that the projection plane is at $z=0$. In Fig. 2.19, the shaded projection planes are arbitrarily specified.

Summary of the viewing pipeline. Before scan-conversion, an OpenGL model will go through the following transformation and viewing processing steps:

- *Modeling*: each vertex of the model will be transformed by the current matrix on the top of the MODELVIEW matrix stack

- *Normalization*: after the MODELVIEW transformation, each vertex will be transformed by the current matrix on the top of the PROJECTION matrix stack

- *Clipping*: each primitive (point, line, polygon, etc.) is clipped against the clipping planes in homogeneous coordinates

- *Perspective division*: all primitives are transformed from homogeneous coordinates into cartesian coordinates

- *Viewport transformation*: the model is scaled and translated into the viewport for scan-conversion

2.4.3 An Example of Viewing in OpenGL

Viewing transformation is carried out by the OpenGL system automatically. For programmers, it is more practical to understand how to specify a viewing volume through *glOrtho()* or *glFrustum()*, and to make sure that your models are in the viewing volume after being transformed by the MODELVIEW matrix. The following descriptions explain Example 2.12.

1. *glutInitWindowSize()* in *main()* specifies the display window on the screen in pixels.

2. *glViewport()* in *Reshape()* specifies the rendering area within the display window. The viewing volume will be projected into the viewport area. When we reshape the drawing area, the viewport aspect ratio (*w/h*) changes accordingly.

3. *glOrtho()* or *glFrustum()* specify the viewing volume. The models in the viewing volume will appear in the viewport area on the display.

4. The first matrix we multiply on the MODELVIEW matrix stack, after loading the identity matrix, is a translation along the z axis. This translation can be viewed as the last transformation in modeling coordinates. That is, after finishing all modeling and transformation, we move the origin of the modeling coordinates (and all the models after being transformed in the modeling coordinates) along z axis into the center of the viewing volume. **When we analyze a model's transformations, logically speaking, the order of transformation steps are bottom-up from the closest transformation above the drawing command to where we specify the viewing volume**.

5. In *display()*, you may think that a robot arm is calculated at the origin of the modeling coordinates. Actually, the robot arm is translated along z axis $-(zNear+zFar)/2$ in order to put the arm in the middle of the viewing volume.

6. Another way of looking at the MODELVIEW matrix is that the matrix transforms the viewing method instead of the model. Translating a model along the negative z axis is like moving the viewing volume along the positive z axis. Similarly, rotating a model along an axis by a positive angle is like rotating the viewing volume along the axis by a negative angle. **When we analyze a model's transformation by thinking about transforming its viewing, the order of transformation steps are topdown from where we specify the viewing volume to where we specify the drawing command. We should remember that the signs of the transformation are logically negated in this perspective.**

/* Example 2.12.robotSolar.c: 3D transformation/viewing */

```
void display(void)
{
    glClear(GL_COLOR_BUFFER_BIT | GL_DEPTH_BUFFER_BIT);

    // draw a robot arm from the origin
    drawRobot(A, B, C, alpha, beta, gama);

    glutSwapBuffers();
}


static void Reshape(int w, int h)
{
    float zNear=w, zFar=3*w;

    glClearColor (0.0, 0.0, 0.0, 1.0);
     glEnable(GL_DEPTH_TEST);

    // viewport lower left corner (0,0), aspect ratio w/h
    glViewport (0, 0, w, h);

    // hardware set to use projection matrix stack
    glMatrixMode (GL_PROJECTION);
    glLoadIdentity ();
    //glOrtho(-w/2, w/2, -h/2, h/2, zNear, zFar);
    glFrustum(-w/2, w/2, -h/2, h/2, zNear, zFar);

    // hardware set to use model transformation matrix stack
    glMatrixMode (GL_MODELVIEW);
    glLoadIdentity ();
    // the origin is at the center between znear and zfar
    glTranslatef (0., 0., -(zNear+zFar)/2);
}
```

3
Color and Lighting

Chapter objectives:

- Introduce RGB color in the hardware, eye characteristics, and gamma correction

- Understand color interpolation and smooth shading in OpenGL

- Set up OpenGL lighting: ambient, diffuse, specular, and multiple light sources

- Understand back-face culling and surface shading models

3.1 Color

In a display, a pixel color is specified as a red, green, and blue (RGB) vector. The RGB colors are also called the *primaries*, because our eye sees a different color in a vector of different primary values. The RGB colors are additive primaries — we construct a color on the black background by adding the primaries together. For example, with equal amounts of R, G, and B: G+B $\Rightarrow$ cyan, R+B $\Rightarrow$ magenta, R+G $\Rightarrow$ yellow, and R+G+B $\Rightarrow$ white. RGB colors are used in the graphics hardware, which we will discuss in more detail.

Cyan, magenta, and yellow (CMY) colors are the complements of RGB colors, respectively. The CMY colors are subtractive primaries — we construct a color on a white background by removing the corresponding RGB primaries. Similarly, with equal amounts of R, G, and B: C = RGB - R, M = RGB - G, and Y = RGB - B.

The CMY colors are used in color printers. Adding certain amounts of CMY inks to a point on a white paper is like removing certain amounts of RGB from the white color at that point. The resulting color at the point on the paper depends on the portions of individual inks. Black ink is used to generate different levels of greys replacing using equal amounts of CMY inks.

3.1.1 RGB Mode and Index Mode

If each pixel value in the frame buffer is an RGB vector, the display is in *RGB mode*. Each pixel value can also be an index into a color look-up table called a *colormap*, as shown in Fig. 3.1. Then, the display is in *index mode*. The pixel color is specified in the colormap instead of the frame buffer.

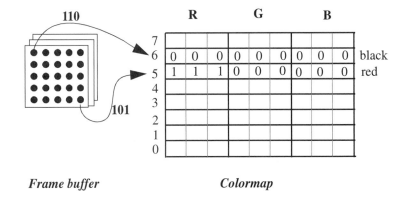

Frame buffer   *Colormap*

Fig. 3.1 Color-index mode and colormap

Let's assume that we have 3 bits per entry in the frame buffer. That is, the frame buffer has 3 *bitplanes*. In RGB mode, we have access to 8 different colors: black, red, green, blue, cyan, magenta, yellow, and white. In index mode, we still have access to only 8 different colors, but the colors can vary depending on how we load the colormap. If the graphics hardware has a limited number of bitplanes for the frame buffer, index mode allows more color choices, even though the number of colors is the same as that of RGB mode at the same time. For example, in the above example, if we have 12 bitplanes per entry in the colormap, we can choose 8 colors from $2^{12} = 4096$ different colors. The colormap does not take much space in memory, which had been a significant advantage when fast memory chips were very expensive. In GLUT, we use *glutInitDisplayMode(GLUT_INDEX)* to choose the index mode. RGB mode is the default. Index mode can also be useful for doing various animation tricks. However, in general, since memory is no longer a limitation and RGB mode is easier and more flexible, we use it in the examples. Also, in OpenGL programming, each color component (R, G, or B) value is in the range of 0 to 1. The system will scale the value to the corresponding hardware bits during compilation transparent to the users.

3.1.2 Eye Characteristics and Gamma Correction

A pixel color on a display is the emission of light that reaches our eye. An RGB vector is a representation of the *brightness* level that our eye perceives. The *intensity* is the amount of physical energy used to generate the brightness. Our eye sees a different color for a different RGB vector. We may not have noticed, but certain colors cannot be produced by RGB mixes, and hence cannot be shown on an RGB display device.

The eye is more sensitive to yellow-green light. In general, the eye's sensitivities to different colors generated by a constant intensity level are different. Also, for the same color, the eye's perceived brightness levels are not linearly proportional to the intensity levels. To generate evenly spaced brightness levels, we need to use logarithmically-spaced intensity levels. For example, to generate n evenly-spaced brightness levels for a color component λ (which represents R, G, or B), we need corresponding intensity levels at

$$I_{i\lambda} = r^i I_{0\lambda} \text{ for } i=0, 1, ..., n\text{-}1, \qquad \text{(EQ 50)}$$

where $I_{0\lambda}$ is the lowest intensity available in the display hardware and $r=(1/I_{0\lambda})^{1/(n-1)}$.

For a CRT display monitor, $I_{i\lambda}$ depends on the energy in voltage that is applied to generate the electrons lighting the corresponding screen pixels (phosphor dots):

$$I_{i\lambda} = KV^\gamma. \qquad \text{(EQ 51)}$$

The value of γ is about 2.2 to 2.5 for most CRTs. Therefore, given an intensity $I_{i\lambda}$, we can find the corresponding voltage needed in the hardware:

$$V = (I_{i\lambda}/K)^{1/\gamma}. \qquad \text{(EQ 52)}$$

This is called *gamma correction*, since γ is used in the equation to find the voltage to generate the correct intensity. Without gamma correction, the brightness levels are not even, and high brightness pixels appear to be darker. Different CRTs have different K's and γ's. Instead of calculating the voltages, CRT manufactures can build up a look-up table for a CRT (in the CRT monitor or in the corresponding graphics card that refreshes the CRT) by measuring the corresponding brightness levels and voltages. In the look-up table, the indices are the brightness levels and the values are the corresponding voltages.

Usually, the hardware gamma correction allows software modifications. That is, we can change the contents of the look-up table. Today, most color monitors have hardware gamma corrections. Due to different material properties (phosphor composites) and gamma corrections, the same RGB vector appears in different colors and brightness on individual monitors. Effort is needed to make two CRT monitors appear exactly the same.

To simplify the matter, since the difference between the intensity and the brightness is solved in the hardware, we use the intensity to mean the brightness or the RGB value directly. Also, we use I_λ to represent the brightness level i of an RGB component directly. That is, I_λ represents a perceived brightness level instead of an energy level.

3.2 Color Interpolation

In OpenGL, we use *glShadeModel(GL_FLAT)* or *glShadeModel(GL_SMOOTH)* to choose between two different models (flat shading and smooth shading) of using colors for a primitive. With *GL_FLAT*, we use one color that is specified by *glColor3f()* for all the pixels in the primitive. For example, in Example 3.1, if we call *glShadeModel(GL_FLAT)*, only one color will be used in *drawtriangle()*, even though we have specified different colors for different vertices. Depending on the OpenGL systems, the color may be the color specified for the last vertex in a primitive.

For a line, with *GL_SMOOTH*, the vertex colors are linearly interpolated along the pixels between the two end vertices. For example, if a line has 5 pixels, and the end point colors are (0,0,0) and (0,0,1), then, after the interpolation, the 5 pixel colors will be (0,0,0), (0,0,1/4), (0,0,2/4), (0,0,3/4), and (0,0,1), respectively. The intensity of each RGB component is interpolated separately. In general, given the end point intensities ($I_{\lambda 1}$ and $I_{\lambda 2}$) and the number of pixels along the line (N), the intensity increment of the linear interpolation is:

$$\Delta I_\lambda = \frac{I_{\lambda 2} - I_{\lambda 1}}{N - 1}.$$

(EQ 53)

That is, for each pixel from the starting pixel to the end pixel, the color component changes ΔI_λ.

For a polygon, OpenGL first interpolates along the edges, and then along the horizontal scan-lines during scan-conversion. All we need to do to carry out interpolation in OpenGL is to call *glShadeModel(GL_SMOOTH)* and set up different vertex colors.

/* **Example 3.1.shading.c: OpenGL flat or smooth shading** */

```
void drawtriangle(float *v1, float *v2, float *v3)
{
   glBegin(GL_TRIANGLES);

      glColor3f(1,0,0); glVertex3fv(v1);
      glColor3f(0,1,0); glVertex3fv(v2);
      glColor3f(0,0,1); glVertex3fv(v3);

   glEnd();
}


void drawColorCoord(float zlen)
{
   glBegin(GL_LINES);
      glColor3f(1,1,1); glVertex3f(0,0,0);
      glColor3f(0,0,1); glVertex3f(0,0,zlen);
   glEnd();
}


void display(void)
{
   cnt++;
   glClear(GL_COLOR_BUFFER_BIT | GL_DEPTH_BUFFER_BIT);

// alternating between flat & smooth
   if (cnt % 50 == 0) glShadeModel(GL_SMOOTH);
   if (cnt%100 == 0) glShadeModel(GL_FLAT);

   drawColorCoord(1.);
   drawtriangle(vdata[0], vdata[1], vdata[2]);

   glutSwapBuffers();
}
```

3.3 Lighting

A pixel color is a reflection or emission of light from a point on a model to our eye. Therefore, instead of specifying a color for a point directly, we can specify light sources and material properties for the graphics system to calculate the color of the point according to a lighting model. The real world lighting is very complex. In graphics, we adopt simplified methods (i.e., lighting or illumination models) that work relatively fast and well.

We use the OpenGL lighting system as an example to explain lighting. The OpenGL lighting model includes four major components: ambient, diffuse, specular, and emission. The final color is the summation of these components. The lighting model is developed to calculate the color of each individual pixel that corresponds to a point on a primitive. The method of calculating the lighting for all pixels in a primitive is called the *shading model*. As introduced in Section 3.2, OpenGL calculates vertex pixel colors and uses interpolation to find the colors of all pixels in a primitive when we call *glShadeModel(GL_SMOOTH)*. If we use *glShadeModel(GL_FLAT)*, only one vertex color is used for the primitive. However, the vertex colors are calculated by the lighting model instead of being specified by *glColor()*.

3.3.1 Lighting Components

Emissive Component. The emission intensity of a vertex pixel with an emissive material is calculated as follows:

$$I_{\lambda e} = M_{\lambda emission},\qquad\text{(EQ 54)}$$

where λ is an RGB component or A (alpha), and $M_{\lambda emission}$ is the material's emission property. Each color component is calculated independently. Since the *alpha* value will be discussed in the next chapter, we can ignore it in our current examples. In OpenGL, *emission* is a material property that is neither dependent on any light source nor considered a light source. Emissive material does not emit light, it displays its own color. The vertex's corresponding surface has two sides, the front and the back, which can be specified with different material properties.

In Example 3.2, the material is emitting a white color and all objects will be white until we change the emission material component to something else. Here according to Equation 54, the calculated RGB color is *(1., 1., 1.)*. If we only specify the emission component, the effect is the same as specifying *glColor3f(1., 1., 1.)*.

/* Example 3.2.emission.c: emissive material component */

```
init() {
    float white[] = {1., 1., 1., 1.}; // RGBA

    glEnable(GL_LIGHTING);
    glMaterialfv(GL_FRONT, GL_EMISSION, white);
}
```

When lighting is enabled, *glColor3f()* is turned off. In other words, even though we may have *glColor3f()s* in the program, they are not used. Instead, the OpenGL system uses the current lighting model to calculate the vertex color automatically. We may use *glColorMaterial()* with *glEnable(GL_COLOR_MATERIAL)* to tie the color specified by *glColor3f()* to a material property.

Ambient Component. The ambient intensity of a vertex pixel is calculated as follows:

$$I_{\lambda a} = L_{\lambda a} M_{\lambda a},$$
(EQ 55)

where $L_{\lambda a}$ represents the light source's ambient intensity and $M_{\lambda a}$ is the material's ambient property. Ambient color is the overall intensity of multiple reflections generated from a light source in an environment. We do not even care where the light source is as long as it exists. In Example 3.3, according to Equation 55, the calculated RGB color is *(1., 1., 0.)*.

/* Example 3.3.ambient.c: ambient color */

```
init() {
    float white[] = {1., 1., 1., 1.}; // RGBA
    float yellow[] = {1., 1., 0., 1.};

    glEnable(GL_LIGHTING);
    glEnable(GL_LIGHT0); // enable light source zero
    glLightfv(GL_LIGHT0, GL_AMBIENT, white);
    glMaterialfv(GL_FRONT, GL_AMBIENT, yellow);
}
```

Diffuse Component. The diffuse intensity of a vertex pixel is calculated as follows:

$$I_{\lambda d} = L_{\lambda d} M_{\lambda d} (\boldsymbol{n} \bullet \boldsymbol{L}),$$ (EQ 56)

where $L_{\lambda d}$ is the light source's diffuse intensity, $M_{\lambda d}$ is the material's diffuse property, $\boldsymbol{L}$ is the light source direction, and $\boldsymbol{n}$ is the surface normal direction from the pixel, which is a vector perpendicular to the surface. Here the light source is a point generating equal intensity in all directions. Diffuse color is the reflection from a dull surface material that appears equally bright from all viewing directions.

In OpenGL, $\boldsymbol{L}$ is a unit vector (or normalized vector) pointing from the current vertex to the light source position. The normal is specified by *glNormal*() right before we specify the vertex. As shown in Fig. 3.2, $\cos\theta = \dfrac{\boldsymbol{n} \bullet \boldsymbol{L}}{|\boldsymbol{n}|}$, which is between *0* and *1* when θ is between 0° and 90°. When θ is greater than 90°, the diffuse intensity is set to zero.

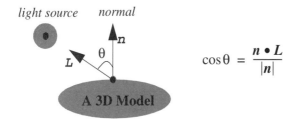

Fig. 3.2 The angle between *L* and *n* at the vertex

The length of the normal is a factor in Equation 56. We can initially specify the normal to be a unit vector. However, normals are transformed similar to vertices so that the lengths of the normals may be scaled. (Actually, normals are transformed by the inverse transpose of the current matrix on the matrix stack.) If we are not sure about the length of the normals, we can call *glEnable(GL_NORMALIZE)*, which enables the OpenGL system to normalize each normal before calculating the lighting. This, however, incurs the extra normalization calculations. Also, the light source position has four parameters: (*x, y, z, w*) as in homogeneous coordinates. If *w* is *1*, (*x, y, z*) is the light source position. If *w* is *0*, (*x, y, z*) represents the light source direction at infinity, in which case the light source is in the same direction for all pixels at different locations. If a point light source is far away from the object, it has essentially the same angle with all surfaces that have the same surface normal direction. Example 3.4 shows how to specify the diffuse parameters in OpenGL.

/* Example 3.4.diffuse.c: diffuse light & material components */

```
init()
{
    //xyzw, light source at infinity
    float position[] = {0., 0., 1., 0.};
    float white[] = {1., 1., 1., 1.}; // RGBA

    glEnable(GL_LIGHTING);
    glEnable(GL_NORMALIZE);

    glEnable(GL_LIGHT0);
    glLightfv(GL_LIGHT0, GL_POSITION, position);
    glLightfv(GL_LIGHT0, GL_DIFFUSE, white);

    glMaterialfv(GL_FRONT, GL_DIFFUSE, white);
}


void drawConeSide(float *v1, float *v2, float *v3)
{
    float v11[3], v22[3], v33[3];
    int i;

    for (i=0; i<3; i++) {
        v11[i] = v1[i] + v3[i]; // normal for cone vertex 1
        v22[i] = v2[i] + v3[i]; // normal for cone vertex 2
        v33[i] = v11[i] + v22[i]; // normal for cone vertex 3
    }

    glBegin(GL_TRIANGLES);

        glNormal3fv(v11);
        glVertex3fv(v1);
        glNormal3fv(v22);
        glVertex3fv(v2);
        glNormal3fv(v33);
        glVertex3fv(v3);

    glEnd();
}
```

Object shading depends on how we specify the normals as well. For example (Fig. 3.3), if we want to display a pyramid, the normals for the triangle vertices v1, v2, and v3 should be the same and perpendicular to the triangle. If we want to approximate a cone, the normals should be perpendicular to the cone's surface. If we assume that the radius of the cone's base and the height of the cone have the same length, then the normals are $n1$=v1+v3, $n2$=v2+v3, and $n3$=$n1$+$n2$. Here, the additions are vector

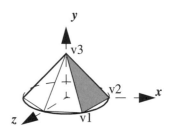

Fig. 3.3 The radius and the height of the cone are the same (unit length)

additions, as in the function *drawConeSide()* in Example 3.4 above. The OpenGL system interpolates the pixel colors in the triangle. We can set all the vertex normals to $n3$ to display a pyramid.

Specular Component. The specular intensity of a vertex pixel is calculated as follows:

$$I_{\lambda s} = L_{\lambda s} M_{\lambda s} \left(\frac{n \bullet (L + V)}{|L + V|} \right)^{shininess}$$

(EQ 57)

where $L_{\lambda s}$ is the light source's specular intensity, $M_{\lambda s}$ is the material's specular property, V is the view point direction from the pixel, and *shininess* is the material's shininess property. Specular color is the highlight reflection from a smooth-surface material that depends on the reflection direction R (which is L reflected along the normal) and the viewing direction V. As shown in Fig. 3.4, $\cos\alpha = \dfrac{n \bullet (L + V)}{|n||L + V|}$, which is between 0 and 1 when α is between $0°$ and $90°$. When θ or α is greater than $90°$, the specular intensity is set to zero. The viewer can see specularly reflected light from a mirror only when the angle α is close to zero. When the *shininess* is a very large number, $(\cos\alpha)^{shininess}$ is attenuated towards zero unless $(\cos\alpha)$ equals one.

The view point, as we discussed in the viewing transformation, is at the origin (facing the negative *z* axis). We use *glLightModeli(GL_LIGHT_MODEL_LOCAL_VIEWER, GL_TRUE)* to specify the view point at *(0, 0, 0)*. However, to simplify the lighting calculation, OpenGL allows us to specify the view point at infinity in the *(0, 0, 1)* direction. This is the default in the same direction for all vertex pixels. Since this assumption is only used to simplify lighting calculations, the view point is not changed for other graphics calculations, such as projection. Example 3.5 shows how to specify the specular parameters in OpenGL.

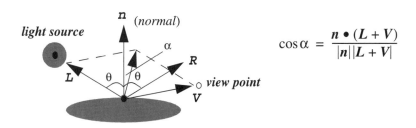

$$\cos\alpha = \frac{n \cdot (L+V)}{|n||L+V|}$$

Fig. 3.4 **The angle between *n* and (*L+V*) at the vertex**

/* Example 3.5.specular.c: specular light & material components */

```
init() {
    float position[] = {0., 0., 1., 0.};
    float white[] = {1., 1., 1., 1.}; // RGBA

    glEnable(GL_LIGHTING);
    glEnable(GL_NORMALIZE);

    glEnable(GL_LIGHT0);
    glLightfv(GL_LIGHT0, GL_POSITION, position);
    glLightfv(GL_LIGHT0, GL_SPECULAR, white);

    glMaterialfv(GL_FRONT, GL_SPECULAR, white);
    glMaterialf(GL_FRONT, GL_SHININESS, 50.0);
}
```

3.3.2 OpenGL Lighting Model

Both the light source and the material have multiple components: ambient, diffuse, and specular. The final vertex color is an integration of all these components:

$$I_\lambda = I_{\lambda e} + I_{\lambda a} + I_{\lambda d} + I_{\lambda s}. \qquad \text{(EQ 58)}$$

We can simplify Equation 58 as:

$$I_\lambda = I_{\lambda e} + I_{\lambda L},$$ (EQ 59)

where $I_{\lambda L} = I_{\lambda a} + I_{\lambda d} + I_{\lambda s}$. While ambient, diffuse, and specular intensities depend on the light source, emissive intensity does not. OpenGL scales and normalizes the final intensity to a value between 0 and 1.

In previous examples, even though we didn't specify all the components, OpenGL used the default values that are predefined. If necessary, we can specify all different lighting components (Example 3.6). Fig. 3.5 is a comparison among the different lighting component effects from the examples we have discussed.

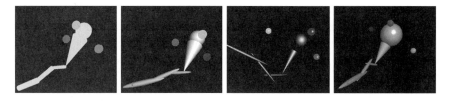

Example 3.3:   *Example 3.4:*   *Example 3.5:*   *Example 3.6:*
Ambient/Emissive   **Diffuse**   **Specular**   **Multiple components**

Fig. 3.5 **The OpenGL lighting components and integration**

/* Example 3.6.materials.c: multiple light and material components */

```
init() {

    float position[] = {0., 0., 1., 0.};
    float white[] = {1., 1., 1., 1.};
    float whitish[] = {.7, .7, .7, 1.};
    float black[] = {0., 0., 0., 1.};
    float blackish[] = {.2, .2, .2, 1.};

    glEnable(GL_LIGHTING);
    glEnable(GL_NORMALIZE);
    glEnable(GL_LIGHT0);
```

```
glLightfv(GL_LIGHT0, GL_POSITION, position);
glLightfv(GL_LIGHT0, GL_AMBIENT, whitish);
glLightfv(GL_LIGHT0, GL_DIFFUSE, white);
glLightfv(GL_LIGHT0, GL_SPECULAR, white);

glMaterialfv(GL_FRONT, GL_AMBIENT, blackish);
glMaterialfv(GL_FRONT, GL_DIFFUSE, whitish);
glMaterialfv(GL_FRONT, GL_SPECULAR, white);
glMaterialf(GL_FRONT, GL_SHININESS, 100.0);
}
```

Movable Light Source. In OpenGL, a light source is invisible. If the light source is directional at infinity with $w=0$, it is always fixed. Otherwise, the light source position is transformed as a geometric object by the current matrix when it is specified. In other words, if the matrix is modified at run time, the light source can be moved around like an object. Lighting is calculated according to the transformed position. To simulate a visible light source, we can specify the light source and draw an object at the same position. As in Example 3.7, the light source and the sphere are transformed by the same matrix. We may specify the sphere's emission property to correspond to the light source's parameters, so that the sphere looks like the light source.

/* Example 3.7.movelight.c: movable light source */

```
void drawSolar(float M, float m)
{
    float position[] = {0., 0., 0., 1.};

    glPushMatrix();

        // the moon rotates around the earth
        glRotatef(m, 0., 1., 0.);

        glTranslatef(M, 0., 0.);

        glLightfv(GL_LIGHT0, GL_POSITION, position);

        // the center of the sphere is at the origin
        drawSphere();

    glPopMatrix();

}
```

Spotlight Effect. A real light source may not generate equal intensity in all directions:

$$I_\lambda = I_{\lambda e} + f_{spot} I_{\lambda L} \qquad \text{(EQ 60)}$$

where f_{spot} is called the *spotlight effect factor.* In OpenGL, it is calculated as follows:

$$f_{spot} = (-L \bullet D_{spot})^{spotExp} \qquad \text{(EQ 61)}$$

where (*-L*) is a unit vector pointing from the light source to the vertex pixel, D_{spot} is the direction of the light source, and *spotExp* is a specified constant. As shown in Fig. 3.6, $\cos\gamma = \dfrac{(-L) \bullet D_{spot}}{|D_{spot}|}$. When the *spotExp* is a large number, $(\cos\gamma)^{spotExp}$ is attenuated towards zero and the light is concentrated along the D_{spot} direction.

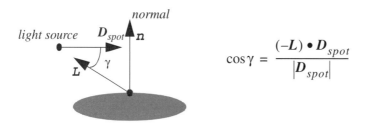

Fig. 3.6 The angle between (*-L*) and D_{spot}

The light source may have a *cutoff angle* as shown in Fig. 3.7, so that only the vertex pixels inside the cone area are lit. There is no light outside the cone area. To be exact, the cone area is infinite in the D_{spot} direction without a bottom.

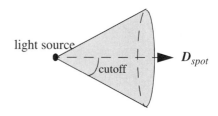

Fig. 3.7 The light source cutoff angle

Example 3.8 shows how to specify spotlight parameters. The D_{spot} direction vector is also transformed by the current modelview matrix, as the vertex normals.

/* Example 3.8.spotlight.c: spotlight effect */

```
void drawSolar(float M, float m)
{
    float position[] = {0., 0., 0., 1.};
    float spot_direction[] = {-1., 0., 0., 1.};

    glPushMatrix();
        // "Moon" rotating around the "Earth"
        glRotatef(m, 0.0, 1.0, 0.);
        glTranslatef(M, 0., 0.);

        glLightf(GL_LIGHT0,GL_SPOT_CUTOFF,30.0);
        glLightfv(GL_LIGHT0,GL_SPOT_DIRECTION,spot_direction);
        glLightf(GL_LIGHT0,GL_SPOT_EXPONENT,2.0);
        glLightfv(GL_LIGHT0, GL_POSITION, position);

        drawSphere();
    glPopMatrix();
}
```

Light Source Attenuation. The intensity from a point light source to a vertex pixel can be attenuated by the distance the light travels:

$$I_\lambda = I_{\lambda e} + f_{att}f_{spot}I_{\lambda L},$$

(EQ 62)

where f_{att} is called the *light source attenuation factor*. In OpenGL, f_{att} is calculated as follows:

$$f_{att} = \frac{1}{A_c + A_l d_L + A_q d_L^2},$$

(EQ 63)

where d_L is the distance from the point light source to the lit vertex pixel, A_c, A_l, and A_q are constant, linear, and quadratic attenuation factors. Example 3.9 shows how to specify these factors.

/* Example 3.9.attlight.c: light source attenuation effect */

```
void drawSolar(float M, float m)
{
    float position[] = {0., 0., 0., 1.};

    glPushMatrix();
        // moon rotate around the "earth"
        glRotatef(m, 0.0, 1.0, 0.);
        glTranslatef(M, 0., 0.);
        glLightf(GL_LIGHT0,GL_CONSTANT_ATTENUATION, 1.0);
        glLightf(GL_LIGHT0,GL_LINEAR_ATTENUATION,0.0002);
        glLightf(GL_LIGHT0,GL_QUADRATIC_ATTENUATION,0.0001);
        glLightfv(GL_LIGHT0, GL_POSITION, position);
        drawSphere(position);
    glPopMatrix();
}
```

Multiple Light Sources. We can also specify multiple light sources:

$$I_\lambda = I_{\lambda e} + \sum_{i=0}^{k-1} f_{atti} f_{spoti} I_{\lambda Li}, \qquad \text{(EQ 64)}$$

where k is the number of different light sources. Each light source's parameters and position can be specified differently. There may be fixed as well as moving light sources with different properties. The emission component, which is a material property, does not depend on any light source. We can also use *glLightModel()* to specify a global ambient light that does not depend on any light source. Fig. 3.8 is a comparison among the different lighting component effects from the examples we have discussed.

/* Example 3.10.lights.c: fixed and multiple moving light sources */

```
init() {
    float position[] = {0., 0., 1., 0.};

    glEnable(GL_LIGHTING);
    glEnable(GL_NORMALIZE);
    glEnable(GL_CULL_FACE);
```

```
glEnable(GL_LIGHT0);
glEnable(GL_LIGHT1);
glEnable(GL_LIGHT2);
glEnable(GL_LIGHT3);
...
// fixed light source
glLightfv(GL_LIGHT0, GL_POSITION, position);

// lights 1, 2, and 3 are specified as local
//        and movable positions
}
```

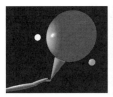 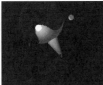  

Example 3.7:
**Moving light
source**

Example 3.8:
**Spotlight
effect**

Example 3.9:
**Light source
attenuation**

Example 3.10:
**Multiple light
sources**

Fig. 3.8 The OpenGL light sources: moving, spotlight, and attenuation

3.4 Visible-Surface Shading

Shading models are methods for calculating the lighting of a surface instead of just one vertex or point pixel. As we discussed, OpenGL provides flat shading and smooth shading for polygonal surfaces. A polygon on a surface is also called a *face*. We will discuss some issues related to improving the efficiency and quality of face shading.

3.4.1 Back-Face Culling

We can speed up drawing by eliminating some of the hidden surfaces before rendering. Given a solid object such as a polygonal sphere, we can see only half of the faces. The visible faces are called *front-facing* polygons or *front faces*, and the invisible faces are called *back-facing* polygons or *back faces*. The invisible back faces should be eliminated from processing as early as possible, even before the z-buffer algorithm is called. The z-buffer algorithm, as discussed in Section 2.3.3 on page 37, needs significant hardware calculations. Eliminating back-facing polygons before rendering is called *back-face culling*.

In OpenGL, if the order of the polygon vertices is counter-clockwise from the view point, the polygon is front-facing (Fig. 3.9). Otherwise, it is back-facing. We use *glEnable(GL_CULL_FACE)* to turn on culling and call *glCullFace(GL_BACK)* to achieve back-face culling. Therefore, if we use back-face culling, we should make sure that the order of the vertices are correct when we specify a face by a list of vertices. Otherwise, we will see some holes (missing faces) on the surface displayed. Also, as in

$$n = (v2 - v1) \times (v3 - v2)$$

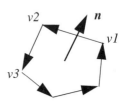

Fig. 3.9 A front face and its norma

the following function (Example 3.10), we often use the cross product of two edge vectors of a face to find its normal *n*. An edge vector is calculated by the difference of two neighbor vertices. The correctness of the surface normal depends on the correct order and direction of the edge vectors in the cross product, which in turn depend on the correct order of the vertices as well. The faces that have normals facing the wrong direction will not be shaded correctly.

```
void drawBottom(float *v1, float *v2, float *v3){
    // normal to the cone or cylinder bottom
    float v12[3], v23[3], vb[3];
    int i;

    for (i=0; i<3; i++) { // two edge vectors
        v12[i] = v2[i] - v1[i];
        v23[i] = v3[i] - v2[i];
    }

    // vb = normalized cross prod. of v12 X v23
    ncrossprod(v12, v23, vb);
    glBegin(GL_TRIANGLES);
        glNormal3fv(vb);
        glVertex3fv(v1); glVertex3fv(v2); glVertex3fv(v3);
    glEnd();
}
```

Given a hollow box or cylinder without a cover, we will see both front and back faces. In this case, we cannot use back-face culling. We may turn on lighting for both front and back faces: *glLightModeli(GL_LIGHT_MODEL_TWO_SIDE, TRUE)*. If we turn on two-side lighting, each polygon has two sides with opposite normals and OpenGL will decide to shade the side that the normal is facing the view point. We may also supply different material properties for both the front-facing polygons and the back-facing polygons: *glMaterialfv(GL_FRONT, GL_AMBIENT, red); glMaterialfv(GL_BACK, GL_AMBIENT, green)*.

3.4.2 Polygon Shading Models

The appearances of a surface under different shading models differ greatly. Flat shading, which is the simplest and fastest, is used to display a flat-face object instead of a curved-face object. In approximating a curved surface, using flat shading with a finer polygon mesh turns out to be ineffective and slow. Smooth shading (also called Gouraud shading), which calculates the colors of the vertex pixels and interpolates the colors of every other pixel in a polygon, is often used to approximate the shading of a curved face. To eliminate intensity discontinuities, the normal of a vertex is often calculated by averaging the normals of the faces sharing the vertex on the surface. In general, we try to specify a vertex normal that is perpendicular to the curved surface instead of the polygon. Also, we may specify normals in the directions we prefer in order to achieve special effects.

Another popular shading model, the normal-vector interpolation shading (called Phong shading) calculates the normals of the vertex pixels and interpolates the normals of all other pixels in a polygon. Then, the color of every pixel is calculated using a lighting model and the interpolated normals. Phong shading is much slower than Gouraud shading and therefore is not implemented in the OpenGL system.

Phong shading allows specular highlights to be located in a polygon while Gouraud shading does not. In contrast, if a highlight is within a polygon, smooth shading will fail to show it, since the intensity interpolation makes it such that the highest intensity is only possible at a vertex. Also, if we have a spotlight source and the vertices fall outside the cutoff angle, smooth shading will not calculate the vertex colors and thus the polygon will not be shaded.

All of the above shading models are approximations. Using polygons to approximate curved faces is much faster than handling curved surfaces directly. The efficiency of polygon rendering is still the benchmark of graphics systems. In order to achieve better realism, we may calculate each surface pixel's color directly without using interpolations. However, calculating the lighting of every pixel on a surface is in general very time consuming.

3.4.3 Ray Tracing and Radiosity

Ray tracing and *radiosity* are advanced global lighting and rendering models that achieve better realism, which are not provided in OpenGL. They are time-consuming methods so that no practical real-time animation is possible with the current graphics hardware. Here we only introduce the general concepts.

Ray tracing is an extension to the lighting model we learned. The light rays travel from the light sources to the view point. The simplest ray tracing method is to follow the rays in reverse from the view point to the light sources. A ray is sent from the view point through a pixel on the projection plane to the scene to calculate the lighting of that pixel. If we simply use the lighting model (Equation 64) once, we would produce a similar image as if we use the OpenGL lighting directly without ray tracing. Instead, ray tracing accounts for the global specular reflections among objects, and calculates the ray's recursive intersections that include reflective bounces and refractive transmissions. Lighting is calculated at each point of intersection. The final pixel color is an accumulation of all fractions of intensity values from the bottom up. At any point of intersection, three lighting components are calculated and added together: current intensity, reflection, and transmission.

The current intensity of a point is calculated using the lighting method we learned already, except that we may take shadows into consideration. Rays (named feeler rays or shadow rays) are fired from the point under consideration to the light sources to decide the point's current intensity using Equation 64. If an object is between the point and a light source, the point under consideration will not be affected by the blocked light source directly, so the corresponding shadows will be generated.

The reflection and transmission components at the point are calculated by recursive calls following the reflected ray and transmitted ray (Fig. 3.10). For example, we can modify Equation 64:

$$I_\lambda = I_{\lambda e} + \sum_{i=0}^{k-1} f_{atti} f_{spoti} I_{\lambda Li} + I_{\lambda r} + I_{\lambda t}, \qquad \text{(EQ 65)}$$

where $I_{\lambda r}$ accounts for the reflected light component, and $I_{\lambda t}$ accounts for the transmitted light component, as shown in Fig. 3.10.

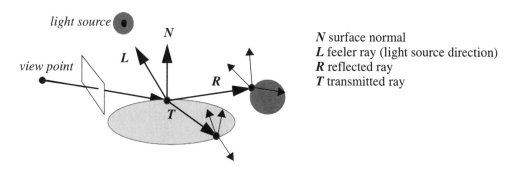

N surface normal
L feeler ray (light source direction)
R reflected ray
T transmitted ray

Fig. 3.10 Recursive ray tracing

The reflection component $I_{\lambda r}$ is a specular component, which is calculated recursively by applying Equation 65. Here, we assume that the "view point" is the starting point of the reflected ray R and the point under consideration is the end point of R:

$$I_{\lambda r} = M_{\lambda s} I_{\lambda},$$
(EQ 66)

where $M_{\lambda s}$ is the "view point" material's specular property. The transmission component $I_{\lambda t}$ is calculated similarly:

$$I_{\lambda t} = M_{\lambda t} I_{\lambda},$$
(EQ 67)

where $M_{\lambda t}$ is the "view point" material's transmission coefficient.

The recursion terminates when a user-defined depth is achieved where further reflections and transmissions are omitted, or when the reflected and transmitted rays don't hit objects. Computing the intersections of the ray with the objects and the normals at the intersections is the major part of a ray tracing program, which may take hidden-surface removal, refractive transparency, and shadows into its implementation considerations.

Radiosity assumes that each small area or patch is an emissive as well as reflective light source. The method is based on thermal energy radiosity. We need to break up the environment into small discrete patches that emit and reflect light uniformly in the entire area. Also, we need to calculate the fraction of the energy that leaves from a patch and arrives at another, taking into account the shape and orientation of both patches. The shading of a patch is a summation of its own emission and all the emissions from other patches that reach the patch. The finer the patches, the better the results are at the expense of longer calculations.

Although both ray tracing and radiosity can be designed to account for all lighting components, ray tracing is view point dependent, which is better for specular appearance, and radiosity is view point independent, which is better for diffuse appearance.

4

Blending and Texture Mapping

Chapter objectives:

- Understand OpenGL blending to achieve transparency, antialiasing, and fog

- Use images for rendering directly or for texture mapping

- Understand OpenGL texture mapping programs

4.1 Blending

Given two color components $I_{\lambda 1}$ and $I_{\lambda 2}$, the blending of the two values is an interpolation between the two:

$$I_\lambda = \alpha I_{\lambda 1} + (1 - \alpha) I_{\lambda 2} \qquad \textbf{(EQ 68)}$$

where α is called the alpha blending factor, and λ is R, G, B, or A. Transparency is achieved by blending. Given two transparent polygons, every pixel color is a blending of the corresponding points on the two polygons along the projection line.

In OpenGL, without blending, each pixel will overwrite the corresponding value in the frame buffer during scan-conversion. In contrast, when blending is enabled, the current pixel color component (namely the source $I_{\lambda 1}$) is blended with the corresponding pixel color component already in the frame buffer (namely the destination $I_{\lambda 2}$). The blending function is an extension of Equation 68:

$$I_\lambda = B_1 I_{\lambda 1} + B_2 I_{\lambda 2} \qquad \textbf{(EQ 69)}$$

where B_1 and B_2 are the source and destination blending factors, respectively.

The blending factors are decided by the function: *glBlendFunc(B1, B2),* where *B1* and *B2* are predefined constants to indicate how to compute B_1 and B_2, respectively. As in Example 4.1 (Fig. 4.1), *B1* = *GL_SRC_ALPHA* indicates that the source blending factor is the source color's alpha value, which is the A in the source pixel's RGBA. That is, B_1 = A, and *B2* = *GL_ONE_MINUS_SRC_ALPHA* indicates that B_2 = 1-A. When we specify a color directly, or specify a material property in lighting, we now specify and use the alpha value as well. In Example

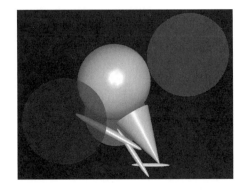

Fig. 4.1 Transparent spheres

4.1, when we specify the material properties, we choose A=0.3 to represent the material's transparency property. Here, if we choose A=0.0, the material is completely transparent. If A=1.0, the material is opaque.

/* Example 4.1.blending.c: transparent spheres */

```
void drawSolar(float E, float e, float M, float m)
{
    float red[] = {1., 0., 0., .3};

    drawSphere(); // opaque sphere
    glEnable (GL_BLEND);
    glBlendFunc (GL_SRC_ALPHA, GL_ONE_MINUS_SRC_ALPHA);
    glMaterialfv(GL_FRONT, GL_AMBIENT, red);
    drawSphere(); // transparent sphere
    glDisable (GL_BLEND);
}
```

4.1.1 OpenGL Blending Factors

Example 4.1 chooses the alpha blending factor as in Equation 68, which is a special case. OpenGL provides more constants to indicate how to compute the source or destination blending factors through *glBlendFunc()*.

If the source and destination colors are (R_s, G_s, B_s, A_s) and (R_d, G_d, B_d, A_d) and the source (src) and destination (dst) blending factors are (S_r, S_g, S_b, S_a) and (D_r, D_g, D_b, D_a), then the final RGBA value in the frame buffer is $(R_sS_r+R_dD_r, G_sS_g+G_dD_g, B_sS_b+B_dD_b, A_sS_a+A_dD_a)$. Each component is eventually clamped to [0,1]. The predefined constants to indicate how to compute (S_r, S_g, S_b, S_a) and (D_r, D_g, D_b, D_a) are as follows:

Constant	Relevant Factor	Computed Blend Factor
GL_ZERO	src or dst	$(0, 0, 0, 0)$
GL_ONE	src or dst	$(1, 1, 1, 1)$
GL_DST_COLOR	src	(R_d, G_d, B_d, A_d)
GL_SRC_COLOR	dst	(R_s, G_s, B_s, A_s)
GL_ONE_MINUS_DST_COLOR	src	$(1,1,1,1)-(R_d, G_d, B_d, A_d)$
GL_ONE_MINUS_SRC_COLOR	dst	$(1,1,1,1)-(R_s, G_s, B_s, A_s)$
GL_SRC_ALPHA	src or dst	(A_s, A_s, A_s, A_s)
GL_ONE_MINUS_SRC_ALPHA	src or dst	$(1,1,1,1)-(A_s, A_s, A_s, A_s)$
GL_DST_ALPHA	src or dst	(A_d, A_d, A_d, A_d)
GL_ONE_MINUS_DST_ALPHA	src or dst	$(1,1,1,1)-(A_d, A_d, A_d, A_d)$
GL_SRC_ALPHA_SATURATE	src	$(f,f,f,1); f=\min(A_s, 1-A_d)$

Depending on how we choose the blending factors and other parameters, we can achieve different effects of transparency, antialiasing, and fog, which will be discussed later.

OpenGL blending achieves nonrefractive transparency. The blended points are along the projection line. In other words, the light ray passing through the transparent surfaces is not bent. Refractive transparency, which needs to take the geometrical and optical properties into consideration, is significantly more time consuming. Refractive transparency is often integrated with ray tracing.

4.1.2 Transparency and Hidden-Surface Removal

It is fairly complex to achieve the correct transparency through blending if we have multiple transparent layers, since the order of blending of these layers matters. As in Equation 69, the source and the destination parameters are changed if we switch the order of drawing two polygons. We would like to blend the corresponding transparent points on the surfaces in the order of their distances to the view point. However, this requires keeping track of the distances for all points on the different surfaces, which we avoid doing because of time and memory requirements.

If we enabled the depth-buffer (z-buffer) in OpenGL, obscured polygons may not be used for blending. To avoid this problem, while drawing transparent polygons, we may make the depth buffer read-only. Also, we should draw opaque objects first, and then enable blending to draw transparent objects. This causes the transparent polygons' depth values to be compared to the values established by the opaque polygons, and blending factors to be specified by the transparent polygons. As in Example 4.2, *glDepthMask(GL_FALSE)* makes the depth-buffer become read-only, whereas *glDepthMask(GL_TRUE)* restores the normal depth-buffer operation (Fig. 4.2).

Fig. 4.2 Depth-buffer read only

/* **Example 4.2.opaque.c: transparency / hidden-surface removal** */

```
void drawSolar(float E, float e, float M, float m)
{
    ...
        drawCone(); // draw opaque object first
        glEnable (GL_BLEND);
        glDepthMask (GL_FALSE); // make depth-buffer read-only
        glBlendFunc (GL_SRC_ALPHA, GL_ONE_MINUS_SRC_ALPHA);
        drawCone();
        glDepthMask (GL_TRUE);
        glDisable (GL_BLEND);
    ...
}
```

Example 4.3 uses transparent cones to simulate the lighting volumes of the moving and rotating spotlight sources.

/* **Example 4.3.translight.c: cones to simulate moving spotlights** */

```
void drawSolar(float E, float e, float M, float m)
{
    ...
```

```
      glRotatef(e+m, 0, 1, 0); // the light source is rotating
      glLightfv(GL_LIGHT1, GL_POSITION, position);
      glLightfv(GL_LIGHT1,GL_SPOT_DIRECTION,spot_direction);
      glLightf(GL_LIGHT1,GL_SPOT_CUTOFF,10.0);

      glEnable (GL_BLEND);
      glDepthMask (GL_FALSE);

      // cone tip 10 degree
      glScalef(1,tan(PI*10/180),tan(PI*10/180));
      drawCone();

      glDepthMask (GL_TRUE);
      glDisable (GL_BLEND);
   ...
}
```

4.1.3 Antialiasing

In OpenGL, antialiasing can be achieved by blending. If you call *glEnable()* with *GL_POINT_SMOOTH*, *GL_LINE_SMOOTH*, or *GL_POLYGON_SMOOTH*, OpenGL will calculate a coverage value based on the fraction of the pixel square that covers the point, line, or polygon edge with specified point size or line width, and multiply the pixel's alpha value by the calculated coverage value. You can achieve antialiasing by using the resulting alpha value to blend the pixel color with the corresponding pixel color already in the frame buffer. The method is the same as the unweighted area sampling method discussed in Section 1.4.1 on page 13. You can even use *glHint()* to choose a faster or slower but better quality sampling algorithm in the system.

4.1.4 Fog

Fog is the effect of the atmosphere between the rendered pixel and the eye, which is called the depth cuing or atmosphere attenuation effect. Fog is also achieved by blending:

$$I_\lambda = f I_{\lambda I} + (1 - f) I_{\lambda f} \qquad \text{(EQ 70)}$$

where f is the fog factor, $I_{\lambda I}$ is the incoming pixel component, and $I_{\lambda f}$ is the fog color. In OpenGL, as in Example 4.4 (Fig. 4.3), the fog factor and the fog color are specified by *glFog*(). The fog color can be the same as, or different from, the background color. The fog factor *f* depends on the distance (*z*) from the view point to the pixel on the object. We can choose different equations if we specify the fog mode to *GL_EXP* (Equation 71), *GL_EXP2* (Equation 72), or *GL_LINEAR* (Equation 73):

$$f = e^{-(density \cdot z)} \qquad\qquad \text{(EQ 71)}$$

$$f = e^{-(density \cdot z)^2} \qquad\qquad \text{(EQ 72)}$$

$$f = \frac{end - z}{end - start} \qquad\qquad \text{(EQ 73)}$$

In Equation 73, when *z* changes from *start* to *end*, *f* changes from 1 to 0. According to Equation 70, the final pixel color will change from the incoming object pixel color to the fog color. We may supply *GL_FOG_HINT* with *glHint()* to specify whether fog calculations are per pixel (*GL_NICEST*) or per vertex (*GL_FASTEST*) or whatever the system has (*GL_DONT_CARE*).

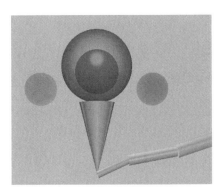

Fig. 4.3 Fog in OpenGL

/* Example 4.4.fog.c: fog and background colors */

```
init() {
   float fogColor[4] = {0.8, 0.8, 0.7, 1.0};

   glClearColor (0.8, 0.8, 0.7, 1.0);

   glEnable(GL_FOG);

   glHint (GL_FOG_HINT, GL_DONT_CARE);
   glFogi (GL_FOG_MODE, GL_LINEAR);
   glFogfv (GL_FOG_COLOR, fogColor);
   glFogf (GL_FOG_START, 1.5*Width);
   glFogf (GL_FOG_END, 3.8*Width);
}
```

4.2 *Images*

We have discussed rendering and scan-converting 3D models. The result is an image, or an array of RGBAs stored in the frame buffer. Instead of going through transformation, viewing, hidden-surface removal, lighting, and other graphics manipulations, OpenGL provides some basic functions that manipulate image data in the frame buffer directly: *glReadPixels()* reads a rectangular array of pixels from the frame buffer into the (computer main) memory, *glDrawPixels()* writes a rectangular array of pixels into the frame buffer from the memory, *glBitmap()* writes a single bitmap (a binary image) into the frame buffer from the main memory, etc. The function *glRasterPos*()* specifies the current raster position (x, y, z, w) where the system starts reading or writing. The position (x, y, z, w), however, goes through the transformation pipeline as a vertex in a 3D model.

The image data stored in the memory might consist of just the overall intensity of each pixel (R+G+B), or the RGBA components, respectively. As image data is transferred from memory into the frame buffer, or from the frame buffer into memory, OpenGL can perform several operations on it. Also, there are certain formats for storing data in the memory that are required or are more efficient on certain kinds of hardware. We use *glPixelStore*()* to set the pixel-storage mode of how data is unpacked from the memory into the frame buffer or from the frame buffer to the memory. Example 4.5 (Fig. 4.4) reads an image from a file, and draws the image into the frame buffer directly as the background of the 3D rendering.

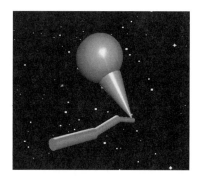

Fig. 4.4 **Image background**

/* **Example 4.5.image.c: write an image into the framebuffer** */

```
void initImage(void) // called once at initialization
{
    read_stars_image();
    // inform the system about image storage format in memory
    glPixelStorei(GL_UNPACK_ALIGNMENT, 1);
}
```

```
void drawImage(float x, float y, float z)
{
    glRasterPos3f(x, y, z);

    glDrawPixels(stars_pixels, stars_pixels,
                 GL_LUMINANCE, GL_UNSIGNED_BYTE, stars_image);
}


void display(void)
{
    glClear(GL_COLOR_BUFFER_BIT | GL_DEPTH_BUFFER_BIT);

    drawImage(-2.4*Width, -2.4*Height, -1.9*Width);
    drawRobot(A, B, C, alpha, beta, gama);

    glutSwapBuffers();
}
```

4.3 Texture Mapping

In graphics rendering, an image can be mapped onto the surface of a model. That is, when writing the color of a pixel into the frame buffer, the graphics system can use a color retrieved from an image. To do this we need to provide a piece of image called *texture*. *Texture mapping* is a process of using the texture pixels (namely *texels*) to modify or replace the model's corresponding pixels during scan-conversion. Texture mapping allows many choices and is fairly complex. Here we only introduce some basics.

4.3.1 Pixel and Texel Relations

Let's consider mapping a square texture onto a rectangular polygon (Example 4.6).

First, we need to specify the corresponding vertices of the texture and the polygon. In OpenGL, this is done by associating each vertex in the texture with a vertex in the polygon, which is similar to the way of specifying each vertex normal. Given a point (s, t) in the 2D texture, the s and t are in the range of $[0, 1]$. *glTexCoord2f(s, t)* corresponds to a point in the texture. In our example, the points are the vertices of the texture and the OpenGL system stretches or shrinks the texture to map exactly onto the polygon.

Second, given a pixel location in the polygon, we can find its corresponding point in the texture. This point may be on a texel, on the line between two texels, or in the square with four texels at the corners. The resulting texel of the point needs to be calculated. The simplest method is to choose the texel that is nearest to the point as the mapping of the pixel. We can also linearly interpolate the four texels according to their distances to the point to find the mapping of the pixel. In OpenGL, when the texture is smaller than the polygon, the system stretches the texture to match the polygon (magnification). Otherwise, the system shrinks the texture (minification). Either way the texels corresponding to the pixels after stretching or shrinking need to be calculated. The algorithms to calculate the mapping are called the magnification or minification filters. Again, we can choose either nearest or linear algorithms in OpenGL to calculate the corresponding textures.

Third, at each pixel, the calculated texel color components can be used to either replace or modulate pixel color components. If the texels replace the pixels, lighting will not affect the appearance of the polygon. If the texel components are used to modulate the pixel components, each texture color component is multiplied by the corresponding pixel color component, and the original color and shading of the polygon are partially preserved.

Example 4.6 maps an image to a polygon. Although Example 4.5 and Example 4.6 look the same, the approaches are totally different.

/* Example 4.6.texture.c: simple texture mapping */

```
void initTexture(void)
{
    read_stars_image();
    glPixelStorei(GL_UNPACK_ALIGNMENT, 1);

    // specify the mapping between pixel & corresponding texels
    glTexParameteri(GL_TEXTURE_2D,
            GL_TEXTURE_MAG_FILTER, GL_NEAREST);
    glTexParameteri(GL_TEXTURE_2D,
            GL_TEXTURE_MIN_FILTER, GL_NEAREST);

    // specify the texture
    glTexImage2D(GL_TEXTURE_2D, 0, GL_LUMINANCE,
        stars_pixels, stars_pixels, 0,
            GL_LUMINANCE, GL_UNSIGNED_BYTE, stars_image);
}
```

```
void drawTexture(float x, float y, float z)
// the back ground stars
{
    // specify that the texels replace the pixels
    glTexEnvf(GL_TEXTURE_ENV,
              GL_TEXTURE_ENV_MODE, GL_REPLACE);

    glEnable(GL_TEXTURE_2D);

    glBegin(GL_QUADS);

        glTexCoord2f(0.0, 0.0); glVertex3f(x, y, z);
        glTexCoord2f(0.0, 1.0); glVertex3f(-x, y, z);
        glTexCoord2f(1.0, 1.0); glVertex3f(-x, -y, z);
        glTexCoord2f(1.0, 0.0); glVertex3f(x, -y, z);

    glEnd();

    glDisable(GL_TEXTURE_2D);
}


void display(void)
{
    glClear(GL_COLOR_BUFFER_BIT | GL_DEPTH_BUFFER_BIT);

    drawTexture(-2.4*Width, -2.4*Height, -1.9*Width);

    drawRobot(A, B, C, alpha, beta, gama);

    glutSwapBuffers();
}
```

4.3.2 Texture Objects

If we use several textures in the same program (Fig. 4.5), we may load them into texture memory and associate individual texture parameters with their texture names before rendering. This way we do not need to load textures and their parameters from the disk files during rendering, which would otherwise be very slow. In OpenGL, this is done by calling *glGenTextures()* and

Fig. 4.5 Multiple texture objects

glBindTexture(). When we call *glGenTextures()*, we can generate the texture names or texture objects. When we call *glBindTexture()* with a texture name, all subsequent *glTex*()* commands that specify the texture and its associated parameters are saved in the memory corresponding to the named texture. The following program segment is part of Example 4.7.

```
static GLuint iris_tex, stars_tex, earth_tex;

static GLubyte iris_image[iris_pixels][iris_pixels][3];
static GLubyte stars_image[stars_pixels][stars_pixels];
static GLubyte earth_image[earth_pixelx][earth_pixely][3];


void initTexture(void)
{
    read_stars_image();

    read_earth_image();

    glPixelStorei(GL_UNPACK_ALIGNMENT, 1);

    glGenTextures(1, &earth_tex);
    glBindTexture(GL_TEXTURE_2D, earth_tex);

    glTexParameteri(GL_TEXTURE_2D,
            GL_TEXTURE_MAG_FILTER, GL_LINEAR);

    glTexParameteri(GL_TEXTURE_2D,
            GL_TEXTURE_MIN_FILTER, GL_LINEAR);

    glTexImage2D(GL_TEXTURE_2D, 0, 3,
            earth_pixelx, earth_pixely,
            0, GL_RGB, GL_UNSIGNED_BYTE, earth_image);

    glGenTextures(1, &stars_tex);
    glBindTexture(GL_TEXTURE_2D, stars_tex);

    glTexParameteri(GL_TEXTURE_2D,
            GL_TEXTURE_MAG_FILTER, GL_LINEAR);
    glTexParameteri(GL_TEXTURE_2D,
            GL_TEXTURE_MIN_FILTER, GL_LINEAR);

    glTexImage2D(GL_TEXTURE_2D, 0, GL_LUMINANCE,
            stars_pixels, stars_pixels,
        0, GL_LUMINANCE, GL_UNSIGNED_BYTE, stars_image);

}
```

4.3.3 Texture Coordinates

In OpenGL, *glTexCoord2f(s, t)* corresponds to a point in the texture, and *s* and *t* are in the range of [0, 1]. If the points are on the boundaries of the texture, then we stretch or shrink the entire texture to fit exactly onto the polygon. Otherwise, only a portion of the texture is used to map onto the polygon. For example, if we have a polygonal cylinder with four polygons and we want to wrap the texture around the cylinder (Example 4.7), we can divide the texture into four pieces with *s* in the range of [0, 0.25], [0.25, 0.5], [0.5, 0.75], and [0.75, 1.0]. When mapping a rectangular texture onto a sphere around the axis, texture geodesic distortion happens — especially towards the poles.

If we specify *glTexCoord2f(2, t)*, we mean to repeat the texture twice in the *s* direction. That is, we will squeeze two pieces of the texture in *s* direction into the polygon. If we specify *glTexCoord2f(1.5, t)*, we mean to repeat the texture 1.5 times in the *s* direction. In order to achieve texture repeating in *s* direction, we need to specify the following: *glTexParameteri(GL_TEXTURE_2D, GL_TEXTURE_WRAP_S, GL_REPEAT)*. In OpenGL, the texture should have width and height in the form of 2^m number of pixels, where the width and height can be different.

/* Example 4.7.texobjects.c: texture objects and coordinates */

```
void textureCoord(float *v, float *s, float *t)
{ // given the vertex on a sphere, find its texture (s,t)

    float x, y, z, PI=3.14159, PI2=6.283;

    x = v[0]; y = v[1]; z = v[2];

    if (x>0) {
        if (z>0) *s = atan(z/x)/PI2;
        else *s = 1 + atan(z/x)/PI2;
    }
    else if (x<0)
        *s = 0.5 + atan(z/x)/PI2;
    else {
        if (z>0) *s = 0.25;
        if (z<0) *s = 0.75;
        if (z==0) *s = -1.0;
    }

    *t = acos(y)/PI;
}
```

```
void drawSphereTriangle(float *v1, float *v2, float *v3)
{
   float s1, t1, s2, t2, s3, t3;

   textureCoord(v1, &s1, &t1);
   textureCoord(v2, &s2, &t2);
   textureCoord(v3, &s3, &t3);

   // for coord at z=0, distortion happens more
   if (s1 == -1.0) s1 = (s2+s3)/2;
   else if (s2 == -1.0) s2 = (s1+s3)/2;
   else if (s3 == -1.0) s3 = (s2+s1)/2;

   glBindTexture(GL_TEXTURE_2D, earth_tex);
   glTexEnvf(GL_TEXTURE_ENV,
             GL_TEXTURE_ENV_MODE, GL_MODULATE);

   glBegin(GL_POLYGON);
      glTexCoord2f(s1, t1);
      glNormal3fv(v1);
      glVertex3fv(v1);
      glTexCoord2f(s2, t2);
      glNormal3fv(v2);
      glVertex3fv(v2);
      glTexCoord2f(s3, t3);
      glNormal3fv(v3);
      glVertex3fv(v3);
   glEnd();
}


void subdivideCylinder(float *v1,
            float *v2, int depth, float t1, float t2)
{
   float v11[3], v22[3], v00[3] = {0, 0, 0}, v12[3];
   int i;

   if (depth == 0) {
      glColor3f(v1[0]*v1[0], v1[1]*v1[1], v1[2]*v1[2]);
      drawBottom(v2, v1,  v00); // draw the cylinder bottom

      for (i=0; i<3; i++) { v11[i] = v1[i]; v22[i] = v2[i];
      }
      // the height of the cone along z axis
      v11[2] = v22[2] = 1;

      glBindTexture(GL_TEXTURE_2D, iris_tex);
      glTexEnvf(GL_TEXTURE_ENV,
          GL_TEXTURE_ENV_MODE, GL_REPLACE);
```

```
    // draw the side rectangles of the cylinder
    glBegin(GL_POLYGON);
        glNormal3fv(v2);
        glTexCoord2f(t1, 0.0); glVertex3fv(v1);
        glTexCoord2f(t2, 0.0); glVertex3fv(v2);
        glNormal3fv(v1);
        glTexCoord2f(t2, 1.0); glVertex3fv(v22);
        glTexCoord2f(t1, 1.0); glVertex3fv(v11);
    glEnd();

    v00[2] = 1;
    drawBottom(v00, v11, v22); // draw the other bottom

    return;
}

v12[0] = v1[0]+v2[0];
v12[1] = v1[1]+v2[1];
v12[2] = v1[2]+v2[2];
normalize(v12);
subdivideCylinder(v1, v12, depth - 1, t1, (t2+t1)/2);
subdivideCylinder(v12, v2, depth - 1, (t2+t1)/2, t2);
}


void drawCylinder(void)
// draw a unit cylinder with bottom in xy plane
{
    subdivideCylinder(vdata[0], vdata[1], depth, 0, 0.25);
    subdivideCylinder(vdata[1], vdata[2], depth, 0.25, 0.5);
    subdivideCylinder(vdata[2], vdata[3], depth, 0.5, 0.75);
    subdivideCylinder(vdata[3], vdata[0], depth, 0.75, 1.0);
}


drawArm(float End1, float End2) {
    float scale;
    scale = End2-End1;

    glPushMatrix();
        glRotatef(90.0, 0.0, 1.0, 0.0);
        glScalef(scale/5.0, scale/5.0, scale);

        // roate the texture image IRIS
        glRotatef(cnt, 0.0, 0.0, 1.0);
        drawCylinder();
    glPopMatrix();
}
```

5
Advanced Topics

Chapter Objectives:

- Wrap up basic computer graphics principles and programming

- Briefly introduce some advanced graphics concepts and methods

5.1 Introduction

We have covered basic graphics principles and OpenGL programming. A graphics system includes a graphics library and its supporting hardware. Most of the OpenGL library functions are implemented in hardware, which would otherwise be very slow. Some advanced graphics functions built on top of the basic library functions, such as drawing curves and curved surfaces, are also part of the OpenGL library or the OpenGL Utility library (GLU). GLU is considered part of the OpenGL system to facilitate complex model construction and rendering.

On top of a graphics library, many graphics methods and tools (namely high level graphics packages) are developed for certain capabilities or applications. For example, mathematics on curve and surface descriptions are used to construct curved shapes, constructive solid geometry (CSG) methods are used to assemble geometric models through logical operations, recursive functions are used to generate fractal images, visualization methods are developed to understand certain types of data, simulation methods are developed to animate certain processes, etc. In this chapter, we wrap up the first part of the book by briefly introducing some advanced graphics concepts. In the second part of the book, we introduce and compile specific graphics tools in more detail.

5.2 *Graphics Libraries*

A *low-level graphics library* or package is a software interface to graphics hardware. All graphics tools or applications are built on top of a certain low-level graphics library. High-level graphics tools are usually easier to learn and use. An introductory computer graphics course mainly discusses the implementations and applications of low-level graphics library functions. A graphics programmer understands how to program in at least one graphics library. OpenGL, Direct3D, and PHIGS are well-known low-level graphics libraries. *OpenGL* and Direct3D are currently the most widely adopted 3D graphics APIs in research and applications.

A *high-level graphics library*, which is often called a *3D programming tool library* (e.g., OpenInventor, discussed in Chapter 12), provides the means for application programs to handle scene constructions, 3D file imports and exports, object manipulations, and display. It is an API toolkit built on top of a low-level graphics library. Most high-level graphics libraries are categorized as animation, simulation, or virtual reality tools.

5.3 *Visualization*

Visualization employs graphics to make pictures that give us insight into the abstract data and symbols. The pictures may directly portray the description of the data or completely present the content of the data in an innovative form. Users, when presented with a new computed result or some other collection of online data, want to see and understand the meaning as quickly as possible. They often prefer understanding through observing an image or 3D animation rather than from reading abstract numbers and symbols.

5.3.1 Interactive Visualization and Computational Steering

Interactive visualization allows visualizing the results or presentations interactively in different perspectives (e.g., angles, magnitude, layers, levels of detail, etc.), and thus helps the user to better understand the results on the fly. Interactive visualization systems are most effective when the results of models or simulations have multiple or dynamic forms, layers, or levels of detail, which help users interact with visual presentations and understand the different aspects of the results.

For scientific computation and visualization, the integration of computation, visualization, and control into one tool is highly desirable, because it allows users to interactively "steer" the computation. At the beginning of the computation, before any result is generated, a few important pieces of feedback will significantly help in choosing correct parameters and initial values. Users can visualize some intermediate results and key factors to steer the computation in the right direction. With *computational steering*, users are able to modify parameters in their systems as the computation progresses, and avoid errors or uninteresting output after long tedious computation. Computational steering is an important method for adjusting uncertain parameters, moving the simulation in the right direction, and fine tuning the results.

5.3.2 Data Visualization: Dimensions and Data Types

A visualization technique is applicable to certain data types (discrete, continual, point, scalar, or vector) and dimensions (1D, 2D, 3D, and multiple: *N*-D). *Scatter Data* represent data as discrete points on a line (1D), plane (2D), or in space (3D). We may use different colors, shapes, sizes, and other attributes to represent the points in higher dimensions beyond 3D, or use a function or a representation to transform the high dimensional data into 2D/3D. *Scalar Data* have scalar values in addition to dimension values. The scalar value is actually a special additional dimension that we pay more attention to. 2D diagrams like histograms, bar charts, or pie charts are 1D scalar data visualization methods. Both histograms and bar charts have one coordinate as the dimension scale and another as the value scale. Histograms usually have scalar values in confined ranges, while bar charts do not carry this information. Pie charts use a slice area in a pie to represent a percentage. 2D contours (iso-lines in a map) of constant values, 2D images (pixels of *x*-*y* points and color values), and 3D surfaces (pixels of *x*-*y* points and height values) are 2D scalar data visualization methods. Volume and iso-surface rendering methods are for 3D scalar data. A *voxel* (volume pixel) is a 3D scalar datum with (x, y, z) coordinates and an intensity or color value. *Vector Data* include directions in addition to scalar and dimension values. We use line segments, arrows, streamlines, and animations to present the directions.

- *Volume rendering* or visualization is a method for extracting meaningful information from a set of 2D scalar data. A sequence of 2D image slices of human body can be reconstructed into a 3D volume model and visualized for diagnostic purposes or for planning of treatment or surgery. For example, a set of volumetric data such as a deck of Magnetic Resonance Imaging (MRI) slices or Computed Tomography (CT) can be blended into a 2D X-ray image by firing rays through the volume and blending the voxels along the rays. This is a rather costly operation and the blending methods vary. The concept of volume rendering is also to extract the contours from given data slices. An iso-surface is a 3D constant intensity surface represented by triangle strips or higher-order surface patches within a volume. For example, the voxels on the surface of bones in a deck of MRI slices appear to have the same intensity value.

• From the study of turbulence or plasmas to the design of new wings or jet nozzles, flow visualization motivates much of the research effort in scientific visualization. Flow data are mostly 3D vectors or tensors of high dimensions. The main challenge of flow visualization is to find ways of visualizing multivariate data sets. Colors, arrows, particles, line convolutions, textures, surfaces, and volumes are used to represent different aspects of fluid flows (velocities, pressures, streamlines, streaklines, vortices, etc.)

• The visual presentation and examination of large data sets from physical and natural sciences often require the integration of terabyte or gigabyte distributed scientific databases with visualization. Genetic algorithms, radar range images, materials simulations, and atmospheric and oceanographic measurements are among the areas that generate large multidimensional multivariate data sets. The data vary with different geometries, sampling rates, and error characteristics. The display and interpretation of the data sets employ statistical analyses and other techniques in conjunction with visualization.

• The field of *information visualization* includes visualizing retrieved information from large document collections (e.g., digital libraries), the Internet, and text databases. Information is completely abstract. We need to map the data into a physical space that will represent relationships contained in the information faithfully and efficiently. This could enable the observers to use their innate abilities to understand through spatial relationships the correlations in the library. Finding a good spatial representation of the information at hand is one of the most challenging tasks in information visualization.

Many forms and choices exist for the visualization of 2D or 3D data sets, which are relatively easy to conceive and understand. For data sets that are more than 3D, visualization methods are challenging research topics. For example, the Linked micromap plots are developed to display spatially indexed data that integrate geographical and statistical summaries (http://www.netgraphi.com/cancer4/).

5.3.3 Parallel Coordinates

The *parallel coordinates* method represents *d*-dimensional data as values on *d* coordinates parallel to the *x*-axis equally spaced along the *y*-axis (Fig. 5.1, or the other way around, rotating 90 degrees). Each *d*-dimensional datum corresponds to the line segments between the parallel coordinates connecting the corresponding values. That is, each polygonal line of (*d-1*) segments in the parallel coordinates represents a point in *d* dimensional space. Parallel coordinates provide a

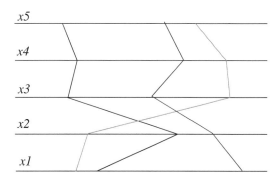

Fig. 5.1 Parallel coordinates: an example

means to visualize higher order geometries in an easily recognizable 2D representation. It also helps find the patterns, trends, and correlations in the data set.

The purpose of using parallel coordinates is to find certain features in the data set through visualization. Consider a series of points on a straight line in Cartesian coordinates: *y=mx+b*. If we display these points in parallel coordinates, the points on a line in Cartesian coordinates become line segments. These line segments intersect at a point. This point in the parallel coordinates is called the *dual* of the line in the Cartesian coordinates. The point~line duality extends to conic sections. An ellipse in Cartesian coordinates maps into a hyperbola in parallel coordinates, and vice versa. Rotations in Cartesian coordinates become translations in parallel coordinates, and vice versa.

Clustering is easily isolated and visualized in parallel coordinates. An individual parallel coordinate axis represents a 1D projection of the data set. Thus, separation between or among sets of data on one axis represents a view of the data of isolated clusters. The *brushing* technique is to interactively separate a cluster of data by painting it with a unique color. The brushed color becomes an attribute of the cluster. Different clusters can be brushed with different colors and relations among clusters can then be visually detected. Heavily plotted areas can be blended with color mixes and transparencies. Animation of the colored clusters through time allows visualization of the data evolution history.

The grand tour method is used to search for patterns by looking at the high-dimensional data from all different angles. That is, to project the data into all possible d-planes through generalized rotations. The purpose of the grand tour animation is to look for unusual configurations of the data that may reflect some structure from a specific angle. The rotation, projection, and animation methods vary depending on specific assumptions. There are visualization tools that include parallel coordinates and grand tours: ExplorN (ftp://www.galaxy.gmu.edu/pub/software/ExplorN_v1.tar), CrystalVision (ftp://www.galaxy.gmu.edu/pub/software/CrystalVisionDemo.exe), and XGobi (http://www.research.att.com/areas/stat/xgobi/).

5.4 Modeling and Rendering

Modeling is a process of constructing a virtual 3D graphics object (computer model, or model) from a real object or an imaginary entity. Creating graphics models requires a significant amount of time and effort. Modeling tools make creating and constructing complex 3D models fast and easy. A graphics model includes geometrical descriptions (particles, vertices, polygons, etc.) as well as associated graphics attributes (colors, shadings, transparencies, materials, etc.), which can be saved in a file using a standard (3D model) file format. Modeling tools help create virtual objects and environments for CAD (computer-aided design), visualization, virtual reality, simulation, education, training, and entertainment.

Rendering is a process of creating images from graphics models. 3D graphics models are saved in computer memory or hard-disk files. The term *rasterization* and *scan-conversion* are used to refer to low-level image generation or drawing. All modeling tools provide certain drawing capabilities to visualize the models generated. However, in addition to simply drawing (scan-converting) geometric objects, rendering tools often include lighting, shading, texture mapping, color blending, ray tracing, radiosity, and other advanced graphics capabilities. For example, the *RenderMan* Toolkit includes photorealistic modeling and rendering of particle systems, hair, and many other objects with advanced graphics functions such as ray tracing, volume display, motion blur, depth-of-field, and so forth. Many powerful graphics tools include modeling, rendering, animation, and other functions in one package.

Basic modeling and rendering methods were discussed in previous chapters. Here we introduce some advanced modeling and rendering techniques.

5.4.1 Curves and Surfaces

To describe a sphere, we can save a list of vertices on the surface of the sphere. However, it would be probably more efficient and accurate to save just the sphere equation and calculate the vertices of the surface when needed. Parametric mathematical equations are used to generate smooth curves and curved surfaces. Cubic parametric functions are the lowest-degree curve functions that are non-planar in 3D. Therefore, we can use Hermite, Bezier, B-spline, NURB, natural cubic spline, and other mathematical equations or methods, which are abundant in math or graphics books and literature.

5.4.2 Sweep Representations

We can create a 3D volume by sweeping a 2D area along a linear path normal to the area. *Sweeping* is implemented in most graphics modeling tools. The generated model contains many vertices that may be eliminated. Algorithms are developed to simplify models and measure the similarity between models. A model can also be represented with multiple levels of detail for use with fast animations and high-resolution rendering interchangeably.

5.4.3 Instances

In a hierachical model, there are parts that are exactly the same. For example, all four wheels of a car can be the same model. Instead of saving four copies of the model, we save just one primitive model and three *instances*, which are really pointers to the same primitive. If we modify the primitive, we know that the primitive and the instances are identically changed.

5.4.4 Constructive Solid Geometry

Constructive Solid Geometry (CSG) is a solid modeling method. A set of solid primitives such as cubes, cylinders, spheres, and cones are combined by union, difference, and intersection to construct a more complex solid model. In CSG, a solid model is stored as a tree with operators at the internal nodes and solid primitives at the leaves. The tree is processed in the depth-first search with a corresponding sequence of operations, and finally, rendering. CSG is a modeling method that is often used to create new and complex mechanical parts.

5.4.5 Procedural Models

Procedural models describe objects by procedures instead of using a list of primitives. Fractal models, grammar-based models, particle system models, and physically-based models are all procedural models. Procedural models can interact with external events to modify themselves. Also, very small changes in specifications can result in drastic changes of form.

5.4.6 Fractals

A *fractal* is a geometric shape that is substantially and recursively self-similar. Theoretically, only infinitely recursive processes are true fractals. Fractal models have been developed to render plants, clouds, fluid, music, and more. For example, a grammar model can be used to generate self-similar tree branches: T -> T | T[T] | (T)T | (T)[T] | (T)T[T], where square brackets denote a right branch and parentheses denote a left branch. We may choose a different angle, thickness, and length for the branch at a depth in the recursion with flowers or leaves at the end of the recursions.

5.4.7 Particle systems

Particle systems are used to model and render irregular fuzzy objects such as dust, fire, and smoke. A set of particles are employed to represent an object. Each individual particle generated evolves and disappears in space, all at different times depending on its individual animation. In general, a particle system and its particles have very similar parameters, but with different values:

- Position (including orientation in 3D space and center location x, y, and z)

- Movement (including velocity, rotation, acceleration, etc.)

- Color (RGB) and transparency (alpha)

- Shape (point, line, fractal, sphere, cube, rectangle, etc.)

- Volume, density, and mass

- Lifetime (only for particles)

- Blur head and rear pointers (only for particles)

The position, shape, and size of a particle system determine the initial positions of the particles and their range of movement. The movements of the particles are restricted within the range defined by their associated particle system. The shape of a particle system can be a point, line segment, fractal, sphere, box, or cylinder. The movement of a particle system is affected by internal or external forces, and the results of the rotations and accelerations of the particles as a whole. A particle system may change its shape, size, color, transparency, or some other attributes as it evolves. The lifetime defines how long a particle will be active. A particle has both a head position and a tail position. The head position is usually animated and the tail position follows along for motion blur.

In general, particle systems are first initialized with each particle having an original position, velocity, color, transparency, shape, size, mass, and lifetime. After the initialization, for each calculation and rendering frame, some parameters of the particles are updated using a rule base, and the resulting particle systems are rendered. Fig. 5.2 summarizes the applications that employ particle systems. Structured particle systems are often used to model trees, water drops, leaves, grass, rainbows, and clouds. Stochastic particle systems are often used to model fireworks, explosions, snow, and so forth. Oriented particle systems are often used to model deformable and rigid bodies such as cloth, lava flow, etc.

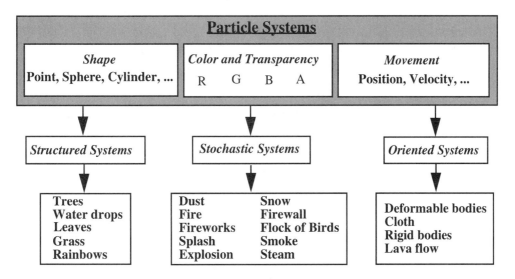

Fig. 5.2 **Applications of particle systems in computer graphics**

5.4.8 Image-based Modeling and Rendering

Image-based modeling or rendering uses images or photographs to replace geometric models. This technique achieves shorter modeling times, faster rendering speeds, and unprecedented levels of photorealism. It also addresses different approaches to turn images into models and then back into renderings, including movie maps, panoramas, image warping, light fields, and 3D scanning.

It has been observed that the rendering process can be accelerated significantly by reusing the images to approximate the new frames instead of rendering them from the geometric model directly. The rendering error introduced by the approximation, which determines whether or not an image must be refreshed, can be calculated by comparing the image to the object's geometry.

Given the view position and direction, we can use a texture image mapped onto a polygon with transparent background to replace a complex model such as a tree, building, or human avatar. The polygon is called a *billboard* or *poster* if it is always perpendicular to the view point.

We can integrate image-based rendering and model-based rendering in one application. For example, we can use images to render avatar body parts and employ geometrical transformations to move and shape the parts. A human-like avatar geometric model consists of joints and body segments. The 3D positions of these joints, governed by the movement mechanism or pre-generated motion data, uniquely define the avatar's gesture at a moment. The entire animation process is used to find the joint coordinates of each frame in terms of animation time.

If we project every segment of the 3D avatar separately onto the projection plane, the synthesis of these projected 2D images will be the final image of the 3D avatar we actually see on the screen, provided the segment depth values are taken into account appropriately. Therefore, avatar walking can be simulated by the appropriate transformations of the avatar segment images. From this point of view, the avatar's walking is the same as its segments' movements in the 3D space. Here, the basic idea is to reuse the snapshot segment images over several frames rather than rendering the avatar for each frame from the geometric model directly. The complicated human-like 3D avatar model is used only for capturing body segment images when they need to be updated. The subsequent animation frames are dynamically generated through 2D transformations and synthesis of the snapshot segment images.

5.5 Animation and Simulation

Computer *animation* is achieved by refreshing the screen display with a sequence of images at more than 24 frames per second. *Keyframe* animation is achieved by using pre-calculated keyframe images and in-between images, which may take a significant amount of time, and then displaying (playing back) the sequence of generated images in real time. Keyframe animation is often used for visual effects in films and TV commercials, where no interactions or unpredictable changes are necessary. Interactive animation, on the other hand, is achieved by calculating, generating, and displaying the images simultaneously on the fly. When we talk about *real-time animation*, we mean the virtual animation occurring in the same time frames as real world behavior. However, for graphics researchers, real-time animation often simply implies the animation is smooth or interactive. Real-time animation is often used in virtual environments for education, training, and 3D games. Many modeling and rendering tools are also animation tools, which are often associated with simulation.

Simulation, on the other hand, is a software system we construct, execute, and experiment with to understand the behavior of the real world or imaginary system, which often means a process of generating certain natural phenomena through scientific computation. The simulation results may be large datasets of atomic activities (positions, velocities, pressures, and other parameters of atoms) or fluid behaviors (volume of vectors and pressures). Computer simulation allows scientists to generate the atomic behavior of certain nanostructured materials for understanding material structure and durability and to find new compounds with superior quality. Simulation integrated with visualization can help pilots learn to fly and aid automobile designers in testing the integrity of the passenger compartment during crashes. For many computational scientists, simulation may not be related to any visualization at all. However, for many graphics researchers, simulation often simply means animation. Today, graphical simulation, or simply simulation, is an animation of a certain process or behavior that is often generated through scientific computation and modeling. Here we emphasize an integration of simulation and animation — the simulated results are used to generate graphics models and control animation behaviors. It is far easier, cheaper, and safer to experiment with a model through simulation than with a real entity. In fact, in many situations, such as training space-shuttle pilots and studying molecular dynamics, modeling and simulation are the only feasible methods to achieve the goals. *Real-time simulation* is an overloaded term. To computational scientists, it often means the simulation time is the actual time in which the physical process (under simulation) should occur. In automatic control, it means the output response time is fast enough for automatic feedback and control. In graphics, it often means that the simulation is animated at an interactive rate of human perception. The emphasis in graphics is more on responsiveness and smooth animation rather than strictly accurate timing of the physical process. In many simulation-for-training applications, the emphasis is on generating realistic behavior for interactive training environments rather than strictly scientific or physical computation.

5.5.1 Physics-Based Modeling and Simulation: Triangular Polyhedra

A *polyhedron* is an arbitrary 3D shape whose surface is a collection of flat polygons. A *regular* polyhedron is one whose faces and vertices all look the same. There are only five regular polyhedra: the *tetrahedron* — 4 faces with three equilateral triangles at a vertex; the *cube* — 6 faces with three squares at a vertex; the *octahedron* — 8 faces with four equilateral triangles at a vertex; the *dodecahedron* — 12 faces with three pentagons at a vertex; and the *icosahedron* — 20 faces with five equilateral triangles at a vertex. The regular polyhedron models can be found in many books and graphics packages. However, the complex polyhedron model requires effort to be constructed.

Physics-based modeling (also called physically-based modeling) is a modeling method that employs physics laws to construct models. Here, we use the physics-based modeling method to construct some polyhedra. Given an arbitrary number n, we construct a triangular polyhedron model of n vertices such that the distance from each vertex to the origin equals one, and the distances between the neighboring vertices are as far distant as possible. Let's assume that the radius of the polyhedron is one. The method includes the following steps:

1. Generate n arbitrary vertices *vtx[i]* in 3D space for $i=0$ to n-1. Each vertex is an imaginary object with mass M.
2. Normalize the vertices so that the distance from each vertex to the origin is one. The vertices can be viewed as vectors. A normalized vector has unit length.
3. Establish a physical relation between each pair of vertices by connecting them with an imaginary spring. The spring is at rest when the distance between the vertices is two, which is the farthest distance on a sphere of unit radius. Otherwise, the spring will apply an attracting or repelling force on the two vertices. According to Hooke's law, the spring force on vertex i from all vertices j is

```
f[i].x = f[i].y = f[i].z = 0;
```

```
for (j = 0; j < n; j++) if (i != j) {
  f[i].x = f[i].x + K*(direction.x*2 - vtx[i].x + vtx[j].x);
  f[i].y = f[i].y + K*(direction.y*2 - vtx[i].y + vtx[j].y);
  f[i].z = f[i].z + K*(direction.z*2 - vtx[i].z + vtx[j].z);
}
```

where K is the spring coefficient and *direction* is a unit vector along vertex i and j. Since x, y, and z components are basically the same and independent, in the rest of the discussion we only present the x component.

As we know, a spring will bounce back and forth forever if there is no damping force. Therefore, we add an air friction force proportional to the vertex's velocity. The vertices will eventually converge to stable coordinates after a number of iterations:

```
f[i].x = f[i].x - K1*dv[i].x;
// K1 is the velocity damping coefficient
```

4. Calculate the new coordinates of the vertices after a short period DT according to the physics relation: for each vertex,

```
ddv[i].x = f[i].x/M;
// the acceleration
```

```
dv[i].x = dv[i].x + ddv[i].x*DT;
// the new velocity and
```

```
vtx[i].x = vtx[i].x + dv[i].x*DT;
// the new position.
```

5. Repeat Steps 2 to 4 until a satisfactory condition is reached. Draw the current polyhedron. A satisfactory condition can be, for example, that each vertex velocity is smaller than some criterion.

The samples and source code for the above modeling method are at: http://graphics.gmu.edu/polyhedra/

In the program, we can construct and display an equilateral triangle, a tetrahedron, an octahedron, or an icosahedron (Fig. 5.3) by simply specifying 3, 4,

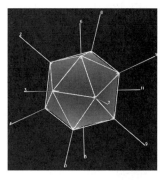

Fig. 5.3 An icosahedron

6, or 12 vertices respectively. We can also construct many specific irregular polyhedra. From the above example, we know that we can achieve many different shapes by specifying different physics relations among the vertices and the origin. This method is totally different from the traditional methods used to construct polyhedron models. Instead of using mathematical relations to find out the exact vertex coordinates, it relies on physics relations to dynamically construct the models. The construction process is a simulation of the designed physics relations. Many complex models could be constructed easily this way. Today, physics-based modeling is employed in some advanced graphics modeling tools for constructing certain 3D models.

5.5.2 Real-time Animation and Simulation: a Spider Web

The display refresh rate is the rate of reading from the frame buffer and sending the pixels to the display by the video controller. A refresh rate at 60 (frames per second) is smoother than one at 30, and 120 is marginally better than 60. However, if the image frame rate is much lower, the animation could be jittery. Sometimes, it is an easy-to-be-rendered model that takes time to be constructed. Sometimes, it is an easy-to-be-constructed model that takes time to be rendered. To achieve smooth animation, we need high performance algorithms as well as graphics hardware to efficiently carry out modeling, simulation, and graphics rendering. Graphical simulation, or simply simulation, animates certain processes or behaviors generated through scientific computation and modeling. A *simulation model* is a physics or math description of the simulated entity or system. Simulation can be used to achieve a static graphics model like a polyhedron, or dynamic behavior like a waving spider web. In the above example of modeling polyhedra, the simulation model describes the physical relationships among the vertices. The simulated results are used to generate the graphics models and control the animation behavior. That is, the simulation model describes the graphics model, and the graphics model is the simulation result.

A real-time simulation is a simulation where the time is the actual time in which the physical process (under simulation) occurs. Many real-time simulation systems are *event-driven*, in which the evolution of the simulation is determined by the complexity of both the computation and the graphics rendering. A real-time simulation can be synchronized with a wall clock, so that the simulation proceeds accurately on the physical time scale we perceive. The simulation will appear at the same speed on different computing platforms. The method is as follows. A variable (lastTime) is used to record the last time the simulation updated its state. Each time the simulation begins to update its state, it reads the computer's clock to get the current time (currentTime) and subtract lastTime from currentTime to determine the period between the current time and the last time when the state was updated. This period, the time slice passed — together with the simulation's old state — determines the simulation's new state. At the same time, lastTime will be updated to currentTime.

Real-time simulation often employs a wide range of physical laws that are functions of time. To retain numerical stability and to limit the numerical offset error, many activities cannot be calculated with a time slice bigger than a threshold. However, varying time slices between states can be so large that the numerical computation of the physics-based model diverges. Our solution to this problem is as follows. Let's assume that DT satisfies numerical stability and at simulation state m the time slice is DT_m. When DT_m is larger than DT, DT_m can be divided into a number of DTs and the physical phenomena can be simulated DT_m/DT times. The residue of the time division can be added to the next simulation period.

As an example, we simulate a spider walking on a web in real time synchronized with the wall clock. Again, we use springs to construct the simulation model. The data structure for the web is as in Fig. 5.4. The modeling method mainly includes the following steps:

1. Generate *4* vertex arrays *a[i], b[i], c[i], and d[i]* in 3D space for *i*=0 to *n-1*. Each vertex is an imaginary object with mass *M*.

2. Fix the end points of the vertex arrays.

3. Rotate the web into an orientation of your choice. The vector *down* is a fixed direction pointing towards the ground after the rotation.

4. Establish a physical relationship between neighboring vertices by connecting them with a spring line, as in Fig. 5.4. The spring is at rest when the distance between the vertices is zero. Otherwise, the spring will apply an attracting force on the two neighboring

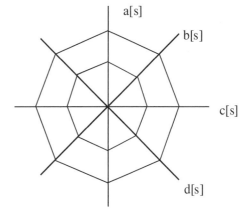

Fig. 5.4 **A spiderweb data structure**

vertices. According to Hooke's law, the spring force *Fa[i]* on vertex *a[i]* includes 4 components (in x, y, and z direction, respectively; here we only show the force in x direction):

```
Fa[i].x = K*(a[i+1].x - a[i].x) + K*(a[i-1].x - a[i].x);
// the force generated by
// the 2 springs along the diagonal line

Fa[i].x = Fa[i].x + K1*(b[i].x-a[i].x)+
         K1*(d[S-1-i].x-a[i].x);
// the force generated by
// the 2 springs along the circle line

Fa[i].x = Fa[i].x - K2*da[i].x;
// the air damping force according to
// the velocity of a[i]

Fa[i].x = Fa[i].x + gravity*down.x;
// the gravity force so the web will be
// drawn towards the ground

If (spider is at a[i])
    Fa[i].x = Fa[i].x + spiderWeight*down.x;
// the spider's weight. The spider is
// moving around on the web
```

5. Calculate the new coordinates of the vertices after a period

```
DTm = period() + (DTm % DT);
```

where *period()* returns the clock time passed since last time we updated the vertices, and *(DTm % DT)* is the remainder time from the last simulation. We repeat the following simulation *(DTm/DT)* times (except the acceleration, which only calculates once):

```
dda[i].x = fa[i].x/M;
// the acceleration

da[i].x = da[i].x + dda[i].x*DT;
// the new velocity and

a[i] = a[i]+da[i]*DT;
// the new position
```

6. Draw the current spider and web.

7. Move the spider. Repeat Steps 3 to 7.

Fig. 5.5 is a snapshot of the simulation result: a spider walking on the web. We may have multiple spiders in the environment as well. The samples and source code for the above modeling method are on line at: http:// graphics.gmu.edu/spider/

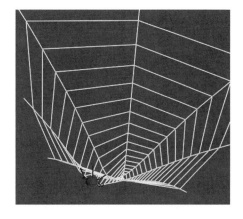

Fig. 5.5 A simulation of a spider web

5.5.3 The Efficiency of Modeling and Simulation

Fortunately, in the above example the simulation and graphics rendering are both fast enough on an ordinary PC to achieve the web and spider behavior in real time. More often than not, the simulation efficiency and the physical and visual realism are contradictory to the point that we cannot achieve both. To achieve real time, we sacrifice the physical realism and/or the visual quality by simplifying the complex physics-based model and/or the graphics rendering method. The 3D graphics rendering speed is often the bottleneck of real-time simulation. The bottom line is that the associated processing loads must not reduce the system update rate below what we consider to be real time (24 frames per second). We can improve the simulation efficiency by changing the software or hardware, or both, to accommodate real time. A real-time graphics simulation pipeline is a loop that includes the following major processes:

1. Handle user input (keyboard, mouse, external sensors, VR trackers, etc.);

2. Calculate the new state of the simulation model;

3. Pre-process 3D objects (collision detection, clipping/culling, organization, etc.);

4. Render the virtual world. Repeat Steps 1 to 4.

Software Methods. For Step 2, we can simplify the simulation model to the point that it satisfies the minimum requirements, or use a simpler model that achieves the partial requirements. For Step 3, where there are different algorithms that provide collision detection and other graphics preprocessing functions, we can choose the most efficient algorithms. For Step 4, we have different rendering methods that will significantly change the efficiency. For example, we can use polygons instead of curved surfaces, shaded polygons instead of texture mapped polygons, flat polygons instead of shaded polygons, wire-frame objects instead of polygonal objects, etc. Choosing graphics rendering methods to improve efficiency often requires more understanding of the graphics system.

Hardware Methods. Many low-level graphics functions are implemented in the hardware on a graphics card. In fact, without a graphics card, no graphical simulation can be in real time. However, not all graphics cards are the same. Some functions are expensive to implement in hardware. The prices on the graphics cards are different. Therefore, it is important to know what graphics functions are necessary, and to purchase the card that comes with the necessary functions. For example, if a simulation application requires large-number polygon rendering, we may choose a specially configured intensive-polygon-rendering hardware. If a simulation requires frequent texture mapping, we will need texture mapping hardware. Texture mapping would be extremely slow if there were no hardware support. Some high performance graphics cards, such as Intense3D Wildcat 5110, have very large dedicated texture memory and frame buffers for hardware texture mapping. Hardware makes it possible to achieve advanced graphics effects such as lighting, texture mapping, volume rendering, antialiasing, and scene accumulation in real time.

5.6 Virtual Reality

Virtual Reality (VR) extends the 3D graphics world to include stereoscopic, acoustic, haptic, tactile, and other kinds of feedback to create a sense of immersion. A 3D image is like any ordinary picture we see, but a stereo image gives a strong sense of depth in 3D. It is generated by providing two slightly different views (images) of the same object to our two eyes separately.

The head-mounted device (HMD), the ImmersaDesk/CAVE, and the VREX stereo projectors are different kinds of display devices for stereo images. An HMD like VR8 has two separate display channels/screens to cover our two eyes. An ImmersaDesk or CAVE has only one channel, like an ordinary display screen, except that it displays two different images alternatively for our two eyes. Lightweight liquid crystal shutter glasses are worn by the viewer. These glasses activate each eye in succession. The glasses are kept synchronized with the two images through an infrared emitter. CAVE is the predecessor of ImmersaDesk, which is more expensive and has multiple display screens surrounding the viewer. Usually it has four walls (left, right, front, and ceiling walls). An ImmersaDesk can be considered to be a movable/flip-able one-wall CAVE. VREX's stereo projectors generate two images at the same time that can be viewed through lightweight, inexpensive polarized glasses.

The key hardware technologies for achieving VR are real-time graphics generators, stereo displays/views, tracking sensors, sound machines, and haptic devices. Real-time graphics (computer) and stereo displays (HMD, ImmersaDesk, CAVE, or VREX projectors) allow the user to view stereoscopic scenes and animation, and provide the user a sense of immersion. Tracking sensors, which get the position and orientation of the user's head, hands, body parts, or other inputs, enable the user to manipulate models and navigate in the virtual environment. Sound machines provide a sense of location and orientation of certain objects and activities in the environment. Like sound machines, haptic devices vibrate and touch the user's body, generating another feedback from the virtual environment in addition to stereoscopic view and 3D sound, enhancing the sense of immersion.

Some VR software tools are available that recognize well-defined commercial tracking sensors, sound machines, and haptic devices, in addition to functions for developing 3D virtual environments. SunMicrosystem's Java3D and Sense8's WorldToolKit are cross-platform software development systems for building real-time integrated 3D applications. MultiGen-Paradigm's Vega is a real-time visual and audio simulation software tool that includes stereo imaging. OpenInventor (based on SGI's Inventor standard) is a real-time programming system that sits on top of a graphics library. Lincom's VrTool is an OpenInventor-based toolkit used to provide a rapid prototyping capability that enables VR users to quickly get their application running with the minimum amount of effort. These VR tools are scene-graph based programming environments. *Scene-graph* is a data structure that describes 3D objects and environments.

Often non-immersive 3D graphics systems are also called VR systems. VRML (Virtual Reality Modeling Language) is a web-based 3D scene description language based on Inventor's 3D scene-graph structure. ActiveWorlds and DIVE (Distributed Interactive Virtual Environment) are internet-based multi-user VR systems where participants navigate in 3D space and see, meet and interact with other users and applications.

5.7 Graphics on the Internet: Web3D

The Internet has been the most dynamic new technology in the past decade. Many web-based 3D modeling, rendering, and animation tools have emerged. It is not difficult to foresee that Web3D will be the future of education, visualization, advertising, shopping, communication, and entertainment. Currently, most Web3D tools are individual plug-ins for a general web browser. Most of the tools are built on OpenGL or Direct3D, such as VRML browser and the Java3D programming environment.

5.7.1 Virtual Reality Modeling Language (VRML)

VRML is a scene description language that presents 3D objects and environments over the Internet. It is also a file format that defines the layout and content of a 3D world. VRML worlds usually have the file extension *.wrl* or *.wrl.gz* as opposed to *.html*. When a web browser sees a file with the *.wrl* file extension, it launches the VRML engine, which is usually a plug-in viewer. A VRML file containing complex interactive 3D worlds is similar to an ordinary HTML page in size.

5.7.2 Java3D

Java3D by Sun Microsystem, is a scene-graph based 3D API that runs on multiple platforms, which can be deployed over the Internet. 3D graphics can be easily integrated with Java applications and applets. VRML and other 3D files can be loaded into the Java3D environment, which are controlled and manipulated according to the program and user interactions.

On top of lower graphics libraries, many new web-based 3D API engines similar to Java3D have been developed by individuals and companies. VRML, HTML, Java, Java3D, Streaming Media, and dynamic database are evolving technologies, which will enable a new kind of 3D Hypermedia Web site.

6
Low-Level Graphics Libraries

Chapter Objectives:

- Introduce some basic graphics libraries
- Compile a reference list of low-level graphics libraries

6.1 Introduction

A low-level graphics library or package is a standard that defines the graphics functions. It is a software interface to graphics hardware, namely the application programmer's interface (API). It provides a set of graphics functions or output subroutines, which can specify primitive geometric models and their attributes to digitize and display. Some graphics subroutines or functions are integrated with special graphics hardware to improve the speed efficiency. Therefore, some graphics libraries are device dependent, which are implemented on specific platforms. Every graphics tool or application is built on top of a specific low-level graphics library.

6.2 OpenGL and Mesa

OpenGL is the most widely adopted device-independent 3D graphics API. It was first developed by SGI from its early device dependent GL (graphics library). Now the OpenGL Architecture Review Board (ARB) with leading computer companies controls the OpenGL technology standard (http://www.opengl.org). We have used OpenGL as an API to introduce the basic graphics principles in *Part I* of this book.

Mesa was developed by Brian Paul to simulate OpenGL functions on UNIX platforms that did not support OpenGL at the time (http://www.mesa3d.org/). Today, Mesa is the most convenient OpenGL API on Linux and an open software implementation for learners as well as developers to use and study.

6.3 Direct3D/DirectX

Microsoft's Direct3D is the de facto standard 3D graphics API for the Windows platform. It has an OpenGL-comparable feature set. Both Direct3D and OpenGL are widely supported by PC hardware graphics card vendors. Direct3D is part of DirectX, which is a set of APIs (DirectDraw, DirectSound, DirectPlay, Direct3D, DirectInput), available as COM (Component Object Model) objects. These APIs provide objects and functions for developing real-time, high-performance games and other applications on the Windows platform.

6.4 PHIGS and GKS-3D

PHIGS and GKS-3D are international standards that were defined in the 1980s. Some high-level graphics packages have been developed on PHIGS or GSK-3D. Many OpenGL and Direct3D functions have been evolved from the PHIGS or GKS-3D functions.

6.5 QuickDraw3D and XGL

QuickDraw3D is a relatively new graphics library that is implemented on top of QuickTime by Apple Computer. XGL is a graphics library developed by SUN Microsystems. An XGL application runs within a window environment managed by an X11 compatible server, such as the X11 server within Sun's OpenWindows environment. Both QuickDraw3D and XGL include drawing 3D primitives directly.

7
Visualization

Chapter Objectives:

- Introduce different visualization methods and tools
- Compile a reference list of visualization tools

7.1 Introduction

Visualization, the use of computer graphics to gain insight into complex phenomena, is a powerful instrument. Many visualization tools, built on top of a graphics library, are developed for certain applications, such as AVS for spatial and engineering data, Star-CD for CFD data, and 3DVIEWNIX for medical image data. Some of them are more general, while others are more specific to certain types of data. They provide insightful visualization solutions, but they more or less lose the flexibility of a low level graphics library as a general tool. We need either to find a good match of the visualization tool to our application, or to develop our own visualization application from a graphics library.

Visualization employs graphics to make pictures that give us insight into certain abstract data and symbols. The pictures may directly portray the description of the data, or completely present the content of the data in an innovative form. Many commercial and free visualization software packages exist in different application areas: medical imaging, computational fluid dynamics visualization, large-data-set visualization, information visualization, etc. It is difficult to categorize visualization tools since most of the tools contain a variety of functions covering many different applications. Many tools have overlapping visualization functions. Some tools include the capabilities to do interactive modeling, animation, simulation, and graphical user interface construction. In the following, we briefly introduce several visualization tools as examples for different applications.

7.2 Multipurpose Visualization Tools

AVS/Express, IRIS Explorer, Data Explorer, MATLAB, PV-WAVE, Khoros, and VTK are multiple purpose visualization commercial products. AVS/Express has applications in many scientific areas, including engineering analysis, CFD, medical imaging, and GIS (Geographic Information Systems). It is built on top of OpenGL and runs on multiple platforms. IRIS Explorer includes visual programming environment for 3D data visualization, animation and manipulation. IRIS Explorer modules can be plugged together, which enable users to interactively analyze collections of data and visualize the results. IRIS Explorer is build on top of OpenInventor, an interactive 3D object scene management, manipulation, and animation tool. OpenInventor has been used as the basis for the emerging Virtual Reality Modeling Language (VRML). The rendering engine for IRIS Explorer and OpenInventor are OpenGL. IBM's Data Explorer (DX) is a general-purpose software package for data visualization and analysis. OpenDX is the open source software version of the DX Product. DX is build on top of OpenGL and runs on multiple platforms. MATLAB was originally developed to provide easy access to matrix software. Today, it is a powerful simulation and visualization tool used in a variety of application areas including signal and image processing, control system design, financial engineering, and medical research. PV-WAVE integrates charting, volume visualization, image processing, advanced numerical analysis, and many other functions. Khoros is a software integration, simulation, and visual programming environment that includes image processing and visualization. VTK is a graphics tool that supports a variety of visualization and modeling functions on multiple platforms. In VTK, applications can be written directly in C++ or in Tcl (an interpretive language).

7.3 Volume Rendering

Volume rendering or visualization is a method of extracting meaningful information from a set of volumetric data. It is also called imaging if the volumetric data are images. A sequence of 2D image slices of a body part can be reconstructed into a 3D volume model and visualized for diagnostic purposes or for planning treatment or surgery. For example, a set of volumetric data such as a deck of Magnetic Resonance Imaging (MRI) slices or Computed Tomography (CT) can be blended into a 2D X-ray image by firing rays through the volume and blending the voxels (volume pixels) along the rays. This is a rather costly operation and the blending methods vary.

The concept of volume rendering is also to extract the contours from given data slices. An isosurface is a 3D constant intensity surface represented by triangle strips or higher order surface patches within a volume. For example, the voxels on the surface of bones in a deck of MRI slices appear to be same intensity value. The Marching Cubes algorithm, which was introduced by Lorenson and Cline, examines each cubic element in the volume data and determines what the topology of an isosurface passing through this element would be.

3DVIEWNIX, Volumizer, ANALYZE, and VolVis are 3D imaging and volume rendering tools. The NIH's Visible Human Project (http://www.nlm.nih.gov/research/ visible/visible_human.html) has created anatomically detailed 3D representations of the human body. The project has included the efforts of several universities and resulted in many imaging tools.

7.4 Vector Field and Fluid Flow

Tecplot, StarCD, FAST, pV3, FIELDVIEW, EnSight, and Visual3 are CFD (Computational Fluid Dynamics) visualization tools. Fluid flow is a rich area for visualization applications. Many CFD tools integrate interactive visualization with scientific computation of turbulence or plasmas for the design of new wings or jet nozzles, the prediction of atmospheric and oceanic activities, and the understanding of material behaviors.

7.5 Large Data Sets

The visualization of the large data sets from physical and natural sciences employ statistical analyses, cartography, Computer Aided Design (CAD), multiresolution analyses, and Geographic Information Systems (GIS) techniques. The integration of multidisciplinary data and information (e.g. atmospheric, oceanographic, and geographic) into visualization systems will help and support cross-disciplinary explorations and communications. The variety of data comes with different data geometries, sampling rates, and error characteristics.

NCAR, Vis5D, FERRET, GNUplot, and SciAn are software tools for visual presentation and examination of datasets from the physical and natural sciences, often requiring the integration of terabyte or gigabyte distributed scientific databases with visualization.

8
Modeling and Rendering

Chapter Objectives:

- Introduce different modeling, rendering, and animation tools
- Compile a reference list of modeling tools
- Compile a reference list of rendering tools

8.1 *Modeling*

Modeling is a process of constructing a 3D model from a real object or an imaginary entity. Modeling tools help create virtual objects and environments for CAD (computer-aided design), visualization, education, training, and entertainment. MultigenPro is a powerful modeling tool for 3D models and terrain generation/editing. AutoCAD and MicroStation are popular for 2D/3D mechanical designing and drawing. 3D Studio Viz is a multifunction tool for architectural and industrial designs. Rhino3D is for freeform curve surface models.

8.2 *Rendering*

Rendering is a process of creating images from graphics models. 3D graphics models are generated on the fly or loaded in computer memory from hard-disk files. The terms rasterization and scan-conversion are used to refer to low-level image generation. All modeling tools provide certain drawing capabilities to visualize the models generated. However, in addition to simply drawing (scan-converting) geometric objects, rendering tools often include lighting, shading, texture mapping, color blending, raytracing, radiosity, and other advanced graphics capabilities. For example, RenderMan Toolkit includes photorealistic modeling and rendering of particle system, hair, and many other objects with advanced graphics functions such as raytracing, volume display, motion blur, depth-of-field, and so forth. Some successful rendering tools were free (originally developed by excellent researchers at their earlier career or school years), such as POVRay, LightScape, Rayshade, Radiance, and BMRT. POVRay is a popular raytracing package across multiple platforms that provides a set of geometric primitives and many surface and texture effects. LightScape employs radiosity and raytracing to produce realistic digital images and scenes. Rayshade is an extensible system for creating ray-traced images that includes a rich set of primitives, CSG (constructive solid geometry) functions, and texture tools. Radiance is a rendering package for the analysis and visualization of lighting in design. It is employed by architects and engineers to predict illumination, visual quality and appearance of design spaces, and by researchers to evaluate new lighting technologies. BMRT (Blue Moon Rendering Tools) is a RenderMan-compliant raytracing and radiosity rendering package. The package contains visual tools to help users create RenderMan Input Bytestream (RIB) input files.

8.3 Multipurpose Tools: Modeling, Rendering, and Animation

Many powerful graphics tools include modeling, rendering, animation, and other functions into one package, such as Alias|Wavefront's Studio series and Maya, SoftImage, 3DStudioMax, LightWave, and TrueSpace. It takes serious course training to use these tools. Alias|Wavefront's Studio series provide extensive tools for industrial design, automotive styling, and technical surfacing. Its Maya is a powerful and productive 3D software for character animation that has been used to create visual effects in some of the hottest recent film releases, including *A Bug's Life* and *Titanic*. SoftImage3D provides advanced modeling and animation features such as NURBS, skin, and particle systems that are excellent for special effects and have been employed in many computer games and films, including stunning animations in *Deep Impact* and *Air Force One*. 3DStudioMax is a popular 3D modeling, animation, and rendering package on the Windows platform for game development. Its open plug-in architecture makes it an idea platform for third party developer. LightWave is a powerful tool that has been successfully used in many TV feature movies, games, and TV commercials. TrueSpace is another popular and powerful 3D modeling, animation, and rendering package for the Windows platform.

9
Animation and Simulation

Chapter Objectives:

- Introduce different animation and simulation tools
- Compile a reference list of animation tools
- Compile a reference list of simulation tools

9.1 Animation

Animation is an integral part of interactive computer graphics. Most visualization, modeling, rendering, and simulation tools, such as OpenInventor, Maya, Lightwave3D, and Activeworlds, include animation. In traditional storyboard animation, a high-level sequence of sketches are first developed, then keyframes and soundtrack are decided upon, the keyframes where sounds occur are correlated, and finally the inbetweenings are interpolated between keyframes. In computer graphics, animation is mostly interactive geometry or image transformations.

Computer animation is achieved by drawing frames of different images at more than 24 frames per second. To achieve smooth animation, we need high performance algorithms as well as graphics hardware to carry out scene modification and rendering efficiently. 3D Choreographer is an animation program designed for non-artists. Outlining your animation is as simple as casting "Actors," drawing "Paths," and issuing "Scripts." Poser 4 is a 3D-character animation and design tool for artists and animators. AnimationMaster is a spline based animation program that provides advanced features like inverse kinematics, raytracing, image mapping, and modeling of complex organic and mechanical objects. b3d Studio is an editing and production package for 3D animated movies. Motivate 3D is primarily an animation tool for developing 3D games and interactive multimedia titles.

9.2 *Simulation*

A simulation is a process of constructing, executing, and visualizing a model to collect pertinent information about the behavior of a real-world or imaginary system. Here the model is a math, physics, or engineering representation of the system with its many characteristics. A graphical simulation emphasizes animation and visualization of the simulation process. A real-time simulation is one in which the time seems to be the actual time in which the physical process under simulation occurs. In graphics, it often means that the simulation is smoothly animated. Many real-time simulation systems are event-driven, in which the evolution of the simulation is determined by the complexity of both the computation and the graphics rendering.

Many animation tools, interactive game engines, and virtual environment enabling systems, such as Softimage, NetImmerse, Genesis3D, WorldUp, and ActiveWorlds, are also simulation tools, because they provide the means and environments to achieve significant simulations. IRIS Performer is a toolkit for real-time graphics simulation applications. It simplifies development of complex applications such as visual simulation, flight simulation, simulation-based design, virtual reality, interactive entertainment, broadcast video, CAD, and architectural walk-throughs. Vega is MultiGen-Paradigm's software environment for real-time visual and audio simulation, virtual reality, and general visualization applications. It provides the basis for building, editing, and running sophisticated applications quickly and easily. 20-sim is a modeling and simulation program for electrical, mechanical, and hydraulic systems or any combination of these systems. Mathematica is an integrated environment that provides technical computing, simulation, and communication. Its numeric and symbolic computation abilities, graphical simulation, and intuitive programming language are combined with a full-featured document processing system. MATLAB and Khoros contain modeling and simulation functions.

10
Virtual Reality

Chapter Objectives:

- Introduce different virtual reality methods and tools
- Compile a reference list of virtual reality tools

10.1 *Virtual Reality*

Virtual Reality (VR) can be divided into two categories: immersive VR and non-immersive VR. In an immersive VR system, users wear head-mounted devices (HMD) or special glasses to view stereoscopic images. The viewpoint usually follows the viewer's head movement in real time. In a non-immersive VR, which is usually a lot cheaper, users usually do not wear any device, and the viewpoint does not follow the user's head movement. But users navigate in the virtual world through input devices interactively and the image is usually a first-person view. In a VR system, navigation allows a user to move around and to view virtual objects and places, and interaction provides an active way for a user to control the appearance and behavior of objects.

A VR system is also a simulation system that describes and simulates certain real-world activities in various areas such as training, education, and entertainment. Therefore, many simulation tools like Vega and WorldUp are also VR tools. A VR system always repeats the following processing steps:

1. Handle user inputs from various devices — keyboard, mouse, VR trackers, sensors, voice recognition systems, etc.

2. Calculate the new state of the objects and the environment according to the simulation models.

3. Pre-process 3D objects including collision detection, levels of detail, clipping/culling, etc.

4. Render the virtual world.

In Step 2, different VR applications may use different simulation models. No matter what application a VR system implements, the software to handle the other three steps, a high-level graphics library called a VR tool (or VR toolkit), is always needed. Therefore, VR tools are usually independent of the applications. A VR system is usually a VR application implemented on top of a VR tool, which provides an API for the VR application to manipulate the objects according to the simulation models. VR tools are likely to be device dependent, built on low-level basic graphics libraries with interfaces to sensory devices.

Some VR tools, such as MR Toolkit, OpenInventor, and WorldToolkit, only provide APIs embedded in certain programming languages for VR developers. It requires more knowledge and programming skills to employ these toolkits, but they provide more flexibility in application implementations. Others, such as Alice and WorldUp (often called VR simulation tools), provide graphical user interfaces (GUIs) for the developers to build applications. Developers achieve virtual worlds and simulations by typing, clicking, and dragging through GUIs. Sometimes simple script languages are used to construct simulation processes. VR simulation tools allow developing a VR system quicker and easier, but the application developed is an independent fixed module that cannot be modified or integrated in a user-developed program. A VR simulation tool is generally developed on top of a VR toolkit, so it is one level higher than the VR toolkit in the VR software levels.

11
Web3D Tools and Networked Environment

Chapter Objectives:

- Introduce Web3D and distributed interactive simulation in a networked environment
- Compile a list of Web3D tools

11.1 Web3D

Web3D tools are graphics tools that deliver graphics through web browsers over the Internet. Many web-based 3D modeling, rendering, and animation tools emerged recently. It is not difficult to foresee that Web3D will be the future of education, visualization, advertising, shopping, communication, and entertainment. Currently, most Web3D tools are individual plug-ins for a general web browser. Most of the tools, such as VRML browser and the Java3D programming environment, are built on OpenGL or Direct3D. Individuals and companies have developed many new Web-based 3D API engines (similar to Java3D) on top of lower-level graphics libraries.

11.2 Distributed Interactive Simulation

In addition to Web3D tools, networked virtual environments have been developed to simulate highly interactive activities in critical mission training. Unlike Web3D tools, which develop applications for independent users without real-time constraints, distributed interactive simulation (DIS) systems immerse networked users in the same virtual environments across the network in real time.

In a distributed interactive virtual environment, multiple nodes (computer simulators) at different locations have the same entities (objects) and activities (behavior). NPSNET (www.npsnet.org/), MUVE (http://www.virtual.gmu.edu/muvees/), ExploreNet (http://www.cs.ucf.edu/ExploreNet/) are examples of such kind of environments. Today, most DIS environments call for a centralized infrastructure to control and manage information. The High Level Architecture (HLA) with a Run Time Infrastructure (RTI), which builds upon and generalizes the results in DIS, is advocated by the US government. HLA allows for nodes to coordinate the execution and exchange of information through the RTI.

There are two layers of communications in DIS/HLA: communicating between the multiple nodes at the network communication layer and synchronizing physical activities on top of the network communication. The low-level communication protocol determines the efficiency and reliability of the message transmission. The high-level time synchronization is vital for achieving fast DIS. Better solutions to these problems will improve the usability and speedup the simulation in DIS/HLA. For example, in Doom — a simple distributed multi-player game system — each node simply *broadcasts* the location of each entity that it maintains. Communication delay for time synchronization is ignored.

11.3 Synchronization in a DIS

When implementing a DIS/HLA, the commonly accepted approach to limit the rate of simultaneous updating of multiple nodes on a distributed simulation network is termed *Dead Reckoning*. Dead Reckoning is a method of position/orientation estimation that predicts and approximates the behavior of simulated entities among the networked nodes. Dead Reckoning's estimations eliminate the need for sending every change in position/orientation until a pre-specified threshold is exceeded; then, the behavior of the entities that changed is updated by new data sent across the network. In a DIS/HLA, an entity is either an *object* or a *ghost*. An object is the master entity running on its host node where the user controls its activities. Its copies running on other networked nodes are called its (Dead Reckoning) ghosts. The user has no control over the activities of ghosts, which proceed according to their object's original parameters (position, orientation, velocity, acceleration, etc). A ghost is running on the host node as well, so that Dead Reckoning algorithm can compare the parameters of the object and the ghost on the host node to estimate the errors in the networked ghosts, and update the ghosts with the object's parameters if necessary.

In a Dead Reckoning process, the logical time step used has to be synchronized (or uniform) across the network. The time management to synchronize the networked activities has been a major research issue. Centralized control and event-driven methods use time step ticks (heartbeats) to achieve the synchronization. In an event-driven system, the evolution of the simulation is determined both by the computational complexity of simulated objects and by the rapidity of network communication to update the behavior of those objects. Simulations involving close coordination of entities over long distances across multiple network nodes are not practical due to the introduction of unpredictable, but significant, latencies. The Clock Reckoning strategy uses system clocks to synchronize distributed entities across the network. Here, the physical time and simulation time are all unified under wall clock time.

11.3.1 The Clock Reckoning — Wall Clock Synchronization

The Clock Reckoning strategy uses a wall clock to synchronize distributed entities across the network. Each entity will have a local variable (lastTime) used to record the last time this entity updated its state. Each time an entity begins to update its state, it reads the host node's clock to get the current time (currentTime) and subtracts lastTime from currentTime to determine the period between the current time and the last time when the state was updated. This value is the time-step passed; its value together with the entity's old state uniquely determines its new state. At the same time, lastTime will be updated to currentTime. Overall, each entity proceeds at its own pace synchronized by a uniform time scale of the wall clock. No time step ticks are needed.

The next stage of the Clock Reckoning strategy involves synchronizing state-updates across multiple nodes, providing inter-entity synchronization across the network. When an entity receives a network update message, it must compute the network delay between the time when the message was sent and when it is received. The sending node can include a time stamp — the currentTime of the entity's state data. Assuming the system clocks have the same wall clock time, the receiving node can read its clock to get the local currentTime, and subtract the time stamp currentTime in the received data from the local currentTime to determine the network delay. Again, this value is the time step that determines the new state (together with the update state in the received data.)

Now, how are the node system clocks synchronized to the wall clock? A simple solution is as follows: a portable hardware called *wallClock* is designed that can be plugged into a node to synchronize the system clock time to its own time. Many wallClocks can be made, synchronized, and sent to multiple hosts. Fig. 11.1 shows that a wallClock is used to synchronize multiple hosts in a simplified DIS network.

The synchronization mechanism does not require transmitting event-driven heartbeat ticks, yet the time elapsed between events is accurately communicated. The time steps vary at different nodes yet the time order is guaranteed. All nodes can smoothly and accurately simulate a predictable physical activity despite unpredictable network latencies. So this time synchronization protocol is applicable to certain physics-based simulation.

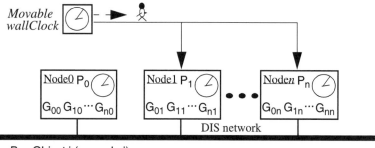

P_i = Object i (on node i)
G_{ij} = Ghost of Object i on node j

Fig. 11.1 Time synchronization in a simplified DIS

12
3D File Formats

Chapter Objectives:

- Introduce the relationships between 3D programming tool libraries and file formats
- Survey graphics file formats and format converting tools
- Compile a list of file format converting tools

12.1 Introduction

Today, people live not only in the real world, but also in 3D virtual worlds. We spend time on virtual reality systems, graphics games, films of imaginary worlds and characters, Web-based 3D environments, and distributed interactive simulations. People represented by 3D avatars can travel in virtual worlds and meet with one another over the Internet. Advances in graphics software and hardware have enabled many new applications, and many virtual worlds are constructed with different models and activities.

In order to reuse constructed models and to transmit virtual worlds across the Internet and on different platforms, 3D graphics files are created to save models, scenes, worlds, and animations. However, graphics developers have created many different 3D graphics file formats for different applications. Here, we survey and list some popular 3D graphics file formats, programming tool libraries that understand different formats, authoring tools that create virtual worlds and save them in graphics files, and format conversion tools that transform files from one format into another. We hope to provide a panoramic view of 3D virtual world technologies to facilitate 3D modeling, reuse, programming, and virtual world construction.

The relationships in an ordinary high-level 3D graphics tool are shown in Fig. 12.1. A 3D graphics tool is built on top of other 3D graphics tools or a low-level graphics library. Therefore, at the bottom of any graphics tool is a low-level graphics library. Low-level graphics libraries such as OpenGL or Direct3D are the rendering tools that actually draw 3D models into the display. 3D models can also be stored and transmitted as 3D graphics files. 3D authoring tools are modeling tools

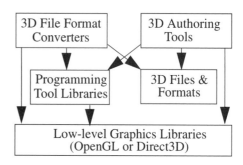

Fig. 12.1 Relationships in 3D graphics tool

that provide users with convenient methods to create, view, modify, and save models and virtual worlds. In general, a 3D authoring tool includes a 3D browser. 3D browsers or viewers are graphics tools that read, analyze, and convert 3D graphics files into the tools' internal formats, and then display the converted worlds to the user. 3D graphics viewers, authoring tools, and format converters may access 3D files directly, or go through programming tool library functions.

12.2 3D File Formats

There are different names for virtual worlds or environments. A virtual world is a scene database, which is composed of hierarchical 3D scenes, for example, as in OpenInventor. A 3D scene is an ordered collection of nodes that include 3D models, attributes, animations, and so forth. 3D graphics file formats are storage methods for virtual worlds. Due to the complexities of virtual worlds, 3D file formats include many specifications about how 3D models, scenes, and hierarchies are stored. In addition, different applications include different attributes and activities, and thus may require different file formats. The Center for Innovative Computer Applications at Indiana University has a good collection of 3D format specifications (http://www.cica.indian.edu/graphics/object_specs/.)

Over the years, many different 3D graphics file formats have been developed that are in use today, as in Tab. 12.1 on page 131. DFX, VRML, 3DS, MAX, RAW, LightWave, POV, and NFF are probably the most commonly used formats. Searching on the Internet, we found 80–90% of 3D models and scenes are in these formats.

12.3 3D Programming Tool Libraries

3D programming tool libraries provide powerful and easy-to-use functions for programs to handle 3D file imports and exports, model and scene constructions, and virtual world manipulations and display. They are also called high-level graphics libraries, built on top of low-level graphics libraries, but they are really primitive functions for higher-level graphics applications. They make sophisticated 3D file formats and virtual world hierarchies easy to handle, and thus reduce application developers' programming efforts. Many high-level graphics tools are built on top of certain programming tool libraries. Usually, a 3D programming tool library supports one 3D file format by providing a series of functions that an application program can call to store, import, parse, and manipulate 3D models or scenes. Tab. 12.2 on page 133 is a list of 3D programming tool libraries. If we develop our own 3D applications, we save much time and effort by using a 3D programming tool library. In general, for the same file format, commercial products with customer service are much more reliable than freeware tools.

12.4 3D Authoring Tools

3D graphics authoring tools, which in general are modeling tools as discussed in Chapter 8, free us from constructing complicated objects, worlds, and dealing with complicated specifications of 3D graphics file format definitions and make our 3D world construction job much easier.

3D authoring tools usually have good user interfaces, which provide rich object editing tools (such as object extruding, splitting, and cutting, etc.) and flexible manipulation approaches. Using these tools, you can construct complicated 3D models conveniently even without knowing the 3D file formats.

12.5 3D File Format Converters

There are many 3D file formats in use. Every 3D file-format has its specific details. People have created and are still creating huge amounts of 3D models and 3D scenes with different 3D graphics file formats. Without knowing clearly the 3D file format specifications, is it possible — or is there a shortcut for us — to use these different formatted 3D resources and import (reuse) them into our own 3D worlds? Fortunately, the answer is: yes. We can employ the 3D graphics file format conversion tools, as shown in Tab. 12.1 on page 131. By the way, many 3D authoring tools also provide certain 3D file format conversion functions.

Some attributes and properties of the 3D models or scenes may be lost during the format converting. This is because some specifications of a 3D file format can't be translated into another 3D file format; the converters just throw these specifications away. So we should not anticipate that all the details of the 3D models or scenes will be fully translated from one 3D file format to another. Here we briefly introduce a couple of commonly used tools. A detailed list of the tools is provided later.

12.5.1 Built-In and Plug-In VRML Exporters

VRML is the standard 3D file format on the Web. Many 3D file converters can convert different file formats to VRML format. Many 3D authoring tools have the capability to import 3D models from some other file formats, and export 3D scenes to VRML file format. Here is a list of authoring tools that support VRML export: Alias/ Wavefront's Maya, AutoCAD's Mechanical Desktop, Bentley MicroStation, CAD Studio, Kinetix's VRML Exporter (a free plug-in for 3D Studio MAX), Lightwave, Poser, and SolidWorks.

12.5.2 Independent 3D File Format Converters

Some independent 3D file format conversion tools, such as Crossroads 3D and 3DWinOGL, are free. Others are commercial products with reliable technique supports, such as Interchange and NuGraf.

12.6 References

(Those formats with a star in front of their names are the most commonly used ones.)

Tab. 12.1: 3D Graphics File Formats

Name	Extension	Application/Developer	Reference
3DMF	.3dmf, .t3d	Quickdraw 3D package / Apple	http://www.info.apple.com/qd3d/3DMFspec.html
3D2	.3d2	Stereo CAD-3D 2.0 package for the Atari ST	http://www.cica.indiana.edu/graphics/object_specs/3D2.format.txt
*3DS	.3ds, .prj, .mli, .asc	Autodesk 3D Studio / Autodesk LTD	http://www.dcs.ed.ac.uk/home/mxr/gfx/3d/3DS.spec
AVS	.geom, .prop, .scr	AVS commercial high-end visualization environment	http://www.avs.com
BYU	.byu	Movie BYU format (Creator: Brigham Young University)	http://www.cica.indiana.edu/graphics/object_specs/BYU.format.txt
CDF	.cdf	Cyberspace Description Format	http://vrml.wired.com/proposals/cdf/cdf.html
COB	.cob	Calgaro/TrueSpace	http://www.caligari.com/
DX	.dx	Used by IBM Data Explorer soft	http://www.ibm.com/
*DXF	.dxf	used by *AutoCAD* & other CAD tools	http://www.mcwi.com/dxf13/dxf_01.html;
FFIVW	.ffivw	File Format for the Interchange of Virtual Worlds	http://vrml.wired.com/proposals/ffivw.html
FIG	.fig	Used by REND386/AVRIL	http://www.dcs.ed.ac.uk/home/mxr/gfx/3d/FIG.spec
FLT	.flt	MulitGen's OpenFlight format	http://www.multigen.com/
GLC	.glc		http://www.dcs.ed.ac.uk/home/mxr/gfx/3d/GLC.spec
HDF		Hierarchical Data Format / University of Illinois	http://hdf.ncsa.uiuc.edu/
*IGES	.iges	Used by many commercial programs including *Autocad* and *Alias*	http://www.cica.indiana.edu/graphics/object_specs/IGES.ptr.txt
INVENTOR IV-VRML	.iv	Used by SGI's *Inventor* graphics programming package.	http://www.sgi.com/tech/Inventor/VRML/VRMLDesign.html.
LABYRINTH-VRML	.vrml	Labyrinth Virtual Reality Markup Language Format	http://vrml.wired.com/proposals/labspec.html
*LWLO, OB, SC	.lwlo, .lwob, .lwsc	Lightwave 3D file formats	http://www.dcs.ed.ac.uk/home/mxr/gfx/3d/LWLO.txt http://www.dcs.ed.ac.uk/home/mxr/gfx/3d/LWSC.txt
*MAX	.max	3D Studio Max	http://www.3dmax.com/
MAZ	.maz	Division Ltd.	http://www.dcs.ed.ac.uk/home/mxr/gfx/3d/MAZ.spec
MGF	.mgf	Materials and Geometry Format	http://radsite.lbl.gov/mgf/HOME.html
MSDL	.msdl	Manchester Scene Description Language / University of Manchester	http://www.cica.indiana.edu/graphics/object_specs/msdl/MSDL.format.html

Tab. 12.1: 3D Graphics File Formats (Cont'd.)

Name	Extension	Application/Developer	Reference
*NFF, ENFF	.nff, .enff	Used by a variety of programs including Sense8 World Toolkit etc.	http://www.cica.indiana.edu/graphics/object_specs/NFF.format.txt
NURBS	.txt, .nurbs	Spline surface format / University of Utah	http://www.cica.indiana.edu/graphics/object_specs/NURBS.format.txt
*OBJ	.obj (ASCII), .mod (binary)	Used by the *Wavefront* suite of high-end animation packages	http://www.cica.indiana.edu/graphics/object_specs/OBJ.format.txt
OFF	.off	A 3D mesh Object File Format	http://www.cica.indiana.edu/graphics/object_specs/OFF.format.txt
*OOGL	.oogl, .off, .list, .tlist, .grp, .inst	Object Oriented Graphics Library	http://www.cica.indiana.edu/graphics/object_specs/OOGL.format.txt
PLG	.plg	Used by REND386/AVRIL	http://www.dcs.ed.ac.uk/home/mxr/gfx/3d/PLG.spec
PLY	.ply	Used by the *ZipPack* polygon mesh "zippering" package on the SGI	http://www.cica.indiana.edu/graphics/object_specs/PLY.format.txt
*POV	.pov, .pob	Persistence of Vision Ray Tracer (POV-Ray)	http://www.cica.indiana.edu/graphics/object_specs/POV.format.txt
QD3D		Apple's QuickDraw 3D format	http://www.apple.com/quicktime/
RADIANCE	.rad, .oct	Used by the *Radiance* public domain radiosity renderer for Unix	http://www.cica.indiana.edu/graphics/object_specs/radiance/radiance.format.html
*RAW	.raw	Open Standard	Used by shareware tools available on the Internet
Rayshade	.ray, .shade	*Rayshade* public domain ray tracer	
*RIB	.rib	Used by the *Renderman* commerical renderer by Pixar	http://www.cica.indiana.edu/graphics/object_specs/RENDERMAN.ptr.txt
RWX	.rwx	*MEME* virtual reality system	
SCENE	.scene	for the storage and interchange of 3D geometric information.	http://www.cica.indiana.edu/graphics/object_specs/scene/scene.html
SCN	.scn	This format was designed to replace SFF used by the *Rtrace* raytracer	http://www.cica.indiana.edu/graphics/object_specs/scn/SCN.format.html
SCULPT	.scene	Used by *Sculpt3D* on the Amiga	http://ctiweb.cf.ac.uk/cticbe/resguide/sculpt3d.html
SDL	.sdl	Scene Description Language by Alias	http://www.aw.sgi.com/
SDML	.sdml	"Spacial Data Modeling Language", used by the *CLRMosaic* for SGI.	http://www.cica.indiana.edu/graphics/object_specs/SDML.html
SGO	.sgo	Used by the *IRIS Showcase* package for Silicon Graphics workstations	http://www.cica.indiana.edu/graphics/object_specs/inventor/InventorTranslator.ps
STRATA		Used by the *StrataVision* package on the Macintosh.	http://www.strata3d.com/
TDDD	.tddd	Used by the Impulse's *Imagine* and *Turbo Silver 3.0* raytracers	http://www.cica.indiana.edu/graphics/object_specs/TDDD.format.txt
TrueSpace	.obj, .cob, .scn	Used by TrueSpace software	http://www.caligari.com/ftp/pub/trueSpace/info/format.rtf
VID	.vid	Amiga VideoScape format	
VIZ	.viz .BIZ, .VTX	Used by Division's dVS/dVISE	http://www.dcs.ed.ac.uk/home/mxr/gfx/3d/VIZ.spec

Tab. 12.1: 3D Graphics File Formats (Concluded)

Name	Extension	Application/Developer	Reference
*VRML	.wrl	Virtual Reality Modeling Language	Version 2.0 specification at http://www.vrml.org/technicalinfo/specifications/vrml2.0/index.htm
Wavefront	.obj. .tri	Alias|WaveFront company products	http://www.aw.sgi.com/
WLD	.wld	Used by REND386/AVRIL	http://www.dcs.ed.ac.uk/home/mxr/gfx/3d/WLD.spec
X3D	.x3d, .obj	*x3d 2.0* and the *xdart* renderer	http://www.cica.indiana.edu/graphics/object_specs/X3D.format.txt
YAODL	.ydl, .yaodl	Silicon Graphics *Powerflip*	http://www.cica.indiana.edu/graphics/object_specs/YAODL.format.txt

Tab. 12.2: 3D Programming Libraries

3D Library Name	Description	Platform	Price	Reference
3D-MasterSuite (TGS)	Libraries that help build interactive 3D applications in C++ or Java. Support OpenInventor, VRML, etc.	Windows95/98/NT Solaris, AIX, Interix, HP-UX, OS/2	Contact TGS company	http://www.tgs.com/
Activate - VRML2 Toolkit for C/C++ Developers	C/C++ toolkit for that provides support formatting VRML2 support to 3D MS-Windows products.	Windows95/98/NT	$21,000	http://www.3dweb.com/html/products.html
Apprentice	OpenInventor emulator library Some functions not implemented	Windows95/98/NT C++ library	Free in Visual C++	www.mrpowers.com/Apprentice/
Coin	An OpenGL based 3D graphics rendering library. The API is based on the OpenInventor API.	platform independent. C++ library.	Released under QPL	Http://www.sim.no/coin.html
Crystal Space	A free 3D engine (6DOF with portal technology). Well documented.	Linux, Windows, OS/2, SGI, Solaris, Macintosh	Free, source code available	http://crystal.linuxgames.com
FxEgine	A 3d graphics library that uses the glide API.	Windows95/98/NT Linux	Free Source available	http://welcome.to/3dfxPS/
Genesis3D	A free and open source 3D graphics engine targeted at game developers	Windows95/98/NT	Free	www.wildtangent.com/genesis/download.php3
GIZMO	3D Scene Graph & effect visualisation toolkit for C++ programmers; Support .3ds, .flt, and GIZMO formats	Linux, IRIX Windows95/98/NT	Free Trial	http://www.linux3d.net/gizmo3d/
Jun for Smalltalk	A 3D Graphics Library with Topology and Geometry	Windows95/98/NT Linux; Mac OS	Free	http://www.srainc.com/Jun/Main_e.htm
OBSIDIAN	3D virtual world libary, support Multiplayer Client-Server architecture.	Linux	Free, source available	http://www.zog.net.au/computers/obsidian/
OpenInventor (SGI)	OpenInventor package by SGI	IRIX UNIX C library	Contact SGI	Http://www.sgi.com/Technology/Inventor/

Tab. 12.2: 3D Programming Libraries (Concluded)

3D Library Name	Description	Platform	Price	Reference
OpenInventor for C++ or Java (TGS)	OpenInventor library by TGS Recently OpenInventor for Java and for Mac have also been released.	Windows95/98/NT Unix; OS/2, C++ library, Java library	Contact TGS	Http://www.tgs.com/ Products/openinv-index.html
OpenWorlds Libraries	A C++ libraries that bring 3D graphics, sound, and Web support	Windows, UP-UX, SGI IRIX, Solaris	Trial version $250	http:// www.openworlds.com/
Panard Vision	A fast generic high quality 3D renderer	UNIX/X Windows, Linux, Windows	Panard Vision	http://pvision.planet-d.net/
Pryan	C++ library similar to OpenInventor, 100% compatible with its syntax.	Linux/Mesa, SUN, SGI	Free source available	sal.kachinatech.com/F/3/ PRYAN.html
QUESA	High level graphics library compatible with Apple's QuickDraw 3D API. Support QD3D format.	Mac OS, Linux, Windows95/ 98/NT	Free Source code available	http:// quesa.designcommunity. com/
RenderIT 3D	3D graphics C++ library built on top of DirectDraw and Direct3D; Support 3DS, DXF and DirectX formats	Windows95/98/NT	$995	http://www.indotek.com/ sales_r3d.html
Scene	OpenInventor library in C++	GNU/Linux Windows95/98/NT	Free source available	scene.netpedia.net/ download/download.html
SoFree	A free implementation of Open-Inventor (based on OpenGL or Mesa)	HP-UX, Linux, SunOS, Windows	Free	Http://www.lal.in2p3.fr/SI/ SoFree/
WorldToolKit	A cross-platform software development tool. 3D format is NFF.	Windows95/98/NT SGI, Sun, HP-UNIX	Contact Sense8	http://www.sense8.com

(Note: r/w in the file format field means import and output of the file format is supported)

Tab. 12.3: 3D File Format Converters

Converter Name	Description	Platform	Price	Reference
3DwinOGL	Converts between multiple different file formats	Windows95/98/NT	Free	http://www.stmuc.com/thbaier/ tools.html
3Space Converter	Converts CAD/CAM file formats to formats that 3Space Assistant can read and display	Windows95/98/NT	Contact TGS	http://www.tgs.com/Products/ converter-index.html
AccuTrans 3D	3D Studio (.3ds, .asc, .prj) – r/w AutoCAD DXF (.dxf) – r/w Imagine (.iob) – r/w LightWave (.lwo) – r/w TrueSpace (.coa, .cob) – r/w VRML 1.0 & 2.0 (.wrl) – r/w Wavefront (.obj) – r/w	Windows95/98/NT	$60.00	http://web3d.about.com/ compute/web3d/gi/dynamic/ offsite.htm?site=http:// www.unibase.com/%7E4dsol/ accutrans/at3d1.html

Tab. 12.3: 3D File Format Converters (Cont'd.)

Converter Name	Description	Platform	Price	Reference
Clayworks	Unspecified	Linux Windows95/98/NT	Free	http://members.aol.com/ luthercode/clay/index.html
Crossroads 3D	Converts between multiple file formats	Windows95/98/NT	Free	http://home.europa.com/~keithr/ crossroads/
Dx2VRML	IBM Data Explorer (.dx) – r VRML 2.0 (.wrl) – r	Portable	Free	http://www.tc.cornell.edu/ Visualization/contrib/cs490-04to95/ckline/dx2vrml/ dx2vrml_v1.2.tar.gz
DxfToIv	Converts DFX to Inventor	Portable	Free	ftp://ftp.sgi.com/sgi/inventor/1.0/ DxfToIv.tar.Z
Image2VRML	Converts Image format to VRML format	Unspecified	Free	ftp://ftp.sdsc.edu/pub/vrml/ software/geom_trans/
Interchange(tm) 5.5	See the introduction in the paper	Windows95/98/NT	$495+	http://www.viewpoint.com/ interchange/
IV2Pov	Converts Inventor format to POVray format	SGI IRIX Source available	Free	http://www.hammerve.com/ NewHome/FreeStuff/ Converters/
IV2Ray	Converts Inventor format to Rayshade	SGI IRIX Source available	Free	http://www.hammerve.com/ NewHome/FreeStuff/ Converters/
IV2Rib	Converts Inventor format to Rib	SGI IRIX Source available	Free	http://www.hammerve.com/ NewHome/FreeStuff/ Converters/
lwtoiv	Converts Lightwave file to Inventor file	SGI IRIX	Free	http://amber.rc.arizona.edu/ vrml.html#Converters
Materialize 3D!	3D Studio (.3DS) – r; AutoCAD (.DXF) – r/w; Direct3D X (DirectX) – r /w; POVray – w	Windows95/98/NT	$79	http://www.indotek.com/ material.html
NuGraf Version 2.2	More powerful than PloyTrans V2 (from the same company)	Windows95/98/NT	$495 PC	http://www.okino.com/conv/ filefrmt.htm
Obj2wrl	Wavefront (.obj) – r VRML1.0 (.wrl) -- w	Windows95/98/NT	Free	ftp://ftp.sdsc.edu/pub/sdsc/ graphics/vrml/obj2wrl.tar.gz
Off2VRML	OFF – r VRML1.0 -- w	Write in Perl language	Free	http:// EDNET.GSFN.NASA.GOV/ Mathews/Objects/off2vrml.pl.txt
PatchDance	QuickTime3D (.3DMF) - - r/w VRML1.0 and 2.0 – r/w DFX – r/w	Power Macintosh	Free	http://www.patchdance.com/

Tab. 12.3: 3D File Format Converters (Concluded)

Converter Name	Description	Platform	Price	Reference
PloyTrans V2	Alias Triangle (.tri) -- r/w Apple 3D Metafile(.3dmf, .3dm) – r/w 3D Studio R4 (.3ds) – r/w 3D Studio Max (.max) – r/w CAD 3D (.3d2) –r Autocad (.dfx) – r/w DirectX – w IGES (.iges) – r/w Image (.ima) – r/w Lightwave (.lw) – r/w OpenFlight (.flt) – r/w OpenGL C code – w POVray (.pov) – w Software (.hrc) -- r/w TrueSpace (.cob, .scn) – r/w Wavefront (.obj) – r/w VRML1.0 and 2.0 (.wrl) – w	Windows95/98/NT UNIX	$395 PC, $495 UNIX	http://www.okino.com/
Sced	POVray RenderMan RayShade Radiance VRML2.0	Multiple platforms	Free Source Avaialbe	http://http.cs.berkeley.edu/ ~schenney/sced/sced.html
VRML1to2	VRML 1.0 – r VRML 2.0 – w	Windows95/98/NT	Free	http://vs.spiw.com/vs/ vrml1to2E.html
Vrml2pov	VRML2.0 (wrl) – r POVray (pob, pov) – w (but any animation specifications are ignored)	Portable, tested on Windows95/98/NT and SGI IRIX	Free	http:// www.chemicalgraphics.com/ paul/vrml2pov/
VRMLConvert	Converts *Mathematica* 3D graphics into VRML format	Multiple platforms	Free	http://www.ma.iup.edu/ MathDept/Projects/ VRMLConvert/
wadtoiv	Converts Doom wad file (and, optionally, a patchwad) to OpenInventor format	SGI IRIX Source available	Free	http://www-white.media.mit.edu/ ~kbrussel/wadtoiv.html

Appendix:
Graphics Software Tools

Appendix Objectives:

- Provide a comprehensive list of graphics software tools.

- Categorize graphics tools according to their applications. Many tools come with multiple functions. We put a primary category name behind a tool name in the alphabetic index, and put a tool name into multiple categories in the categorized index according to its functions.

A.1. Graphics Tools Listed by Categories

We have no intention of rating any of the tools. Many tools in the same category are not necessarily of the same quality or at the same capacity level. For example, a software tool may be just a simple function of another powerful package, but it may be free.

Low-level Graphics Libraries

Visualization Tools

Modeling Tools

Rendering Tools

Animation Tools

Simulation Tools

Virtual Reality Tools

Web 3D Tools

3D File Format Converters

A.II. Alphabetical Listing and Description of Graphics Tools

Note: please contact the company or vendor for the actual prices. The prices listed are for reference and comparison only. When there is no available price for a tool, the number of "$" signs indicates the range of the price. For example, "$$$" indicates the price of the tool is in the range of $100–$999.

20-sim

1. PLATFORMS, PRICES, AND SUPPLIER/CREATOR

- Windows 95 / 98 / NT 4 / ME / 2000
- 20-sim 3.1 pro
  - corporate: $4000; academic: $800; classroom kit: $4000
- 20-sim 3.1
  - corporate: $2000; academic: $400; classroom kit: $2000
- 20sim.com (CLP): http://www.20sim.com/index.html

2. APPLICATIONS

- 20-sim is a modeling and simulation program that runs under Windows. With 20-sim you can simulate the behavior of dynamic systems, such as electrical, mechanical, and hydraulic systems — or any combination of these

- 20-sim has been developed at the Control Laboratory of the University of Twente, as successor of the famous TUTSIM package. It fully supports graphical modeling, allowing to design and analyze dynamic systems in a intuitive and user friendly way, without compromising power

- 20-sim is officially MATLAB enabled. 20-sim allows for a close interaction with MATLAB and Simulink in both modeling and simulation

3. EXAMPLES/SAMPLES

- http://www.mathworks.com/products/connections/product_main.shtml?prod_id=288

- http://www.20sim.com/products/images/win_linix.jpg

- http://www.20sim.com/products/images/win_oscar.jpg

4. FUNCTIONS

- Modeling:
  - Systems can be modeled using iconic diagrams, block diagrams, bond graphs and equation descriptions. These descriptions can be fully coupled to create hybrid models
  - Fully observable, unlimited hierarchical model structure
  - Active support of top-down, inside-out and bottom-up modeling
  - Create your own model icons with the Icon Editor and see them in the Windows Explorer
  - Multiple libraries with a large set of domain-oriented submodels. Use the Explorer for library management
  - Add graphical elements (rectangles, text ..., etc.) to models
- Rendering:
  - Cameras: The viewpoint of the animation is determined by inserting a camera object. Several of these camera objects can be inserted in the same animation window to allow the user to switch the active camera at runtime
  - Lights: ambient, point, directional, parallel, and spotlight objects
  - fogging and texture mapping (with transparency and filtering) to create highly realistic animations
  - The basic predefined animation objects are lines, circles, squares, cubes, spheres, cylinders and cones
- Simulation:

- 20-sim contains powerful simulation algorithms for solving ordinary differential equations (ODE) and differential algebraic equations (DAE). It has a variety of numerical integration methods: one-step, multistep and multiorder

- Animation:
  - Simulation results in 20-sim Pro can now be shown as 3D animation. Any variable of a 20-sim model can be connected to 3-dimensional objects to show animated output
  - The Animation Engine in 20-sim is based on Microsoft Direct3D technology. This means that it automatically takes full control of 3D-hardware if present, or just uses software rendering when necessary
  - With 20-sim Pro, the results of a simulation can be shown in a graphical model as well. During a simulation, the thickness and color of signals and bonds will correspond with the values they carry. In a bond graph, these values can be the effort, flow, or power of the bonds

- File Formats:
  - Export of data and models to MATLAB. Direct connection with the MATLAB workspace

5. WEB RESOURCES

- Official site: http://www.20sim.com/products/20sim.htm

- A good introduction:
  http://www.mathworks.com/products/connections/
  product_main.shtml?prod_id=288

- An excellent review: http://www.rt.el.utwente.nl/clp/products/files/
  20sim3Danim.PDF

3D Builder Pro

1. PLATFORMS, PRICES, AND SUPPLIER/CREATOR

- PC

- AAY! Palisades Research: http://www.aay.com/ (No longer supports)

2. APPLICATIONS

- Convert a 2D picture into a 3D model. 3D builder will combine information from a large number of photos and extract information from all the pictures to merge to a single 3D model and obtain 3D measurements at specified locations

3. EXAMPLES/SAMPLES

- http://www.aay.com/gallery.htm

4. WEB RESOURCES

- http://www.aay.com/features.htm

3D CANVAS

1. PLATFORMS, PRICES, AND SUPPLIER/CREATOR

- Window 95/98/NT
- $49.95
- Amabilis, Inc.: http://www.amabilis.com

2. APPLICATIONS

- 3D Canvas is a real-time 3D modeling and animation tool that incorporates an intuitive drag-and-drop approach to 3D modeling. Complex models can be constructed from simple 3D primitives, or created using 3D Canvas' Object Building Tools. Since 3D Canvas imports many popular 3D file formats, many of the public domain 3D models available on the internet can be incorporated in user's scenes

3. EXAMPLES/SAMPLES

- Gallery for 3D Canvas: Tricycle: http://www.amabilis.com/gallery/gallery1-2.htm
- Midnight Flyer: http://www.amabilis.com/gallery/gallery1-5.htm
- Dinosaur Head: http://www.amabilis.com/gallery/gallery1-3.htm
- Kirby and Bad Guy: http://www.amabilis.com/gallery/gallery1-4.htm
- http://www.davidcedrone.com/html/cnvs3d.html
- http://www.erinet.com/dolphin
- http://www.digitalcanvas3d.com/frameset.html

4. FUNCTIONS

- Modeling:
  - Objects: cube, sphere, cone, cylinder, torus, NURBS, spline

- Transformation: bending, twisting, taping, drag and drop scaling, rotating, moving
- Editing and manipulations (vertex, edge, face, polygon, curves, objects): lathing, extruding, deforming, sculpting, texture wrap orientation, deformation tool, painting tool, beveling, face and point editing, building tool, modeling tool

- Rendering:

  - Cameras: adjustable, movable
  - Lights: point, parallel point and spotlight, shadow, ambient, directional
  - Optical effects: transparency, fog, shadow, ambient, specular, and emissive light
  - Materials: palette, shadow, blend, skin, composite, particle surfaces
  - Before and after rendering: smooth, flat and wireframe rendering, fog, including linear, exponential and exponential squared

- Animation:

  - Controllers: keyframe
  - Advanced animations: inverse kinematics, skeletal deformation, blend channels, expressions, soft and hard body dynamics, character animation
  - Basic Animation

- File Formats:

  - Importing file formats: 3DS, POVRay, COB, DXF, WRL
  - Exporting file formats: 3DS, POVRay, COB, DXF, WRL

5. WEB RESOURCES

- 3D Canvas — Product of Amabilis: http://www.amabilis.com/products.htm

- Program Files: http://www.programfiles.com/index.asp?ID=7181

- Dave Central: http://www.davecentral.com/12595.html

- Digital Canvas 3D: http://www.digitalcanvas3d.com

3D Choreographer

1. PLATFORMS, PRICE, AND SUPPLIER/CREATOR

- Windows 9x/NT

- $159.00 Standard Version / $310.00 Deluxe Version

- Animated Communications: http://www.3dchor.com

2. APPLICATIONS

- 3D Choreographer is an animation program designed for non-artists. At the heart of 3D Choreographer is the LCDA (Layered Command Driven Animation). Outlining animation involves casting "Actors," drawing "Paths," and issuing "Scripts."

3. EXAMPLES/SAMPLES

- Animation power, team building: http://www.3dchor.com/3d/teams.htm
- 3d Choreographer PowerPoint Example: http://www.3dchor.com/3d/powerpoint.html

4. FUNCTIONS

- Modeling:
  - Objects: the animation in 3D Choreographer is built around three components a) Actors, b) Paths and c) Scripts.Actors are the objects that will be moving in the animation along the paths you create and the scripts will tell them what to do at any given point
  - Transformation: smile, run, walk, wave, fly, yawn, somersault, and dance or put hands on hips, raise eyebrows...
  - Editing and Manipulating: Cast the Actor. These can be 3D or 2D. All of 3D Choreographer's Actors are customizable so you can change the color of their hair, shirt, race, etc. Move the Actor, turn him from side-to-side, and rotate the head or arm
- Rendering:
  - Materials: Move the Path (Point), and you automatically reposition the Actor. The next part is to create a Script.This Script will tell the Actor what he is to do along the Path. Since there is a library of Scripts included it's just a matter of selecting what you want your Actor to be doing
  - Rendering: 3D Choreographer can handle more than 256 colors, support wrapping bitmaps on actors, and produce Video for Windows and QuickTime movies.The resolution is determined by the user but is limited to a maximum of 640 by 480 pixels. FLC files support up to 256 colors, AVI allows up to 16 million colors
- Animation:
  - Controllers: key-based, systems
  - Advanced animations: The animations are formatted as 8-bit FLC or 8 to 24 bit AVI files. The FLC files can be played from within 3D Choreographer or with Aaplay.exe, a player provided with the package. AVI files can be played with a run-time version of Video for Windows also included with 3D Choreographer. Single frames of an animation can be exported as BMP files at user selected resolution and with up to 16 million colors
- File Formats:

- Importing file formats: BMP
- Exporting file formats: AVI, FLC, JPG, DVP, Adobe Premiere, MOV

5. WEB RESOURCES

- Software review: http://www.kckps.k12.ks.us/techplan/reviews.html
- Press and Awards: http://www.3dchor.com/3d/pressrel.html

3D DREAMS (Shells 3D Author)

1. PLATFORMS, PRICE, AND SUPPLIER/CREATOR

- PC
- Free to download
- Shells Interactive: http://www.shellsinteractive.com;
  http://www.doitin3d.com/3ddreams/

2. APPLICATIONS

- 3D modeling, animation, and interoperation with Macromedia Director. Easy, powerful and fast creation of interactive 3D content

3. EXAMPLES

- http://mindstorms.lego.com/robohunter/
- http://www.aquileia2000.com/
- http://www.iprint.com/
- http://www.sharperimage.com/

4. FUNCTIONS

- Modeling: It can create images on each frame with the options of skewing, changing color, tweaking, and aligning
- Animation: It will convert a series of frames into high-quality animation
- User Interaction: You can add buttons so the users can control the animation
- Import: bitmap, PICT, Palette, SOund, Director Movie, Director Cast, AVI, FLC and FLI, script, quicktime, text, animated gif, shockwave flash
- Export: It can export the popular media formats BMP, AVI, and MOV

5. WEB RESOURCES

- Product Information at:
    - http://www.doitin3d.com/3ddreams/
    - http://developer.intel.com/drg/web/testimonials/viewpoint.htm
- Download Freeware at:
    - http://www.DoItIn3D.com/3ddreams/download/3ddreamsv2.5rc2.exe
- Examples at:
    - http://www.sharperimage.com/
    - http://www.iprint.com/
    - http://www.aquileia2000.com/
    - http://mindstorms.lego.com/robohunter/

3D Exploration

1. PLATFORM, PRICES, AND SUPPLIER/CREATOR

- PC
- 3D Exploration Discovery Edition — US $49
    - 3D Exploration Enterprise Edition — US $249 (available as ESD and Physical Product)
- Right Hemisphere: http://us.righthemisphere.com/

2. APPLICATIONS

- 3D Exploration is an easy-to-use tool with a Windows Explorer-like interface for Web searching, viewing and 3D rendering. It supports most popular 2D and 3D file formats. The Enterprise Edition allows translation between many different formats with animation included, as well as publishing to many different 3D Web formats. 3D navigation tools let you instantly explore 3D objects and scenes from any angle. You can even use 3D Exploration to present a slide show of a folder's images or create high quality renderings of 3D objects and scenes for use in any other graphic applications. It is extremely fast and includes Open GL hardware acceleration support. Full support for the nVidia GeForce 3-based graphics cards is included.

    The 3D Exploration Enterprise Edition allows you to Browse, View, Render and

Translate. All of the features enabled for the 3D Exploration Discovery Edition are included in the Enterprise Edition but the translate feature is also enabled.

- 3D Viewer/Translator supporting all popular 3D/2D file formats
- Allows creation of 2D/3D slide shows for presentations
- Enterprise edition generates C++ code for transformations performed in viewer
- Tool for students to experiment with OpenGL features and view effects
- Web Search
- Optional .dds file support for Direct X
- MAX import/export plug-in available for Enterprise Edition Only (3DS Max required)
- W3D (Macromedia Shockwave 3D file) export plug-in added
- MTX (Viewpoint media) import/export plug-in added
- HTML publish plug-in added (based on Viewpoint media)

3. EXAMPLES/SAMPLES

- http://us.righthemisphere.com/products/3dexplore/screenshots.htm

4. FEATURES

- Discovery Edition

  - Browse and view and thumbnail 2D image files Browse 3D objects and materials High speed Open GL 3D acceleration support Load and view most any 2D or 3D file format Dynamic viewpoint control Create 2D and 3D slide shows Multiple rendering modes, solid, points, wireframe, transparent etc. Individual object rendering control Full screen mode operation High quality ray tracing output with shadows and reflection High quality Anti-aliased Z-Buffer 3D rendering output Create and browse 3D thumbnails View files contained in Zip and Rar archives directly without unpacking them History of browsed files Reads animation and scene attributes such as lighting and camera definitions Drag and drop 2D and 3D objects to and from other applications Launch applications directly from 3D Exploration Merge multiple 3D files for viewing

- Enterprise Edition — Includes all of the features of the Discovery Edition, plus...

  - Publish 3D content for Web-based presentations using Viewpoint Media File format support or Macromedia Shockwave 3D. Viewing support for Maya .mb, .ma and 3D Studio Max .max native files (available as optional plug-ins). Allows modifications and saving of 3D file attributes such as textures and geometry transformations Allows translation between different 3D file formats including animation support between many formats Allows batch conversion of files

- Right Hemisphere Developed Plug-ins

  Maya Binary and Maya ASCII
  .mb — Import with animation — Requires Maya*
  .ma — Import with animation — Requires Maya*

  max — Import/Export.
  This plug-in allows 3D Exploration to load *.max files. It only works with Enterprise Edition and requires 3DS Max 3 or 4.
  http://www.righthemisphere.com/products/3dexplore/plugins.htm

  .dds — Import only — Requires Direct X 8.0
  *Optional Plug-ins that require Enterprise Edition

- 3rd Party Plug-ins...

  AIR Portal
  This plug-in provides a very affordable full quality Renderman rendering solution directly from within 3D Exploration. Such features as global illumination and hemispherical lighting are supported. Drag and drop Renderman shaders directly onto 3D Exploration models for the highest quality rendering possible. Ideal for animators, industrial designers, architects and anyone involved in high quality 3D presentation or entertainment graphics. Features include:

- Renderman RIB export plug-in for 3D Exploration
  Global illumination
  Area and hemispherical lighting
  Renderman shader support including displacement mapping
  For more information, see http://www.sitexgraphics.com/id41.htm and
  http://www.sitexgraphics.com/airportal.zip
  Wild Tangent

- 3D Exploration System Requirements
  3D Exploration works with Windows 95, 98, NT and 2000.
  The software requires a Pentium 166 MHz CPU or better and at least 16 MB of RAM.
  A 3D graphics hardware accelerator is recommended

5. WEB RESOURCES

- http://us.righthemisphere.com/3dexploration/

3D Grapher

1. PLATFORMS, PRICES, AND SUPPLIER/CREATOR

- Windows 95/98/NT/2000 or higher
  - High color or true color display recommended
  - OpenGL compatible 3D accelerator recommended
- 30 day trial period, then $24.95 registration fee
- RomanLab Software: http://www.romanlab.com

2. APPLICATIONS

- Illustrating and solving complex mathematical equations in 2D and 3D
- A picture and animation creator. This program can also be used as a fast way to create 3D pictures and movies

3. EXAMPLES/SAMPLES

- 3D Grapher Graphs Gallery: http://www.romanlab.com/3dg/graphs.htm

4. FUNCTIONS

- Creates animated 2D and 3D equation and table-based graphs
- Unlimited number of graphs can be plotted using different colors and lighting conditions
- Plots functions with 1 to 3 independent variables including a time variable for animation
- Supports Cartesian, polar, cylindrical or spherical coordinates
- Real-time graphs animation, rotating, moving and zooming
- Tracing and displaying the mouse cursor position on a plane or 3D coordinates
- Contains a built-in expression calculator
- Has convenient and understandable help

5. WEB RESOURCES

- RomanLab Software's mailing list: http://www.romanlab.com/maillist.htm
- Author: Roman Nikolaev: roman@romanlab.com
- Webpage 3D Grapher information: http://www.romanlab.com/3dg/

3D IMPACT! Pro

1. PLATFORM, PRICES, AND SUPPLIER/CREATOR

- Windows 95/98/2000/NT/ME
- $79
- CrystalGraphics, Inc.: http://www.crystalgraphics.com

2. APPLICATIONS

- 3D IMPACT! Pro enhances webpages with extraordinary 3D graphics and animations with over 145 highly-detailed, pre-built 3D objects, organized in a customizable object gallery. It enables Web developers, video enthusiasts and others to add the impact of 3D titles, logos, objects, buttons and pictures to webpages, banner ads, videos and presentations

3. EXAMPLES/SAMPLES

- http://www.crystalgraphics.com/web/web.gallery.asp
- http://www.crystalgraphics.com/web/3dimpactpro.features.asp
- http://www.haave.net/william/images/3d/glass_egg.JPG
- http://www.haave.net/william/images/3d/maler2.jpg
- http://www.haave.net/william/images/3d/shaker_spark.gif
- http://www.haave.net/william/images/3d/sveits.jpg

4. FUNCTIONS

- Modeling:
  - Objects: Line, Arcs, Circle, Splines, Polygon and 2D Shapes
  - Transformations: Scaling, rotation, and translation
  - Editing and Manipulations: Create and manipulate lightbulbs, spotlights, sunlight and ambient lighting with powerful lighting tools. Users have control to get the lighting effects they want. Motion paths use smooth spline motion algorithms
- Rendering:
  - Cameras: Simple, two-parameter camera
  - Lights: Point Lighting, Spotlighting, Lightbulbs and Ambient Lighting
  - Rendering Effects: soft-edged shadows, object reflections, ray-traced refractions, bumpiness, shininess, transparency, sparkles, perspective and embossing

- Materials: Soft-edged object-to-object shadows and drop shadows. Mapping tools include texture, bump, reflection and transparency mapping. Maps and backgrounds may be animated
- Formats
  - Importing and Exporting file formats: GIF, JPEG, PNG, TGA, TIFF, AVI, BMP and PCX
- Animation:
  - Controllers: key-based, systems
  - Advanced animations: Can easily preview and adjust a still or animated GIF's visual quality and file size right within the program, making it a snap to minimize download times
- Additional Features
  - Convert 2D Artwork into 3D: Create an outline of a 2D logo, using the automatic outline tool, so it can be animated in 3D
  - Sparkle Effects: 3D IMPACT! Pro can add sparkles to highlights automatically

5. WEB RESOURCES
- http://www.crystalgraphics.com/web/3dimpactpro.main.asp
- http://downloads.mediadna.zdnet.com/info/com
- http://www8.techmall.com/techdocs/
- http://www.davecentral.com/
- http://softseek.zdnet.com/Internet/
- http://www.davecentral.com/graph3d.html
- http://www.simplythebest.net/gold/gocrysta.html
- http://msdn.microsoft.com/downloads/tools/crystal/3DPro.asp

3D INSTANT WEBSITE

1. PLATFORMS, PRICES, AND SUPPLIER/CREATOR

- PC
- FREE
- SolidWorks Company: http://www.solidworks.com

2. APPLICATIONS
- 3D Instant Website enables users to quickly and easily create and publish live webpages with 3D interactive content

- Enables users to publish interactive 3D images with a single mouse clickShare SolidWorks Models or Drawings with other users without the need to manually install additional viewers or CAD software
- Complete control; SolidWorks 3D Instant Website provides the freedom to review, delete and administer published websites in a secure environment

3. EXAMPLES/SAMPLES

- http://www.solidworks.com/3dinstantwebsite/gallery.cfm
- http://www.solidworks.com/3dinstantwebsite/more_gallery.cfm
- http://www.mcadcafe.com/MCADVision/GRAPHICS/direct_3d2.jpg
- http://www.mcadcafe.com/MCADVision/GRAPHICS/direct_3d4.jpg
- http://www.mcadcafe.com/MCADVision/GRAPHICS/direct_3d5.jpg

4. FUNCTIONS

- Viewing: 3D Instant Website supports several standard 3D interactive viewing formats
  - Solidworks eDrawings; CATweb; MetaStream; RealityWave
- Customizable Templates: 3D Instant Website provides easy-to-use, customizable templates for providing informational content
  - Basic Templates — allow users to enter webpage titles, design descriptions, related Web links, and company information
  - Collaborative Templates — enable users to invite anyone with a Web browser to review and comment on the design
- Sharing your website
  - Use your email address book to allow others to review your website, providing everyone with the visual information they need to provide you with "instant" feedback
  - Reviewers have the ability to approve and reject your design and add comments instantly

5. WEB RESOURCES

- http://www.creativepro.com/story/news/10786.html
- http://www.cad3d.it/script/news/notizie/80.htm
- http://www.engineeringtalk.com/news/sol/sol114.html
- http://www.hexapods.com/phpnews/viewer.php3?artid=2035
- http://www.sgi.com/newsroom/press_releases/2000/december/solidworks.html

3D Invigorator

1. PLATFORM, PRICE, AND SUPPLIER/CREATOR

- PC / Macintosh
- $595.00
- ZAXWERKS: http://www.zaxwerks.com

2. APPLICATIONS

- The 3D Invigorator is a modeling, rendering, and animation system for producing broadcast and film quality titles, logos and 3D graphical elements. It operates as a standalone tool or plug-in to major rendering and animation tools such as AE (After Effects) and Maya. You can create 3D graphics inside your compositing environment, enabling you to combine multiple layers of 2D and live 3D at will. Well regarded in the industry for its ease of use and quick turn around of 3D graphics

3. EXAMPLES/SAMPLES

- http://www.zaxwerks.com/Zaxwerks_Images/InvigAE_screenshot_NBC.jpg
- http://www.adobe.com:82/products/plugins/illustrator/invigorator.html

4. FEATURES

- Modeling:
  - Texture mapping of scanned and painted images onto any surface. Models can be updated with one click, leaving all textures and animation intact, by simply replacing the original vector file that the models were based on
  - Create custom Object Styles so entire shape and material setups can be reapplied with a single click
  - Completely object oriented material setup. Drag and Drop to apply materials from libraries. Create your own libraries of materials. Edit a material style and the change is applied everywhere the material was used
  - Application of any AE layer or pre-comp onto any surface. This enables movies to be "painted" onto objects. It also enables any image or stack of images to be layered in AE, mixed using various Apply modes, and then applied as bump, reflection or texture maps onto any object
  - High quality antialiasing. Special anti-flicker video antialiasing
- Rendering:
  - Draft mode rendering. A typical scene renders RAM previews in real time on a G4 533

– All animation is handled in the standard After Effects (AE) timeline, so all AE animation techniques can be used including: Keyframe assistants, Motion Math and copy and pasting of keyframes and sequences. Works well with AE Favorites enabling entire animation sequences to be saved and reused over and over

- File Formats:
  – Any raster-based format that After Effects can open can be used as a texture map or texture movie applied to any 3D object
  – Direct support for ai. (Adobe Illustrator) vector formats. 3D Invigorator will use any shape that Illustrator or any vector plug-in can make — Hundreds of thousands of sources of raw material from vector clip art websites
  – Pro version imports 3D models into After Effects. Supports OBJ, 3DS, LWO, C4D, FACT and DXF models

5. WEB RESOURCES

- http://www.zaxwerks.com/AEInvig_Resources.html

- http://www.adobe.com:82/store/plugins/pages/3dinvigorator.html

- Books: http://www.zaxwerks.com/3DInvigAE_UserGuide.pdf

- Related articles: http://msp.sfsu.edu/Instructors/rey/aepage/aetips.html

3D Magic (also called Pixel 3D)

1. PLATFORMS, PRICES, AND SUPPLIER/CREATOR

- Windows 95, 98, and NT 4.0

- $$$

- 3D Magic: http://store.yahoo.com/forwarddesign/pix3dmag.html

2. APPLICATIONS

- 3D Magic creates 3D logos and graphics for Websites or documents. It loads and saves 23 different 3D file formats. You can also use auto-tracing to trace images into 3D logos

3. EXAMPLES/SAMPLES

- http://store.yahoo.com/forwarddesign/enfornigdrea.html

- http://store5.yimg.com/I/forwarddesign_1551_328251

- http://www.forwarddesign.com/3dobjects.htm
- http://www.modelmagic3d.com/

4. WEB RESOURCES
- http://www.forwarddesign.com/links.htm
- http://www.forwarddesign.com/3dobjects.htm
- http://www.3dmagic.com/catalog/3dmagic.html

3D MeNow

1. PLATFORMS, PRICES, AND SUPPLIER/CREATOR
- Windows NT/95/98/2000/ME
- $49.00
- bioVirtual: http://www.biovirtual.com/

2. APPLICATIONS
- 3DMeNow is a modeling and animation tool for 3D real time humans. 3DMeNow is used to build realistic talking avatars

3. WEB RESOURCES
- Software Releases: http://www.biovirtual.com/products_f.htm
- Press Releases: http://www.biovirtual.com/press_f.htm
- Frequently Asked Questions: http://www.biovirtual.conmm/messageboard/faq_f.htm
- Article: http://www.biovirtual.com/newsarchive/pcformat_f.htm

3D STUDIO MAX

1. PLATFORM, PRICE, AND SUPPLIER/CREATOR
- PC

- $$$$$
- Discreet, a division of Autodesk: http://www2.discreet.com

2. APPLICATIONS

- A multifunction 3D modeling, rendering, and animation tool. It has been used for many purposes, including special effects in films and advertisements, and complex objects in virtual environments

3. EXAMPLES/SAMPLES

- http://www.3dlinks.com/gallerydisplay.cfm?sid=3D%20Studio%20Max
- http://www.3dlinks.com/gallerylinks.cfm
- http://www.3dmax.com/gallery/index.cfm?SubCat=Still

4. WEB RESOURCES

- http://usuarios.tripod.es/max3d/3dstudio.html
- http://www.3dlinks.com/books_max.cfm
- http://www.zdnet.com/pcmag/features/software/1519/3d-r6.htm
- http://3dgraphics.about.com/cs/3dstudiomax/?once=true&

3D Studio VIZ

1. PLATFORM, PRICE, AND SUPPLIER/CREATOR

- PC
- $$$$$
- Discreet, a division of Autodesk: http://www2.discreet.com/index-nf.html

2. APPLICATIONS

- 3D Studio VIZ is a modeling tool for architectural and interior design, land planning and civil engineering, mechanical assembly visualization, and industrial product design

3. EXAMPLES/SAMPLES

- samples for VIZ: http://www.3dmax.com/shop/ProductInfo.cfm?ID=4#Samples

- 3D Links Gallery: http://www.3dlinks.com/
  gallerydisplay.cfm?sid=3D%20Studio%20VIZ

4. WEB RESOURCES

- Stories and Case Studies:
  http://www3.autodesk.com/adsk/autoindex/0,,544532-123112-146824,00.html
- Books: http://www.3dlinks.com/books_viz.cfm
- Other resources for 3DSVIZ: http://pointa.autodesk.com/portal/welcome.jsp

3D Styler

1. PLATFORMS, PRICES, AND SUPPLIER/CREATOR

- Windows 3.1, 95, and NT
- Freeware
- 3D Styler was originally written by Krecik and Tomala in 1993 as the part of their thesis at the Institute of Computer Science, Warsaw University of Technology in Poland: http://www.xortech.com.pl/~tomala/3dstyler/

2. APPLICATIONS

- 3D Styler supports hierarchical data structure and CSG operators, different rendering algorithms, rendering of shadows, light sources, different material, light and shape editors

3. EXAMPLES/SAMPLES

- Trade Mark: http://www.xortech.com.pl/~tomala/3dstyler/TM.jpg
- Shadow Example: http://www.xortech.com.pl/~tomala/3dstyler/Shadows.jpg

4. 3DSTYLER SUPPORTS THE FOLLOWING:

- hierarchical data structure and CSG operators
  - Example: 1000 Cubes http://www.xortech.com.pl/~tomala/3dstyler/10x10x10.gif
- rendering algorithms: hidden-line, flat-, Gouraud-, and Phong-shading
  - Example: Chess Hidden Lines
    http://www.xortech.com.pl/~tomala/3dstyler/ChessHiddenLine.gif

- Example: Chessboard Phong Lines
  http://www.xortech.com.pl/~tomala/3dstyler/ChessPhong.jpg
- rendering of shadows
  - Example: Desk-Lamp Flat Shaded
    http://www.xortech.com.pl/~tomala/3dstyler/LampFlat.jpg
  - Example: Desk-Lamp Phong Shaded
    http://www.xortech.com.pl/~tomala/3dstyler/LampPhong.jpg
- light sources: ambient, directional, positional and spot-light
  - Example: All Figures http://www.xortech.com.pl/~tomala/3dstyler/AllFigures.jpg
  - Example: Space Balls http://www.xortech.com.pl/~tomala/3dstyler/Balls.jpg
- material, light and shape editors
  - Example: Desk with Chess Board and Lamp
    http://www.xortech.com.pl/~tomala/3dstyler/Desk.jpg

5. WEB RESOURCES

- Graphic Utilities: http://www.bergen.org/AAST/ComputerAnimation/Files_Utils_PC.html
- 3D Gallery: http://www.webbrain.com/brains/Mozilla/Top/Computers/Graphics/3D/3D_Gallery/links.html

3D Win

1. PLATFORM, PRICES, AND SUPPLIER/CREATOR

- PC, Windows
- $56.00
- 3D Win: http://www.stmuc.com/thbaier/

2. APPLICATIONS

- 3DWin is a small utility for Windows 95/98/ME/NT4/W2K to convert 3D files to a number of other 3D formats

3. EXAMPLES/SAMPLES

- http://www.stmuc.com/thbaier/gallery.html

4. FUNCTIONS

- 3DWinOGL features:
  - D Quad OpenGL views with mouse support
  - various OpenGL settings
  - UV view with material preview
  - multiple camera views
  - light view
  - multiple shading options for active and inactive objects (textured, colored, transparent and grey shading)
  - interactive manipulation of objects (mesh optimizing and transformations)
  - drag and drop
  - merge multiple scenes
  - exchange materials
  - selective export
  - Difference demo/registered version: enabled 3D file export
- Formats
  - Import: Generic ASCII format (*.raw); 3dStudio (*.3ds, *.prj); Lightwave (*.lwo, *.lws); Autodesk (*.dxf); WaveFront (*.obj); Protein Data Bank (*.pdb); Direct X (*.x); LightWave (*.lwo, *.lws); Quake MDL (*.mdl, *.md2); LDraw (*.dat); 3DS MAX (*.ase); Rhino (*.3dm); VRML97 (*.wrl)
  - Export: Generic ASCII format (*.raw); 3dStudio (*.3ds, *.asc); Autodesk (*.dxf); VRML 1.0/2.0 (*.wrl); POV-Ray and Moray (*.inc, *.udo); WaveFront (*.obj); OpenGL (*.C); Renderman/BMRT (*.rib); Lightflow (*.py); Direct X (*.x); LightWave (*.lwo, *.lws); Quake MDL (*.mdl, *.md2); Digistar (*.vla)

5. WEB RESOURCES

- http://www.crosswinds.net/~draven2561/spatch/hmsp1.html (SPatch)

- http://www.68k.org/~chris/objmot.html (Maple)

- http://ccwf.cc.utexas.edu/~nfolse/unijoint (Autocad)

- http://members.xoom.com/coyotz/tutorial/objects.html (Bryce)

- http://www7.50megs.com/grafix/tut_1.html (polygon optimization)

- http://www.users.zetnet.co.uk/logs/ImGall/raytrace/clip.htm (Povray)

- http://www.who3d.com/tutorials/Conversion30.html (mesh smoothing)

3DAnywhere

1. PLATFORMS, PRICES, AND SUPPLIER/CREATOR

- PC Windows 95/98/NT/2000
- Free (may no longer be supported)
- Monfort Software Engineering Ltd.: http://www.3danywhere.com

2. APPLICATIONS

- 3DAnywhere is a fast, flexible, customizable, and efficient system for publishing 3D scenes on the Web

3. EXAMPLES/SAMPLES

- 3DAnywhere Gallery: http://www.3danywhere.com/3da/index/index.html

4. WEB RESOURCES

- Download 3DAnywhere for free at: http://www.3danywhere.com/download/index.html
- Documentation: http://www.3danywhere.com/docs/index.html

3DField

1. PLATFORMS, PRICES, AND SUPPLIER/CREATOR

- Windows 95/98, NT, and 2000
- List Price: Shareware($50.00)
- 3DField: http://field.hypermart.net/

2. APPLICATIONS

- 3DField is a contouring surface plotting program that quickly converts data into contour maps and surface plots. From its interface, 3DField does the following: Interpolates X, Y, Z data points onto a grid orthogonal or within an arbitrary border; Displays data points on a plane; Graphically displays 2D/3D data arrays; Builds color and black/white isoline contour maps; Creates maps of any size compatible with Microsoft Office; Imports and exports polylines; and finally, outputs maps to emf, wmf, bmp, gif, jpg, png file formats. The map list, which can be shown always-on-top in tree view on the left, allows you to easily switch back and forth between Color Isolines, Locate Points, Simple Isolines, Color Cells, Circle Values, Direchlet Tesselations and Delauney Triangles. The program also provides a zoom navigator that lets you magnify specific areas of maps. The easy-to-use and well-put-together 3DField comes complete with a comprehensive, click-through Help file in HTML format

3. EXAMPLES/SAMPLES

- http://field.hypermart.net/3DView.htm
- http://field.hypermart.net/Help/convert.htm
- http://field.hypermart.net/digitize/ColorMars.jpg

4. FUNCTIONS

- Surface plotting features
  - Interpolates X, Y, Z data points onto a grid, orthogonal or within an arbitrary border
  - Displays data points on a plane
  - Graphically displays 2D/3D data arrays
  - Builds color and black/white isoline (contour) maps
  - Allows map editing to personal taste
  - View and zoom BMP, GIF, PNG and JPG images
  - Automatically and manually digitize image
  - 3D View
  - Creates maps of any size compatible with Microsoft Office 97
  - Digitize image
  - Input TRIANGLES data
- File Formats:
  - Import and export polylines
  - Output maps as EMF, WMF, BMP, GIF, JPG file formats

5. WEB RESOURCES

- http://field.hypermart.net/Lib/index.htm
- http://field.hypermart.net/Help/automatic_digitize_image.htm
- http://field.hypermart.net/Help/3d_view.htm

3dom (a 3D Object Modeler)

1. PLATFORM, PRICE, AND SUPPLIER/CREATOR

- UNIX (or Linux) platform
- Free to download: http://threedom.sourceforge.net//download.html
- Source Forge: http://sourceforge.net/

2. APPLICATION

- 3dom is a 3D modeler that includes constructive solid modeling, reality-based material representation, scripting through Python bindings, etc.

3. EXAMPLES/SAMPLES

- http://threedom.sourceforge.net//shots/quadview.png
- Create solid objects from a true-type font: http://threedom.sourceforge.net//shots/ftt.png
- http://threedom.sourceforge.net//shots/shot_main.jpg
- http://threedom.sourceforge.net//shots/shot_csg.jpg
- The color selector: http://threedom.sourceforge.net//shots/shot_colorselector.jpg
- http://threedom.sourceforge.net//shots/shot_sor.jpg
- http://threedom.sourceforge.net//shots/shot_python.jpg

4. WEB RESOURCES

- 3dom (a 3D Object Modeler): http://threedom.sourceforge.net/
- http://www.gv.kotnet.org/~kdf/3dom/
- Linux (3dom): http://linux.davecentral.com/3576_graphed.html
- Other link of Web-page for 3dom: http://www.dom.zip.com.au/3d/3dabout.html

3DVIEWNIX

1. PLATFORM, PRICES, AND SUPPLIER/CREATOR

- UNIX/X, SGI, Sun, PC, on a variety of platforms

- $1,000
- Medical Image Processing Group, Department of Radiology, University of Pennsylvania: http://www.mipg.upenn.edu

2. APPLICATIONS

- 3DVEWNIX is a transportable, software system that has state-of-the-art capabilities for visualizing, manipulating, and analyzing multidimensional, multimodality image information. It is a tool to promote widespread use of 3D imaging and cooperative research (technical and applied) in 3D imaging. 3DVIEWNIX can handle rigid, non-rigid, static, and dynamic objects and object assemblies. It is used for variety of purposes: MR brain image analysis in Multiple Sclerosis, in late-life depression, tumor volume quantification; MR angiography with uncluttered display and artery/vein separation; mammographic image analysis for cancer risk assessment, lesion detection; craniofacial soft tissue display with skin peeled; kinematic analysis of the tarsal joints and of the glenohumoral joint via MRI; MR image intensity standardization

3. EXAMPLES/SAMPLES

- http://www.mipg.upenn.edu/~Vnews/3dviewnix_movies.html
- http://wuarchive.wustl.edu/graphics/graphics/packages/3dviewnix/ MPEG_MOVIES
- http://www.mipg.upenn.edu/~Vnews/3dviewnix_ftp.html

4. FUNCTIONS

- Visualization:
    - Slice: Sophisticated form of slice display
    - Multiple input volumes of any dimensionality can be handled simultaneously
    - Multiple color maps
    - Surface Rendering: Multitudes of methods
    - Multiple objects with translucency and color
    - Based on the notion of a structure system: A structure system may be a collection of static objects, dynamic rigid objects, dynamic non-rigid objects or any of these coming from multiple modalities
    - Viewing properties of objects can be changed independently
    - Volume Rendering: Interactive rendering, Interactive color modification, Interactive measurement of fuzzy surfaces
- Manipulation:
    - One of the most sophisticated set of operations in 3DVIEWNIX
    - A variety of complex operations including cut away, reflect, separate, move, surface marking, measure, animation

- Analysis:

  Measurement:

  - A variety of image intensity-based measurements such as density profile, time density curves, region-of-interest statistics and their variation with time

  Registration:

  - Based on matching homologous features — points, curves, entire surfaces
  - For merging information from multiple modalities
  - For motion description and analysis

  Motion Analysis:

  - Rigid object assemblies
  - Animation of motion and its quantification
  - Comparison of motion of two assemblies of objects such as two joints
  - Relationship between moving surfaces

- Preprocessing:

  Volume-of-Interest:

  - To specify subset of the n-dimensional (nD) volume image

  Interpolation:

  - To create isotropically sampled data of lower or higher resolution than input

  Filtering:

  - A variety of forms of enhancing and smoothing filters
  - Used for filtering surfaces, for normal estimation, for interpolation, and volume rendering

  Thresholding:

  - Multiple intervals can be specified

  Segmentation:

  - 2-feature cluster partitioning
  - Quick gesture-controlled (user-guided) boundary segmentation

  Classification:

  - 1-feature multiple material classification for opacity assignment
  - 2-feature multiple material classification for opacity assignment

  Boundary Formation:

  - Connected, oriented, closed 3D surfaces are formed
  - Surfaces may have any resolution

  Image Algebra:

  - Image addition, subtraction, logical operation

- Additional Features:

  - Measurement, registration and motion analysis

5. WEB RESOURCES

- http://www.sis.ucm.es/3dviewnix/tutorial/tutorial_contents.html
- http://wuarchive.wustl.edu/graphics/graphics/packages/3dviewnix
- http://biocomp.stanford.edu/3dreconstruction/software/3dviewnix.html
- http://www.interlog.com/~aceze/3d/index.html
- http://www.3dsite.com/n/sites/3dsite/cgi/ftp-index.html

AC3D

1. PLATFORM, PRICE, AND SUPPLIER/CREATOR

- Windows, Linux, and SGI-IRIX
- $39.95
- Author: Andy Colebourne at Lancaster University, England: http://www.comp.lancs.ac.uk/computing/users/andy/ac3d.html

2. APPLICATIONS

- AC3D is a popular 3D object/scene modeler. It's is very easy to use but powerful too — anyone can create good looking 3D objects in minutes. It outputs POV-Ray, VRML (1 and 2), RenderMan, Dive, Massive and other formats

3. EXAMPLES/SAMPLES

- http://www.comp.lancs.ac.uk/computing/users/andy/ac3d.html#Examples
- AC3D User Pages Gallery: http://www.eilers.net/ac3d/

4. FUNCTIONS

- Multi platform program — AC3D file format compatible across platforms
- Easy to use intuitive interface
- 4 views — 3 orthographic and one 3D at once or individual views
- Named objects can be searched for within a scene
- Navigate/Zoom around the 2d views with cursor keys and other single key presses
- Hierarchical view window
- Hide/unhide objects for easier/faster editing of complicated scenes

- Built-in fast OpenGL 3D renderer with adjustable field-of-view — instantly see results of your actions in 3D. Spin the model or switch into *walk mode* for Quake-style control

- Headlight and up to 7 other positionable lights

- 24-bit color palette with adjustable diffuse; ambient; emissive; specular; shininess; and transparency

- Texture mapping support with real-time rendering

- Adjustable 2D and 3D grid guide lines with grid-snap function

- Edit at different granularity — groups, objects, vertices

- Full polygon editing

- Manipulate individual surfaces:
  - insert/remove vertices
  - make holes
  - spike
  - spline
  - bevel
  - triangulate
  - flip
  - group into new objects

- Create new surfaces/objects around any selection (Convex hull)

- Configurable to use external renderers such as Povray and BMRT

- Attach URLs to objects for use in VRML files

- Attach string data to objects to be used as scripting in Dive or special directives for POV or renderman

- Supports many output/input formats including:
  - 3D-studio
  - Lightwave
  - Alias triangle
  - DXF
  - VRML1 and 2 and Inventor
  - Povray
  - RIB
  - Triangles
  - Direct X (via plug-in)

- Extrude and revolve 2D lines to make 3D shapes

- scale a selection to a specific size

- flip a selection (mirror) about X, Y, or Z axis

- Optimize duplicate vertices and surfaces

- Simple documented file formats allow easy conversion from other forms of data — ideal for visualizing your own data in 3D

- Plug-in interface (registered versions only) with source code for existing plug-ins and a software development kit

5. WEB RESOURCES

- AC3D users webpages: http://www.eilers.net/ac3d/

- Project ac3dloader: http://ryan.entrophica.org/projects/ac3dloader/index.jsp

- http://www.on-the-web.ch/3dc/

- Manuals:

- http://www.comp.lancs.ac.uk/computing/users/andy/ac3d/man/ac3dman.html

- http://wwwzenger.informatik.tu-muenchen.de/~gdv/ac3dman/ac3dman.html

AccuRender

1. PLATFORM, PRICE, AND SUPPLIER/CREATOR

- Windows 95/98/2000/NT/XP

- $95–$495: http://www.accurender.com/purchase.htm

- Robert McNeel and Associates: http://www.accurender.com/ www.mcneel.com

2. APPLICATIONS

- AccuRender creates life-like images from 3D models inside AutoCAD R14 and 2000/2000i/2002, Architectural Desktop, Mechanical Desktop, Revit, or Rhino (www.flamingo3d.com). AccuRender uses ray tracing and radiosity technologies to create high quality, photorealistic, still, panorama, and animation image files

3. EXAMPLES/SAMPLES

- 3D Gallery of models created with AccuRender provided by AccuRender: http://www.accurender.com/gallery/index.htm

- 3D Gallery of models created with AccuRender provided by Asuni CAD (in Spanish): http://www.asuni.es/accurender/galeria.asp?Producto=ACC

- 3D Gallery of models created with AccuRender provided by DrcAuto.: http://www.drcauto.com/products/accurenderlt/gallery1.html

4. FUNCTIONS

- Features:

  - Calculates light, shadows, materials, transparency, diffusion, reflection, ClearFinish, and refraction, from a surface's properties. Uses both ray tracing and radiosity to create sophisticated single-frame images, panoramas, and animations. Automatically calculates indirect light, hard and soft shadows, color bleeding, reflections, translucency, transparency, refraction, depth of field, and depth attenuation. Supports multiprocessors and background processing. Includes realistic mathematically-generated 3D plants with seasonal variation, giving realistic foliage, shadows, and reflections. Viewpoint animation for walking through and flying around model. Optimization by adaptive spatial subdivision. Progressive-refinement rendering algorithms with on-screen preview. Two- and three-point perspective projections. Produces panorama files. When viewing a panorama file, you can move around within the rendered image

- Image quality:

  - Combine radiosity and ray tracing for highest quality images. True specular reflection and transparency. Shadow casting from all light sources. Soft shadow edges, blurry reflection, and translucency. Refraction and simulated caustics. Depth of field. Depth attenuation for transparent materials. Antialiasing by adaptive stochastic sub-pixel sampling with extensive user control. 24- or 32-bit color output (16.7 million colors plus alpha channel for background). Resolution up to 16,000 by 16,000 pixels, not limited screen resolution. WYSIWYG 256, 32,000, or 16.7 million color display

- Lighting:

  - Distant, point, spot, linear, rectangular, and goniometric lights; user-defined light fixtures; sun, ground, sky lighting. Extensive light fixture library (over 300). Physically-based light sources and illumination algorithms. Manufacturers photometric (IES) data supported for light fixtures. Accurate daylighting simulation (sun, sky, ground, and cloud cover components). Exact solar time calculator. Graphical adjustment of spot focus for spotlights
  - Shadow casting on/off by object. Adjustable sun light color in RGB or degrees Kelvin. Intensity specified in watts, lumens, or max candelas

- Lighting Analysis:

  - Display pseudo-color image of the luminance or illuminance. Interactively meters any surface luminance

- Environment:

  - Background options include automatic sky, solid color, gradient colors, and image map. Library of background images. Ground plane with materials. Procedural clouds. Depth cue control. Clipping plane support. Haze

- Animation:

- Viewpoint animation (for walk-through and fly-by animation). Preview using OpenGL. Multiple complex 2D or 3D polyline target and camera paths. Pans and zooms. Sunlight animation for daily or seasonal shadow studies. AVI file output, or TGA, TIFF, JPEG, or BMP individual frames

- Materials:

  - Extensive materials library. Multiple library support. Assign materials by layer, object, or block. Interactive material editor with "live" ray-traced preview of several materials at the same time. Physically-based material properties (reflectivity, transparency, and index of refraction) Depth attenuation control for transparent materials. Customizable 3D procedural textures, including marble, granite, wood, tile, mask, blend, and ClearFinish. Complex materials with multiple procedural textures. 3D procedural bump maps, including fine and coarse textures, and waves. RGB and HSB color systems. Color, transparency, and bump mapping. Tiled, decal, and background bitmaps. Planar, cylindrical, and spherical projections for decals Multiple bitmaps per object. Support for TGA, BMP, TIF, and JPEG file formats

- Landscaping:

  - Extensive library of fractal-generated 3D plants including wet and dry climate plants, cold and warm climate plants, ground cover, and house plants. Bitmap masks define foliage geometry. Generated from simple wireframe objects while rendering. Tag any block as a plant. Specify size by height or trunk diameter. Pruning tools for removing lower branches
  - Foliage density control. Interactive plant editor for creating or modifying plants. Seasonal controls, global or individual

- Application Interface:

  - Access to AccuRender features with AutoLISP

5. WEB RESOURCES

- AccuRender Website: http://www.accurender.com

- Asuni CAD Website: http://www.asuni.es/accurender/index.asp

- DrcAuto Website: http://www.drcauto.com/products/accurenderlt/

AccuTrans 3D

1. PLATFORMS, PRICES, AND SUPPLIER/CREATOR

- Windows 95 / 98 / Me / NT / 2000

- $20.00

- AccuTrans 3D by MicroMouse Productions; Website: http://www.micromouse.ca/

2. APPLICATIONS

- The primary application of AccuTrans is to translate 3D geometry information between different file formats that are used by many popular modeling programs. During translation, the integrity of information such as positional and rotational data and material attributes is maintained

3. EXAMPLES/SAMPLES

- Screen Shots of how files are imported: http://www.micromouse.ca/screenshots.html

- Screen Shots of how files are saved: http://www.micromouse.ca/Export.gif

- Avatar Animation Tutorial: http://www.micromouse.ca/avatars.html

4. FUNCTIONS

- File Format Conversions:
  - The following is the list of formats that AccuTrans 3D can read and write to:

File Format	File Extension	Read	Write
3D Metafile	.3dmf	No	Yes
3D Studio	.3ds, .asc, .prj (read only)	Yes	Yes
AutoCAD DXF	.dxf	Yes	Yes
Imagine	.iob	Yes	Yes
Turbo Silver (Amiga)	.ts	Yes	Yes
LightWave	.lwo	Yes	Yes
Lightscape	.lp	Yes	Yes
POV-Ray 3.0	.pov	No	Yes
RealiMation Version 4.1	.rbs	Yes	Yes
RenderWare	.rwx (ASCII only)	Yes	Yes
Scenery Animator (Amiga)	.land	Yes	Yes
Sculpt (Amiga)	.scene	Yes	Yes
StereoLithography	.stl (ASCII and Binary)	Yes	Yes
trueSpace	.coa, .cob	Yes	Yes
TrueType Font	.ttf	Yes	No
USGS 1-degree DEM	.dem	Yes	No
USGS STDS	functionality will be added	Yes	No
USGS GTOPO30	.dem	Yes	No

VideoScape (Amiga)	.geo	Yes	Yes
VistaPro	. dem	Yes	Yes
VRML 1.0 and 2.0	.wrl (ASCII only)	Yes	Yes
Wavefront	.obj	Yes	Yes

- Landscapes:
  - Digital Elevation Model can be read into 3D meshes that can be saved to any 3D supported file format. AccuTrans 3D reads the following file formats: Scenery Animator, VistaPro, USGS 1- degree DEM and USGS GTOPO30 files
  - Elevations are sampled at regular intervals of every 1000 meters for GTOPO30 files and 30 meters for other files
- Support for Animation:
  - AccuTrans 3D provides an interesting tutorial of how 3D meshes of an Avatar body can be created and animated in different frames and viewed
- Modeling:
  - Objects while read can be assigned to different sub objects
  - Scale 3D object when either reading or writing files
  - Convert coplanar triangular faces into Quads

5. WEB RESOURCES

- 3D Model World: http://www.3dmodelworld.com/
- Comparative Tools: http://oct31.de/aw/
- http://grafix.www7.50megs.com/

ACIS 3D (Geometric Modeler and Deformable Modeling)

1. PLATFORM, PRICE, AND SUPPLIER/CREATOR

- Multiple: http://www.spatial.com/products/Toolkit/ACIS_Tech_Specs.htm
- Free trial
- Spatial Corp.: http://www.spatial.com/

2. APPLICATIONS

- ACIS 3D Geometric Modeler is a solid modeling component, providing software developers—Original Equipment Manufacturers (OEMs) — with the underlying 3D modeling functionality necessary for creating innovative and high-performance software applications

- Deformable Modeling is an interactive sculpting tool for creating and manipulating free-form curves and surfaces. Local and global editing features allow for the easy manipulation of B-spline and NURB curves and surfaces, enabling a very high level of artistic design, while retaining the ability to generate a precise machinable surface

3. EXAMPLES/SAMPLES

- Links to Solutions: http://www.spatial.com/products/Toolkit/toolkit.htm

4. FUNCTIONS

- ACIS 3D Geometric Modeler:

  Open, object-oriented C++ architecture that enables robust 3D geometric modeling capabilities. ACIS integrates wireframe, surface, and solid modeling functionality with both manifold and non-manifold topology, and offers a rich set of geometric operations for the construction and manipulation of complex 3D models. Spatial has improved the existing functionality of ACIS and added new features with Version 7.0:

  - 1. Ruled Skinning – creates surfaces from two or more profile curves, placing ruled surfaces in-between each section of the profiles
  - 2. Skinning to Planar Normal – constrains the take-off vector for each profile to that profile's planar normal
  - 3. Branched Skinning – creates surfaces with profiles that can resolve at two or more branches
  - 4. Patterns – repetitive geometry can be re-created
  - 5. Binary Compatibility of SAB Files (Enhanced)
  - 6. Blending (Enhanced)
  - 7. History Streams (Enhanced)
  - 8. Memory Management (Enhanced)

- Deformable Modeling:

  Deformable Modeling is a more powerful alternative to traditional surfacing techniques such as control point manipulation and lofting, and is intuitive, requiring less manipulation, time and user knowledge while producing a higher-quality result. Functionality includes:

  - 1. Full, Multisurface Capabilities
  - 2. Advanced Control of Surface Shape
  - 3. Continuity Control Along Edges
  - 4. Global and Local Deformations

- File Formats:
  - Importing file formats: 3D CAD models (ACIS SAT IGES, STEP, VDA-FS, CATIA, Pro-E, and more)
  - Exporting file formats: ACIS SAT IGES, STEP, VDA-FS, CATIA, Pro-E, and more
  - Additional file formats: others formats may be available

5. WEB RESOURCES

- Press/Publications: http://www.spatial.com/press_room/inthepress

- Example Article, Daratech Industry Brief:
  http://www.daratech.com/spatial_001201.htm

- Evaluate Products — Free of charge
  http://www.spatial.com/downloads/downloads

- A list of resources on the net:
  http://www.mcadcafe.com/MCADCafe/Tools/HTML/DB_0319.html

- A PC Magazine article: http://www.startmag.com/news_9909/99092713.asp

ActiveWorlds

1. PLATFORMS, PRICES, AND SUPPLIER/CREATOR

- PC using Windows 95/98/2000/NT, Macs, Unix (SUN or Linux 2.2)

- $$$

- Activeworlds.com, Inc. http://www.activeworlds.com

2. APPLICATIONS

- Networked virtual environments for interactive shopping, gaming, and chatting. ActiveWorlds server allows a developer to create 3D worlds where users can shop, chat, and explore

3. EXAMPLES/SAMPLES

- Activeworlds related links http://www.dlcwest.com/~rpatter/tyrell4bb.htm

- Cool Worlds http://activeworlds.com/tour/cool.html

- Female citizens (avatars) http://activeworlds.com/tour/female.html

- Related tools http://www.insead.fr/CALT/Project/AWJavaBots

- Special characters http://activeworlds.com/tour/special.html

4. WEB RESOURCES

- Technical support http://www.activeworlds.com/tech/index.html
- Online Help Manual http://www.activeworlds.com/help/index.html
- Newsletter http://www.activeworlds.com/newsletter/0401/index.html
- Frequently Asked Questions http://www.activeworlds.com/help/faq.html

Active Dimensions 3

1. PLATFORM, PRICE, AND SUPPLIER/CREATOR

- PC
- $25.00–$56.00
- BMT Micro, Inc.: http://www.bmtmicro.com/

2. APPLICATIONS

- Active Dimensions 3 is a CAD and 3D modeling tool with several special features. It can render scenes in either wireframe, flat, Gouraud, or true Phong shading. It has thirty-one preset surfaces which are categorized as extruded regular polygons, inverse kinematics capable joints, platonic solids, 3D primitives, and rounded cubes, cylinders and diamonds

3. EXAMPLE/SAMPLES

- Gallery: http://members.spree.com/technology/microtools/gallery.html

4. WEB RESOURCES

- http://members.spree.com/technology/microtools/documentation.html
- Review: http://the-internet-eye.com/reviews/Oct99/ActiveDimensions3/default.htm
- http://davecentral.com/3437.html

Adobe Dimensions

1. PLATFORM, PRICE, AND SUPPLIER/CREATOR

- PCs and Macintosh computers
- $125
- Adobe www.adobe.com

2. APPLICATIONS

- Complex 3D rendering and modeling software, containing tools such as surface properties commands, lighting effects, extrusions, masks, guides, paths, and more. Allows the user to turn any object into a professional 3D object by offering both raster and crisp, resolution-independent PostScript output

3. EXAMPLES/SAMPLES

- http://www.adobe.com/print/gallery/spollen/main.html
- http://www.adobe.com/print/spotlights/pinsard/main.html
- http://www.efuse.com/Design/untitled.html#Dimensions

4. FUNCTIONS

- Lighting and Shading:
  - Position the lights freely, at any angle or from behind
  - Apply unlimited light sources and with individual intensities
  - Three shading techniques: flat, Gouraud (diffuse), or Phong (plastic)
  - Customize the shading with ambient, highlight, or shininess controls, and specify shade colors
- 3D Rendering:
  - Draw 2D images and then convert them to 3D by adding depth to them or by revolving them around an axis
  - Create basic 3D shapes (primitives) using the program's drawing tools. Primitives include cubes, spheres, cones, and cylinders
  - Ability to wrap raster images on a 3D surface
  - Combine two or more simple objects to build more detailed models
- Transformation:
  - Align Object Centerpoints, Align Surface Centerpoints, Align Surface Orientation, and Align Surface Planes
- File Formats:
  - Importing file formats: .PSD .AI .EPS .TIF .BMP Macintosh PICT
  - Exporting file formats: .AI .PSD .EPS . TIFF .BMP QuickDraw 3D (3DMF)

5. WEB RESOURCES

- Product information: www.adobe.com/products/dimensions/main.html
- An article at: http://www.techweb.com/winmag/library/1997/1101/winla112.htm

AIR (Animation and Image Rendering)

1. PLATFORMS, PRICES, AND SUPPLIER/CREATOR

- Windows 95/98/NT/2000/ME; Linux
- Single-user license: $300; Single-user educational license: $100; Educational site license: $1000
- SiTexGraphics: http://www.sitexgraphics.com

2. APPLICATIONS

- AIR is used for 3D image rendering and animation. AIR offers fast scanline rendering with optional ray tracing that enables users to render high-quality images of 3D scenes. Plug-ins are available for many popular modeling, animation, and visualization packages, and additional plug-ins are in development. AIR accepts scenes exported from modeling and animation programs in RIB format

3. EXAMPLES/SAMPLES

- Demo Version: http://www.sitexgraphics.com/airsetup.exe

4. FUNCTIONS

- Rendering:
  - Fast Scanline Primary Rendering
  - Ray tracing for sharp shadows, reflections, and refraction
  - Global Illumination using irradiance
  - Programmable Shading: support for the RenderMan Shading Language
  - Depth of Field effects simulating the limited focal range of a physical camera
  - Motion Blur
  - Texture Mapping using mip-maps for efficient, anti-aliased texture generation
  - Shadows using ray tracing or shadow maps
  - Reflections using ray tracing or environment maps
  - Hemispherical Lighting
  - Area Lights
  - Advanced Anti-Aliasing and Gamma Correction for high-quality output

- Rich set of Geometric Primitives: convex and concave polygons with holes, quadrics, bicubic patches, trimmed NURB surfaces, subdivision meshes, and CSG objects
- Levels of Detail
- Animation:
  - Key frame and procedural animation
- File Formats:
  - Importing file formats: RIB
  - Exporting file formats: TIFF, BMP, TGA, JPEG, and PNG

5. WEB RESOURCES
- RenderMan Newsgroup: comp.graphics.rendering.renderman
- RenderMan Repository: http://www.renderman.org

Aladdin 4D

1. PLATFORMS, PRICES, AND SUPPLIER/CREATOR
- Amiga
- $280
- Nova Design, Inc.: http://www.novadesign.com

2. APPLICATIONS
- A 3D modeling, rendering, and animation tool with dolly, truck, and pan capabilities and infinite surface layering. Some advanced features include procedural textures, real world gasses, particle systems, and path-based animation

3. EXAMPLES/SAMPLES
- Directory of 3D Models: ftp://ftp.novadesign.com/aladdin/3D_Models/
- Directory of 3D Pictures: ftp://ftp.novadesign.com/aladdin/Pictures/
- Example of 3D Animation: ftp://ftp.novadesign.com/aladdin/Animations/

4. FUNCTIONS
- Modeling:
  - Spline modeling tools

- Extensive modeling tools including Extrude, Path Extrude, Lathe, Bevel, Mirror, Clone, Subdivide and more
- Works in an unlimited number of layers/spaces
- Creates organic objects with spline curves

- Rendering:
  - Multilevel supersampling antialiasing
  - Motion blur with controllable passes
  - Fully customizable lens flare and 3D flare objects
  - Control light attributes including Light Type, Color, Intensity, Falloff, Lens Flare, Shadow Options and more

- Animation:
  - Camera can use one or more targets which control zoom, tilt and direction and even pan from one target to the next, all under spline control
  - Paths also control rotation, scaling, mechanical waves, deforms and instancing, and can be linked for complex motion
  - Animate lights, lens flares, textures, objects, even camera attributes
  - Advanced motion controls including Spline Controls, Velocity, Shifting, and Scaling
  - Enhanced lens flare controls with complete customization and animation

- Lighting/Shading:
  - Shading can be facet, Gouraud or Phong. Other attributes are timelined so objects can change reflectivity, color, transparency, hardness, etc. during the animation by spline controls
  - Unlimited lights of any type
  - Lights use attribute lists that can be animated to change color and strength
  - True photoreal soft shadows and user optimizable ray-traced shadows
  - Conic lights (Spotlights) with full controls and targeting
  - Negative lights

- File Formats:
  - Image loaders/savers for the following formats: IFF/ILBM (palette mapped and 24-bit formats), JPEG, and Framestore
  - 3D Object loaders and/or savers for the following formats: Aladdin4D, Lightwave3D, GEO, EPS, DEM, Draw4D-Pro, and Draw4D

5. WEB RESOURCES

- Tutorials for Aladdin 4D: www.novadesign.com/Newsletters/RMAU/index.html

- Aladdin 4D Newsletter Archive: www.novadesign.com/Newsletters/Alad/index.html

Alice

1. PLATFORMS, PRICES, AND SUPPLIER/CREATOR

- Windows NT/98/95/2000
- Free
- Stage 3 Research Group http://www.alice.org/stage3/ at Carnegie Mellon University

2. APPLICATIONS

- Alice is primarily a scripting and prototyping environment for 3D object behavior. By writing simple scripts, Alice users can control object appearance and behavior, and while the scripts are executing, objects respond to user input via mouse and keyboard
- Alice Authoring Tool comes with the Alice Development Environment, and a collection of 3D objects and textures. It uses Python, a full-featured programming language with vast capabilities: http://www.python.org

3. EXAMPLES/SAMPLES

- http://www.alice.org/demos/demos.htm
- Alice Plug-in: http://www.python.org

4. FUNCTIONS

- Rendering:
    - texture map movie — a series of images that are displayed in sequence
    - Billboarding and Transparent Textures
- Modeling:
    - Accurate collision detection
    - 3D primitives import
    - Advanced texture placement
    - Real world dimensions
- Animation:
    - Animated textures(AVI)
- Internet support:
    - 3D Bookmarks
    - In-place editing
    - Level of detail
    - 3D sound
    - Polygon reduction

- Import and Export:
    - many common 3D file formats include DXF, 3DS, OBJ etc.
    - Head-Mounted Display (HMD): 640 x 480 VGA resolution

5. WEB RESOURCES

- http://www.alice.org/advancedtutorial/
- http://www.alice.org/links.htm

Amapi 3D

1. PLATFORMS, PRICES, AND SUPPLIER/CREATOR

- Windows 95/ 98/ NT4.0 / 2000 / ME / XP
- Mac OS 8.6 — 9.x, Mac OS X in Classic mode
- List Price: $399.00 (various upgrades/side grades/educational discounts available)
- Eovia, a TGS Company: http://www.eovia.com/amapi

2. APPLICATIONS

- Amapi 3D, a NURBS modeler, simplifies the creation and editing of complex geometric shapes by offering a large selection of advanced tools
- A complete 3D solution for modeling, shading, scene building, basic animation, hybrid ray-traced and cartoon rendering

3. EXAMPLES/SAMPLES

- http://www.eovia.com/amapi/demo.htm#
- http://www.eovia.com/amapi/user_project.htm
- http://www.tgsmirror1.com/tutorials.html

4. FUNCTIONS

- Modeling:
    - Object catalog: display a specified directory through the catalog, get project information (modification date, size), create and manage bookmarks
    - Global deformers — taper, bend, twist, interpolation smoothing on polygonal curves, chaikin smoothing on polygonal curves, cubic smoothing on polygonal curves, breaks and tensions control of smoothing

- Spherical deformation, mold (smooth deformation), wrap an object, stretch points, snap a part of the object to a specific location, merge points, edit tangents on NURBS curves, delete points / edges / facets
- Global and local Bezier smoothing, doo, catmul smoothing, loop, butterfly, approximation smoothing on polygonal, curves, rectangular / triangular / diamond-shaped tessellation, polygon reduction, cut by plane, extract parts of curves and surface, boolean operation between and surfaces or volumes, radius / tessellation / angle control of chamfers, chamfers on points of a polyline, chamfer on points and edges of a mesh
- Generates smooth rounded and filled edges, polygon, corners, or shape intersections
- Model rounded, natural organic shapes by creating a mesh over a set of an unlimited number of connected curves

- Rendering:

  - Cameras: move, change, set, create, specify the field of vision — global parameters of rendering (define, saving, render, select, anti-aliasing)
  - Light: set the quality of the shadow, the shading area, noise of the shadow, specify a light color, creation of a bulb light, sun light, spotlight, change the light source name, light source type, specify direction of the beam of light, area of decreasing light propagation
  - Dynamic Geometry: Amapi 3D constructs a history of complex surfaces. This allows the user to dynamically edit an object by acting on its outline, profile or its basic structure. Transformation a vase into a flower of bottle, controlling the facial expressions of characters, modify the dimensions of an industrial object Amapi works with a large number of tools
  - Color ramp — shaded breakpoints in the color ramp, change color of a breakpoint, manage the balance for the each breakpoint of the colormap, browse the list of the color ramps (select, add, delete a color ramp from the list)
  - Decimation reduces the density of complex meshes while preserving their key datapoints and polygons. This feature creates model with varying levels, reduced file size
  - Texture-layer, wood, marble, checker, grid, brick, radial, smooth, ramp radial, noise ramp; replace: mix, add, subtract, lighten, darken, multiply
  - Material editor: display a preview of the entire scene, save / recall / delete a point of view, preview preferences (ray, tracing, shadows display)
  - Rendering parameters: background image, environment, snap an object to specific location, lay out a facet of an object onto the facet of another object
  - Primitives: sphere and Geodesic spheres (polygonal of NURBS), Ellipsoid, super-ellipsoid, cube and parallelpiped, cylinder, cone, platonic solids, tetrahedron, icosahedron, dodecahedron, grid, height fields

- Animation:

  - Create an animation on a recording tape: create, modify, copy, reproduce delete, convert, move and / or deform the object to be animated (move, rotate, scale, deform, mold, stretch, bend)
  - Play an animation: preview, play, stop, choose if the animation is playing in loop

- Animation parameters: set the size, number, image, export file, record an animation AVI (Windows) QuickTime (Mac)
- Formats
  - Import file: 3DMF, 3D Studio, DXF, IGES, Illustrator 3.0, OBJ, Open Inventor, STL, VRML
  - Export file: 3D Studio, 3DGF, 3DMF, 3Space, AMAPI 3D 4.1, Artlantis Render, Cinema 4D, Lightwave, OBJ, BMP, DXF, DXF 2D, FACT (Mac), Illustrator 3.0, Lightwave, NeMo, OBJ, Open Inventor, PICT, POV 3.0, RayDream Studio, RenderMan, Strata Studio Pro, Truespace 2.0, HPGL
  - New import / export formats: Carrara export, OBJ import and export with NURBS, STL import, VRML 2 compliance in import and export, FLASH, SHOCKWAVE-3D
- Additional Features
  - Support of UV mapping for construction primitive and NURBS
  - Environment mapping and new reflection management
  - Progressive fog
  - Ray-traced and Shadow-mapped soft shadows with attenuation
  - Gain and Bias control on algorithmic textures

5. RESOURCES

- http://www.eovia.com/amapi/index.htm
- http://www.eovia.com/amapi/full_features.htm
- http://www.eovia.com/amapi/product_tour/hybrid_render.htm
- http://bondiboard.macpublishing.net/2000/09/reviews/amapi.html
- http://www.staigerland.com/amapi/samples.html
- http://www.tgsmirror1.com/Marketing

AMIRA

1. PLATFORMS, PRICES, AND SUPPLIER/CREATOR

- Windows 95/98/2000 and NT4, PC Linux, SGI Irix 6.5, Sun Solaris 2.7, HP-UX 10.20
- Standard: $1000.00; Developer: $6000.00
- Template Graphics Inc.(TGS): http://www.tgs.com/index.html

2. APPLICATIONS

- AMIRA is a 3D visualization and modeling system. It allows visualization of scientific datasets from various application areas, for example medicine, biology, chemistry, physics, or engineering. AMIRA provides methods to generate 3D grids from voxel data representing an image volume, and it includes a general purpose interactive 3D viewer. AMIRA's state-of-the-art visualization techniques allow you to gain detailed insight into data. Graphics hardware support is utilized to display even very large datasets at interactive speed. Powerful automatic and interactive segmentation tools support processing of 3D image data. Novel, fast, and robust reconstruction algorithms make it easy to create polygonal models from segmented objects. In addition, true volumetric tetrahedral meshes can be generated, suitable for advanced finite-element simulations. Simulation results as well as other data defined on a variety of different grids can be investigated using a large set of powerful visualization methods

3. EXAMPLES/SAMPLES

- http://www.tgs.com/Amira/index.html
- Website gallery: http://amira.zib.de/gallery2/
- Another gallery: http://www.interpatec.co.kr/amiragallery.htm

4. FUNCTIONS

- Modeling:
  - Objects: slices (orthogonal / oblique), pseudo-coloring on arbitrary surfaces, colorwash display, isosurfaces on tetrahedral and hexahedral grids, direct volume rendering, line probe / point probe, 2D-plotting facilities, illuminated field lines, line integral convolution, view-dependent depth-sorted transparency, data type conversion, reconstruction of non-manifold surfaces from 3D image data, surface simplification, registration / matching of 3D images
  - Transformation: Parameters, like slice numbers or orientations of cutting planes, can be adjusted directly by clicking into the 3D presented geometry
  - Editing and manipulations (vertex, edge, face, polygon, curves, objects): AMIRA allows the user to visualize an arbitrary number of datasets at once. Different visualization techniques may be freely combined in a single 3D view, or multiple viewers may be used to analyze and compare different datasets. Different visualization modules can be tightly coupled, for example slicing modules are able to clip the geometry of any other module, or may operate on the same slice without z-buffer fighting
- Rendering:
  - Cameras: Animate camera, adjustable, movable; multiple lights can be used in AMIRA

- Digital Image Filters: AMIRA includes gaussian blur, median filter, unsharp masking, contrast-limited adaptive histogram equalization, and noise reduction filters
- Materials: computes and shows contours for a 3D label field on a 2D cutting plane, performs a surface smoothing by shifting its vertices, takes a surface and randomly distributes a number of short line segments on it, colorwash module helps you to visualize two scalar fields in combination, e.g., medical images like CT data and a temperature distribution

- Animation:
  - Controllers: key-based, procedural, compound, system
  - Animation sequences: Animation sequences can be generated and can be integrated into technical and marketing documents, presentations, local HTML files, remote URLs or online training. An easy-to-use camera path editor is included

- File Formats:
  - ACR-NEMA/DICOM, AVS Field, AVS UCD Format, AMIRA Mesh Format, BMP Image Format, DXF, Encapsulated Postscript, Fluent UNS, HxSurface, Hypermesh, Icol, Inventor, JPEG Image Format, Leica Microscope #D TIFF, Leica Microscope Slice Series, PNG Image Format, PSI format, Ply Format, Raw Data, SGI-RGB Image Format, STL, Stacked-Slices, VRML

5. WEB RESOURCES

- http://amira.zib.de/usersguide/index.html
- http://amira.zib.de/usersguide/description.html
- http://www.tgs.com/Amira/index.html

Amorphium

1. PLATFORMS, PRICES, AND SUPPLIER/CREATOR

- PC/Mac
- $49.95 for Basic Version; 149.95 for Full Version
- Play: http://www.amorphium.com/

2. APPLICATIONS

- Powerful yet simple 3D modeling, rendering, and animation tool. Amorphium has a nice set of features that include: the ability to create Organic 3D Sculpting and 3D Painting in real time, and 3D Model Detailing and Texture mapped objects. Amorphium emulates real-world objects, entirely eliminating the complex user interfaces which often baffle the 3D newcomer

3. EXAMPLES/SAMPLES

- http://www.3d-journal.com/reviews/061499/amorphium.html
- http://www.macoroni.f2s.com/articles/05/amorphium.html

4. FUNCTIONS

- Organic 3D Sculpting:
    - Modeling: polygon-based
    - Primitives: cylinder, sphere, block, cube, tetrahedron, text, doughnut, cone, both side plain mesh, and imported 3D object from another program
    - 3D distortions: Rotate, Bank, Scale, Stretch, Center, Variable Undo, Noise, Smooth, Waves, Tsunami, Equalize, Contrast, Bottle, Bulge, Button, Belly, Flatten, Spikes, Shear, Bend, Radial Shear, Taper, Twist and Twirl
    - Tools: Brush, Smudge, Spheric brush, Normal brush, and Smooth tools in any of twenty-six 3D shapes — all with adjustable Flux, Radius, Pressure, Symmetry, Tilt, and Depth. Tools are used for distortions, 3D painting, and masking operations
- Rendering:
    - Cameras: can be moved up and down and rotated round the object
    - Lights: angle adjustable sun Lighting
    - Materials: Morphing, Texture mapping, HeightShop, and Painting
    - Texture mapping effects: Opacity, Lightness, Contrast, Hue with rotation, and Saturation
    - Before and after rendering: Antialiasing, Shadows, Back picture, Fog, and Smoke
- Animation:
    - Controllers: Procedural
    - Animation Features: Ghosting, mirroring, duplication, pivot point, inverse kinematics, deformation, morphing, text character animation, motion blur
- File Formats:
    - Model Import and Export: Supports industry-standard file formats, including FACT, DXF, 3DS, LWO, VRML (1 and 2) and OBJ
    - Texture Import and Export: BMP, JPEG, PNG, GIF, TIFF, PICT and QuickTime movie file formats are supported

5. WEB RESOURCES

- http://www.3dcafestore.com/amorphium.html
- http://216.246.51.202/forums/amorphium/
- http://www.egroups.com/group/amorphium-users

Analyze

1. PLATFORMS, PRICES, AND SUPPLIER/CREATOR

- Windows 95/98/NT/2000/ME, UNIX (Sun, SGI, HP, IBM, DEC Alpha), or Intel-based Linux
- Mayo Foundation: http://www.mayo.edu/bir/
  Analyze Direct: http://www.analyzedirect.com

2. APPLICATIONS

- Analyze is an integrated, comprehensive software system developed by the Biomedical Imaging Resource, useful in a variety of multimodality, multidimensional biomedical imaging and scientific visualization applications. These integrated suites of complementary tools for fully interactive display, manipulation, and measurement of multidimensional biomedical images have been used in applications involving many different imaging modalities, including CT, MRI, SPECT, PET, ultrasonic and digital microscopy

3. EXAMPLES/SAMPLES

- The Biomedical Imaging Resource at the Mayo Clinic: http://www.mayo.edu/bir/
- Segmentation: http://www.analyzedirect.com/products/tour/images/screenshots/Segmented Objects.jpg
- Image Fusion:
  http://www.analyzedirect.com/products/tour/images/screenshots/Fusion.jpg
- Volume Render:
  http://www.analyzedirect.com/products/tour/images/screenshots/Volume Render.JPG

4. FUNCTIONS

The following summarizes the advanced algorithms and major features of the Analyze software system:

- Analyze Main Control Panel:
    - Launching pad for all Analyze programs, either from menus or power bar icons
    - Configurable, multiple power bar(s) for iconic representations of programs
    - Control canvas for loaded volume images with iconic representation of images
    - Configurable loaded volume location for multiple, independent sessions
    - System resource monitor (disk, memory, time, etc.)
    - Powerbar editor and icon layout facility
    - Support for multiple user preferences (interface options, etc.)

- Image Data Retrieval and Management:
    - Import/export of standard image file formats and many commercial scanner formats
    - Conversion to/from over 30 standard image formats, including the DICOM standard
    - Template for specification of image information for unknown formats
    - Automated construction of volume image files from groups of individual image files
    - High fidelity, rapid image compression/decompression using wavelets
    - Access to tape devices for I/O of image data in many formats
    - Graphical file manager with iconic representation of images and other file types
    - Direct drag and drop to/from the Analyze file manager and other Analyze programs

- Image Data Loading and Storing:
    - Support for native image file formats without need for conversion
    - Volume image resizing based on automated isotropic sampling (noncubic resizing)
    - Interactive subregioning, flipping, and padding of volume image
    - Data type conversion with intensity windowing or thresholding
    - Direct output to any supported file format

- 2D Image Generation and Display:
    - Interactive reformatting and display of multiplanar images
    - Interactive intensity windowing
    - Interactive dissection and intersection through 3D volumes
    - Interactive oblique images through 3D volumes
    - Image volume reformatting along any arbitrary oblique axis
    - Interactive generation of "curved" images and radial images
    - Cine movie displays with multiple panels, variable size, and speed control

- 3D Image Generation and Display:
    - Fully interactive volume rendering of 3D images
    - Both transmission and reflection ray casting models
    - Depth, gradient, composited and Phong shaded surfaces

– Voxel and object compositing with transparency
– Divergent perspective ray casting/rendering
– Interactive colorizing and voxel texture mapping
– Interactive, graphical control of all divergent viewing specifications
– Control of multiple viewing positions (cameras)
– Sequence generation between camera positions for cine fly-throughs (e.g., virtual endoscopy)
– Variable illumination and angle-of-view
– Variable render masks and dynamic preview modes
– Radial cylindrical and stereo-pair rendering
– Maximum intensity, integrated and surface projections
– Numerical projection rendering
– Multiplanar dissection and subregioning
– Interactive orthogonal and oblique sectioning
– Manual editing and automatic definition of objects
– Rendering of combined or individual segmented objects
– Interactive rendered object manipulation
– Mirror image rendering for independent objects
– Linear and curvilinear surface measurements
– Direct surface area and volumetric measurements
– Powerful, flexible movie generator with control of frame-to-frame updates of volume rendering parameters (e.g., rotations, dissections, dissolutions, etc.)

- 3D Model Generation and Display:

– Automatic extraction of contours from isosurfaces or objects
– Output to common contour file formats (IGES, SLC, ASCII list)
– Surface extraction from voxel-based structures using advanced algorithms:
– Deformable model with adaptive surface fitting for surface extraction
– Marching cubes surface extraction
– Based on user-specification of a given number of desired polygons (polygonal budget)
– Output to common surface file formats (IGES, DXF, OBJ, IV, STL, VRIO, VRML, POLY, PATRAN)
– Model viewer for viewing multiple extracted surfaces (wireframe and shaded)

- Image Processing:

– Image Calculator — metaphor of hand-held calculator for powerful algebraic and boolean operations on images
– Formula design and execution for customized 2D and 3D image processing
– Image algebra for combining images from formulas
– Mathematical, logical, and transcendental operations
– 3D matrix operations and geometric transformations
– Linear and adaptive histogram operations
– Spatial and frequency domain image processing
– User-defined convolution kernels
– Inhomogeneity correction based on statistical means filtering
– Interactive, graphic-based design of custom filters
– 2D and 3D FFT (Fast Fourier Transformation) and deconvolution routines
– Image transformation and compression using wavelets

- Image Segmentation:

  - Interactive manual object segmentation
  - 2D and 3D region growing for object segmentation
  - 2D and 3D math morphology for object segmentation
  - Automatic edge contour extraction
  - Automated segmentation based on 3D morphological processing
  - User definition of bounded region on selected image(s) within volume to condition segmentation
  - Output of binary or masked grayscale segmented volume to other Analyze programs

- Image Registration and Fusion:

  - Fusion (registration and integration) of multimodal images
  - Intra- and inter-modality registration
  - Registration using advanced normalized mutual information maximization
  - Permits registration without need for prior segmentation
  - Registration using surface matching of common surfaces
  - Efficient section-to-section registration for 3D volumes of serial images
  - Interactive plotting and measurement of line and trace profiles
  - Interactive definition of multiple regions of interest
  - Selection and automatic sampling of regions of interest
  - Measurement of dimensions and densities
  - Measurement of regional shape and texture
  - ASCII data file format for exporting to standard analysis programs
  - Analysis of tree structures (lengths, branching angles, cross-sectional areas)
  - Surface area and volume measurement by stereology

- Ancillary Functionality:

  - Interactive screen editor with text, labels and graphics
  - Hardcopy printing of text and images, including full color postscript
  - Extensive interactive color definition and manipulation

- Documentation:

  - Online, context sensitive help documentation and tutorials
  - Documentation in HTML format, use with Web browsers

- File Formats:

  - Analyze-Specific File Formats: AnalyzeAVW, AnalyzeAVW Volume Files, Analyze Image (7.5), Analyze Object Maps, Analyze (7.5) Screen Files
  - Standard Radiological File Formats: DICOM, ACR-NEMA, PAPYRUS, INTERFILE
  - Vendor-Specific Radiological File Formats: GE Advantage, GE Signa MRI, GE 9800 CT, GE Advance PET, GE Starcam, Siemens CT, Siemens MAGVIS, Siemens/CTI PET, IMATRON (EBCT), SMIS
  - Common Raster File Formats: BMP, GIF, TIFF, PBM, PGM, PPM, PNG, TARGA, PIC, SGI rgb, Sun Rasterfiles, XBM, XWD, PostScript
  - Common Movie File Formats: QUICKTIME, YUV
  - Output surface file formats: Alias, IGES, SLC, ASII list, DXF, OBJ, IV, STL, VRIO, VRML, POLY, SSD, POGO, PATRAN, Inventor, Autocad

5. WEB RESOURCES

- http://www.mayo.edu/bir/
- http://www.analyzedirect.com/
- http://www.bmtp.akh-wien.ac.at/people/backwe1/HSL/HelpDocs/ AnalyzeAVW.html
- http://www.mrc-cbu.cam.ac.uk/Imaging/analyze.htm

Anfy 3D

1. PLATFORM, PRICES, AND SUPPLIER/CREATOR

- PC (Java)
- Freeware
- Anfy Team: http://anfyteam.com/indexen.html

2. APPLICATIONS

- Anfy 3D is software designed for creating 3D images for the Web. Can be used to easily create interactive 3D worlds, presentations, and rotating 3D letters with Java

3. EXAMPLES/SAMPLES

- http://anfyteam.com/panfy3d.html
- http://anfyteam.com/an3d/index.html

4. FUNCTIONS

- Modeling:
  - Objects: cube, sphere, cone, cylinder and extrusion
  - Transformation: translation, rotation, scaling, zoom, pan
- Rendering:
  - Cameras: adjustable, movable
  - Lights: real-time omni lights, lightballs/flares
  - Materials: blend, transparent
  - Before and after rendering: antialiasing, motion blur, gaussian blur, blur-motion, real-time fog
- Animation:

       − Controllers: key or mouse based
       − Animations: antialiasing, double-buffering, motion blur, merge and explode
- File Formats:
       − .spz (Anfy 3D editor files)

5. WEB RESOURCES

- http://anfyteam.com/indexen.html

- http://anfyteam.com/panfy3d.html

- http://javaboutique.internet.com/anfyjava/

ANIM8OR

1. PLATFORMS, PRICES, AND SUPPLIER/CREATOR

- PC

- Freeware

- R. Steven Glanville: http://www.anim8or.com/main/index.html

2. APPLICATIONS

- Anim8or is a 3D modeling and character animation program. Objects can be easily created and manipulated by dragging, rotating, scaling, using illumination, Phong, animation, etc. Primitive shapes are included, and users find that Anim8or nicely integrates with industry-leading modeling packages (3D Studio, Lightwave, etc.), file formats

3. EXAMPLES/SAMPLES

- www.anim8or.com/gallery/gallery5/index.html

- www.geocities.com/mard_rhi/Pics.html

- www.geocities.com/elimar48/animator.html

- http://www.paula.univ.gda.pl/~fizws/anim8or/

- http://www.geocities.com/lanceart/

- http://members.aol.com/beyondvr/carpet.html

- http://www.angelfire.com/in/ezekeal/

4. FUNCTIONS

- Modeling:
  - Objects: spheres, cylinders, platonic solids, polygons, splines, extrusion, lathing
  - Transformation: translation, rotation, scaling, mirroring, modifiers, subdivision
- Rendering:
  - Cameras: adjustable, movable
  - Lights: attenuation, Phong, Gouraud
  - Materials: blend, morpher, ray trace, two-sided texture mapping
  - Before and after rendering: antialising, transparency, perspective matching, fog, motion blur
- Animation:
  - Advanced animation: character animation, warps, pivot point, motion blur
  - Basic animation
- File Formats:
  - Importing file formats: 3DS, LWO, OBJ
  - Exporting file formats: 3DS, JPG, BMP, AVI

5. WEB RESOURCES

- http://www.geocities.com/lanceart/article03.html
- http://interneteye3d.com/Tutorials/2000/sept/posermorph/
- http://www.npwt.net/%7eduanem/gallery/index.html
- http://www.geocities.com/elimar48/
- http://www.npwt.net/~duanem/tutor1/
- http://www.geocities.com/mard_rhi/
- ListServ: MajorDomo@mgarts.net

Animation Master

1. PLATFORMS, PRICES, AND SUPPLIER/CREATOR

- PC Windows and Mac
- $299
- Hash Inc.: http://www.hash.com/index.asp

2. APPLICATIONS

- A spline based modeling and animation tool with advanced features like inverse kinematics, ray tracing, image mapping, and modeling of complex organic and mechanical objects
- Offers sculpting features, animation tools, rendering etc. Can be used for making movies, 3D story boards, building virtual reality, business presentations etc. Features like drag and drop, customizable interface, powerful motion, ability to build libraries of actions and characters that can be reused, makes it ideal for amateur animators, professional artists, and even studios

3. EXAMPLES/SAMPLES

- Sample images created with Animation Master:
  - Still image galleries: http://www.hash.com/gallery/stills1.asp
  - Animation galleries: http://www.hash.com/gallery/movies1.asp

4. FUNCTIONS

- Modeling:
  - Model with flexible Hash patches
  - Point-and-click sculpting for object creation
  - Model over a Rotoscope image
  - Seamlessly integrates "bones" into low-density, unibody models
  - Un attach; disconnect "attached" points while modeling
  - Perspective Modeling
  - Nested Hide
  - "Lasso" or free form group tool
  - Choose D3D or Conix OpenGL shaded real-time mode when modeling instead of wire frame
  - Bias Handles for easy control of spline curvature
  - Optimized DXF export
  - Object manipulators for translating scaling and rotating
  - variable lathe cross sections
  - Uniform Normal Face Control for Polygonal output
  - Flip or Mirror a selected group of points around any axis
  - "Distortion Mode" Deformation Tool
- Animation:
  - Patch-based animation
  - Bones motion offers lifelike bouncing and twisting
  - Complete skeletal and muscle control features
  - Inverse Kinematics (IK) for creating skeletal based motion
  - Character animation with lip-synch via muscle motion
  - Stride length to prevent a character's feet or tires from slipping as they move
  - Action Overloading; applying layers of Actions to a character so that it can "walk," "talk," and "clench" its fists simultaneously
  - Action Range; choose only a range of frames, Hold, or Wait from an Action
  - Rotoscope facial movement in Muscle with sequenced backgrounds

- Poses; save and open single Skeletal or muscle key frame
- Lock Bones to lock masses in space while adjusting the rest of the Character
- Many different kinds of real-time constraints for perfect anchoring, picking up objects, and animated paths; Including: Aim At, Kinematic, Path, Translate To, Orient like, Aim Roll At, Spherical Limits, Surface, Scale Like and Scale to Reach
- Rotoscoping
- Action blending
- Kinematic rotational stiffness
- Animated camera rotoscopes
- Hard and soft body dynamics; including cloth, springs, masses and collision detection between objects

- Rendering:

  - Ray tracing of transparency, reflections, and shadows
  - Mirrors with adjustable settings
  - Alpha buffer rendering for combining computer animation with live action
  - Multiple levels of antialiasing for animation or film
  - 32-bit, variable, unlimited resolution rendering
  - Transparency Averaging
  - Image Maps can be antialiased
  - Shadow Maps
  - Gamma Correction
  - Motion Blur
  - Extensive render status meters
  - Radiosity
  - Ray-traced or Z-buffer soft shadows
  - Bloom
  - Soften
  - Up-Rez
  - Over Sampling
  - Dither
  - Dynamic Range (gamma correction)
  - Line Geometry
  - No "anti-alias" option. (Game Sprites)
  - Film Tint; presets like "black and white" or "sepia tones"
  - Stereo rendering
  - Shadow buffers and "Shadow Only" buffers
  - Exportable lighting maps
  - Selectable soft shadow color
  - Fully customizable toon or anime style shader/render

- Materials and Object Attributes:

  - Ability to apply custom textures, images and object Attributes to individual patches
  - Image Maps Locked to the surface through use of UV coordinate system
  - Glass with Refraction and Caustics
  - Image types include color, bump, transparency, reflectivity, diffuse, specular, ambiance, mirror, gradient and cookie-cut maps
  - Integrated Algorithmic Perlin Materials Editor

- Displacement and Fractal Maps
- Edge Transparency
- See through Decaling
- Tileable Image Maps
- Spherical, cylindrical, and planar projection mapping
- Material Effector Objects
- JPEG and TIFF support
- Transparent Density
- Translucency
- Reflection Falloff
- Material "Bump" attribute

- Image formats supported:

  - Load: TARGA, JPEG, TIFF, PICT (mac only), AVI (pc only), Quicktime
  - Save: TARGA, PICT (mac only), AVI (pc only), Quicktime

5. WEB RESOURCES

- Online Manual: http://www.hash.com/htmlHelp/index.html

- Tutorials: http://www.hash.com/users/jsherwood/tutes/tutorials.html

- Free Models: http://www.eggington.net/Hash/Models/

- http://www.hash.com/htmlHelp/HTMLHelp/index.htm

- http://www.amazon.com/exec/obidos/ASIN/1584500425/o/qid=974504702/sr=2-1/104-4774156-6056738

- http://www.graphicssoft.about.com/compute/graphicssoft/gi/dynamic/offsite.htm?site=http://macworld.zdnet.com/2000/08/reviews/animation%5Freview.html

- http://www.alphalink.com.au/~kandt/am2000.html

- http://www.dlf.org.au/

- http://www.tradey.com.au/darcy/

ANIMATION STAND

1. PLATFORMS, PRICES, AND SUPPLIER/CREATOR

- Mac, SGI, and Windows (95, 98, ME, NT 4, and 2000)

- Cinema: $5,995; Professional: $595; Personal $15 on CD-ROM, or free download from the website

- Linker Systems: http://www.linkersystems.com
  and http://www.animationstand.com

2. APPLICATIONS

- a complete 2D animation tool for scanning, painting and compositing 2D animation. It can be used from start to finish on an animation project, from viewing pencil tests through final, composited output. It has been used in video and film projects for animation and quality special effects

3. EXAMPLES/SAMPLES

- gallery: http://www.animationstand.com/gallery

- image sample on homepage: http://www.animationstand.com

4. FUNCTIONS

- Animation:
  - Multiplane camera controls of cel art including trucks, pans, wipes, zooms, slow in, slow out, fade and dissolve during move
  - User-created, curve-, spline-, and example-based motion paths
  - Sub-pixel antialiasing and motion
  - Automatic drop shadows
  - No frame or layer limit. No picture size limit
  - Linear keying
  - Sound synchronization: "Beat" marking. Frame/sound correlation. Squash/ stretch sound with or without frequency shift. Multiple concurrent sound tracks
  - Optical and Special Effects: Unlimited effects in one pass. Multiple exposures. Transparencies. Controlled, in-motion fades. Mattes, gels, glow. Rack focus. Backlight
- Ink and paint:
  - Coloring: CMYK color separations, named colors, Paint with textures
  - Saturation control, invert luminance, find lines, RGB/HSV color block
  - Rendering: Antialiasing, Pixelize, blur, smudge images, unlimited light sources, 3D rendering (Mac Only),3D shading
  - Modes: Acrylic, variable blend, gel, mask, paint from another document, soft edge, alpha channel, darkest color, lightest color, faded edges, partial
  - color modes, definable wash types and patterns, palette color spread
  - Modeling: 6 forms of document selection options through marquee and lasso, expand or shrink selection, fill with selection, select with polygon, etc. Partial undo and revert. Rotate, twist, resize, bend, flip, tilt, squash, and stretch
  - Auto-Painter built-in. ArtDirector built-in
- other key features:
  - Automatic cel painting
  - Production cost reporting

      − Easy output to film, HDTV, video, QuickTime, and files
      − ScanLink built-in

5. WEB RESOURCES:

- Main website: http://www.animationstand.com/

- Manuals and tutorials: http://www.animationsttand.com/products/ requestForm2.html

- An article: http://www.animationstand.com/news/articles/billDavis.html

- News and Press Releases: http://www.animationstand.com/news

- News article: http://www.digitaleditor.com/news/articles/00725-2.shtml

Arius3D

1. PLATFORMS, PRICES, AND SUPPLIER/CREATOR

- PC

- $1600 onwards…

- ARIUS3D Limited; Website: http://www.arius3d.com

2. APPLICATIONS

- Arius3D creates digital copies of real world objects. Images are highly detailed (better than 50 microns) and the color is perfect. Ambient light has no impact — the shaders are in real color. The images can be intelligently built to whatever resolution and accuracy is required enabling images to be shown in 3D on the Web. The patented method uses three laser wavelengths: red, green and blue, to capture simultaneously the geometric and the reflectance coordinates, that is X,Y, Z, R, G, B values. Resolution in the x,y planes is better than 50 microns and in the z plane 10 microns. Using laser illumination and unique layout allows the recording of accurate and repeatable measurements that cannot be matched by competing digital/video recording devices

3. EXAMPLES/SAMPLES

- http://www.arius3d.com/dynamic-frameset.html?imaging.html

4. FUNCTIONS/FEATURES

- Modeling:
  - Arius3D creates digital copies of real world objects
  - Transformation: translation, rotation, scaling, cloning, align, array, mirror, and spacing
- Rendering:
  - Gaming platforms are setting a new standard for texture and polygon resolution. Arius3D color scanning technology allows for the capture of extremely accurate geometry and color which can be either triangulated and decimated to a lower polygon count or selectively modeled from the point cloud. The color information derived from the scan can either be rendered out and created as a texture over-laid on a lower polygon count model, or can be reduced in size and used directly as a texture map
  - True color
    Because the light source is the lasers themselves, Arius3D scanning is not affected by ambient light and shadows are not an issue
  - Registration
    Measurement of the geometry and the color is achieved by the same laser beams, at the same time. Arius3D technology allows perfect registration between the 3D data and the color data
  - Pixel Resolution
    Arius3D technology can achieve at least 5,000 by 5,000 pixels across its field of view
  - Color Measurements
    Color readings are repeatable. The use of laser for color measurements means that reliable and repeatable values are obtained
- Animation:
  - Basic Animation
  - Extremely high resolution textures are derived from the scans
  - Traditional scanning methods create a black and white 3D image. Arius3D's technologies allow animators to start with detailed, photorealistic geometry. Each point captured has an exact R, G, B value
- File Formats:
  - Universal inputs:
    Supports input of ASCII point data from virtually all 3D scanners and digitizers. Accepts direct input of file formats from Cyberware, Digibotics, Hymarc, and Steinbichler systems, as well as IGES point clouds (type 106 and 116). Uses integrated plug-n-play interface with Immersion MicroScribe digitizers. Imports polygonal file formats such as STL (rapid prototyping), OBJ (Alias|Wavefront), 3DS (3D Studio Max), DXF (AutoCAD), VRML (Web format), and LW (Lightwave)
  - For files intended for the Web, Studio can create Viewpoint (formerly Metastream) interactive 3D. The Viewpoint file format preserves the macro geometry and color of an object, but discards the micro geometry (the bump map) of the surface detail, and heavily compresses the data to keep file sizes small enough to stream easily over the Web

5. WEB RESOURCES:

- http://www.arius3d.com/new/newsletter/page_1a.htm
- http://www.arius3d.com/news.html
- Books: www.geomagic.com/news/articles/pdf/ed200009.3Dphotography.pdf
- Related articles:
- http://www.geomagic.com/products/ecommerce/applications.php3
- http://cma.zdnet.com/texis/techinfobase/techinfobase/edit.html
- http://www.archimuse.com/mw2001/exhibit/ex_100000608.html

ARTlantis Render

1. PLATFORMS, PRICES, AND SUPPLIER/CREATOR

- PC, Macintosh
- $495.00
- The Abvent Group: http://www.abvent.com/us/default.asp

2. APPLICATIONS

- ARTlantis Render is a photorealistic rendering and animation system

3. EXAMPLES/SAMPLES

- Links Gallery for ARTlantis Render: http://www.abvent.com/us/press/July3.asp
- ARTlantis Render links on related tools:
  http://www.abvent.com/us/gallery/link/default.asp

4. FUNCTIONS

- Features:
  - Global illumination; real-time previewing; ray tracing; animation; procedural shaders; batch renderings; 2D and 3D background images; refraction and reflection; Heliodon lighting; soft shadows; ambiance effects; virtual reality panoramas; depth of field
- Modeling/Rendering/Animation:
  - With ARTlantis, every single element can be modified, interactively, at any moment and visualized instantaneously in the preview window

- Fast, precise and flexible fine-tuning of any 3D scene results in images and animations of incredible realism and atmosphere. Shaders are applied by a single drag and drop, whether they are predefined "ARTlantis shaders" or new textures created by the user
- The library of shaders is organized by families, which facilitates their installation, distribution and management. The user can create his or her own library of shaders and update them easily. Each modification of shaders is entirely graphic: from the choice of color to the adjustment of reflection, everything is controlled, interactively, by a simple cursor
- The final presentation of the project can be a still image, an animation, or a virtual reality panorama
- Complete control is available at any moment, for all types of operations: creating and editing animation sequences, manipulating camera parameters and behavior, setting speed and timing, sun-light studies, linking sequences and exploring panoramic views are just a few of them
- A multitude of functions, such as the integration of a background 3D image, the application of 3D atmosphere effects, or the setting of depth of field, the user can personalize his or her presentations and obtain highly realistic results

- File Formats:

  - Importing file formats: Communicating directly with CAD Software (ArchiCAD, VectorWorks, AutoCAD, form•Z, CadSoft, ChiefArchitect, ARC+, Amapi, ZOOM…), ARTlantis can import most of the standard file formats (DXF, DWG, 3D Studio, IGES, VRML, Electric Image, RIB, etc.)
  - Export file formats: saves images and animations in most common file formats: TIFF, PICT, TGA, BMP, AVI, EPIX (Piranesi), QuickTime Movie, QuickTime VR Panorama and VR object; and manages alpha channels as well

5. WEB RESOURCES

- Discussion Forums: http://forums.architosh.com/ forumdisplay.phtml?forumid=6&daysprune=

- Review: http://www.macworld.com/1998/06/reviews/4353.html

AVS5

1. PLATFORMS, PRICES, AND SUPPLIER/CREATOR

- UNIX-DEC, HP, IBM, SGI, and SUN workstations

- $1,495 — locked academic price; $1,745 — floating

- Advanced Visual Systems Inc.: http://www.avs.com/

2. APPLICATION

- AVS5 is Advanced Visual Systems' original visual programming product. AVS5 consists of a comprehensive suite of data visualization and analysis techniques that incorporates both traditional visualization tools such as 2D plots and graphs and image processing as well as advanced tools such as 3D interactive rendering and volume visualization

3. EXAMPLES/SAMPLES

- http://www.avs.com/solution/success/technology/index.htm
- http://www.avs.com/solution/success/application/index.htm
- http://www.avs.com/solution/success/industry/index.htm

4. FUNCTIONS

- Data Viewer:
    - Easy-to-use Data visualization
    - Point and click menu interface
    - Comprehensive suite of visualization techniques
    - Extensible application with pre-packaged networks
- Geometry Viewer:
    - Interactive 3D geometric display
    - Choice of render modes: wireframe, wurface
    - Surface transparency and reflectance
    - Multiple light sources
    - 2D/3D texture mapping
    - Multiple viewports
- Image Viewer:
    - Real-time image pan and zoom
    - Region of interest operations
    - Flip book animation
    - 8-bit, 16-bit, and 24-bit Support
    - Look-up table operations
    - Data resizing operations
- Graph Viewer:
    - Line, bar, scatter, and area Plots
    - Contour plots
    - Variable line type and plot color
    - Variable axis range and scale
    - Titles, axes labels and legends
- Advanced Visualization Techniques:
    - Streamlines and particle advection
    - Image processing

- Volume rendering
- Isosurfaces and slice planes
- Comprehensive finite element data visualization
- Presentation:
  - Image labeling and annotation
  - PostScript and encapsulated PostScript output
  - AVS animator for high quality animations
  - Wide range of video and print output options

5. WEB RESOURCES

- http://www.avs.com/products/AVS5/avs5.htm

AutoCAD 2000

1. PLATFORM, PRICE, COMPANY

- PC

- N/A

- Autodesk: http://www.autodesk.com

2. APPLICATIONS

- AutoCAD is a 2D/3D computer assisted-design tool. It is used by architects, engineers, and draftsmen to produce highly detailed schematics for objects such as ships, buildings, and manufacturing components

3. EXAMPLES/SAMPLES

- Scenic Production: http://www.panix.com/jviii/jv3acad.html

- DWF Drawing: http://www.webfooters.com/dwfdrawing.html

4. WEB RESOURCES

- http://www3.autodesk.com/adsk/section/0,,284288,00.html

- AutoCAD Resource Guide: http://www.acad.co.uk/

- Mastering AutoCAD: http://www.omura.com/autocad/linksaec.htm

b3d Studio Pro

1. PLATFORM, PRICE, AND SUPPLIER/CREATOR

- PC Windows 98, NT4, or 2000
- $995.00 — single license; Free — trial version
- Brilliant Digital Entertainment: http://www.b3d.com

2. APPLICATIONS

- b3d Studio is an editing and production package for 3D animated movies. It brings together 3D animation, audio, model gestures, effects, and interactivity, all into a single-scene time line. It can be used to create multiscene, multipath movies that offer both interactivity and variety — from 3D banner ads to music webeos, to multiepisode Web movies or CD ROM training. b3d Studio gives users a range of compression, streaming, caching, and other features to optimize movies for delivery over the Internet

3. EXAMPLES/SAMPLES

- b3d showcase: http://www.b3d.com/showcase.asp?memberID=0
- Case study of a 3D Web banner ad: http://www.b3d.com/case_studies.asp
- b3d Studio resources and home page:
  http://www.brilliantdigital.com/productdetails.asp?ProductFamily=1
- b3d Studio samples and examples:
  http://www.digimation.com/asp/product.asp?product_id=25

4. FUNCTIONS

- Creating models for 3D animated movies:
  - Create reusable animation, models and morph targets from the model files
  - Control character gestures and emotions
  - Model once; use in multiple projects and scenes
  - Cache models and textures on users' machines for one-time download
  - Scale models to match user's CPU
- Adding and editing events:
  - Insert effects: camera control, fade, reusable animation, lights, sprites, URL links, volume control
  - Insert resources: audio, animation, subtitle, bitmaps
  - Preview immediately using the only real-time rendering engine available
  - Edit multiple windows and scenes
  - Use shortcuts with markers, message palette and timeline

- Visual plotting and story branching:

    - Draw lines from scene to scene to set story path
    - See links to scenes launched by icon or hotspot clicks

- Auto-lipsyncing with visual editing:

    - Auto-lipsync using advanced waveform and text analysis with the click of a button
    - Enhance sync using dialog text
    - Preview and edit lipsync
    - Redo lipsyncing from within the timeline

- Compression and streaming:

    - Set automatic animation key reduction and geometry compression
    - Split files into upfront downloads and streamable parts
    - Optimize for 28k, 56k, 128k or CD-ROM delivery
    - Auto-create optimal caching for episodic delivery

- Having plug-ins to 3D Studio Max:

    - Correct textures and other display
    - Create objects fixed in camera view
    - Create objects always facing camera

5. WEB RESOURCES

- An review article: http://ipw.internet.com/development/rich_media/937849958.html

- A company using b3d to create interactive 3D banner ads: http://www.mindgel.com/main.htm

- http://www.web3d.org/vrml/wb31.htm

bCAD

1. PLATFORM, PRICE, AND SUPPLIER/CREATOR

- PC

- bCAD ST (Standard) full CD edition: $595

- ProPro Group, Inc., located in Novosibirsk, Russia; Company Website: http://propro.ru/

2. APPLICATIONS

- bCAD is an integrated software tool for computer drawing, 3D modeling and designing, and supporting realistic visualization for designers, engineers, and architects. Aiming for multipurpose user, this powerful software supports 3D graphic solutions: 2D drawing, 3D modeling, material, object snap, modification, realistic rendering, and OpenGL supports

3. EXAMPLES/SAMPLES

- http://propro.ru/bcad/gallery/gallery.html
- http://www.3dsite.com/cgi/bcad/gallery/gallery.html
- http://www.3dsite.com/ism/mmarket/items/bcad/coffepot-small.html

4. FUNCTIONS

- Modeling:
  - 2D-objects: lines, circles, arcs, ellipses, rectangles, polylines, polygons, hatching
  - 3D-objects: boxes, spheres, dishes, domes, torus, cylinders, cones, single 3D faces, fractal surfaces, meshes, surfaces and extrusion, TrueType 3D texts
  - Transformation: translation, rotation, scaling, mirror, antialiasing
  - Modification: erase, move, copy, rotate, mirror, stretch, group/ungroup, delete, add, fillet, smooth curve, decurve, chamfer (on vertex, edge, line, polyline, polygon, curves, meshes), construct 3D solid modeling as intersection, subtraction, union, merge, bend, twist, collision detection, line of intersection, 3D dimensions and coordinates
- Rendering:
  - Cameras: dynamic camera adjustment
  - Lights: spot studio lights, spot and omni internal lights, ambient, Z-buffer Phong with shadow casting, texture Gouraud rendering
  - Materials: color, shininess, mirror reflection, roughness, transparency, self-illumination, rotation and scaling texture images
  - More materials: ray tracing, raster and procedural textures and bumps (planar, spherical, cylindrical, solid and entire mesh), reflection mapping, correct interpretation of the smoothing groups, hidden lines removal, object hierarchy
  - Supporting OpenGL real-time preview: interactive navigation through 3D space, walk-through playback in real time, mesh optimizing for speed, Gouraud, flat and wire frames modes, customizing background
- Animation:
  - Basic animation: walk-through, key-frames
- File Formats:
  - Importing textures from BMP/GIF/JPEG/TGA/CEL/PIC files

– Importing of ready-to-render models from the native 3D Studio files, including material settings, textures, bump and reflection maps, correct usage of the smoothing groups
– Export/Import of DWG/DXF R10-12 by user choice, of 3D meshes to/from 3D Studio 3DS ASC
– Export of raster images to BMP, TIFF, GIF, PCX, JPEG, TGA
– Export of vector drawings to HPGL, EPS

5. WEB RESOURCES

- • - http://propro.ru/

- • - http://www.3dcafestore.com/bcad.html

- • - http://www.pcplus.co.uk/article.asp?ID=3369

- • - http://www.3dsite.com/3dsite/cgi/bcad/download.html

Behemot Graphics Editor

1. PLATFORM, PRICE, CREATOR/SUPPLIER

- • Windows 95/98/NT, Linux/Intel, Macintosh

- • Freeware

- • Behemot: http://www.behemot.com, by Sergio Perani

2. APPLICATIONS

- • Behemot Graphics Editor is a graphics program which allows modeling and rendering 3D objects and scenes

3. EXAMPLES/SAMPLES

- • Images and animations: http://www.behemot.com/images/index.html

4. FUNCTIONS

- • Modeling:
  – Objects: primitives (box, sphere, cone, cylinder, etc.), triangle mesh, NURBS, Bezier surface, CSG, blob, skeleton, and others (Curve: polyline, Bezier, NURBS)
  – Transformation: translation, rotation, scaling, sweep, intersection, and subtraction

– Editing and manipulations (vertex, edge, face, polygon, curves, objects):
   customizable vector fields, deformation field and graph

- Rendering:

  – Lamp: point and area
  – Shading: boundary representation (with Phong interpolation), ray tracing
  – Materials: Bezier mesh, texture and bump mapping, depth bitmap, layers
  – Before and after rendering:
     antialiasing, preview, convert text to solid objects

- Animation:

  – Basic: modeling in wireframe or shaded mode, lining objects via a skeleton
     wire frame to move easily, modify b-rep, blob, and NURBS models
  – Advanced: complex modeling and animation through integrated Prolog
     scripting

- File Formats:

  – Importing file formats: RT, DXF, 3DS
  – Exporting file formats: RT, DXF, VRML 1.0, MPEG, BMP

- Editing:

  – Integrated environment: editor + render
  – Polyline, Bezier and NURBS curve editing, extended sweep
  – Deformation field
  – Events to model and animate objects
  – Layers
  – Integrated Prolog language

5. WEB RESOURCES

- Online manual: http://www.behemot.com/doc/manual/index.html

- http://www.listsoft.com/progs/pr155.htm

Beyond 3D

1. PLATFORMS, PRICES, AND SUPPLIER/CREATOR

- 32-bit Windows environment

- $$$$

- Uppercut Software: http://www.uppercutsoftware.com/

2. APPLICATIONS

- Beyond 3D is a modeling, ray tracing, and animation tool

3. EXAMPLES/SAMPLES

- Beyond 3D Gallery:
  http://www.uppercutsoftware.com/gallery/images/gallery.html

4. WEB RESOURCES

- Beyond 3D Website: http://www.uppercutsoftware.com/beyond/
- Beyond 3D Applications: http://www.beyond-3d.com/beyond/ext_who.htm

Blender

1. PLATFORMS, PRICES, AND SUPPLIER/CREATOR

- Most platforms: PC, Linux, SGI, Sun, Mac, etc.
- Free
- NaN Technologies BV: http://www.blender3d.com

2. APPLICATIONS

- Blender Creator is a fully integrated 3D creation suite. Blender features a versatile animation system, contemporary modeling principles, an advanced rendering engine, character animation tools, an editor for post-production and tools for creating and playback of real-time interactive 3D
- Blender is a 3D package integrating a real-time 3D (game-) engine for interactive editing of real-time content. Its 1.5Mb file size makes for quick and easy downloading, while its compatibility with OpenGL eliminates the need for costly high-end graphics machines
- Blender's game engine is designed around a solid physics simulation system, all forces such as gravity, impacts from weapons, character interactions and collision detection are handled automatically by the software. The game engine allows playback of content created by all modeling and animation tools in Blender. Game logic can be edited with a GUI or can be scripted using the industry standard Python scripting language
- Blender can be used to create commercials and other broadcast quality content, as well as multimedia and interactive 3D content for PCs and workstations

3. EXAMPLES/SAMPLES

- Image Gallery from the Blender Website: http://www.blender.nl/gallery/index.php
- More images made by Blender: http://www.medialab.chalmers.se/people/jmo/blender/

4. FUNCTIONS

- Modeling:
  - Objects: spline, polygonal, parametric, NURBS, subdivision surfaces
  - Transformation: translation, rotation, scaling, cloning, mirror, and spacing
- Rendering:
  - Camera: movable
  - Lights: attenuation, volumetric lighting, Phong, and flat shading, shadows
  - Materials: texturing, Bump mapping, alpha blending, multitexturing, complex 3D materials, reflective
  - Before and after rendering: antialiasing, motion blur, fog, environment maps, shadowing, compositing/video editing
- Animation:
  - Controllers: key-based, procedural, compound, system
  - Advanced animations: trajectory, ghosting, pivot point, morphing, space warps, character animation, motion, blurBasic Animation
- File Formats:
  - Importing file formats: BLEND, JPG, TGA, VRML, DXF
  - Exporting file formats: BLEND, JPG, AVI, VRML, DXF

5. WEB RESOURCES

- Blender Learning Path: http://www.blender.nl/support/learning.php#learningpath
- Blender Knowledge base: http://helium.homeip.net/support/browse.php
- Blender fan site: http://www.blendermania.com/
- Iceman tutorial index: http://205.152.62.12/gruff/
- Raysite, a blender user with information about the product: http://www.rash.f2s.com/
- Fan site with tutorials: http://www.blendedplanet.com/
- Blender artist site: http://www.rocket3d.com/

Blueberry 3D

1. PLATFORMS, PRICES, AND SUPPLIER/CREATOR

- Windows 95/98/2000/NT
- Blueberry3D Viz $2490 U.S.; Price for Blueberry3D TE and Blueberry3D GE are not available
- Sjöland and Thyselius: http://www.st.se/; http://www.blueberry3d.com/

2. APPLICATIONS

- Interactive modeling and visualization of detailed 3D terrain. Blueberry3D is an advanced tool with which user can design and create their own virtual landscape or automatically generate it from real map data. Where the resolution of the map data is limited, Blueberry3D uses mathematical fractals to extend the data and create smaller details automatically. Coarse terrain-class rasters are sufficient to create terrain in which every leaf of all trees is visible.

3. EXAMPLES/SAMPLES

- http://www.blueberry3d.com/Gallery.html

4. FUNCTIONS

- High detail level
- Large areas — small database
- Scalability
- Powerful terrain design
- Unique terrain
- Beautiful roads
- Advanced physics engine

5. WEB RESOURCES

- http://www.st.se/blueberry/applications.html
- http://www.blueberry3d.com/

BMRT (Blue Moon Rendering Tools)

1. PLATFORMS, PRICE, AND SUPPLIER

- IRIX 6.x, Solaris/SunOS, Windows, Linux, DEC OSF1
- BMRT is free for all uses
- Larry Gritz: http://www.bmrt.org/ (Blue Moon Rendering Tools)

2. APPLICATIONS

- Furnishes a completely implemented renderer of the Pixar RenderMan Interface. Although the rendering tools include basic rendering, scan-line rendering and OpenGL rendering, the most exciting part of the BMRT is its ability to render using the cutting-edge techniques of radiosity and ray tracing

3. EXAMPLES/SAMPLES

- http://www.exluna.com/products/gallery
- http://rhinoman.renderology.com/gallery.html
- http://www.k-3d.com/gallery/
- http://www.k-3d.com/gallery/old/images.html
- http://www.linuxgazette.com/issue17/more-musings.html
- http://www.renderman.org/RMR/rmBlockers/uber/index.html
- http://ourworld.compuserve.com/homepages/scorpius/bmrt.htm

4. FUNCTIONS

- Modeling:
  - Objects: planar convex polygons, general planar concave polygons with holes, collections of planar convex or general planar concave polygons with holes which share vertices (polyhedra), bilinear patches and patch meshes, bicubic patches and patch meshes with an arbitrary basis, non-uniform rational B-spline surfaces of arbitrary degree (NURBS), quadric surfaces, torii, and disks. SOURCE: http://www.pixar.com/products/renderman/toolkit/RISpec/section5.html
  - Transformation: Transform, ConcatTransform, Perspective, Translate, Rotate, Scale, Skew, Projection SOURCE: http://www.pixar.com/products/renderman/toolkit/RISpec/section6.html
- Rendering:
  - Cameras: adjustable, movable

- Lights: ambient, diffuse, specular, Phong, distantlight pointlight, spotlight, area light sources
- Materials: constant, matte, metal, shinymetal, plastic, painted plastic
- More materials: texture mapping, bump mapping, environment mapping, cube mapping, shadow mapping
- Before and after rendering: fog, depth queue

- File Formats:

  - Programing formats: C (Renderman API), SL (Shading Language)
  - Pencil-Test format: RBI

5. WEB RESOURCES

- www.pixar.com/products/renderman/toolkit/Toolkit/index.html
  [Pixar's Renderman Interface Spec]

- http://users.info.unicaen.fr/~karczma/docs/bmrtdoc/rayserver.html
  [talks about using PRMAN instead of BMRT for rendering]

- http://www.project-borg.org/
  [LITERALLY: BMRT rendering GUI organization]

- http://www.k-3d.com/k3d/index.html
  [Site for K-3D's modeling tool for BMRT rendering]

- http://www.rhino3d.com/bmrt.htm
  [Site for Rhino's modeling tool for BMRT rendering]

- http://www.faqs.org/faqs/graphics/renderman-faq/
  [Monthly Renderman/BRMT FAQ Postings]

- http://www.vidi.com/bmrt/bmrt.html
  [3D Joy can use BMRT with a Renderman plug-in]

Body Paint 3D

1. PLATFORMS, PRICES, AND SUPPLIER/CREATOR

- Windows 95/98/ME/NT/2000, or Macintosh OS 7.61+

- $595.00

- Maxon (German company): http://www.maxoncomputer.com

2. APPLICATIONS

- Tool for creating high-quality detailed textures. Body Paint is more than a Photoshop, it's a painter as well. Body Paint 3D eliminates the arduous task of placing textures by guesswork and bringing various material channels into harmony with each other. Artists can paint and draw directly onto 3D objects and see the results immediately

3. EXAMPLES/SAMPLES

- Gallery for Body Paint 3D:
  - Raybrush Reflection:
    http://www.maxoncomputer.com/product/bp-features/pics_hires/raybrush_reflection.jpg
  - Fisch collage:
    http://www.maxoncomputer.com/product/bp-features/pics_hires/fisch_collage.jpg
  - Kopfcollage:
    http://www.maxoncomputer.com/product/bp-features/pics_hires/kopfcollage.jpg
  - Zombi screenshot:
    http://www.maxoncomputer.com/product/bp-features/pics_hires/zombi_auge_screenshot.jpg
  - Exhaust_rusty:
    http://www.maxoncomputer.com/product/bp-features/pics_hires/exhaust_rusty.jpg
  - Customizable Interface:
    http://www.planet3dart.com/features/2001_1/bodypaint3d/CustomizableInterface.jpg
  - Birdy screenshot:
    http://www.planet3dart.com/features/2001_1/bodypaint3d/birdy_screenshot.jpg

4. FUNCTIONS

- Modeling:
  - Objects: polygon, sphere, NURBS, cylinder, planar, cube
  - Transformation: array, move, scale, rotate, shear, resize, distort
  - Editing and manipulations (vertex, edge, face, polygon, curves, objects): Raybrush, eyedropper tools, edit points or polygons, dragnet tools, tiling U/V, interactive mapping (planar, cylindrical, spherical, box, shrink, frontal, spatial, analytical mapping), hierarchical navigation
- Rendering:
  - Cameras: adjustable, movable
  - Lights: shadow, tube, three-point lighting
  - Optical effects: len flares, reflectivity, bump, transparency, specularity paint, color, environment, motion blur, glow, shine, opacity, smooth, shadow

    – Materials: ray trace, skin, woods, dirt, displacement, top/bottom, left/right, back/front, Cel-render mode, bump, specular color, luminence, diffusion, alpha

    – More materials: ray-traced maps, texture mapping, bump map, specular map, interactive mapping, optical mapping, optimal mapping

    – Before-and-after Rendering: layer, blending modes, motion blur, smooth, wireframe rendering, antialiasing, filter, isoparms

- Animation:

    – Controllers: keyframe, mouse

    – Advanced animations: soft and rigid body dynamics, skeletal deformation, blend channels, blur (motion, gaussian, radial)

    – Basic animation: graph, programmatic (C.O.F.F.E.E similar to C++ language or JAVA)

- File Formats:

    – Importing file formats: C4D, OBJ, 3DS, QD3D, VRML 1&2, LWO/LWS, DXF

    – Exporting file formats: C4D, OBJ, 3DS, QD3D, VRML 1&2, DXF

5. WEB RESOURCES

- Review: http://www.digitmag.co.uk/reviews/display_review.cfm?ReviewID=65

- http://www.maxoncomputer.com/product/art-features/features.html

- Internet Eye3D: http://www.interneteye3d.com/Reviews2001/Feb/BodyPaintMac/

- Planet 3D Art: http://www.planet3dart.com/sections.php?op=viewarticle&artid=25

- Body Paint 3D in Mac: http://www.critical-depth.com/reviews/bpmac/bpmac-review.html

- Body Paint 3D in PC: http://www.critical-depth.com/reviews/bppc/bppc-review.html

Breeze Designer

1. PLATFORMS, PRICES, AND SUPPLIER/CREATOR

- PC (Windows 95, 98, 2000, and NT)

- Freeware

- http://www.imagos.fl.net.au

2. APPLICATIONS

- Breeze Designer is a 32-bit 3D model and design tool for Windows platform. The program has been written to interface primarily with the Persistance of Vision Raytracer (POV-Ray version 2.0 and 3.0), there is also support to export to a number of other popular renderers including Pixars's RenderMan

3. EXAMPLES/SAMPLES

- http://www.imagos.fl.net.au/breeze/bdload.htm
- http://www.imagos.fl.net.au/breeze/gallery.htm

4. FUNCTIONS

- Modeling:
    - Modeling primitives; cube, sphere, cone, cylinder, torus, bicubic "Bezier" patches
    - Text objects using TrueType fonts
- Rendering:
    - Render and view from within program
    - Isosurfaces; blobs (metaballs)
    - Heightfields, spline paths and extruded shapes
    - Surfaces of revolution (sweeps)
    - Object grouping with CSG support
    - Keyframe animation support, with tween function and spline paths
    - Transition position, scale, and rotation between frames
- Architecture:
    - Multiple model views and zoom factors
    - Built-in macro language
    - Built-in texture builder
    - Built-in shaded preview
- File Formats:
    - Import Autodesk 3D-Studio 3DS format models
    - Import AutoCAD 2D and 3D DXF files
    - Export POV Raytracer, RenderMan RIB, VRML scene, Polyray, AutoCAD DXF
    - Support for OpenGL with texture mapping for Windows NT, Windows 95/98
    - Online help and tool tips support
    - Third party plug-in module support

5. WEB RESOURCES

- http://www.unrealized.com/main/
  tools.html?display_section=Modeling#921640246

- http://www.povray.org/ftp/pub/povray/utilities/modellers/breeze/BreezeDesigner.html
- http://www.mirco-schoel.de/bryce/tools_e.htm#breeze

Bryce 3D

1. PLATFORMS, PRICE, AND SUPPLIER/CREATOR

- PC (Windows 9x/NT), Mac (PowerMac)
- $199 for Corel Bryce 4.0
- Corel (Bryce formerly distributed by MetaCreations): http://www.corel.com/

2. APPLICATIONS

- Bryce is a 3D environmental rendering, modeling, and animation tool primarily used for creating and rendering landscapes and various realistic terrain/water/skies to be used in conjunction with other products, such as Photoshop, RayDream, etc. This tool can also be used for creating panoramic videos of the 3D scene using QuickTime. The easy interface of Bryce allows for photorealistic scenery to be created by novice-to-advanced users

3. EXAMPLES/SAMPLES

- http://members.nbci.com:80/coyotz/html/main.html
- http://www.navpoint.com/~steve/gallery.html
- http://www.metasynth.com/BRYCEART/PAGES/galleryBryce.html

4. FUNCTIONS

- Modeling:
  - Objects: 3D Primitives, fractal terrain meshes, pre-defined terrain objects
  - Transformation: translation (Reposition), rotation (Rotate), scaling (Resize), clone (Copy/Paste)
  - Editing and Manipulations: vertex manipulation (to perform transformation), Group, scatter (Disperse)
- Rendering:
  - Camera: position movable
  - Lights: shadow, radial light, spotlight, square spotlight, parallel light

- Materials: Texture mapping, bump-mapping, predefined or importable material textures
- Render: Anti-aliased, Ray traced

- Animation:

  - Keyframe based
  - Quicktime Movie or QTVR for repositioned camera

- File Formats:

  - Import
  - 3D Formats: 3D Studio (.PRJ)/(.3DS); AutoCAD (.DXF); Direct X 3D (.X); Heightfield (.HF); Haines and WTK (.NFF); LightWave (.LWO)/(.LWS); Portable Greyscale Map (.PGM); TrueSpace (.COB)/(.SCN); USGS DEM (.DEM); USGS SDTS (.DDF); VideoScape (.VSA); VistaPro DEM (.DEM); VRML1 (.WRL); Wavefront (.OBJ); World Construction Set (.ELEV)
  - 2D Formats: BMP; JPEG; PICT; Adobe Photoshop; Targa; TIFF
  - Export
  - 3D Formats (Textured Terrain Objects): 3D Studio (.3DS); AutoCad (.DXF); DirectX 3D (.X); Heightfield (.HF); Haines and WTK (.NFF); Infini-D 4.0 (.ID4); LightWave (.LWO)/(.LWS); MetaStream; Portable Greyscale Map (.PGM); RayDream Studio (.RDS); RayShade Height Field Export; trueSpace (.COB); USGS DEM (.DEM); VideoScape (.VSA); VRML1 (.WRL); Wavefront (.OBJ)
  - 2D Formats: BMP; Adobe Photoshop; PICT; TIFF
  - Plug-Ins allow for more formats

5. WEB RESOURCES

- http://www.watchfuleye.com/bryce.html

- http://easyweb.easynet.co.uk/~jba/br/brframe.html

- http://www.ruku.com/bryce1.html

- http://www.geocities.com/SoHo/Gallery/2780/linkstutorial.html

- http://www.3dlinks.com/tutorials_bryce.cfm

- http://www.halcyon.com/alrives/brycetips/

Calimax

1. PLATFORMS, PRICE, AND SUPPLIER/CREATOR

- Windows platform
- Calimax is Freeware

- Individually made by Andreas Koepke: http://www.calimax.de/english/Index.htm

2. APPLICATIONS

- Calimax Modeller is a 32-bit 3D modeling tool for Windows 95 and NT 4.0. It gives you an easy-to-use graphical user interface for interactive modeling scenes for the Persistance of Vision Raytracer (POV-Ray version 2.0 and 3.0)

3. EXAMPLES/SAMPLES

- Samples from Calimax homepage:
  http://www.calimax.de/images/chess.jpg
  http://www.calimax.de/images/fog4.jpg

4. FUNCTIONS

- Finite solid primitives

- Infinite solid primitives

- Built-in texture editor

- Light source

- Constructive solid geometry

- Camera

- Environment

- Halo

- In/output (extension *.cm)
    - the fileformat is compatible with POV Ray. but Calimax Modeller reads files written with the Calimax Modeller itself only
    - pov 2.x style
    - pov 3.0 style* (different #include section)
    - It is possible to save and load single parts of a scene, so that a scene can be a collection of several predefined scene scripts

5. WEB RESOURCES

- 3D Animation Utilities: http://www.povray.org/links/3D_Animation_Utilities/

- FAQS: http://www.povray.org/links/3D_Magazines_Lists_and_FAQ's/

Carrara Studio (RayDream and Infini-D)

1. PLATFORMS, PRICES, AND SUPPLIER/CREATOR

- PC and Macintosh
- $349.99
- MetaCreations: http://www.metacreations.com/;
  now Eovia, a TGS company: http://www.eovia.com/

2. APPLICATIONS

- Carrara studio is a complete 3D solution for modeling, shading, scene building, animation, rendering, and special effects. It is built for the creative professional who is advancing into the world of 3D. In addition to all the normal tasks a 3D modeler can accomplish, this software package can create 3D static images and generate VRML for use in Website development, etc.
- Because the best features of the Infini-D and RayDream products were incorporated into Carrara, those two products have been discontinued and will no longer be supported

3. EXAMPLES/SAMPLES

- Wolfgang's 3D gallery: http://www.wolfdd.org/3dgallery01.html

4. FUNCTIONS

- Modeling:
  - Objects: spline, vertex, text, terrain, formula
  - Transformation: translation, rotation, scaling, cloning, align, array, mirror, and spacing
  - Editing and manipulations (spline): center, fill, break apart, ghost, group, ungroup
  - Editing and manipulations (vertex): weld, link, unlink, deform, subdivide, ghost, magnet (append to various objects)
  - Editing and manipulations (text): depth, alignment, scaling, spacing
  - Editing and manipulations (terrain): erode, raise, invert, smooth
- Rendering:
  - Cameras: adjustable, movable
  - Lights: directional, spot, ambient, animatable, angular cutoff, shadow, soft shadow, pulsating
  - Materials: shading, highlight, layer list, shininess, texture mapping, color, transparency, glow
  - More materials: preprogrammed maps, procedural mapping
  - Extra control: antialiasing frames and lines, motion blur, fog

- Animation:
  - Particle system: bound, free, lifetime, velocity, emit duration, freeze, bounce, gravity, angle, friction
  - Atomize, bend, explode, dissolve, shatter, shear
  - Animation options: physics-based, procedural-based; align, slide, oscillate
- File Formats:
  - Importing file formats: RDS, DXF, OBJ, 3DMF, 3DS
  - Exporting file formats: DXF, OBJ, 3DMF, VRML 2, MTS (MetaStream, a MetaCreations format), 3DS
  - 2D file format import: GIF, JPEG, PICT (MAC), BMP, PCX
  - 2D file format export: GIF, JPEG, PICT (MAC), BMP, PCX

5. WEB RESOURCES

- Book review: http://the-internet-eye.com/reviews2000/Jul/CarraraBible/default.htm

- Book: http://www.netstoreusa.com/cbbooks/076/0764506560.shtml

- Review on Carrara: http://maccentral.macworld.com/news/9908/31.carrara.shtml

CINEMA 4D XL

1. PLATFORM, PRICES, AND SUPPLIER/CREATOR

- PC

- $1695

- Maxon Computer Inc.: http://www.maxon.net

2. APPLICATIONS

- 3D modeling, animation and rendering

3. EXAMPLES/SAMPLES

- 3D Links Gallery Index for Cinema 4D: http://maxon.net/usa/index.html

- 3D Links Gallery on related tools: http://www.3dlinks.com/gallerylinks.cfm

4. FUNCTIONS

- Modeling:

- Objects: Hyper NURBS, Instances with hierarchies and animation, Metaballs/Metasplines/Metaparticles, Symmetry
- Transformation: modification, rotation, scaling, move variation, align, spacing, mirror, optimize, subsidize, triagulate
- Editing and manipulations: Matrix extrude, new deformation object (bend, twist, bulge, shear), Inner and outer distance, radius control

- Rendering:

  - Sound: 2D/3D sound rendering including Doppler effect, microphone object, loudspeaker object, customizable sound
  - Lights: shadow, volumetric noise, colored edge falloff, inner and outer color control
  - Materials: asynchronous material dialog, directly available procedure shaders
  - More materials: color/texture per channel mixing with transitions, textures supported in OpenGL, mapping modes MIP and SAT
  - Multiprocessor rendering with near-scale performance, materials per polygon, multiple render setting per document

- Animation:

  - Live expressions, interactive expressions, layer system, hide and lock, multiple selection in timeline, Lasso selection, motion grouping, sound display, power slider, parameter recording

- Interface:

  - Customizable: layouts, keyboard shortcuts, icon, palettes, view windows, dialogues
  - Navigation tools: move, scale, rotation handles

5. WEB RESOURCES

- A list of resources on the net: http://www.senduptheflares.com

- A PC Magazine article: http://www.cinema4d.com/stuff/cebit2001.html

ClayWorks

1. PLATFORMS, PRICE, AND SUPPLIER/CREATOR

- PC DOS/Windows

- Free

- Tim Lewis: http://www.clayworks3d.com/clay/index.html

2. APPLICATIONS

- A 3D modeling and rendering tool

3. EXAMPLES/SAMPLES:

- http://www.clayworks3d.com/clay/screens.html

4. FUNCTIONS

- Modeling:
  - Objects: spline, polygonal, parametric, and metaball primitives
- Interface:
  - Highly flexible, custom interface
  - Services offered: clipboard and drag and drop

5. WEB RESOURCES

- http://www.clayworks3d.com/clay/index.html

Corel Dream 3D

1. PLATFORMS, PRICE, AND SUPPLIER/CREATOR

- Corel Dream 3D is available with Corel Draw on Windows and Macintosh systems
- $$$$
- Corel Corporation: http://www.corel.com/

2. APPLICATIONS

- Corel Dream 3D is a spline-based 3D modeling and rendering package

3. EXAMPLES/SAMPLES

- CorelDream 3D: http://www.3dshop.com/cgi-bin/Gallery/show?Vehicle=99
- http://library.thinkquest.org/29033/create/creating.htm

4. WEB RESOURCES

- http://www.corelmag.com/ADS/dremprom.html

- http://www.corel.com/products/graphicsandpublishing/draw8/dream3d.htm

Cosmo Create

1. PLATFORMS, PRICES, AND SUPPLIER/CREATOR
- SGI workstation (IRIX 6.5 or higher); ports for other platforms available
- $$$$
- SGI: http://www.sgi.com/software/cosmo/create.html

2. APPLICATIONS
- Cosmo Create is a modeling tool that combines 3D and 2D modeling, animation, multimedia, user interaction, VRML and HTML authoring, and WWW posting together in one package

3. EXAMPLES/SAMPLES
- A link page to galleries: http://illustration.inaustralia.com/links.html
- Computer Associate's gallery: http://cosmosoftware.com/galleries/

4. WEB RESOURCES
- A complete tutorial: http://www.uvigo.es/servicios/atic/seinv/manuais/cosmocreate/
- A review: http://ipw.internet.com/clients_servers/vrml/916162499.html

Cosmo Worlds

1. PLATFORMS, PRICES, AND SUPPLIER/CREATOR
- SGI workstation, IRIX 6.2 operating system or better with 64 MB; Windows version available
- List Price: $$$$; SGI workstation system can apply for one year temporary license for free

- SGI: http://www.sgi.com

2. APPLICATIONS

- Modeling: replicating, stretching, scaling, combining tools are provided. You can import existing geometry, choose a model from a vast library coming with the system, or create your own shapes from scratch. Animation: you can easily achieve animation by setting key frames — the system animator tool automatically interpolates the rest (many interpolating algorithms are provided). In the animation, you can also set proximity sensors, collision detectors, or other lifelike interactive behaviors with the integrated script editor so that you design your animation easily and conveniently

3. WEB RESOURCES

- http://www.sgi.com/software/cosmo/worlds.html
- http://www.zdnet.com/pcmag/firstlooks/9805/f980515a2.htm
- http://www.hiddenline.com/wireframe/word/grotto/cosmoworlds-tutorial.html

CRYONICS

1. PLATFORM, PRICE, AND SUPPLIER/CREATOR

- PC
- $30
- Cryonetwork: http://207.87.26.15/cryonics.htm; http://www.cto.it/Games/mdonetworks/cryonics/cryonics.htm; or http://www.mdnetworks.it/cryonics.htm

2. APPLICATIONS

- Cryonics is a tool to implement interactive 3D websites and virtual worlds, and to receive cyber-visitors in the form of 3D avatars
- Visitors will be able to meet through the 3D avatars, communicate among themselves by means of chat, talk, listen and organize games, all in real time
- Cryonics is intended for anyone who wants to build a virtual 3D space and share it with Web surfers. Users can chat, communicate, interchange, view, show, listen, create links, organize games — all in real time

3. EXAMPLES/SAMPLES

- Cryopolis: http://www.cryopolis.com/
- Cathédrale: http://artdelespace3d.ifrance.com/artdelespace3d/html/cathedrale.html
- Dessin 3D: http://le-village.ifrance.com/cryonic3000/dessin3d.htm
- Odissea: http://www.ctonet.it/giochi/cryonics.php
- Cryonics 3D: http://www.elecplay.com/reviewfull_333.html
- Cryopolis: http://www.cryopolis.com/

4. WEB RESOURCES

- 3D News: http://www.3dsite.com/n/sites/3dsite/newsletter/issues/11/sec5.html
- The cutting edge: http://www.webresort.net/bgezal/pictures.shtml
- Software Programming: http://www.softguide.de/prog_r/pr_0506.htm
- Some Facts About Cryonics: http://sites.netscape.net/shootingstar170/cryonics
- StradaNove: http://www.stradanove.net/news/testi/cybernews-00a/yasom0302004.html
- A convivial community: http://164.109.24.241/Cryopolis.com_eng/habiter.htm
- Philip K. Dick's *Ubik*: http://web1.interplay.com/ubik/
- Related Link: http://www.cryo-interactive.de/links.html

Crossroads

1. PLATFORMS, PRICES, AND SUPPLIER/CREATOR

- Windows 95 or Windows NT 4.0
- Freeware
- Keithr: http://home.europa.com/~keithr/

2. APPLICATIONS

- 3D file format conversion utility for Windows 95 and Windows NT

3. EXAMPLES/SAMPLES

- http://www.sun.com/jiro/enabled/mf/crossroads/crossroadsconsanmf.html

- http://www.crossroads.com/products/scsi/

4. FUNCTIONS

- Modeling:
    - Use of a geometry engine that can convert CSG, and other complicated primitives into polygons
    - Enable key Internet, Intranet, and e-commerce applications
    - Effectively and efficiently store, manage, and ensure the integrity and availability of the data
- Rendering:
    - A Direct X writer
    - A Lightwave reader/writer
    - An Imagine reader/writer
    - Better support for finding surface normals
    - Bitmap texture support
    - Rendered Preview
- File Formats:
    - Supported Import Formats: 3D Studio (3DS), 3DMF ASCII (T3D), 3DMF Binary (B3D), AutoCAD (DXF), "C" code, Direct X, Imagine, Lightwave, Megahedron (SMPL), POVRay V2.2, POVRay V3.0, RAW Triangle, TrueSpace (cob), VRML (V1.0), VRML (V2.0), Wavefront (obj), WorldToolkit (nff)

5. WEB RESOURCES

- http://home.europa.com/~keithr/

- http://www.sun.com/jiro/enabled/mf/crossroads/

CrystalGraphics PowerPlugs

1. PLATFORMS, PRICES, AND SUPPLIER/CREATOR

- PCs using Windows NT/95/98/2000/ME — compatible with Microsoft PowerPoint 97 or 2000, and DirectX 5.0

- $$$

- Crystal Graphics http://www.crystalgraphics.com/corporate.profile.html

2. APPLICATIONS

- 3D graphics and animations tool used with Microsoft PowerPoint, presentations, webpages, and videos
- 3D effects for changing pages or screens and synchronized sound effects are built into transition slides

3. EXAMPLES/SAMPLES

- Drop In: http://www.crystalgraphics.com/images/products/3dsensations/ Drop_In.html
- Gallery: http://www.crystalgraphics.com/ products.powerplugs.transitions.volume1.3.html#
- Revolving Door: http://www.crystalgraphics.com/images/products/3dsensations/ Revolving_Door.html
- Slab Tilt: http://www.crystalgraphics.com/images/products/3dsensations/ Slab_Tilt.html
- Swing: http://www.crystalgraphics.com/images/products/3dsensations/ Swing.html
- Tumbling Away: http://www.crystalgraphics.com/images/products/3dsensations/ Tumbling_Away.html
- Web Hosting tool: http://webmaster.tophosts.com/html4/transitions.htm

4. WEB RESOURCES

- Press releases: http://www.crystalgraphics.com/corporate.press.html
- FAQs: http://www.crystalgraphics.com/ products.powerplugs.transitions.techfaq.html
- http://www.crystalgraphics.com/products.powerplugs.transitions.ownersclub.html

Cult3D

1. PLATFORMS, PRICES, AND SUPPLIER/CREATOR:

- PC: Windows 95/98/NT; Mac: MacOS (PPC); Other: BeOS R4, HP-UX 10.10, SunOs2.4, AIX 4.0

- Non-commercial uses: Free; for other types of license: http://www.cult3d.com/order/
- Cycore: http://www.cycore.com; For Cult3d website see: http://www.cult3d.com/

2. APPLICATIONS

- Cult3D helps create interactive objects on the Web. Objects can be imported from Maya, 3D Studio Max and 3D Studio Viz. Functionality, sound, animation and numerous effects can than be added to the objects. Companies selling items are able to create interactive 3D models of the objects for customers
- E-commerce — Gives clients a "feeling" for the product, by allowing them to interact with the product online. Example: http://www.palm.com/products/palmv/
- Distance learning — Turns training applications into interactive simulations
- Entertainment — Helps to attract customers to companies' websites by allowing these sites to host interactive 3D games. Example: http://www.lego.com/justbuild

3. EXAMPLES/SAMPLES

- http://www.worldof3d.com
- http://www.cult3d.com/gallery/index.html
- http://www.compaq.quokka.com/index2.html
- http://www.auran.com/koolthingz/trainz/visualz.htm
- http://www.dturf.com/c_cooldigs/cool_index.htm
- http://www.replicanation.com/library.html
- http://www.cult3d.com/3dsites/default.asp

4. FILE FORMATS

- Importing: 3D Studio Max, Alias Wavefront Maya, Strata 3D, and Image Modeler
- Exporting: c3d

5.   WEB RESOURCES

- http://www.cult3d.com/designers/pletMaya.pdf
- http://www.webreference.com/3d/lesson86/
- http://industry.java.sun.com/javanews/stories/print/0%2C1797%2C13474%2C00.html
- http://www.worldof3d.com/
- http://www.cult3d.com/howto/virtual.asp

CyberMotion 3D-Designer

1. PLATFORM, PRICE, SUPPLIER/CREATOR

- PC
- $89.00
- Reinhard Epp Software, Germany: http://www.3d-designer.com/index.html

2. APPLICATIONS

- CyberMotion 3D-Designer is a professional 3D tool for modeling, animation systems, and rendering 3D objects that includes a multiwindow graphical user interface, integrated 3D-modeler, ray tracer, particle systems with shadows, reflections and transparencies, and volumetric lighting. It can be used for many purposes, such as games, personal creativity, or even by authors to illustrate their ideas

3. SAMPLES/EXAMPLES

- http://www.3d-designer.com/en/galery/galery.htm#picture_galery
- http://www.3d-designer.com/en/galery/galery.htm#avi_galery

4. FUNCTIONS

- Modeling:
  - Objects: Build your own objects with the built-in editor for: extrude-, sweep-, spiral-, analytical-, functional-, fractal-, or text objects or just load file formats such as DXF or RAW
  - Editing and manipulation: There are tools for manipulating individual points and facets, such as delete or add points/facets, triangulate facets, magnetic deformation
- Ray Tracing:
  - Ray trace renderer: Create photorealistic images and animations with real refraction and shadows. Special effects, such as motion blur, depth-sharpness, atmosphere, real particle systems with shadows, reflections and transparencies, volumetric lighting, depth-sharpness, and lens and luminosity flares, can also be incorporated
- Materials:
  - Material editor: create your own surface, or modify from the libraries. Provides settings for colors, reflection, transparency, self-illumination, bitmap, bump map, and procedural textures
- Animations:

- Animated objects: each object can be animated including camera, lights, light effects like lens flares, background, and particle systems
- New key: a new key is generated automatically if an object is moved, scaled, rotated, or if the parameters of light or backgrounds are changed in any frame
- More complex animation, such as animated robots, skeletons, or joined human models

- Particle Systems:

  - Objects copying: Create one reference object for thousands of copies and animate them automatically, for example: explosions, snowfall, whirlwind, volcanic eruption, swarms of insects, birds, fishes, or water bubbles

- File Formats:

  - Import format: DXF or RAW format
  - Export format: VRML2.0 format

5. WEB RESOURCES

- http://www.3d-designer.com/en/links/links.htm

- http://www.3d-designer.com/en/news/news.htm

Deep Paint 3D

1. PLATFORMS, PRICES, AND SUPPLIER/CREATOR

- Windows NT 4.0, Windows 95, 98, and 2000

- $795.00

- Right Hemisphere: http://www.us.righthemisphere.com/

2. APPLICATIONS

- Deep Paint 3D is a 3D texturing and painting tool. It provides authentic artistic media — such as oils, watercolors, crayons, and pastels — which can be brushed directly onto 3D models. It is designed for film, television, game development, or Web design. Deep Paint 3D fits into existing work environments and provides a seamless workflow integration with 3D Studio Max, Maya, Softimage, Lightwave 3D. Other file formats supported for import and export are .OBJ/.MTL, .3DS, and .LWO. Complete with a bi-directional interface to Photoshop and special support for the Wacom Intuos or compatible pressure sensitive tablet.

3. EXAMPLES/SAMPLES

- Deep Paint 3D and Texture Weapons Gallery Artists:
  http://www.us.righthemisphere.com/gallery/deep_paint_3d_gallery.htm
- Still images:
  http://www.dynamic-realities.com/gallery/index.html
- Examples:
  http://www.us.deeppaint3d.com/gallery/deep_paint_3d_gallery.htm
- Wonderful Demonstration of the product:
  http://www.the-internet-eye.com/HOWTO/1999/dpposertut/
- Example:
  http://www.critical-depth.com/dp3d-review-3.html
- http://www.planet3dart.com/features/
  feature.php?year_month=2000_6&article=deeppaint3d&page=2
- Example from The Deep Paint webpage that illustrates the progression from
  model to the final painted object: http://www.us.deeppaint3d.com/gallery/
  dpaint3d/bill_fleming/bf_frankievo.jpg

4. FEATURES

- Tool for 2D and 3D Artists:
  Deep Paint 3D plugs into Photoshop, making it a fully-functional 2D and 2.5D
  professional artistic paint system

  - Deep Paint 3D supports other Photoshop plug-ins
  - Artistic Tools: True airbrush; Oils; Watercolors; Colored and charcoal pencils;
    Felt pens; Chalks; Pastels; Gouache; Acrylics; Impasto; Textures
- Artistic and Industrial Design Rendering:

  - By using the familiar Photoshop layer concept with variable opacity settings,
    users can trace or clone up from layers below to create new art from existing
    photographs or images. Deep Paint 3D is ideal for architects and industrial
    designers wishing to create painterly artistic product or concept renderings
- Standard Features Include:

  - Seamless workflow with Softimage, 3D Studio Max, and Maya plug-ins and a
    2-way material-to-Photoshop link
  - Color, bump, shine and glow effects rendered in real time as you paint
  - Paint up to 5 material channels with paint or textures simultaneously
  - Multilayer support for bump, color, shine, opacity, and glow channels
  - Smooth airbrush, oil, watercolor, charcoal, colored pencils, felt pens, chalks,
    pastels, gouache, acrylics, impasto, texture, and image paints
  - Photoshop plug-in filter support
  - Create and save your own texture And image paints
  - 2D and 2½D paint mode with UV unwrapping

  - Paint across multiple materials and objects
  - Dynamic 3D zoom, pan, and rotate
  - 3D masking and selection tools, including a 3D polygon selection tool
  - Line, circle, polygon, and text tools
  - Advanced undo capability

5. WEB RESOURCES

- An article: http://www.digitalanimators.com/HTM/Reviews/PamR/Pam_deeppaint1.htm

- Review in Dynamic Realities: http://www.dynamic-realities.com/products/deeppaint3D/

- http://www.us.deeppaint3d.com/dpaint3d/product_information.htm

- Planet3D: http://www.planet3dart.com/features/feature.php?year_month=2000_6&article=deeppaint3d&page=2

DesignCAD 3000

1. PLATFORMS, PRICE, AND SUPPLIER/CREATOR

- Windows 95, 98, Millennium, NT 4.0, and 2000 systems

- $299.95

- UPPERSPACE: http://www.upperspace.com/

2. APPLICATIONS

- Animation, Solid Modeling, Integrated 2D/3D modes, and other features allow the user to create complex and detailed presentations

- DesignCAD 3000 is used primarily in professional engineering, drafting, and architectural applications; also used as a personal CAD system for casual and household drawings

3. EXAMPLE/SAMPLES

- http://img.cmpnet.com/windows/reviews/software/2000/11/DESCAD1.gif

- http://www.comeplan.be/Flamand/designcad.htm

- http://www.designcad.com/

- http://www.designcad.com/gallery/gallery.htm

4. FUNCTIONS

- Modeling:

  - Objects: polygonal, patch, spline curve, lines, circles, planes, spheres, cylinders, cones, and so on
  - Transformation: scaling, rotation, align, array, cloning, mirror, and slice
  - Features: Insert door and window, Double line mode, Snap locator, Tangent snap, Chamfer command, Section copy command, Ortho mode toggle, Trim multiple lines, Slice by curved surface, Expanded solid operations, Enhanced spiraling, Hide/shade all views, Cut corner command, Cut edge command, Walk-through mode
  - Editing and manipulations (solid objects and surfaces): stacking, booleans, snap, grid, point selection, slice, solid subtraction, union, intersection, interference checking, curved surface, linear extrusion, extrusion along a curve, circular sweep, patches, trim, scale, fillet, and the "hammer" command

- Rendering:

  - Cameras: movable, adjustable
  - Lights: ambient lighting, multiple independent light sources, volumetric lighting, three levels of shading including flat, Gouraud, and Phong
  - Materials: wireframe, hidden line, Entity tree, Dimension text
  - Additional materials: 3D walk-through animation with recorded AVI files, textures, realistic 3D texture mapping, anti-aliasing, hidden line removal

- Animation:

  - Controllers: model and viewpoint, key frames, procedural, system
  - Advanced animation: animation fluid movement can be observed, rotate a crankshaft, show pistons pumping up and down, detailed construction process
  - Basic animation

- Customization:

  - Write, develop, and execute programs with BasicCAD
  - Record and execute timesaving macros
  - New OLE interface is improved and twice as fast as DesignCAD 97
  - Customize keyboard shortcuts for any menu command or executable file
  - Customizable with Microsoft Visual Basic and Visual C++
  - Developer's Kit available for creating special features and functions

- Direct scanner support:

  - Enables users to scan documents and place them into drawings as bitmaps. Auto Trace command can be used to convert the bitmaps into vectors for direct incorporation into a drawing

- File Formats:

  - Importing file formats: DXF, DWG, IGS, WMF, HPGL, XYZ
  - Exporting file formats: DXF, DWG, IGS, RIB, VRML, WPG, WMF
  - Load image file formats: JPG, BMP, TIF, TGA, PCX, Photoshop, Macintosh Picture, Kodak Photo Image, Windows Metafile, PNG, WPG, EPS, AWD
  - Export animations created in DesignCAD: AVI, VRML

5. WEB RESOURCES

- http://www.designcad.com/press/productinfo.htm
- http://www.winmag.com/reviews/software/2000/11/1121.htm
- http://www.cadonline.com/features/1100budgetcad/design.htm
- http://www.etracks.com/consumer/ID/UP-DCADPRO3.shtml
- http://www.comeplan.be/Flamand/nouveautes.htm
- http://www.engineeringzones.com/3dcad.htm
- http://downloads.excite.ca/business/adnload/132685_46104.html
- http://brightnet.office.tucows.com/preview/132683.html
- http://www.designcad.com/press/DC3KPR.HTM

DesignStudio 9.5

1. PLATFORMS, PRICES, AND SUPPLIER/CREATOR

- Platforms: Windows NT, Windows 2000, IRIX, Sun Solaris
- $5495.00
  - Normal price: $15,000
  - Product Support: $2,200 (includes free updates every 6 months)
  - Student version: $995/year (http://www.journeyed.com; 1800-874-9001 x316)
- Alias|Wavefront: http://www.aliaswavefront.com/en/Home/homepage.html

2. APPLICATIONS

- DesignStudio is a powerful suite of 3D software, used for design and styling in the automotive, marine, aircraft, sporting equipment, children's toy, and fashion accessory markets. Package includes tools to aid in many aspects of styling and design projects, such as sketching, 2D/3D integration, surface modeling, visualization, rendering, and animation

3. EXAMPLES/SAMPLES

- http://www.cadserver.co.uk/common/viewer/archive/2000/Apr/10/feature3.phtm
- http://www.cadonline.com/spectrum/spotlight/1100dspot/1100dspot.htm
- http://aw.aliaswavefront.com/design/features/ds_eval/pages/get_eval/index_02.html

4. WEB RESOURCES

- HighEnd3d: http://www.highend3d.com
- CadServer: http://www.cadserver.co.uk/
- MCADVision: http://www.mcadcafe.com/MCADVision/feature/Trends.html

DESIGN WORKSHOP PRO

1. PLATFORMS, PRICE, AND SUPPLIER/CREATOR

- PC, Macintosh
- $$$$
- Artifice, Inc.: http://www.artifice.com/dw_pro.html

2. APPLICATIONS

- 3D CAD modeling, rendering, and animation tool (using QuickDraw and other packages like Visionair Builder) that includes generating polygonal objects, curve surfaced objects, and particle systems with advanced rendering and animation options. It allows for walkthroughs of 3D models and gives interior and outdoor light sources and automatic texture mapping. It has been used for many purposes, including special effects in films and advertisements, and complex object in virtual environments

3. EXAMPLES/SAMPLES

- http://www.artifice.com/gallery.html
- http://www.designcommunity.com/user_gallery.html

4. WEB RESOURCES

- http://www.zdnet.com/downloads/stories/info/0,,000U25,.html
- http://www.ms2000.co.uk/acatalog/MyCOM_Online_Store_Design_WorkShop_247.html
- http://archivue.net/atelier/TECHNIQUE/Outils/Artifice/Artifice.htm (in French, but has some pictures as well)
- Book: http://www.amazon.com/exec/obidos/ASIN/0201700883/o/qid=985812964/sr=8-1/ref=aps_sr_b_1_1/104-0556238-9238303

DICE

1. PLATFORMS, PRICE, AND SUPPLIER/CREATOR

- UNIX, Windows 95/ NT
- None (Government Application)
- Army Research Laboratory: http://www.arl.hpc.mil/SciVis/dice/

2. APPLICATIONS

- The Distributed Interactive Computing Environment (DICE) is a toolkit that helps build applications from existing codes. Dice is composed of three major sections: data organization, runtime visualization, and graphical user interface tools

3. EXAMPLES/SAMPLES

- DICE Interface Example: http://www.arl.hpc.mil/SciVis/dice/Examples

4. WEB RESOURCES

- Developing a full featured application from an existing code using DICE: http://www.arl.hpc.mil/SciVis/dice/Publications/dice98.pdf
- The Visualization Toolkit — VTK homepage: http://www.kitware.com/vtk.html
- Emulating Shared Memory to Simplify Distributed-Memory Programming (NDGM): http://computer.org/cse/cs1997/c1055abs.htm

Director 8.5 Shockwave Studio

1. PLATFORMS, PRICES, AND SUPPLIER/CREATOR

- Windows 95/98/NT/2000; Mac OS 8.1 and above
- $1,199, full version; upgrade $199
- Macromedia, Inc.: http://www.macromedia.com/

2. APPLICATION

- Enables user to develop content and interactive media on the Web, CDs and DVDs

3. EXAMPLES/SAMPLES

- http://dynamic.macromedia.com/bin/MM/showcase/scripts/ showcase_cs_listing_by_query.jsp?product=Director%20Shockwave%20Studio Macromedia Director Shockwave Studio Showcase
- http://www.shockingtheweb.com/ Guide to programming Shockwave
- http://www.splashworks.com/ splashworks.com

4. FILE FORMATS

- 3D Import: W3D, OBJ
- 3D Export: W3D, OBJ
- 2D Import: GIF, BMP, TGA, AVI, FLC, JPG, DIB, AI, PS, EPS, PNG, DDS
- 2D Export: BMP, TGA, AVI, JPG, TIFF, PNG

5. WEB RESOURCES

- http://www.macromedia.com/software/director/Official Page
- http://www.macromedia.com/shockwave/ Macromedia Shockwave
- http://www.openswf.org OpenSWF — information about the SWF file format
- http://www.shockfusion.com Shockfusion
- http://www.shockwave.com/ Shockwave.com

DirectX (Dirct3D)

1. PLATFORMS, PRICE, AND SUPPLIER/CREATOR

- Microsoft Windows 95/98/NT/2000
- Free
- Microsoft: http://www.microsoft.com/directx/

2. APPLICATIONS

- Direct3D is a set of low-level graphics APIs on a Windows platform. It provides emulation for features not present on a given system's hardware, which is transparent to the users

- DirectX is a set of APIs including Direct3D — a low-level graphics library on the Windows platform. DirectX provides a standard platform to application developers, by guaranteeing hardware independence. The components of DirectX are: DirectDraw incorporating 2D drawing and interactions; DirectSound for sound; DirectPlay for networked multiple users; Direct3D for 3D graphics; DirectInput for support of other peripherals like joysticks in the applications

3. EXAMPLES/SAMPLES

- http://www.bysoft.se/sureshot/directxdemo/

- http://www.microsoft.com/directx/homeuser/downloads/default.asp

- http://www.planetblackandwhite.com/images/photo/archive.asp

4. FUNCTIONS

- Direct3D Immediate Mode:
  - Switchable depth buffering (using z-buffers or w-buffers)
  - Flat and Gouraud shading
  - Multiple light sources and types
  - Full material and texture support, including mipmapping
  - Robust software emulation drivers
  - Transformation and clipping
  - Hardware independence
  - Full support on Windows 95, Windows 98, and Windows 2000
  - Support for the Intel MMX architecture

- Direct3DX Utility Library:
  - Setting up a DirectDraw object and Direct3D devices
  - Drawing simple geometric shapes
  - Providing hardware independence for textures
  - Providing color conversions for several surface formats
  - Loading texture files (BMP, TGA, and DDS)
  - Creating cube-map textures for environmental mapping
  - Providing Sprite support (rotation, alpha, scaling, and warping)
  - Performing common 3D mathematical operations

- DirectDraw:
  - The hardware abstraction layer (HAL)
  - Ability to assess the video hardware's capabilities
  - Back buffers
  - 3D z-buffers
  - hardware-assisted overlays with z-ordering
  - Access to image-stretching hardware
  - Simultaneous access to standard and enhanced display-device memory areas
  - Custom and dynamic palettes, exclusive hardware access, and resolution switching

- DirectInput:
  - New services for devices not supported by the Microsoft Win32 API
  - Faster access to input data by communicating directly with the hardware drivers
- DirectMusic:
  - Works with message-based musical data
- DirectPlay:
  - Establishing a connection between computers through a network, over the Internet, or by a modem
  - Communicating through a lobby where participants can meet one another and organize sessions
  - Creating and joining sessions
  - Managing players and groups within a session
  - Harmonizing the session state on different computers through the exchange of messages
- DirectSetup:
  - Simple API that provides one-call installation of the DirectX components
- DirectSound:
  - Enables wave sound capture and playback

5. WEB RESOURCES

- The source for many pointers and tutorials: http://www.gamedev.net/

- http://www.microsoft.com/directx/

- On recent additions to the SDK: http://www.gamespot.com/features/dx7/index.html

- Direct3D immediate mode tutorials: http://www.screel.de/direct3d.net/index.html

- http://dir.yahoo.com/Recreation/Games/Computer_Games/Programming/DirectX/

- An overview: http://www.gamedev.net/reference/programming/features/d3do/

- Book by Peter J. Kovach, *The Awesome Power of Direct3D/DirectX*, Manning Pub. Co., 1997: http://www.manning.com/Kovach/

DIVE (Distributed Interactive Virtual Environment)

1. PLATFORMS, PRICES, AND SUPPLIER/CREATOR

- SGI Irix 5.3 and above, HP-UX 9.0x and 10.x, Solaris 2.4 and above, SunOS 4, Linux 2.x, Windows NT
- Free
- Swedish Institute of Computer Science: http://www.sics.se/

2. APPLICATIONS

- The Distributed Interactive Virtual Environment (DIVE) is an internet-based multi-user VR system where participants navigate in 3D space and see, meet and interact with other users and applications

3. EXAMPLES/SAMPLES

- DIVE Example Images: http://www.sics.se/dive/demos/images
- DIVE Example Movies: http://www.sics.se/dive/demos/movies

4. FILE FORMATS

- Importing file formats: Dive Files (vr, vr.gz, vr.Z), Dive Binary Files (bvr, bvr.gz, bvr.Z), AC3D Files (ac, ac.gz, ac.Z), VRML Files (wrl, wrl.gz, wrl.Z)
- Exporting file formats: Dive Files (vr), AC3D Files (ac), VRML Files (wrl)
- Uses tcl for scripting of motions
- I/O plug-ins available for other formats

5. WEB RESOURCES:

- http://www.sics.se/dive/dive.html
- http://www.sics.se/dive/related
- http://www.mcrlab.uottawa.ca/research/QoS_DIVE_Report.html

DIVERSE

Device Independent Virtual Environments — Reconfigurable, Scalable, Extensible

1. PLATFORMS, PRICES, AND SUPPLIER/CREATOR

- GNU/Linux and IRIX systems
- Free (GNU LGPL and GPL) software: http://www.theaceorb.com/product/benefit.html
- Virginia Tech's University Visualization and Animation Group: http://www.cave.vt.edu/

2. APPLICATIONS

- DIVERSE is a common user interface for interactive graphics and/or VE programs. Using DIVERSE the same program can be run on CAVE ImmersaDesk, HMD (head mounted display), desktop and laptop without modification
- DIVERSE is a common API to VE-oriented hardware such as trackers, wands, joysticks, and motion bases
- DIVERSE provides a "remote shared memory" facility allows data from hardware or computation to be asynchronously shared between both local and remote processes

3. EXAMPLES/SAMPLES

- dgiPf documentation: http://www.diverse.vt.edu/dgiPf/html/dgiPf_Prog_Guide.html
- DTK documentation: http://www.diverse.vt.edu/DTK/html_docs/
- dgiPf example programs: http://www.diverse.vt.edu/dgiPf/prereleases/dgiPf/examples/
- DTK example programs: http://www.diverse.vt.edu/dtk/examples/

4. FUNCTIONS

- DIVERSE is comprised of two components:
  - The DIVERSE graphics interface for Performer (dgiPf) provides a framework to implement 3D Virtual Environment (VE) and desktop graphics applications by augmenting OpenGL Performer
  - The DIVERSE ToolKit (DTK), a separate standalone package, is used by dgiPf to provide access to local and networked (real and virtual) interaction devices

- DIVERSE is designed without the "center of the universe" paradigm; you only use the parts of DIVERSE that you need, without being forced into using a particular design for your code, or having to add unneeded features

5. WEB RESOURCES

- The DIVERSE home page: http://www.diverse.vt.edu/

DMesh

1. PLATFORMS, PRICES, AND SUPPLIER

- Windows 95+

- N/A

- Bruce Lamming: http://www.geocities.com/SoHo/Studios/4500/dmmain.htm

2. APPLICATIONS

- DMesh is a mesh creation and deformation tool for use with 3D modeling, rendering, and animation software. Its primary focus is the generation of smooth-surface mesh objects for use in humanoid and other organic modeling tasks. It uses a proprietary Musculature Definition Language designed specifically to assist in the creation of dynamic musculature systems. Recommended — a third party rendering package: DMesh includes an OpenGL preview and capture option, but more sophisticated modeling and rendering environments are also supported. Direct support for POV-Ray, Moray, Poser, BMRT and PolyRay is included. The RAW file format is supplied for use with other 3D file conversion programs

3. EXAMPLES/SAMPLES

- http://www.geocities.com/SoHo/Studios/4500/mod0009.htm
- http://www.geocities.com/SoHo/Studios/4500/gallery.htm

4. FUNCTIONS

- Export Options:
  - POV-Ray 3.1 and 3.5 (mesh, smooth-mesh, and mesh2 — with associated Moray UDO if desired)
  - POV-Ray DF3 point cloud for use with Media statements

- OBJ — WaveFront format
- RIB — for Renderman compliant systems such as BMRT
- RAW — for use with Polyray and several 3D file format conversion programs
- Multilayered Modeling Environment:
  - Supports a user definable number of layers
  - Designated layers can be activated or deactivated
  - Edit or Preview using a single layer, sets of layers or all layers
  - Individual layers can be additive or subtractive
  - Layers can be independently scaled
- OpenGL Mesh Preview:
  - User definable texture definitions supporting separate declarations for the OpenGL ambient, diffuse, specular, and emission color components
  - Preview image sizing and capture to disk options
  - Support for mouse-controlled panning, rotation and scaling operations
  - View as shaded, wire-frame, or vertex point clouds
  - Preview single layers, sets of layers, all layers or as a skinned object
- Compound Mesh Objects:
  - Export object as a single skinned mesh
  - Export selected layer(s) for skin detailing, clothes, or hair
- Height Field Support:
  - Import existing height-field displacement images
  - Supports multiple height-field images per object
  - Each height-field can be independently scaled
  - Individual height-field images can be additive or subtractive
  - Height-fields can be wrapped around a variety of primitives such as planar, conic, spheric and disc. (The upcoming Shape plug-in module will add support for an unlimited number of user definable shapes.)
- Automatic LOD:
  - All models can be exported at a user definable polygon resolution
  - A few hundred polygons for VRML, real-time or layout environments
  - Tens of thousands for more production oriented environments

5. WEB RESOURCES

- http://www.geocities.com/SoHo/Studios/4500/dmmain.htm

Draw3D

1. PLATFORMS, PRICES, AND SUPPLIER

- Windows 95/98
- Free
- Shervin Emamit: http://www.geocities.com/SunsetStrip/Stage/8513/Draw3D.html

2. APPLICATIONS

- Draw3D is a basic 3D drawing program that allows you to plot 3D points anywhere in space. Once you have your points (called "vectors") placed, you can attach sides (4-sided polygons) to the vectors, to be wherever those vectors are, even if you modify those vectors. You can rotate them, zoom them, or move them however you wish, and the polygons will still be connected to them

3. EXAMPLES/SAMPLES

- http://www.geocities.com/SunsetStrip/Stage/8513/samples.html

4. FUNCTIONS

- Modeling:
  - Objects: Polygons, Vectors, and Primitives (Cubes, Cylinders, and Spheres)
  - Transformation: rotating, zooming, moving
  - Vector manipulation: adding and deleting, change coordinates, make groups out of a selection of vectors, remove unused vectors
  - Polygon manipulation: adding and deleting, polygons facing me, polygons facing away, flat fill, gradient fill
- Rendering:
  - Lighting: Depth based, Angle based; (Depth based makes a darker polygon if it is farther away from you, while Angle based makes a darker polygon if it is facing away from you)
  - Extremely fast at rendering polygons
  - Textures: Modes (edit, select, zoom, move, rotate)
- Viewing:
  - Wireframe mode: View polygons in 3D as lines (lets you see through the object, showing what is inside)
  - Solid mode: View polygons in 3D as filled polygons (lets you visualize the objects better than in wireframe mode)
- Features:
  - Remembers the nine most recent files opened

- Up and down, left and right, and pageup and pagedown rotate the 3D view around the X, Y and Z axis
- Can rotate around current vector
- Can fit Object to view
- Clips the lines so they don't have to be cancelled when they are out of view
- Can have group of vectors
- Can automatically open last file on startup
- Slow drawing modes go back fast when they are finished
- No background Bitmap in Version 3.2

- File Formats:

  - Draw3D has its own file format ".3D", but it also can use Autocad's Drawing Interchange format with the extension '.DXF'. This allows Draw3D to used by other 3D programs. Saving to DXF file will store the data differently, since DXF files use a different vector for each corner of each polygon. This means that if you have an object of 1000 polygons, storing it as — or loading it from — a DXF file will store the details of 1000 polygons, and 4000 vectors (4 vectors for every polygon), but using the ".3D" files will store the details of 1000 polygons, and only about 400 Vectors

5. WEB RESOURCES

- Downloads: http://www.geocities.com/SunsetStrip/Stage/8513/downloads.html

- Functionalities: http://www.geocities.com/SunsetStrip/Stage/8513/Help.html

- Other versions: http://www.twostones.org/soft/draw3d/draw3d_eng.html

- http://www.fortunecity.com/skyscraper/macro/527/draw3d.html

Easymodel

1. PLATFORMS, PRICES, AND SUPPLIER

- Windows 95/98 and higher

- $$$ (shareware, 30 time trial)

- J.Thesing (private developer): http://home.wanadoo.nl/jaap.thesing/easymain.htm

2. APPLICATIONS

- Easymodel is an entry-level modeling tool. It supports multiple file formats, including VRML1, VRML2, AutoCAD, and 3D Studio (import and export)

3. EXAMPLES/SAMPLES

- Easymodel Overview: http://home.wanadoo.nl/jaap.thesing/overview.htm

4. WEB RESOURCES

- Easymodel website: http://home.wanadoo.nl/jaap.thesing/easymain.htm
- http://www.zdnet.com/downloads/stories/info/0,,0019QE,.html
- http://www.rocketdownload.com/Details/Grap/easymodel.htm
- http://www.yippee.net/html/win/graphics/title7593.htm

Effect3D

1. PLATFORMS, PRICES, AND SUPPLIER/CREATOR

- PC Windows 98–2000, NT
- Shareware ($39.95)
- Reallusion: http://www.reallusion.com

2. APPLICATIONS

- Effect3D is a powerful editing tool that lets you create 3D objects, add animation, and use a variety of effects for presentations

3. EXAMPLES/SAMPLES

- 3D Links Gallery Index for Effect3D: http://effect3d.reallusion.com/e3d_gallery.asp
- 3D Links Gallery on related tools: http://www.3dlinks.com/gallerylinks.cfm

4. WEB RESOURCES

- A list of resources on the net: http://www.imagespro.com/programs/1108/
- PC Magazine article: http://www.zdnet.com/downloads/stories/info/0,,001EHL,.html

ElectricImage 3D Universe

1. PLATFORMS, PRICES, AND SUPPLIER/CREATOR

- Power Macintosh 6100 or better;
  Mac OS 7.5 or better
- $995.00
- ElectricImage Company: http://www.electricimage.com

2. APPLICATIONS

- ElectricImage Universe is a 3D modeling, rendering, and animation tool that offers a thoroughly modern user interface and a powerful new high-speed rendering engine, capable of everything from ray-traced reflections and refractions to volumetric shadows

3. EXAMPLES/SAMPLES

- http://www.electricimage.com/gallery/index.html
- http://www.electricimage.com/images/gallery/robots/miller_daniel1.jpg
- http://www.electricimage.com/images/gallery/robots/whittaker_sheldon1.jpg
- http://www.ultirender.com/pages/ohjelmistot/play/ei_interface_bike_1_.htm
- http://www.electricimage.com/images/gallery/vehicles/benesch_troy3.jpg
- http://www.electricimage.com/images/product/ei/8x6interface4.jpg

4. FUNCTIONS

- Modeling:
  - Objects: NURBS, Berzier, spline, polyline, rectangle, circle, ellipse
  - Transformation: translation, rotation, scaling, cloning, mirror, copy, twist, bulge, bend, spacing, and move
  - Editing: face, polygon, curves, skinning, losting, knife, NURBS surfaces, booleans, and lofting
- Rendering:
  - Cameras: roll control, rotoscope layers, projection map, focal length, field of view, focal mode, depth of field, zoom, focus distance
  - Lights: parallel lights, spotlights, tube lights, ambient lights, shadow, Phong, Gouraud
  - Materials: blend, shadow, depth buffer, ray trace, smoothing, Phong, wireframe, flat Gouraud, fog, point, texture mapping, procedural maps, ray-traced maps, reflection, volume shadows

- Before and after rendering: antialiasing, multiframe blur, motion blur, polygons rendering, fog, motion vector blur noise, environment maps, resolution, aspect ratio, color depth

- Animation:
  - Control: Animating is fast and interactive, using direct manipulation or flexible temporal, keyframe, key-index, drop frame, procedural shaders, system, and frame project views
  - Advanced animations: Powerful higher level animation provides for inverse kinematics, function curve editing, Bones, morphing, smart deformations, particle systems, vibration systems, character animation, motion blur and importation of motion capture data

- File formats
  - Importing file formats: EPS, IGES
  - Exporting file formats: IGES
  - Image file formats: IMAGE, Quicktime, PICT

5. WEB RESOURCES

- http://www.ultirender.com/pages/ohjelmistot/play/electric_image_eng.htm

- http://www.electricimage.com/press/UniverseSpecRevised.pdf

- http://www.electricimage.com/universeindex.html

- http://www.dvdirect.com/Prods/ELC/4001.htm

- http://www.kodiak.de/electricimage/electricimagespecial.html

Emotion 3D (Web Edition)

1. PLATFORM, PRICES, AND SUPPLIER/CREATOR

- Windows 95/98/NT/2000

- $34.95 through the Net; $39.95 by FedEx/UPS

- Anark: http://www.anark.com

2. APPLICATIONS

- Emotion 3D delivers a wide variety of special effects, behaviors, and compression technologies. Emotion 3D creates professional Gif animations, JavaScript rollover button more for Websites and PowerPoint presentations

- Emotion 3D provides users with real-time 3D graphics, text, video, and audio in an interactive architecture delivered to the end-user in a high performance stream

3. EXAMPLES/SAMPLES

- http://www.creativesight.com
- http://www.anark.com/gallery/gallery.htm

4. WEB RESOURCES

- http://www.anarkmedia.com
- http://www.jumbo.com/pod/September/090899.html
- http://nmreview.com/reviews/emotion3d/
- http://www.creativepro.com/software/home/1441.html
- http://www.digitalproducer.com
- http://www.mediabuilder.com/10606.html

EnLiten

1. PLATFORMS, PRICE, AND SUPPLIER/CREATOR

- Unix, Linux, Windows 98, NT, 2000, XP
- Free
- CEI: http://www.ceintl.com/

2. APPLICATIONS

- EnLiten is a 3D geometry player for viewing, analyzing, and manipulating complex visualization scenarios. It requires no special software skills and runs on Windows, UNIX and Linux computers. EnLiten allows communication of high-end visualizations in the following application areas: computational fluid dynamics (CFD), finite element analysis (FEA), crash analysis, aerodynamics, and scientific visualization. EnLiten imports EnSight or EnSight Gold scenario files containing 3D models with associated rich geometry. Interactive collaboration between multiple EnLiten and EnSight users over a network is possible

3. EXAMPLES/SAMPLES

- An image's link: http://www.ceintl.com/images/Image11.gif

- Incredible image: http://www.ceintl.com/images/01.jpg

4. FUNCTIONS

- Modeling:
  - Object displays traces as point, spheres, line or ribbons, traces emitters to be built from simple points, lines, rakes, planes, nodes or an arbitrary part
  - Transformation: Rotation, translation and mirror
  - Editing and manipulation: enhances visualization by displaying elevated surface as a variable created by projecting away from a parent part provides individual manipulation and attribute control of analysis mesh or derived (clip planes, isosurfaces, particle traces, etc.) parts allows parts to be copied, cut, merged into a single part, and converted to a new representation enables part copy to be positioned independent of the original part in order to display a different variable

- Rendering:
  - Cameras shows the support of unsteady results data, node positions and structure (connectivity) allows time steps to be changed at the click of a button automatically recalculates and redisplays existing objects to reflect each new state provides interpolation between time steps for low-resolution datasets provides dynamic plots that are linked to the transient display of parent part variables
  - EnLiten allows sites to create their own interfaces to input devices (such as the wand device for the Pyramid System ImmersaDesk.) Line culling for faster line performance. Duplicate edges of polygons are removed. Faster transparency option. New point cloud bounding box option
  - Light shows Transparency (simple screen door or alpha shading), length parameters
  - Particle trace (streamlines), clipping, and isosurface algorithms will execute in parallel when running on a shared-memory architecture machine

- Animation:
  - Enables animation of particles traces, provides animation of plane clips or isosurfaces (sweep through a model), allows "flipbook" animation of transient data allows model (mesh) movement, with or without changing topology, supports load animation, provides keyframe animation for automated model fly-arounds and zooms
  - Object: Scale, rotation, dimension, color, point, shades, and transparency
  - Controller: Mouse, Keyframe, and system
  - Animation: view models and animations in full screen and 3D stereo
  - Basic Animation: embed models and animations in MS PowerPoint, MS Internet Explorer and Netscape

- File Formats:
  - Import File Format: scenario

       – Output File format: NA

5. WEB RESOURCES

- CEI Company http://www.ensight.com/
- Ensight http://www.ceintl.com/ensight.html
- Customers http://www.ceintl.com/customers.html
- EnLiten http://www.ceintl.com/enliten.html

Ensight

1. PLATFORM, PRICES, AND SUPPLIER/CREATOR

- SGI/Irix, HP/HP-UX, Compaq/Tru64, Sun/Solaris, IBM/AIX, Windows 98/NT/ 2000, Linux
- $1,000+
- Computational Engineering International: http://www.ceintl.com/

2. APPLICATIONS

- EnSight is a high-end visualization tool with VR (virtual reality) and parallel post-processing capabilities designed for presenting and analyzing large datasets resulting from computer simulations and testing
- Used by engineers for analyzing or presenting results of engineering Computations in 2D or 3D, also known as post-processing results
- EnSight provides a single interface for the visualization of results data from the most popular packages in Computational Fluid Dynamics(CFD), structural analysis, combustion modeling, thermodynamics, electromagnetics, crashworthiness, atmospherics, particle physics, and injection molding

3. EXAMPLES/SAMPLES

- Automotive showcase: http://www.ceintl.com/autoshowcase.html
- Aerospace showcase: http://www.ceintl.com/aeroshowcase.html
- General engineering showcase: http://www.ceintl.com/genengshowcase.html
- Chemical showcase: http://www.ceintl.com/chemshowcase.html
- Scientific visualization showcase: http://www.ceintl.com/scivizshowcase.html

4. FUNCTIONS

- Geometry:

    - Handles structured, unstructured, hybrid and overlapping meshes
    - Parts can be copied, cut, merged into a single part
    - Analysis mesh or derived parts can be manipulated
    - Allows native structured data to be viewed along constant I/J/K planes
    - Allows geometry to be varied with time, with or without changes to mesh topology
    - Offers 1D, 2D and 3D elements in linear or quadric form

- Transformations:

    - Scaling, rotation, translation by drag and drop technique

- Visualization:

    Contours/Isosurfaces:

    - Displays contour loops of any active variable on any surface
    - Individual loops can be labeled
    - Enables isosurfaces to be created based on scalar variable, vector component, vector magnitude or coordinate
    - Allow dynamic visualization of a range of isovalues

    Particle tracing:

    - Allows streamlines, pathlines, streaklines and surface-restricted ("oil-streak") traces to be created
    - Displays traces as points, spheres, lines or ribbons
    - Allows trace emitters to be built from simple points, lines, planes or the nodes of an arbitrary part
    - Enables streamline emitters to be manipulated with the mouse for interactive trace calculation and display

    Vector arrows:

    - Displays arrows showing direction and magnitude of a vector variable for any part
    - Allows control over color, scale, origin location, projection components, and arrowhead style
    - Provides curved arrows to show the local flow curvature

- Rendering:

    - Transparent effect can be created using alpha shading
    - Lighting parameters

- Animation:

    - Enables animation of particle traces
    - Provides animation of plane clips or isosurfaces (sweep through a model)
    - Allows "flipbook" animation of transient data
    - Allows model (mesh) movement, with or without changing topology
    - Supports load animation
    - Provides Keyframe animation for automated model fly-arounds and zooms

- Supports animation recording
- Quantitative Analysis/Data Query/Plotting:
  - Arbitrary points, nodes, elements and parts can be queried for information
  - Queries can also be performed along a line in space, or on any variable over distance of time
  - The data can be provided in terms of tables or it can be plotted in 2D or 3D plots
- Data Exchange:
  - Supports VRML, JPEG, AVI, and MPEG output for distributing images and animations via the Internet and intranets
  - Outputs advanced "Move-Draw" PostScript, encapsulated PostScript and HP-GL files with compact, high-quality images that maintain screen resolution even when resized within other applications; also supports RGB, PICT and other output formats
  - Supports data formats of ABAQUS, LS-Dyna, KIVA, ANSYS, MSC.Nastran, MSC.Dytran, MSC.Patran, IDEAS, Radioss, Fluent, Star-CD, CFD++, CFX, PLOT3D, TECPLOT, CGNS, CTH, FAST, HDF5, EXODUS/PXI, SILO, MESHTV and various other programs
- Additional Features:
  - Hidden line, line style and thickness can be modified for visual purposes
  - Elements can be shrunken for visual purposes
  - Representation modes: 3D, edge, feature angle, non-visual
  - Shared-memory and distributed parallel processing including Beowulf clusters and multipipe graphics
  - Extensive data reduction through full-featured field calculator with flow, trig, statistical, calculus, arithmetic, and structural functions
  - Stereo viewing
  - Integrated plotting allows plotter and transient animation to be updated in sync

5. WEB RESOURCES

- Ensight into Engineering Analysis: http://www.ceintl.com/esfeatures.html
- Worldwide Distributors: http://www.ensight.com/distributors.html

EON STUDIO

1. PLATFORMS, PRICES, AND SUPPLIER/CREATOR

- Windows 95/98/NT 4.0/2000/ME
- $3,795.00

- EON Reality Inc.: http://www.eonreality.com

2. APPLICATIONS

- EON Studio is a comprehensive tool box for creating and deploying interactive real-time 3D simulations on the Windows platforms. Advanced simulations can be created quickly and easily without the need for programming. Popular application areas include marketing and sales tools, product development, simulation based training, architectural studies, and community planning

3. EXAMPLES/SAMPLES

- EON Studio Personal Edition: http://www.softseek.com/Graphics_and_Drawing/ CAD_3D_Design_and_Modeling/F_57106_index.html

- Architecture: http://www.eonreality.com/download/architecture/ eon_demos_architecture.htm

- 3D-commerce/marketing: http://www.eonreality.com/download/e-commerce/ eon_demos_ecommerce.htm

- E-Learning/Training: http://www.eonreality.com/download/e-learning/ eon_demos_elearning.htm

4. FUNCTIONS

- Modeling:
  - Objects: spline, NURBS, particle systems (e.g. rainfall, explosions), hyperNURBS (subdivision surfaces)
  - Transformation: translation, rotation, drag and drop scaling, array, colliding, sliding, rolling
  - Editing and manipulations (vertex, edge, face, polygon, curves, objects): hierarchical navigation, function-curve editing, development tools, multimedia tools
- Rendering:
  - Cameras: adjustable, movable
  - Lights: shadow, Phong, attenuation
  - Optical effects: rain, waves, shading, explosions, reflections, gravity, pressure
  - Materials: blend, morpher, ray trace (reflection), shadow
  - More materials: texture mapping, environmental mapping, ray-traced maps
- Animation:
  - Controllers: keyframe, mouse, sphereSensor
  - Advanced animations: rigid body dynamics, space warp, morphing, inverse kinematics
  - Basic Animation: graph, programmatic (C++ language, J_script, or VB_script)
- File Formats:

– Importing file formats: 3DS, FLT, VRML, TRI, IGES, SAT, SAB, PAR, DXF, IGS, SLP, DSC, HRC, STL, COB, SCN, DEM, OBJ
– Exporting file formats: 3DS, FLT, VRML, TRI, IGES, SAT, SAB, PAR, DXF, IGS, SLP, DSC, HRC, STL, COB, SCN, DEM, OBJ

5. WEB RESOURCES

- Virtual Reality: http://www.est-kl.com/eonstudio.htm

- Digital River: http://www.digitalriver.com/dr/v2/ ec_MAIN.Entry10?SP=10023&PN=1&V1=162162&xid=33655&DSP=&CUR= 840&CACHE_ID=0

- EON authoring tools: http://www.est-kl.com/eon_authoringtools.htm

- EON Reality Product: http://www.eonreality.com/products/ eon_studio_unique_advantages.htm

- Visualization Software: http://www.ocf.co.uk/products/eon_studio.html

- News: http://www.eonreality.se/mirror/news/news_archive/ news_item_6_23_99.html

- An article: http://www8.zdnet.com/pcmag/features/software/1519/3d-r6.htm

Extreme 3D

1. PLATFORMS, PRICES, AND SUPPLIER/CREATOR

- Windows PC

- $$$$

- Macromedia: http://www.macromedia.com

2. APPLICATIONS

- Extreme 3D seamlessly integrates with other Macromedia products such as Freehand, Authorware, and Director. It starts with a standard set of 3D tools and adds customization features, animation, and realistic previews. Extreme 3D is for Web and multimedia designers

3. EXAMPLES/SAMPLES

- Example Gallery/Tips on using Extreme 3D: http://freespace.virgin.net/garry.c/ E3DWEB/gar_e3d.htm

- Screen shots: http://ewave.seul.org/#screenshots

4. WEB RESOURCES

- Books on Extreme 3D: http://www.puzzlecraft.com/3D/extreme.htm; http://www.boutons.com/books/e3d.html
- PC Magazine reviews: http://www8.zdnet.com/pcmag/issues/1513/pcmg0010.htm

eZ-Motion

1. PLATFORMS, PRICES, AND SUPPLIER/CREATOR

- Power Macintosh and PC
- Mac 8.5, 8.6, 9.0 and Windows 98, NT 4.0, 2000, ME, XP
- $69.99
- Beatware: http://www.beatware.com

2. APPLICATIONS

- Basic 3D or 2D image and animation software for Web developers. Allows the creation of images or animation from scratch or from set templates. Templates come from already-created images in its library

3. EXAMPLES/SAMPLES

- Beatware's Gallery: http://www.beatware.com/products/ez_motion/?page=gallery

4. FUNCTIONS

- Modeling:
  - Objects: Basic objects are contained in a library object have already be created by others are just available for use by the user
  - Transformation: rotation, scaling, alignment
  - Editing and Manipulation: filters, special effects (blending images)
- File Formats:
  - Imports: form Dreamweaver, GoLive, FrontPage, Adobe
  - Exports: gif, Flash, RealVideo

5. WEB RESOURCES

- Beatware: http://www.beatware.com/

FAST (Flow Analysis Software Toolkit)

1. PLATFORMS, PRICE, AND SUPPLIER/CREATOR

- SGI graphics workstation with a zbuffer and an IRIX 4.x or late operating system
- $$$$$ for commercial customers, $200 for educational institutions
- NAS, a division of NASA: http://www.nas.nasa.gov/

2. APPLICATIONS

- FAST is a software environment for analyzing data from numerical simulations. It allow scientists to examine the results of numerical simulations by loading data files, performing calculations on the data, visualizing the results of these calculations, and constructing scenes of 3D graphical objects that may be animated and recorded

3. EXAMPLES/SAMPLE

- Images and animations: http://www.nas.nasa.gov/software/FAST/gallery.html

4. WEB RESOURCES

- Home page for FAST: http://www.nas.nasa.gov/Software/FAST/
- User Guide: http://www.nas.nasa.gov/Software/FAST/RND-93-010.walatka-clucas/
- Other: http://www.openchannelfoundation.org/projects/FAST/

FERRET

1. PLATFORMS, PRICES, AND SUPPLIER/CREATOR

- UNIX, Windows using X windows for display, it also can be installed on a Web browser "web ferret"... it also can be installed for interactive access through a Web browser either with a Web user interface ("Live Access Server") or through the native command line ("web ferret")
- Free
- PMEL, NOAA: http://www.pmel.noaa.gov/

2. APPLICATIONS

- Ferret is an interactive computer visualization and analysis environment designed to meet the needs of oceanographers and meteorologists analyzing large and complex gridded datasets. The model datasets are generally multigigabyte in size with mixed 3- and 4-dimensional variables defined on staggered grids. The features that make Ferret distinctive among these packages are delayed mode evaluation (data transformations are defined as equations then evaluated over the requested region as needed), geophysical formatting, automated memory management for very large calculations, and self-documenting of all outputs generated

3. EXAMPLES/SAMPLES

- http://shark.pmel.noaa.gov/~tmap/PMEL98_review/ferret/Review_projections.gif
- http://www.pmel.noaa.gov/tmap/en82_sa.mpg
- http://ferret.pmel.noaa.gov/Ferret/FAQ/custom_plots/plot_layout.gif

4. FEATURES

- Tool for climate research and data analysis

5. WEB RESOURCES

- http://ferret.pmel.noaa.gov/Ferret/
- http://ferret.pmel.noaa.gov/Ferret/Documentation/Users_Guide/current/fer_html.htm
- http://shark.pmel.noaa.gov/~tmap/PMEL98_review/ferret/
- http://ferret.pmel.noaa.gov/Ferret/Downloads/ferret_downloads.html
- http://ferret.pmel.noaa.gov/Ferret/LAS/ferret_LAS.html

- http://tmap.pmel.noaa.gov/
- http://www.noaa.gov/
- http://www.pmel.noaa.gov/home/technology.shtml
- http://www.met.nps.navy.mil/manual/plotting.html
- Making movie: http://www.pmel.noaa.gov/tmap/en82_sa.mpg

Fieldview

1. PLATFORMS, PRICE, AND SUPPLIER/CREATOR

- SGI, HP, IBM, DEC, and SUN
- $$$$$
- Intelligent Light Company: http://www.ilight.com/fv.htm

2. APPLICATIONS

- Fieldview allows visualization of computational fluid dynamics (CFD) and other data. The program operates on datasets stored as NASA PLOT3D grid and solution files, as well as other data formats such as Fidap, Fluent, Fluent-UNS, Rampant, Flow3D, CFDS Flow3D, Visiun, Compact, GASP, Phoenics, and CFD-2000
- It computes a variety of scalar and vector functions on the field data and represents the results as cutting planes, isosurfaces, vector fields, contour lines and particle paths

3. EXAMPLES/SAMPLES

- Cool image: http://www.ilight.com/flow3d.htm
- Image with Window Media Player: http://www.ilight.com/kiva.htm

4. WEB RESOURCES

- Intelligent Light Company: http://www.ilight.com/nparc.htm
- Merak Company: http://www.merak.com/software/field/FieldView/
- Reference Manual: http://hpc.uky.edu/Docs/software/fieldview/FVReference_Manual7.pdf
- Link to a survey: http://www.tec.army.mil/TD/tvd/survey/FIELDVIEW.html

Flesh

1. PLATFORMS, PRICES, AND SUPPLIER/CREATOR

- Windows 95, Windows 98 or Windows Me
- $3,450
- DIGITS 'N ART's: http://www.dnasoft.com/

2. APPLICATIONS

- Flesh is a 3D paint software that offers powerful modeling capabilities. Designed to bring the freedom of a sculptor's atelier into the virtual environment, Flesh allows a complete hands-on feel to building, working, and texturing any structure or surface

3. EXAMPLES/SAMPLES

- Flesh gallery: http://www.dnasoft.com/gallery/index.html

4. FUNCTIONS

- The ultimate 3D paint software with modeling
- Real-time 3D painting
- Paint in multiple layers/rendering
- Comprehensive painting tools
- Advanced uv texture coordinates control
- Modeling flesh superior 3D modeling tools
- User interface, visualization
- Industry standard file formats
- Model import and export: Softimage [hierarchies, polygons, patches, NURBS surfaces], MAYA [polygons], Alias Wire [hierarchies, polygons, NURBS surfaces], Wavefront [polygons], Prisms [polygons], Image import and export, SGI, TIFF, Softimage, Wavefront, Prisms, RenderMan textures

5. WEB RESOURCES

- http://www.namco.com
- http://www.celestisdesign.com/gallery/dna/index2.html

FORM-Z

1. PLATFORMS, PRICES, AND SUPPLIER/CREATOR

- Windows 95, 98, NT 4.0, or 2000; MAC

- Alone: $1,495; with RenderZone: $1,995; with RenderZone and RadioZity: $2,390

- Automated Design Systems (Autodessys, inc.): http://www.formz.com/

2. APPLICATIONS

- Form-Z is a general-purpose 3D modeling, rendering, and animation program that puts sophisticated solid, surface, and form-manipulating capabilities into the hands of the personal computer user

- Extensive set of 2D/3D form manipulating and sculpting capabilities, many of which are unique

- It is an effective design tool for architects, landscape architects, urban designers, engineers, animators and illustrators, industrial and interior designers, and all design fields that deal with the articulation of 3D spaces and forms

3. EXAMPLES/SAMPLES

- http://www.formz.com/web_site_2000/frames_pages/gallery.htm

- http://www.formz.com/gallery/index_o.html

- http://www.arch.columbia.edu/formz/gallery.html

- http://ds.dial.pipex.com/town/parade/abk95/formz/gallery/guspics/gus.html

- http://lightning.prohosting.com/~formz/gallery.html

4. FUNCTIONS

- Modeling:
  - Derivative objects can be generated from 2D shapes through extrusions
  - Spherical objects, such as platonic solids, soccer balls, and lathed and geodesic spheres, can be generated both interactively and through numeric input; can also be scaled and stretched
  - Terrain models can be generated as true 3D solids. The four available types — mesh, triangulated mesh, stepped, and triangulated contour models — can be freely combined to model rivers, roads, flat areas, and a variety of other topographies
  - Smoothly curved splines and meshed surfaces can be generated and edited interactively using one of a complete set of mathematical methods that include NURBS, B-splines, and Bezier curves

- Metaformz allow you to blend a variety of 3D forms, implemented in form-Z employing the metaballs technology

- Editing:
  - Mesh models both flat and smoothly curved can be created, then edited and reshaped interactively by changing their parameters and their geometry, or by applying one of the many available deformation operations to pull or push an area, or to bend and twist. Image based displacements can be used to imprint a shape on both flat and already meshed surfaces
  - Advanced rounding can be applied to vertices, edges, or both vertices and edges including concave vertices and sequences of edges called stitches. Draft angles can also be applied to surfaces of solids
  - 2D and 3D text (TrueType and PostScript) can be generated as plain text or as text objects. A variety of text placement methods are available, including the placement of text on or between freely unfolding and editable control lines
  - Boolean operations, which include union, intersection, and difference, as well as the composite split operation, can be applied to either 2D shapes or 3D solids. They can be used to compose primitive shapes into arbitrarily complex forms
  - Trim, split, and stitch operations are boolean-like operations that can be applied to surface meshed objects as well as to solids, to cut away a piece, to separate an object into two or more parts, or to connect objects together
  - Both 3D symbols for modeling and 2D symbols for drafting can be defined and stored into symbol libraries. The program actually ships with a few libraries of its own. Symbols can be placed as instances as many times as desirable through a variety of placement options. Also, symbol editing operations allow you to apply global or local changes to instances

- Measurements:
  - The query tool provides the ability to determine information about objects, and to calculate areas, volumes, and distances

5. LINKS/WEB RESOURCES:

- http://www.formz.com

- http://bondiboard.macpublishing.net/1999/06/reviews/formz.html

- http://socrates.berkeley.edu/~lachmi/formZbook/formZbook.htm

- http://www.formz.com/web_site_2000/frames_pages/support.htm

- http://www.castech.fi

Genesis3D

1. PLATFORMS, PRICE, AND SUPPLIER/CREATOR

- PC
- FREE
- Genesis3D, owned by Eclipse Entertainment: http://www.genesis3d.com/

2. APPLICATIONS

- Genesis3D is a real time 3D rendering environment. Genesis3D is used to create gaming environments. Genesis3D is an Open Source engine
- Further information on its application: The engine is designed primarily to render indoor scenes with moderate polygon count at very high performance. It can be used to build reasonably detailed and extensive outdoor scenes provided that care is taken to build those scenes correctly. The engine has support for fast collision detection, and precalculated lighting and visibility testing

3. EXAMPLES/SAMPLES

- GTest, deathmatch arena created to test the functionality of the Gensis3D engine: http://www.genesis3d.com/screenshots.htm
- GDemo1, technological display of Genesis3D: http://www.genesis3d.com/gdemo1.htm

4. FUNCTIONS

- Environment:
  - Fast rendering, radiosity lighting
  - Dynamic RGB lights; dynamic shadows; dynamic fog; dynamic mirrors; dynamic water effects; dynamic texturing effects such as animations, blending, and morphing
  - Translucent world geometry
- Character Animation:
  - Animation based on either a hierarchical or a non-hierarchical bone system
  - Arbitrarily spaced keyframes in time
  - High quality interpolation between keys — second order continuity across orientation keys
  - Sharing of animations across different characters
  - Animations can be blended and mixed or partially applied
  - Animations are optimized to take up minimal space
  - Interpolation and blending subsystems can be used independently to animate other user objects

- Advanced Features:

    - Physics subsystem can be used to control world geometry, or independently to animate other user objects
    - Math support for vectors, matrices, and quaternions
    - Comprehensive support for texture and bitmap formats, mipmaps, and conversions
    - Basic network transport support for multiplayer
    - Fast collisions against the world geometry
    - Multiple worlds can be loaded and rapidly switched between
    - Multiple renders from different cameras can be mixed in a single frame
- Exporting

    - Has the ability to export "Actors" to 3D Studio Max

5. WEB RESOURCES

- Online documentation: http://www.genesis3d.com/docs/index.html

- Genesis3D University: http://www.welcome.to/genesis3d-university/

- 3dfiles.com download page for Genesis3D SDK: http://www.3dfiles.com/utility/genesis3d.shtml

Geometique

1. PLATFORMS, PRICE, AND SUPPLIER/CREATOR

- Windows NT

- Copyrighted Freeware

- Geometique: http://www.geometique.com/

2. APPLICATIONS

- Geometique is a standalone 3D modeling package for the PC that provides the modeling ease of the familiar polygonal environment with the surface quality associated with splines. Through the use of a new geometric primitive, subdivision surfaces, you can create high quality characters and props

3. FUNCTIONS

- Modeling:

    - Cut, copy, paste
    - Grow/shrink selection

- Join, split, inset, bevel, extrude, connect, move normal
- Mesh simplification (decimation)
- CSG (booleans on surfaces)
- Find boundary, pick interior, pick connected, pick geodesic, flip normals, extrude edge, collapse edge, hinge face, bridge (connect faces), fill ring, planarize, undo, redo

- Transformation:

  - Translate, rotate, scale, pivots, bake, deform

- Control:

  - Command based interface, hotkeys, space[Menu], primitives (sphere, torus, cylinder, box, platonics), draw curve, booleans on curves, triangulate curves, uv projection, materials, save subdivision

- Display:

  - Multiwindows perspective, ortho

4. FILE FORMATS

- Import File Formats: import (.gtq(native), .obj, .ply, .3ds)

- Export File Formats: export (.gtq(native), .obj)

- Additional file formats: are available through plug-ins

5. WEB RESOURCES

- http://www.geometique.com/

- Subdivision surfaces: http://grail.cs.washington.edu/projects/subdivision/

- Multiresolution methods for modeling: http://www.multires.caltech.edu/

Geomview

1. PLATFORMS, PRICES, AND SUPPLIER/CREATOR

- Geomview runs on most Unix platforms: Linux, FreeBSD, SGI, Sun either (Sun-OS 4.1.x and Solaris), HP RISC, Dec Alpha, RS/6000, and NeXT. Using either OpenGL or the generic X11 renderer, it can probably also be compiled on other Unix systems

- Free software available under the terms of the GNU Lesser General Public License (GPL): http://www.geom.umn.edu/software/download/geomview.html

- Geoview's homepage: http://www.geomview.org/

2. APPLICATIONS

- Geomview is used to view and manipulate 3D geometric objects. It can also act as a standalone viewer for static objects or as a display engine for other programs which produce dynamically changing geometry. In addition, it displays objects described in a variety of file formats and comes with a wide selection of example objects

3. EXAMPLE/SAMPLES

- http://carp.rutgers.edu/math-undergrad/geomview.html
- http://www.geom.umn.edu/software/orrery/
- http://www.math.smith.edu/Local/GeomMathTutorial
- http://www.cica.indiana.edu/graphics/3D.objects.html#sample
- http://www.cs.cmu.edu/~vaschelp/3d/Geomview/geomview.html#HDR1
- http://noframes.linuxjournal.com/lj-issues/issue23/1115f1.html
- http://noframes.linuxjournal.com/lj-issues/issue23/1115f2.html
- http://noframes.linuxjournal.com/lj-issues/issue23/1115f3.html
- http://www.math.smith.edu/~ahawthor/Geomview/
- http://www.math.smith.edu/~ahawthor/Geomview/res.html
- http://www.geomview.org/docs/html/geomview_10.html#tutorial
- http://www.geom.umn.edu/software/geomview/
- http://www.geom.umn.edu/projects/visualization/crafter.html

4. WEB RESOURCES

- http://www.geomview.org/docs/html/geomview_10.html#SEC13
- http://www.rcc.ait.ac.th/helpdesk/helpdocs/geomview/geomview_3.html
- http://www.cs.princeton.edu/~ah/alg_anim/animation/paragraph3_3_2_0_1.html
- http://www.geom.umn.edu/software/geomview/
- http://www-lmc.imag.fr/lmc-mga/Stefanie.Hahmann/ENSIMAG/geomview.html
- http://www2.linuxjournal.com/lj-issues/issue23/1115.html
- http://www.geom.umn.edu/software/geomview/geomview_toc.html

GKS-3D

1. PLATFORM, PRICE, AND SUPPLIER/CREATOR

- Machine and language independent. Specific implementations are known to have been developed for Silicon Graphics (IRIX), Sun Microsystems (Solaris), Hewlett Packard 9000 700 Series(HP/UX), IBM RS 6000 (Aix), Digital (OpenVMS and DEC UNIX), PC Linux, PC Windows NT/98, Convex, and Cray (Unicos). GKS has language bindings to C, FORTRAN, Pascal, and Ada

- Price

    - Varies. GKS itself is a ISO standard (ISO 7942,8651-1, 8651-4). Specific implementations vary in price according to the vendor
    - CERN (cern.web.cern.ch/CERN/) offers GKSGRAL, an implementation of GKS-3D, to affiliated institutes for DM 28.000 (US $13,000)
    - TGS (http://www.tgs.com) offers GKS implementation for multiple platforms, but pricing is unavailable

- American National Standards Institute (www.ansi.org). GKS is a standard published by ANSI. This is available for free from the ANSI institute. TGS offers GKS for a number of platforms. CERN (cern.web.cern.ch/CERN/) also offers an implementation of GKS-3D called GKS-GRAL through the CERN Program Library Office to affiliated institutions

2. APPLICATIONS

- GKS is a low-level 2D graphics ANSI/ISO standard that defines method to produce computer-generated pictures on vector or raster output devices, and is a high-level API. GKS-3D is an extension to GKS which allows the production of 3D objects. It is similar to PHIGS, but where PHIGS allows the developer to create object hierarchies, GKS is non-hierarchical. Both PHIGS and GKS are also similar to OpenGL, but OpenGL is much more specific in terms of required functionality and is currently much more popular

3. EXAMPLES/SAMPLES

- A GIS system, examine the product ARCINFO at: http://www.esri.com

- A set of example images: http://ngwww.ucar.edu/ng4.2/examples/#GKSExamples

- An example GKS program, written in C: http://vms.sggw.waw.pl/htbin/webbook/DKB0%3a%5bDECW$BOOK%5dd37vaaa8.p27.#126

- A set of Example programs, written in FORTRAN: http://www.cineca.it/manuali/CERN/asdoc/gks_html3/node114.html

- A short sample program, also written in FORTRAN:
  http://www.utoledo.edu/it/vms-guide/vmsgks.html
- How to set up and run a short sample GKS program:
  http://www.inf.aber.ac.uk/publications/documentation/g9.asp#2

4. RESOURCES

- ISO standards related to computer graphics, including those that define GKS:
  http://www.dfmg.com.tw/member/standard/iso/35140.html
- CERN documentation of GKS and GKS-3D:
  http://wwws.irb.hr/~cern/gks_html3/gksmain.html
- DEC Online GKS User's Guide:
  http://vms.sggw.waw.pl/htbin/webbook/
  DKB0:%5BDECW$BOOK%5Dd37vaaa8
- A description of how to use both GKS and PHIGS:
  http://www.inf.aber.ac.uk/publications/documentation/g9.asp#2
- A short online lecture on GKS:
  http://www.maths.bath.ac.uk/~pjw/NOTES/graphics/node112.html
- A FAQ on GKS file formats:
  http://www.faqs.org/faqs/graphics/fileformats-faq/part3/section-58.html
- GKS's viewing pipeline:
  http://www.cs.man.ac.uk/cstechrep/Abstracts/UMCS-86-4-1.html
- Standards — an article:
  http://www.siggraph.org/publications/newsletter//v32n1/columns/carson.html

5. BOOKS

- Hopgood, D., *Introduction to the Graphical Kernel System GKS*, Second Edition Revised for the International Standard, Gallop and Sutcliffe, 1986
- Bono, Peter R., *PC Graphics With Gks: Introduction to Graphics Standards (Gks, Gks-3D, Phigs, Cgi, and Cgm and to Graphics Programming)*, Prentice Hall, New York, 1990

Giram

1. PLATFORMS, PRICES, AND SUPPLIER/CREATOR

- PC X Windows Systems, LINUX, and UNIX
- Free download
- Giram: http://www.giram.org

2. APPLICATIONS

- A Persistence of Vision (POV-ray) modeler

3. EXAMPLES/SAMPLES

- http://www.giram.org/screenshots.html
- http://www.lklug.pdn.ac.lk/software/giram/index.html

4. FUNCTIONS

- Modeling:
    - Primitives: Boxes, cones, cylinders, disc, planes, spheres, super-ellipsoids, triangles, torii, CSG generated objects
    - Transformation: translation, rotation, and scaling can be performed with a mouse
    - Model views: WireFrame, HiddenFaces, or Gouraud views
    - Manipulation: of the above primitives
- Rendering:
    - Cameras: povray camera (exact view, not a perspective approximation)
    - Lights: directed, point and spotlights
- File Formats:
    - Importing file formats: POV scene, AutoCAD DXF file

5. WEB RESOURCES

- Download for free: ftp://ftp.giram.org/pub/
- Linux User's Group: http://www.lklug.pdn.ac.lk/
- http://www.giram.org/
- http://www.giram.org/screenshots.html
- http://www.lklug.pdn.ac.lk/software/giram/
- ftp://ftp.giram.org/pub/
- http://www.lklug.pdn.ac.lk/

GL Studio

1. PLATFORMS, PRICE, AND SUPPLIER/CREATOR

- Windows 98/2000/NT; IRIX 6.3/6.5; Linux (pending release of XFree86 4.0)
- N/A
- Distributed Simulation Technology, Inc.: http://www.simulation.com/index.html

2. APPLICATIONS

- GL Studio is a development tool to create real time 3D animated graphics. It generates portable C++ and OpenGL source code that can run standalone. Basic modeling tools are supported. Multiple formats for texture mapping and digital audio are supported

3. EXAMPLES/SAMPLES

- http://www.simulation.com/products/glstudio/gl_studio_examples.html

4. WEB RESOURCES

- GL Studio Website: http://www.simulation.com/products/glstudio/gl_studio.html
- Brochure: http://www.simulation.com/products/glstudio/docs/GLStudio_Brochure.pdf
- White Papers: http://www.simulation.com/products/glstudio/docs/GLStudio_White_Paper.pdf

GL4Java (OPENGL FOR JAVA)

1. PLATFORMS, PRICES, AND SUPPLIER/CREATOR

- AIX, IRIX, Linux, Macintosh, Solaris, Windows
- Freeware
- Jausoft: http://www.jausoft.com/gl4java/

2. APPLICATIONS

- OpenGL for Java (GL4Java) maps the complete OpenGL 1.2 API and the complete GLU 1.2 API to Java and integrates all management functions, while using the Java-Native-Interface (JNI) and the JDirect-Interface of MSTM-JVM. GL4Java uses the native OpenGL library of the underlying operating System

3. EXAMPLES/SAMPLES

- Examples and applications: http://www.jausoft.com/products/gl4java/gl4java_apps.html

4. FUNCTIONS

- Modeling:
  - Objects: primitives (sphere, cone, cylinder, etc.), NURBS, Bezier and quadratic surfaces, polygonal, linear, points
  - Transformation: translation, rotation, scaling
  - Editing and manipulations (vertex, edge, face, polygon, curves, objects): pixel operations, display lists, perspective and orthogonal projection; color, depth, stencil, and accumulation buffers
- Rendering:
  - Cameras: moveable
  - Lights: attenuation, shadowing, Phong and Gouraud shading, spotlighting
  - Materials: blending, shading, emission
  - More materials: texture mapping, multitexturing, depth testing, filtering
  - Before and after rendering: antialiasing, fog, polygon offset, tessellation
- Animation:
  - Basic: buffer swapping
- File Formats:
  - N/A

5. WEB RESOURCES

- Online manual: http://gl4java.sourceforge.net/docs/html/GL4Java.html

- SourceForge user group: http://www.geocrawler.com/lists/3/SourceForge/704/0/

- Article: http://romka.demonews.com/opengl/doc/opengl_java_eng.htm

GNUPlot

1. PLATFORMS, PRICES, AND SUPPLIER

- UNIX, PC, DOS, Windows, OS/2, Macintosh, Others
- Free
- The GNUplot team: http://www.gnuplot.org

2. APPLICATIONS

- GNUplot is a 2D and 3D plotting tool that has many settings to fine tune your plots. It is a command-driven interactive function plotting program

3. EXAMPLES/SAMPLES

- Surface plot: http://www.gnuplot.vt.edu/gnuplot/gpdocs/binary.htm
- Plot of a whale: http://www.gnuplot.vt.edu/gnuplot/gpdocs/multimsh.htm
- Wireframe examples: http://www.gnuplot.vt.edu/gnuplot/gpdocs/surface1.htm
- Contour wireframes: http://www.gnuplot.vt.edu/gnuplot/gpdocs/contours.htm
- The world graphed by GNUPlot: http://www.gnuplot.vt.edu/gnuplot/gpdocs/world.html
- Index to various examples: http://www.gnuplot.vt.edu/gnuplot/gpdocs/all2.htm

4. WEB RESOURCES

- FAQ: http://www.ucc.ie/gnuplot/gnuplot-faq.html
- Resources: http://www.usf.uni-osnabrueck.de/~breiter/tools/gnuplot/index.en.html
- Documentation: http://www.ucc.ie/gnuplot/gnuplot.html
- Tutorial: http://www.duke.edu/~hpgavin/gnuplot.html
- X front end: http://home.flash.net/~dmishee/xgfe/xgfe.html
- Extensive documentation— online manual of all GNUplot features: http://www.comnets.rwth-aachen.de/doc/gnu/gnuplot37/gnuplot.html
- Online tutorial: http://www.eng.hawaii.edu/Tutor/Gnuplot/

GRAFITTI

1. PLATFORMS, PRICES, AND SUPPLIER/CREATOR

- PC Windows 95, NT 4.0
- Free
- Colbeck Deskip Solutions Ltd.: http://www.cix.co.uk/~colbeck/graffiti.html

2. APPLICATION

- Produces 3D models or draws 2D images onto a 3D model. This software has been used in games for rendering the faces and bodies of characters. This application can be used to modify game characters like Lara Croft of Tomb Raider

3. EXAMPLES/SAMPLES

- http://www.cix.co.uk/~colbeck/graffiti/PROJ.HTM

4. FUNCTIONS

- Modeling:
  - Objects: triangles and textures
  - Editing
- Rendering:
  - Materials: transparency, texture mapping
  - Before-and-After Rendering: antialiasing
- Animation:
  - Basic Animations
- File Formats:
  - Import: Raw triangle form, dib, bmp

5. WEB RESOURCES

- Grafitti Homepage: http://www.cix.co.uk/~colbeck/grafitti.html

GSLib

1. PLATFORMS, PRICES, AND SUPPLIER/CREATOR

- Windows 95/NT with Visual C++; Linux with GNU C++
- $$$$$
- IntegrityWare, Inc.: www.integrityware.com

2. APPLICATIONS

- GSLib is an object-oriented software toolkit with a set of objects and methods to create, edit, query, and analyze geometric representations.GSLib is used in both 2D and 3D applications in CAD, simulation graphics, Web development, animation, game development and medical modeling

3. EXAMPLES/SAMPLES

- http://www.integrityware.com/iwgallery.htm
- GSLib was applied to Rhino3D, another 3D graphics tool. More information and samples can be found at: http://www.rhino3d.com

4. WEB RESOURCES

- Product brochure can be found: http://www.integrityware.com/gsprodde.htm
- Rhino3D gallery: http://www.rhino3d.com/gallery

GURU 3D-CONVERTER

1. PLATFORM, PRICE, AND SUPPLIER

- PC
- $10
- Morgan Gunnarsson: http://hem3.passagen.se/sardonyx

2. APPLICATIONS

- GURU 3D-Converter converts 3D Studio files (.3ds) to the DirectX file (.x) format

3. WEB RESOURCES

- Official website: http://hem.passagen.se/sardonyx/

(IBM) HotMedia

1. PLATFORMS, PRICES, AND SUPPLIER/CREATOR

- Mac OS, Windows. It also supports the Java platform
- Currently available as a free download from IBM
- IBM: http://www-4.ibm.com/software/net.media/

2. APPLICATIONS

- HotMedia is a Java applet technology for placing interactive media on the Web. It supports 3D, panoramas, multitrack animations, and streaming audio and video

3. EXAMPLES/SAMPLES

- Customer Gallery: http://www-4.ibm.com/software/net.media/gallery/gallery.html
- Panorama features: http://www.tiac.net/users/millie/centre/fortpan.htm and http://www.panoguide.com/publish/software/hotmedia.html
- Presentation: http://www.ticsay.net/design/hotmedia.php
- Interactive Advertising: http://www-4.ibm.com/software/net.media/gallery/ia.html
- E-education and e-training: http://www-4.ibm.com/software/net.media/gallery/et.html
- VRML: http://www.laverty.freeserve.co.uk/X3d/impl/hypermedia/hypermedia.htm
- Other examples: http://hearth.com/qtvr/ring/preview.htm

4. WEB RESOURCES

- HotMedia in the News:
    - http://industry.java.sun.com/javanews/stories/story2/0,1072,7637,00.html
      http://www.builder.com/Reviews/HotMedia/ss01.html
      http://www-4.ibm.com/software/net.media/archive.html
      http://industry.java.sun.com/javanews/stories/print/0,1797,7637,00.html
      http://www.techweb.com/wire/story/TWB20001023S0010

- CNET Screen Shots and Discussions:
    - http://www.builder.com/Reviews/HotMedia
- HotMedia Download Sites/Product Specs/User Opinions:
    - http://download.cnet.com/downloads/0-10217-100-2596626.html
- HotMedia Audio Presentation:
    - http://www.ngi.ibm.com/demos/hotmedia/HotAudio_portal_demo.htm

HOUDINI

1. PLATFORMS, PRICES, AND SUPPLIER/CREATOR

- Windows NT (Intel): Version 4.0 with SP3 or later;
  Windows 2000 (Intel);
  SGI Irix: version 6.2 or later;
  Linux (Intel): tested with Red Hat 6.0
- $$$$$$
- Sidefx Company: http://www.sidefx.com/index2.shtml

2. APPLICATIONS

- Houdini is a modeling, rendering, and animation tool. It is used for developing films and games

3. EXAMPLES/SAMPLES

- http://www.dctsystems.freeserve.co.uk/demoTree.html
- http://www.renderman.org/RMR/rmHoudini/
- http://www.dctsystems.freeserve.co.uk/demoExplosion.html
- http://www.dctsystems.freeserve.co.uk/demoCandle.html
- http://www.digitalpostproduction.com/Htm/Articles/Animation/Houdini40/Houdini4_0SneakPeak.htm

4. WEB RESOURCES

- http://www.vislab.usyd.edu.au/resources/guide/houdini/houdini_index.html
- http://www.sidefx.com/houdini/features.shtml
- http://www2.linuxjournal.com/lj-issues/issue66/3522.html

HyperActive (HyperReality and HyperSpace)

1. PLATFORMS, PRICES, AND SUPPLIER/CREATOR

- PC
- N/A
- HyperActive Web: http://www.kaon.com/sitemap.html

2. APPLICATIONS

- HyperReality is a 3D modeling service that creates photorealistic models. The small file size and high-quality textures makes HyperReality models for capturing your products for the Web, compatible with any 3D viewer. HyperSpace is a Java-based 3D viewing tool, a high resolution, fast loading, interactive 3D viewer without a plug-in

3. EXAMPLES/SAMPLES

- Gallery: http://www.kaon.com/hsgallery/index.html
- HyperActive solutions: http://www.kaon.com/Solutions/index.html
- 3D viewing technology: http://www.kaon.com/Solutions/Viewing.html

4. WEB RESOURCES

- http://www.kaon.com/partners.html
- http://www.vislab.usyd.edu.au/resources/guide/houdini/houdini_index.html

HyperFun

1. PLATFORMS, PRICE, AND CONTRIBUTORS

- Platform: Windows 98/NT (HyperFun protocol is platform independent)
- N/A — free software under GPL compatible license
- Contributing authors: http://wwwcis.k.hosei.ac.jp/~F-rep/HF_team.html

2. APPLICATIONS

- HyperFun (http://www.hyperfun.org) is a high-level modeling language-based protocol that can serve well for exchanging 3D, 4D (time-dependent) and multidimensional models between users, modeling systems, and networked computers

- Intended for modeling geometric objects described in the function representation (F-rep) form F(x1, x2, x3, ..., xn) >= 0, which is a single real continuous function of several variables explicitly defined. This includes the classic "implicit" functions due to its generality

- Potential to support advanced interactive "empirical modeling" techniques for collaborative work on the Internet with extensibility

3. EXAMPLES/SAMPLES

- Cartoon cat: http://211.133.251.125/mirror/F-rep/HF_dor.html

- Soft object: http://211.133.251.125/mirror/F-rep/HF_sample.html

- HyperFun Gallery: http://wwwcis.k.hosei.ac.jp/~F-rep/HF_gallery.html

4. FUNCTIONS

- Modeling:
  - A number of tools are available: http://211.133.251.125/mirror/F-rep/HF_tools.html
  - "HyperFun for Windows" is a modeling tool using a Symbolic User Interface with a built-in text editor
  - Standard "F-rep library" of geometric object and transformations is available or users can create their own library of geometric objects written in Hyperfun
  - Composes scenes consisting of a few objects, each defined in its own modeling space; generates images of polygonized or ray-traced elementary shapes, animation sequences, 1D and 2D spreadsheets in accordance with assigned multimedia types
  - "HyperFun Polygonizer" is a modeling tool using a command line interface; produces polygonized images with VRML export
  - "HyperFun for PovRay" is a modeling tool implemented as a plug-in to PovRay Raytracer
  - Plans for a Graphical User Interface are present with "drag and drop" node manipulation along with advanced numerical manipulations
  - Internet based-realization with the HyperFun to Java translator would allow on-the-fly model creations

- Animation:
  - Animation sequences based on strict mathematical definitions
  - Animated spreadsheets of images or 3D objects

- File Formats:

    – Plain text (i.e. TXT)

    – Additional formats would be available through plug-ins

5. WEB RESOURCES

- HyperFun mailing list: http://wwwcis.k.hosei.ac.jp/~F-rep/HF_mail.html

- 3D Links' abstract on HyperFun (scroll down): http://www.3dlinks.com/software_modshare.cfm

- HyperFun project description: http://wwwcis.k.hosei.ac.jp/~F-rep/HF_CGG2.htm

- Documentation: http://www.google.com/url?sa=U&start=8&q=http://www.irtc.org/ftp/pub/anims/2000-01-15/homotopi.txt&e=42

- 128K WMV format animation: http://wwwcis.k.hosei.ac.jp/~F-rep/H5D128.html

- 5 megabyte mpg file: http://www.irtc.org/ftp/pub/anims/2000-01-15/homotopi.mpg

ICA (Internet Character Animator)

1. PLATFORM, PRICE, AND SUPPLIER/CREATOR

- PC

- $179

- Parallelgraphics: http://www.parallelgraphics.com/

2. APPLICATIONS

- Internet Character Animator, or ICA, lets you animate 3D characters for the Internet ranging from sketches to complex games and presentations. You may use ICA to animate a virtual character by setting attributes such as translation, rotation, and scale of part of a character's body at specific key frames. ICA can animate characters created on the basis of the Specification of a Standard Humanoid (version 1.1)

3. EXAMPLES/SAMPLES

- ICA samples link: http://www.parallelgraphics.com/products/ica/examples/

4. FUNCTIONS

- Animation:

Key Frame Animator:

– Endow characters with a variety of expressions, gestures and movements

Animation Organizer:

– Set the sequence and duration of created animations
– Can be published Animated characters on the Web
– Can be created the interface for the first nine animations by a single mouse-click

Compatibility with Island multiuser VRML client:

– Use the characters as your personal Avatar in the Islands scenes

- Supported Formats:

  – VRML97 format
  – H-anim standard

5. WEB RESOURCES

- A list of resources on the net:

  – http://www1.buyonet.com/s/
    b?id=4.53.48&pa=pil&pi=4268&vcpid=63&vrc=1
  – http://www.yippee.net/html/win/developer/title4037.htm
  – http://www.davecentral.com/vrmledit2.html

IDL

1. PLATFORM, PRICES, AND SUPPLIER/CREATOR

- MAC, PC, UNIX, Windows

- $2,350 for PC Windows; Prices for other platforms not available

- Research Systems Inc., a Kodak Company: http://www.rsinc.com/idl/

2. APPLICATIONS

- IDL, the Interactive Data Language, provides software for data analysis, visualization, and cross-platform application development. IDL combines all of the tools you need for any type of project — from "quick-look," interactive analysis and display to large-scale commercial programming projects. All in an easy-to-use, fully extensible environment

3. EXAMPLES/SAMPLES

- http://www.researchsystems.com/gallery/index.cfm

- http://www.rsinc.com/AppProfile/idl_es_ocean.cfm/

4. FUNCTIONS

- 2D Plotting:

    - Line plots, scatter plots, histograms, bar graphics, polar plots, error bars
    - Automatic plots with numerous customizable defaults
    - Log, semilog, and linear scaling
    - Overplot multiple datasets
    - Linestyle, color, and marker type control
    - Ganged plots
    - Vector flow diagrams

- Surface Plotting:

    - Contour plots, regular and irregular grids
    - Mesh surface plots with hidden line removal
    - Shaded surface representations of solids and gridded elevations
    - Surface interpolation of irregularly gridded data points
    - "4D" data display of gridded elevations with overlaid image or user-specified shading
    - User-definable, 3D transformations

- Mapping Functions:

    - Ten geographics mapping transformations with inverses
    - Warp image data into arbitrary projections

- Image Processing:

    - Interactive contrast enhancement
    - Histogram equalization
    - Combine images with other two- and three-dimensional graphics
    - Hardware and/or software zoom and pan
    - Image notation
    - Display images on pseudo-color, true-color and bilevel devices
    - Generalized image arithmetic with pixels of any data type
    - Histogram processing
    - High and low pass filtering, convolution
    - Frequency domain filtering and analysis
    - Median filtering
    - Sobel/Roberts edge enhancement
    - Geometric transformations: magnification, minification, rotation, polynomial warping with regular and irregular grids
    - Thresholding
    - Region of interest selection (any shape)
    - Color quantization: convert true-color images to pseudocolor

5. WEB RESOURCES

- http://www.rsinc.com/idl/
- http://www.researchsystems.com
- http://www.rsinc.com/services/books.cfm
- http://idlastro.gsfc.nasa.gov/homepage.html
- http://www.dfanning.com/

ILLUSION

1. PLATFORMS, PRICES, AND SUPPLIER/CREATOR

- PC
- Version 2.0, $299.99 (upgrade from 1.0, $40)
- Impulse, Inc.: http://www.coolfun.com

2. APPLICATIONS

- Particle effects and composing system. Adds effects to already created animations or uses the present animation as the effect for another animation. Allows for easier addition of 3D effects because it works on a 2D platform

3. EXAMPLES/SAMPLES

- Gallery of AVI and MPG movie: http://www.coolfun.com/illusion/gallery2.htm
- http://www.wibwobweb.com/coolfun/gallery.shtml

4. FUNCTIONS

- Modeling:
  - Objects: Particle Systems (Shadows, Tornado, Repeating Pattern)
- Rendering:
  - Before and After Rendering: Motion Blur
- Animation:
  - Basic Animation

5. WEB RESOURCES

- Illusion tutorials: http://www.coolfun.com/illusion/tutorials.htm
- Further Illusion links: http://www.coolfun.com/illusion/links.htm
- Tutorial, links and hints: http://www.coolfun.com/illusion/
- Forum: http://www.wwug.com/forums/impulse_illusion/

Image Modeler

1. PLATFORMS, PRICE, AND SUPPLIER/CREATOR

- UNIX workstations, Window NT platforms or Pentium II class machines under Windows
- N/A
- REALVIZ: http://www.realviz.com

2. APPLICATIONS

- Production and editing tools that are specifically designed for the image modeling process. Captures and constructs 3D coordinate geometry of real objects from photographic, video, or cinematic images

3. EXAMPLES/SAMPLES

- http://www.realviz.com/products/imagemodeler/index.htm

4. FUNCTIONS

- Modeling:
  - Objects: polygon; transformation: translation, rotation, scaling. Editing and manipulations (polygons, objects): hiding, sculpting
- Rendering:
  - Materials: group facets. More materials: texture mapping
- Animation:
  - Controllers: key-based. Basic animation
- File Formats:
  - Importing file formats: REALVIZ ASCII, MatchMover, DXF, STL

    – Exporting file formats: Softimage, 3DSmax, Maya or Lightwave, REALVIZ
      ASCII, OBJ and VRML
    – Additional file formats: are available through plug-ins

5. WEB RESOURCES
    – http://www.3dlinks.com/press/realviz-23-Feb-2001.cfm
    – http://www.creativepro.com/software/home/1386.html

Imagine

1. PLATFORMS, PRICES, AND SUPPLIER/CREATOR

- PC (Windows 95, 98, and NT)

- $995.00

- Impulse, Inc.: http://www.coolfun.com/INFO/info.html

2. APPLICATIONS

- Imagine is a high-powered 3D animation, modeling, and rendering system.
  Features include: bones, kinematics, ray tracing, procedural textures, particle
  system, special effects, multiple file format support, (3D and image) optimized for
  Windows NT and 95, Amiga, and for the Macintosh

3. EXAMPLES/SAMPLES

- http://www.coolfun.com/contest/archive.html

- http://www.coolfun.com/contest/pix.0011/index.html

- http://www.indrev.com/im5.htm

- http://the-internet-eye.com/reviews/Nov99/Imagine/default.htm

- http://www.coolfun.com/INFO/GALLERY/gallery.html

- http://www.coolfun.com/INFO/PRODUCTS/Imagine/IMTECH/imtech.html

4. FUNCTIONS

- Modeling:
  - Transformation: translation, rotation, scaling, cloning, align, array, mirror,
    bending, molding, spin, spacing, and deformation (objects may be deformed
    by stretch, twist, pinch, taper, bend and shear)

- Built in primitives: Sphere, cone, plane, torus, tube and disk, hemisphere, cube, box, rod. Simple drag and drop to the work surface
- Multiple Editors
- Action Dialog quick view of all stage actors
- Detail Object creation and properties application
- Forms slice object editor
- Objects: detail, forms, spline stage (Spline font and 2D spline object creation), NURBS, particle types may be tetrahedrons, pyramids, octahedrons, cubes, blocks, spheres, dodecahedrons (12 sides) or random. Particles may be of any specified size, or random in nature
- Features: customized toolbars, fracture, grid snap, face colors feature, transparency, radial, axial and planar fog, many controls for lighting, all sorts of shapes, falloffs, intensities, colors, etc. are user controlled
- Adding brushes can get interesting as well. Brushes are 2D images the user may create. Textures are 3D in nature. Imagine ships with 108 textures. Also, it has six light textures such as venetian blinds, French windows, etc. Some textures such as fire and electric have characteristics that may be animated
- Procedural texturing with over 100 textures

- Rendering:

  - Full camera control
  - Lights: attenuation, shadow, volumetric lighting, Phong, Blinn
  - Unlimited animatable light sources where color, intensity, and type can be controlled
  - Materials: blend, composite, double-sided, matte/shadow, morpher, ray trace, shellac, multi/sub-ojbect, top/bottom, texture mapping, procedural maps, ray-traced maps
  - The anti-alias provides sliders that allow the user to reduce the effects of jaggies as much as possible. The options tab provides for everything else
  - Portals, giving a mini view of what to expect prior to committing to a render, also makes work flow faster and easier to visualize
  - There are six different rendering types available

- Animation:

  - Basic animation
  - Backdrop images both static and animated
  - Animations can be easily and quickly created between states in the detail editor however they are not high quality renderings. Imagine does all the tweening
  - Animation bluing shows last position of animated object
  - Stage animation control and object staging
  - Inverse Kinematics for character animation
  - Particle system support, various built-in particles as well as load any object as a particle and full animatable

- File Formats:

  - Importing file formats: Imagine only imports .dxf files

   – Additional file formats: Imagine supports a large variety of file formats. For example after an image is rendered it may be saved in .tga, .bmp, .cmp, 6 flavors of .jpg, .png, .psd, .pct, .ras, .pcx, and .tif. file formats available for backdrops include most of the just mentioned plus .avi, .eps, .ilb, .rg8, and .wmf
   – Imagine and DXF, 3D Studio and Lightwave file format load and save

5. WEB RESOURCES

- http://www.indrev.com/imagine.htm

- http://www.coolfun.com/Products/Imagine/imagine.html

- http://the-internet-eye.com/reviews/Nov99/Imagine/default.htm

- http://www.softpile.com/Multimedia/Animation/Review_04794_index.html

- http://www.coolfun.com/INFO/PRODUCTS/Imagine/imagine.html

Infini-D

1. PLATFORMS, PRICE, AND SUPPLIER/CREATOR:

- Windows, Mac OS

- N/A

- Meta Creations, Corp.: http://www.metacreations.com/

2. APPLICATIONS:

- Infini-D deals with rendering and animation, with a focus on broadcast animation. Rendering speed is faster than most of its competitors. Infini-D supports procedural and composite surfaces as well as standard texture mapping. Procedural surfaces have mathematically defined properties and as such are three dimensional as they run through an object rather than just covering the surface. Composite surfaces are created by using several different maps; this allows ease of application in placing a label to a tin or bottle, for example

3. EXAMPLES:

- http://ctiweb.cf.ac.uk/HABITAT/HABITAT5/Images/Infinid1.gif

- http://www.bodwellinternet.com/troy/port/infinid.html

- http://pages.infinit.net/kot/stills/3d2.html

- http://www.phase2.net/claygraphics/Intro.html

4. FUNCTIONS:

- Animation: has a set of tools used for creating animated deformation. These allow organic animated effects to be assigned to objects directly in the scene and animated over time. The twisting, bulging, and wave effects are all stable and produce interesting results when used with text. Subtle deformations can be created by limiting the effect of the process on an object by using a percentage scale applied to the bounding box of an object. Lighting effects provide the means of generating realistic soft shadows. A gradual transition from one shadow to another can be produced, conferring a more realistic, fuzzy effect. All the standard lighting operations are available within Infini-D, including visible light rays

- Modeling: vertex editing tools allows far more complex organic shapes to be modeled. Vertex editing works well with spline modeling tools in the creation of highly complex objects, such as a face, as individual points can be subtly adjusted

- Rendering: field rendering is also available for outputting to video. Without field interlacing, where an image is split into two fields each with half the image data, images often show a tearing effect when played back

- Plug-ins: Infini-D's plug-in architecture supports third party plug-ins, including many designed for Photoshop and AfterEffects

5. WEB RESOURCES:

- http://ctiweb.cf.ac.uk/HABITAT/HABITAT5/infinid.html
- http://shopper.cnet.com/shopping/resellers/1,10231,0-4773383-311-203751,00.html
- http://www.metacreations.com/
- http://www.3dark.com/resources/books/infinid.html
- http://ctiweb.cf.ac.uk/HABITAT/HABITAT5/Images/
- http://www.bodwellinternet.com/troy/port/infinid.html
- http://pages.infinit.net/kot/stills/3d2.html
- http://www.phase2.net/claygraphics/Intro.html

INSPIRE 3D

1. PLATFORMS, PRICE, AND SUPPLIER/CREATOR

- Power PC/MAC
- $495
- NewTek: http://www.newtek.com/

2. APPLICATIONS

- Models, animates and renders 3D elements in any style and complexity. Use the images you create as single frame print graphics or as lower resolution animation files for multimedia or the Web...or choose from a library of precreated images. Photorealistic or stylized animation images can be created for real-time graphics applications, including VRML 2.0

3. EXAMPLES/SAMPLES

- Newtek's low-bandwidth gallery: http://www.newtek.com/lowfi_index.html
- NewTeknique's images: http://www.newtekniques.com/inspire/
- 3D Interactive's gallery: http://209.196.180.82/3dinteractive/
- Reservoir 3D Center: http://sunflower.singnet.com.sg/~teddytan/gallery.htm
- Lightwave Outpost Official Web Page: http://www.lightwave-outpost.com
- Epic Software's Inspire 3D gallery: http://www.epicsoftware.com/inspire/
- 3D Links Gallery for Inspire 3D: http://members.aol.com/Wilgory/inspir3d.html
- 3D Examples using Simply 3D: http://www.zdnet.com/products/stories/reviews/0,4161,2148462,00.html
- Inspire 3D Demonstrations: http://www.3dinteractive.com/2e.htm

4. FUNCTIONS

- Modeling:
  - Inspire's Modeler retains LightWave's precision modeling tools, which include accurate Boolean operations (scoop out, slice up, or stencil polygons onto the surface of an object based on the surface of another object) and MetaNURBs tools (excellent for modeling organic shapes such as characters, cars, or airplane hulls). However, when you get into the details you see the difference between Inspire 3D and its big sibling; Inspire's reduced tool set doesn't allow you to adjust the level of polygon detail in a MetaNURBs object as you can in LightWave — it's locked at three polygons per patch
- Rendering:

- Inspire 3D comes loaded with Lightwave's rendering engine and is equipped to handle resolutions up to 8,000 x 8,000. Its rendering and modeling capabilities can handle 3D elements from the very simple to the very complex. I was quite impressed by the "high end" assets of the program, the lighting, the motion, the texture, etc. It is very versatile. You can output to a single frame or a full-blown multimedia project
- This program allows the user to create anything from cartoons to very complex animations and output to 16 image formats and 7 model formats. It is loaded with a variety of plug-ins. Other features include spline-based modeling as well as MetaNURBs — just to name a couple. It also contains a library chock full of images (1,600 models, objects and other items) that you can use, create your own, or mix-n-match, it's up to you. You can also use most Lightwave and Photoshop plug-ins as well

- Animation:

  - Inspire 3D can handle 2D, 3D, photographs, and video with 3D with ease. Its front projection mapping makes applying cast shadows over or against a photo or video image very accurate. Using the Motion Graph makes animation easy to achieve. As far as rendering is concerned, Inspire 3D rivals any rendering engine out there in speed and quality. Anti-aliasing is excellent even at its lowest denominator. Unfortunately the highest rendering size is 640 x 480 pixels
  - Animation support is still extensive: bones, displacement mapping, animated textures, spline-based keyframing of objects, lights and camera, and object morphing are all there. Glows, depth of field, and extensive lens flares allow a sophisticated touch to be given to Inspire images, while motion blur can be used either in animation, or to give a feeling of movement to print work

- File Formats:

  - Photoshop, QuarkXPress, Illustrator, Freehand, Director… Inspire 3D is compatible with every one of them and more. You can also use your Photoshop plug-ins with Inspire 3D, which makes working with both programs fast and seamless

5. WEB RESOURCES

- Inspire 3D Tutorial: http://www.creativemac.com/HTM/DynamicMedia/Tutorials/12_1_99/inspire3d_pencil_tutorial/inspire3d_tutorial_page15.htm

- Inspire 3D FAQs: http://web.singnet.com.sg/~teddytan/faq.htm

- Inspire 3D Resources: http://www.fignations.com/resources/ins.html

- Inspire 3D Mailing List: http://www.egroups.com/group/INSPIRE3D

- Tutorials: http://www.newtek.com/lowfi_index.html

- Inspire patches: http://www.newtek.com/lowfi_index.html

- 3D Interactive's FAQ: http://209.196.180.82/3dinteractive/

- Reservoir 3D Center: http://sunflower.singnet.com.sg/~teddytan/gallery.htm

- Lightwave Outpost Official Web Page: http://www.lightwave-outpost.com
- Epic Software tutorial: http://www.epicsoftware.com/high/inspire.stm
- NewTekniques Magazine: http://www.newtekniques.com/
- Serious 3D tutorials: http://www.serious3d.com/

Insta3D Pro

1. PLATFORM, PRICES, AND SUPPLIER/CREATOR

- Windows 95/98/NT/2000
- $800 (Insta3D, $99)
- UtahSoft, Inc.: http://www.insta3d.com/index.html
- http://www.utah3d.com

2. APPLICATIONS

- Insta3D is 3D webpage scene authoring tool for creating 3D text and true 3D charts. Insta3D Pro, moreover, is professional version for broadcasting CG and video editing. It can create stunning 3D effects

3. EXAMPLES/SAMPLES

- Basic Examples from Insta3D: http://www.insta3d.com/example/example.htm
- 3D Formats for MBC's Election Coverage: http://www.insta3d.com/elect2000.htm

4. FUNCTIONS

- Modeling:
  - Objects: Text features include bevels, size, ratio, italics, depth, 2-byte character sets. 3D graph types include bar, line, area and pie charts
  - Transformation: position change, rotation, and scale in 3D space
- Rendering:
  - Materials: Bar, line, volume, pie graph
  - Color: Edit and add a new color on palette
  - Lights: Multiple light, colored light, and spotlight
  - More materials: texture mapping including reflection mapping and sequence mapping
- Animation:

- Controllers: key-based, system
- Basic animation
- Additional Features:

    - TGA sequence image creation
    - Unlimited AVI size
    - Counter object
    - Text: drop shadow and edge
    - Scale screen width option for NTSC output
    - TGA sequence image creation
    - Edge, numerical justification, width justification in text

5. WEB RESOURCES

- http://www.insta3d.com/i3dpro.htm
- http://www.davecentral.com
- http://www.ummah.org.uk/software
- http://www.salemcounty.com
- http://www.fileguru.com/presentation-tools/45.html
- http://www.zdnet.com/downloads/stories/info/0,,0011VX,.html
- http://tucows.cybertours.com/preview/163231.html
- http://softload.narod.ru/graphics_and_drawing/cad_3d_design_and_modeling/review_26932_index.htm

Interchange

1. PLATFORMS, PRICES, AND SUPPLIER/CREATOR

- Windows 3.x, Windows 95 and Windows NT
- $$$$
- Viewpoint Digital: http://www.viewpoint.com/vp/interchange

2. APPLICATIONS

- Converts 3D models between any of 40 common formats

3. EXAMPLES/SAMPLES

- http://astronomy.swin.edu.au/pbourke/3dformats/scene/index.html

- http://www.digitalproducer.com/pages/cool8.htm
- http://www.digitalanimators.com/HTM/Reviews/Viewpoint_review.htm
- http://www.cadonline.com/features/0800blocks/howto.htm

4. FILE FORMATS

- Translate between: 3D Studio, BRender, Alias "polyset", CAD-3D, CADKey CADL, AutoCAD DXF, Imagine, SGI Inventor, LightWave obj and scene, Movie BYU, Haines NFF, PLG, POV-Ray, Prisms, ProE "slp", "RAW" triangles, Rend386 PLG, RenderMan RIB, RenderMorphics, RenderWare, Sculpt, Sense8 WTK NFF, Stereolithography, Alias StyleGuide, Swivel, Symbolics, GDS "things", trueSpace, Vertigo, Vista DEM, VideoScape, VRML

5. WEB RESOURCES

- http://www.gamers.org
- http://www.viewpoint.com/vp/interchange
- http://www.digitalanimators.com/HTM/Reviews/Viewpoint_review.htm
- A detailed: list (http://www.viewpoint.com/vp/interchange/interchange5_5conversion.pdf) of which conversion features are supported by Interchange for each file format

ISA (INTERNET SCENE ASSEMBLER)

1. PLATFORMS, PRICES, AND SUPPLIER/CREATOR

- PC
- $179.95
- ParallelGraphics: http://www.parallelgraphics.com/

2. APPLICATIONS

- Internet Scene Assembler (ISA) is a VRML authoring tool that facilitates the creation of interactive and dynamic 3D scenes for the Web. Both experienced Web designers and relative novices can create exciting 3D environments. Supports e-commerce opportunities by providing realistic and interactive 3D presentations of products. Allows viewers to "touch," "feel," and "test" products. Allows the user to engage in a virtual tour. The range of applications goes from photocopiers to cars and from online manuals to the maintenance of highly complex machinery such as planes

3. EXAMPLES/SAMPLES

- Play with a virtual laptop: http://www.parallelgraphics.com/products/isa/ examples/product-presentation/
- Take a virtual tour created with Internet Scene Assembler: http://www.parallelgraphics.com/products/isa/examples/real-estate/
- Habitat Virtual Village houses created with ISA: http://www.habitatvirtualvillage.com/current_projects/index.htm

4. FUNCTIONS

- Object properties:
  - the objects can be created as touchable, movable, turnable, hidable, highlighted, labeled, linked, looksensitive (detect when a user can see the object), billboarded (allows inclusion of 2D images in the scenes that rotate to always face the camera), collidable, proximity (do something when the camera gets close to the object)
- Object hierarchy:
  - allows the creator to establish the subordination of objects. For example, a table and a vase; with a table as object and a vase as subobject, when the table is moved, the vase is moved as well
- Object gallery:
  - ISA includes pre-built galleries with a range of static and animated objects: figurines, furniture, plants, etc. It also includes the following galleries:
    i. System objects – easily attach lights, texts, and sounds to the objects
    ii. Animated – a collection of objects with predetermined animations
    iii. Characters – a collection of characters animated with Internet Character Animator 1.0
    iv. Room – furniture for home and office
    v. Garden – 3D models of trees, bushes, flowers, etc.
    vi. Traffic – cars and road signs
    vii. Exhibition – contains everything one might need to create their own virtual exhibition: demonstration equipment, furniture, decorative elements and product samples
- Animation:
  - with ISA Keyframe Animator the changes in object sizes, properties, and position are easily accomplished
- File Formats:
  - 3D: VRML 97

- 2D images: GIF, JPG, PNG
- Sounds: WAV, MIDI
- You can also import VRML 1.0 in ISA by using the free Cortona VRML 1.0 Converter

5. WEB RESOURCES

- ISA homepage: http://www.parallelgraphics.com/products/isa/
- To download: http://www.zdnet.com/downloads/stories/info/0,,0017KJ,.html
- Review: http://www.yippee.net/html/win/developer/title2977.htm
- Review: http://tucows.eunet.fi/preview/041-010-001-014C.html

ISB (INTERNET SPACE BUILDER)

1. PLATFORMS, PRICES, AND SUPPLIER/CREATOR

- PC
- $78.95
- ParrallelGraphics: http://www.parallelgraphics.com/

2. APPLICATIONS

- ISB lets you establish virtual exhibitions and galleries, travel, and real estate agencies, as well as fill your homepage with cool content. If you would like to see a realization of the house or city of your dreams, ISB can help you solve the problem. ISB is an extremely useful tool in the study of basic three-dimensional simulation and construction. These are compulsory subjects for most students intending to work in the fields of architecture, building, advertising, and design

3. EXAMPLES/SAMPLES

- Monument: http://www.parallelgraphics.com/products/isb/examples/tatlin/
- Musical Merry-go-round: (work along with ISA): http://www.parallelgraphics.com/products/isa/success/merrygoround1
- The flying car (work along with ISA): http://www.parallelgraphics.com/products/isa/success/landing-strip

4. FUNCTIONS

- Modeling:

  - Building of complex 3D objects and structures from simple elements by merely adding and cutting them. More than 250 various models of houses, trees and furniture are pre-built and ready for use. There are also 40 pictures and 40 movies available for users

- Transforming:

  - A simple way of arranging objects in scenes ("drag and drop"); direct edition of objects in 3D window includes the following: rotation, scale, deformation, mirror, texture mapping

- Textures:

  - Creation and edition textures: drawing, scaling, rotation; also animation textures
  - There are more than 900 various samples in the following categories: Arts, Abstract, Block, Brick, Clouds, Dalle, Floorstone, Floorwood, Grids, Grass, Ground, Leaves, Hightech, Ordinary, Rainbow, Stonedeco, Stonewild, Stucco, Waves, Wood

- Sounds:

  - Sounds of WAV and MIDI formats can be linked to the objects

- Backgrounds:

  - Allows for creation of panoramic images by using pre-built landscapes, selecting background textures, editing background colors

- 3D Texts:

  - 3D texts can be added to the objects and to the scenes. Editing of text includes changes of color, fonts, and execution quality

- Supported formats
  i. VRML 97, VRML 2.0, VRML 1.0
  ii. BMP, GIF, JPG, PNG

5. WEB RESOURCES

- Software archive: http://davecentral.com/10684.html

- User guide: http://www.parallelgraphics.com/products/isb/download/

- Success stories: http://www.parallelgraphics.com/products/isb/successstories/

IRIS Explorer

1. PLATFORMS, PRICE, AND SUPPLIER/CREATOR

- PC Windows (NT/2000); PC Linux (Red Hat 5.x/6.x); Silicon Graphics IRIX 6.x; Sun SPARC Solaris (2.x); DEC Alpha UNIX/Compaq Tru64 UNIX; HP 9000/700 HP-UX; IBM RISC/6000 (AIX)

- N/A

- Numerical Algorithms Group (NAG): http://www.nag.com

2. APPLICATIONS

- 3D data visualization, animation and manipulation tool that uses a point and click interface for programming and developing customized visualization applications. Industry, universities, and research institutions including Nike, CERN, Exa, and the National Institute of Health (USA) use IRIS worldwide. IRIS Explorer utilizes the Open Inventor, Image Vision, and OpenGL libraries, together with NAG's world-class numerical libraries. It is available on a broad range of Windows PC, Unix, and Linux platforms

3. EXAMPLES/SAMPLES

- Several examples can be found at each of these sites:
  http://www.nag.com/visual/IE/iecbb/Posters/Index.html
  http://www.nag.com/visual/IE/iecbb/Posters/examples.html

4. FUNCTIONS

- Modularity:
  - Modules are combined to create powerful visualization applications
  - There are approximately 300 reusable modules in IRIS Explorer 5.0
  - A new search facility allows users to find modules based on functionality
  - Modules can be accessed here: http://www.cc.gatech.edu/scivis/iris/doc/ref/man3/index.htm
  - And here: http://www.scs.leeds.ac.uk/iecoe/main_repository.html
  - And others from this site: http://www.nag.com/visual/IE/iecbb/Upload.html
- Visualization:
  - Pyramid modules — used to visualize unstructured meshes using isosurfaces, contouring, and slicing
  - Vector data — visualized on an unstructured mesh using particle advection
  - Open Inventor scene graph — a collection of geometric primitives
  - Clipping
  - Smoke

- Modules control all visualization techniques. The modules may be used individually or in combinations to form new concepts

- Rendering:

  - Cameras: adjustable, movable — user defined viewpoints for navigation
  - Lights: light sources may be added to the scene
  - Links from objects in the scene to other related material using the VRML Anchor node

- Animation:

  Accepts images in byte lattices and buffers them in an internal image list. Images are interactively added or deleted from the list. Sequences are played back in a custom 24-bit (or 12-bit) window. There are controls for:

  - Single stepping
  - Going forwards and backwards
  - Jumping to a particular image
  - Adjusting the animation delay
  - Looping
  - Saving the image for later animation
  - Generate horizontal or vertical planes from a 3D perimeter or curvilinear lattice

- Manipulation:

  - Maps are built from modules with connections defining the data flow
  - Modules are controlled via parameters
  - Reshape the map by adding other modules

- Internal Libraries:

  - NAG Numerical Library — over 1000 routines
  - Image Vision
  - Open Inventor (VRML)

5. WEB RESOURCES

- IRIS information: http://www.scs.leeds.ac.uk/iecoe/

- IRIS information: http://www.nag.com/Welcome_IEC.html

- Download a demo version: http://www.nag.com/visual/IE/iecbb/IE_Demo.asp

- Magazine for IRIS users: http://www.nag.com/visual/IE/iecbb/Render/Issues.html

iSpace

1. PLATFORM, PRICE, AND SUPPLIER/CREATOR

- Windows
- $99.00
- Caligari: http://www.caligari.com/iSpace/

2. APPLICATIONS

- iSpace is a Web graphics assembly tool designed to help quickly and easily add 3D graphics to an HTML layout on your website. iSpace works seamlessly with your main HTML editor such as Front Page, Dreamweaver, or Adobe GoLive and uses a standard HTML format for input and output of the entire fully formatted page. You can create your objects in trueSpace, the company's primary 3D modeling tool, and import them into iSpace. iSpace1.5 with the Flash plug-in now allows Web designers to incorporate 3D animations into their webpages while maintaining optimal file sizes

3. EXAMPLES/SAMPLES

- http://www.caligari.com/iSpace/mainfirstpage.html
- http://www.caligari.com/iSpace
- Examples and applications: http://www.caligari.com/iSpace/banner1.htm
- Examples with music: http://www.computer-music.com/graphic/iSpace.htm

4. FUNCTIONS

- Modeling:
    - Objects: several libraries of buttons, objects, styles, etc. with more available; custom objects can be imported from trueSpace, backgrounds, borders
    - Transformation: translation, rotation, scaling
    - Editing and manipulations (vertex, edge, face, polygon, curves, objects) through widgets
- Rendering:
    - Cameras: moveable
    - Lights: shadowing, reflections, true lighting, falloff, intensity, occlusion
    - Materials: transparency, blending, shading, bump mapping
    - More materials: texture mapping, depth testing, filtering
    - Before and after rendering: anti-aliasing, individual element, ray tracing
- Animation:
    - Basic and importable

  – Advanced: GIF89 and .avi imbedding, bounce, swing, spiral, spin, orbit, pop, fade, Flash format
- File Formats:
  – Import files: .cob, .sob, .asc, .3ds, .prj, .x, .dxf, .ps, .eps, .ai, .iob, .lwb, .lwo, .geo, .obj, .dib, .bmp, .tga, .jpg, .gif, .avi, .png, .dds, and .tif
  – Export files: .cob, .can, .asc, .3ds, .x, .dxf, .bmp, .tga, .jpg, .gif, .avi, .swf, and .png

5. WEB RESOURCES

- http://www.caligari.com/iSpace.html
- http://www.webscape.com
- http://www.amazing3d.com
- Review: http://www.iboost.com/build/software/reviews/iSpace/1152.htm
- iSpace forum: http://206.79.28.16/discus/messages/2/2.html?988374571
- iSpace manual: http://www.caligari.com/ispacemanual/toc.htm

JAVA 3D

1. PLATFORMS, PRICES, COMPANY

- PC, Mac, SGI IRIX
- Java Jump Start Edition (on subscription at $49.95 a year); for other editions see: http://www.sun.com/developers/tools/sw_overview.html#jumpstart
- Free use available (as per license)
  Download from: http://java.sun.com/products/java-media/3D/download.html
- Sun Microsystems: http://java.sun.com/

2. APPLICATIONS

- Java 3D is an extension to java for displaying 3D graphics. Developers can easily incorporate platform-independent 3D graphics into Java technology-based applications and applets. The Java 3D API provides a set of object-oriented interfaces that support high-level programming

3. GALLERY/SAMPLES

- Some examples:
  http://www.java3d.org/examples/
  http://www.ncsa.uiuc.edu/~srp/Java3D/portfolio/examples.html
  http://www.cs.ubc.ca/~djames/deformable/ArtDefoPics/

4. FUNCTIONS

- Features include animation, grouping, positioning, rotating, scaling, lighting, sound, fog, backgrounds, primitive shapes, concepts of appearance, material, textures, and bounding boxes, coplanar objects, objects built in order based on indexed lists, an ambient-light object, built-in morphing capability, and the ability to specify image depth and 3D textures

- Java 3D includes an extensive set of math classes: vector objects used to store colors, texture coordinates, vertices, and so on; matrix objects, which define a complete three-by-three or four-by-four floating-point transform matrix; and quarternion objects, which store four-component x, y, z, and w coordinates

- Java 3D also provides a view model that enables an application to be viewed with many different devices: computer displays, head-mounted displays and other six-degrees-of-freedom devices, multiple-projection displays, and so on

- (Note: It is very important that Java3D is a higher level language, as a result it does not provide the user with as much flexibility as OpenGL)

5. RESOURCES

- Tutorial: http://developer.java.sun.com/developer/onlineTraining/java3d/
- Object library for Java3D: http://www.ncsa.uiuc.edu/~srp/Java3D/portfolio/
- Implementation Documentation Download: http://java.sun.com/Download4
- Java 3D Online Documentation: http://java.sun.com/products/java-media/3D/forDevelopers/j3dapi/index.html

Jet 3D

1. PLATFORMS, PRICES, AND SUPPLIER/CREATOR

- PC Windows platforms

- Free Open Source License — for either commercial or noncommercial projects as long as the rules stated in the Open Source License are followed. A copy of the Open Source License can be found at:http://www.genesis3d.com/licensing.htm
- Full License Costs $10,000. This license releases you from all splash screen, open source, and logo requirements
- Cheyenne Cloud: http://www.cheyennecloud.com; http://www.jet3d.com/index.htm; http://www.destiny3d.com/

2. APPLICATIONS

- Jet 3D is a state-of-the-art 3D graphics engine built for high performance real-time rendering. It can be used to create complex virtual environments, games, presentations, etc.

3. EXAMPLES/SAMPLES

- Screenshots rendered by Jet 3D engine can be found in the following link: http://www.jet3d.com/screenshots.htm

4. FUNCTIONS

- Environment:
  - Exceptionally fast rendering
  - Radiosity lighting
  - Integrated rigid body physics simulation support for world objects
  - Pre-computed lighting for animating light intensities and simulating caustics
  - Environment uses BSP trees for fast visibility culling
  - Dynamic RGB lights
  - Dynamic shadows
  - Dynamic fog
  - Dynamic mirrors
  - Dynamic water effects
  - Dynamic texturing effects such as procedurals, animations, blending, and morphing
  - Area portals allow selective rendering of world geometry
  - Translucent world geometry for windows, or other effects
  - Spherically mapped sky for seamless sky and horizon
  - 3D sound positioning and attenuation
  - User extendable special effects and particle systems
  - Bitmap and Windows font support for labeling the screen, textures, or bitmaps
- Editor:
  - CSG editor builds geometry optimized for 3D environments
  - Built in keyframe system to animate world geometry
  - Multiple compilation options, including fast recompiles for changes to non-geometrical objects such as lights and entities

- Configurable entity definitions for sharing level data with applications
- Built in physics entity definitions for specifying interactions between physically controlled objects

- Characters:
  - Seamless soft-skin polygonal characters
  - Automatic visibility culling for optimal performance
  - Tools to support character and animation authoring for 3D Studio Max
  - Smoothing group support for high quality shading
  - No limit to the number of materials used to texture or color characters
  - Materials can be animated using tinting, procedurals, animations, blending, and morphing

- Character Animation:
  - Animation based on either a hierarchical or a non-hierarchical bone system
  - Arbitrarily spaced keyframes in time
  - High quality interpolation between keys — second order continuity across orientation keys
  - Sharing of animations across different characters
  - Animations can be blended and mixed or partially applied
  - Animations are optimized to take up minimal space
  - Interpolation and blending subsystems can be used independently to animate other user objects

- Driver Support:
  - Glide
  - D3D (full screen and in a window)
  - Software driver for support on machines without hardware acceleration (full screen and in a window)
  - Built in texture and lightmap caching
  - Takes advantage of 3D hardware that supports multitexturing
  - 2D bitmap overlays

- Other Features:
  - Physics subsystem can be used to control world geometry, or independently to animate other user objects
  - Virtual file system allows file IO access to collection files, memory files, DOS file systems, and user extendable file systems transparently
  - Math support for vectors, matrices, and quaternions
  - Comprehensive support for texture and bitmap formats, mipmaps, and conversions
  - Basic network transport support for multiplayer
  - Fast collisions against the world geometry
  - Volumetric queries to determine the type of volume(s) a box lies in
  - Multiple worlds can be loaded and rapidly switched between
  - Multiple renders from different cameras can be mixed in a single frame
  - High level polygon API for adding persistent or temporary user drawn objects

5. WEB RESOURCES:

- FAQ for using Jet3D is available in this link: http://www.jet3d.com/faq.htm
- Discussion forum is available here: http://server5.ezboard.com/bjet3d

JIG

1. PLATFORMS, PRICES, AND SUPPLIER/CREATOR

- Workstations
- Jig v1.0 — Professional License: $1,050/License/CPU; Student Rate: $100/License/Year; Personal Use Rate: $200/License/Year;
- Steamboat Software, Inc.: http://www.steamboat-software.com

2. APPLICATIONS

- Jig is a fast, extensible, and open general purpose renderer for special effects companies and post production facilities of all sizes. Jig is a comprehensive solution for rendering traditional geometry as well as photorealistic hair, volumes, and particles. Jig is designed to be scalable, performing well on modest workstations as well as large rendering clusters

3. EXAMPLES/SAMPLES

- Traditional Geometry Images:
  http://www.steamboat-software.com/gallery_traditional.html
- Volumetric Images: http://www.steamboat-software.com/gallery_volumes.html
- Hair and Fur Images: http://www.steamboat-software.com/gallery_hair.html
- Cartoon and Line Rendered Images:
  http://www.steamboat-software.com/gallery_toon.html

4. FUNCTIONS

- Fast NURBS Surface Rendering:
- Hair Rendering:
  - Jig includes a comprehensive solution for rendering photorealistic hair. The speed of the rendering algorithm allows it to render millions of hairs in a reasonable amount of time. The sheer number of hairs one can render greatly increases the realism of the final image. The hairs are generated procedurally

in the renderer with a plug-in. As a result, no more than one hair is stored in memory at any given point in time. All attributes of the hair (i.e. color, kink, length, etc.) are mappable with the same layered mapping system used by the shaders. Hair combing may be controlled by sparsely positioning guide hairs on the surface, and interpolating them within the Jig system

- Volume Rendering:
  - The Jig system supports the rendering of volumetric effects such as smoke, clouds, and fire. Volumes may be defined using all the power of the Jig shading system, similar to the layering of maps and shaders. Volumes may also be defined by using large numbers of sub-pixel particles. Jig has the ability to cast shadows from the volumes onto other objects or even themselves (self-shadowing). Self-shadowing is crucial for many effects like smoke and clouds. The volume-rendering algorithm is also extremely efficient in terms of both memory and speed. Many effects that were previously impossible simply because of render time may now be achieved at nominal cost

- Toon Rendering:
  - JigToon provides a method to achieve a traditional 2D cel animation look, complete with lighting and simulated ink-drawn lines. Ink lines may be introduced automatically based on curvature and silhouette. Lines may also be introduced, removed, or colored by the user using the Jig mapping system. With JigToon, the user is equipped with all the tools necessary to achieve a final image that can seamlessly integrate within a classic animation pipeline

5. WEB RESOURCES

- http://www.steamboat-software.com/JIG.html
- http://www.3drender.com/ref/software.htm
- http://www.tenlinks.com/CAD/products/graphics.htm
- http://www.millimeter.com/HTM/Articles/2000/Oct/stepByStep2.htm
- http://www.highend3d.com/jig/

J/View 3Dpro

1. PLATFORMS, PRICES, AND SUPPLIER/CREATOR

- PC
- N/A
- J/View3D Web: http://www.int.com/products/java_toolkit_info/jview3d/j3dpro_product_overview.htm

2. APPLICATIONS

- J/View3DPro is built on top of Java3D, a high performance component that simplifies the task of creating sophisticated interactive data visualizations. Minimal Java programming experience is needed for rapid development of 3D visualization applications with J/View3DPro. No previous Java 3D or DirectX/ OpenGL programming experience is required

3. EXAMPLES/SAMPLES

- View3D Links: http://visualbeans.com/View3D/
- View3D technology: http://www.int.com/

4. WEB RESOURCES

- A list of resources on the net: www.visualbeans.com/
- Books: http://www.catalystpics.co.uk/sitemap.htm
- PC Magazine article: http://www.davecentral.com/javadev4.html
- http://usa.viewstat.nedstatbasic.net/cgi-bin/viewstat?name=javaView3D

K-3D

1. PLATFORMS, PRICES, AND SUPPLIER/CREATOR

- GNU/Linux and Win32
- Free
- K-3D: http://www.k-3d.com/

2. APPLICATIONS

- K-3D is a 3D modeling, animation, and rendering system. Features include creation and editing of geometry in multiple real-time solid, shaded, and texture-mapped views. It is optimized for use with the BMRT rendering engine

3. EXAMPLES/SAMPLES

- http://www.k-3d.com/gallery/index.shtml

4. WEB RESOURCES

- http://www.k-3d.com/
- http://www.linux.org/apps/AppId_4030.html

Khoros

1. PLATFORMS, PRICES, AND SUPPLIER/CREATOR

- DEC/OSF, PC/Linux, SGI/Irix, Sun/Solaris, Windows NT 4.0
- Depending on version: $$$$$
- Khoral Research, Inc.: http://www.khoral.com/

2. APPLICATIONS

- Khoros is an Integrated Development Environment (IDE). It offers a visual programming environment with access to hundreds of data processing and visualization tools. It consists of the geometry library, a number of data processing routines for 3D visualization, and the render software rendering application. Visualization applications include animate, editimage, extractor, getimage, xprism, spectrum

3. EXAMPLES/SAMPLES

- http://www.khoral.com/khoros/khoros2/toolboxes/sampledata.html
- http://www.tnt.uni-hannover.de/soft/imgproc/khoros/khoros1/demos/overview.html

4. WEB RESOURCES

- http://www.tnt.uni-hannover.de/soft/imgproc/khoros/khoros1/
- http://www.sis.ucm.es/dipcourse/html/course-obj.html
- http://www.cs.ioc.ee/~khoros2
- http://www.khoral.com/khoros/

LandForm

1. PLATFORM, PRICE COMPANY

- Windows 95, 98, 2000, and NT (3.51 or 4.0)
- $$$$
- Rapid Imaging Software: http://www.landform.com

2. APPLICATIONS

- LandForm is a general purpose 3D Geographic modeler with image overlay capabilities. It displays topographic map data as 3D surfaces and allows of overlay satellite and aerial imagery on top of the surface

3. EXAMPLES/SAMPLES

- Exploring Mars: http://www.landform.com/pages/exploring-mars.htm (Terrain data from the Viking Orbiter)
- Terrain Modeling: http://www.landform.com/pages/modeling-the-terrain.htm (Modeling the terrain around Hoover Dam)
- Overlaying Images: http://www.landform.com/pages/overlaying-images.htm (Overlaying images from an Aeronautical chart onto data)
- High Resolution: http://www.landform.com/pages/high-resolution.htm (Imagery for an engineering model)
- Combining: http://www.landform.com/pages/combining.htm (Puts Satellite image data together with elevation data from a file)
- VRML Examples generated by LandForm: http://www.landform.com/pages/vrml.htm

4. WEB RESOURCES

- Satellite Imagery and High Resolution DEM data:
  - Spot Satellite: http://www.spot.com/
  - Microsoft TerraServer: http://terraserver.homeadvisor.msn.com/default.asp
  - Image Scans: http://www.imagescans.com/mainindex.html
  - Intermap Technologies: http://www.intermap.ca
  - Atlantis Scientific Inc.: http://www.atlsci.com/
- Source for Aeronautical and Nautical charts: http://www.maptech.com/
- Sources for USGS data:
  - Web GLIS: http://edc.usgs.gov/webglis
  - GISData: http://gisdata.usgs.gov/

- Other Resources:
  - National Elevation Dataset: http://edcnts12.cr.usgs.gov/ned/
  - A Listing of Digital Elevation Data: http://www.geo.ed.ac.uk/home/ded.html
  - The GeoVRML Working Group: http://www.ai.sri.com/geovrml/

LATTICE DESIGNER

1. PLATFORMS, PRICES, AND SUPPLIER/CREATOR

- Pentium PC 166mhz or higher, Windows 95+, Windows NT4.0+

- Free download (has expiration date, for further information, contact company in Japan)

- Lattice Technology, Inc.: http://www.lattice.co.jp/

2. APPLICATIONS

- Lattice Designer is a 3D modeling program that unites the best features of polygon and spline modeling software to create a new 3D graphics paradigm. The result is an easy, intuitive program with powerful accuracy and realism

3. EXAMPLES/SAMPLES

- On website: http://www.lattice3d.com/products.htm

- Modeling sample: http://www.sfc.keio.ac.jp/~daigo/scene2.html

4. FUNCTIONS

- Modeling:
  - Objects: polygon, spline, rounding
  - Transformation: scaling, translation, rotation, dividing, cloning, mirror, spacing, reversing, morphing
  - Editing and manipulations (vertex, edge, face, polygon, curves, objects): twirling, stretching, extruding, autogrid, smoothing, etc.
- Rendering:
  - Cameras: adjustable, movable
  - Lights: attenuation, volumetric lighting, shadow
  - Materials: composite, matte/shadow, morpher, multi/sub-object, top/bottom
- Key characteristics:
  - Calculates a surface and create surface shapes in real time

- User interface realizes practical modeling: users need not care about keeping polygons planar
- Any polygonal shape such as triangle, pentagon, or higher polygons is also accepted
- Standard file format is XVL, creates extremely small file size. DXL and OBJ are also acceptable

5. WEB RESOURCES

- An abstract: http://www.web3d.org/TaskGroups/x3d/lattice/LatticeProposal.html

- Website: http://www.lattice3d.com/

LEGUS3D

1. PLATFORMS, PRICES, AND SUPPLIER/CREATOR

- Windows 9x/NT

- $$$

- Legus3D LLC: http://www.legus3d.com/

2. APPLICATIONS

- Legus3D is a high-level Application Programming Interface (API) with scene graph, networking, sound, input and game logic libraries for creating real-time 3D applications. The scene graph library contains key rendering features such as: BSP, curved surfaces, volumetric lighting, shadows, decals, detail textures, skeletal transformation and animation, and it supports Direct3D and OpenGL rendering. The engine offers complete solution for 3D application developers

3. EXAMPLES/SAMPLES

- http://www.ga-source.com/all/news/bits/00+06+2000/1:31:26.shtml

- http://www.legus3d.com/screenshots/editor02l.jpg

4. WEB RESOURCES

- http://www.legus3d.com/technology.shtml

- http://www.meshes.com/cssgame/engine1.htm

Lightscape

1. PLATFORMS, PRICES, AND SUPPLIER/CREATOR

- Microsoft Windows 95, 98, NT 4.0, or NT 3.51
- $$$$
- Discreet: http://www.lightscape.com http://www.discreet.com

2. APPLICATIONS

- Lightscape is a tool for lighting design and rendering. Lightscape is used by digital content creators to illuminate and render real-time environments for film, broadcast, Web, and interactive gaming applications

3. EXAMPLES/SAMPLES

- Radiosity Demonstration: http://www.lightscape.com/assets/images/radiosity.jpg
- Image by Michael Fowler: http://www.id8media.com/3d_products/lightscape_1.htm
- Gallery: http://www.lightscape.co.uk/gallery/Gallery_16_43/gallery_16_43.html
- "Building": http://www.renderology.com/vault/gallery/images/sgsg363.jpg

4. WEB RESOURCES

- ID8 Media (Retail): http://www.id8media.com/3d_products/Lightscape3.2.htm
- Seiler Instrument: http://www.seilerinst.com/cad/products/lscp.htm
- TV Technology.com: http://www.tvtechnology.com/cv/cv-shamms_lightscape32.shtml
- Cadalyst: http://www.cadonline.com/features/0800render/lightscape.htm
- UK Lightscape Site: http://www.lightscape.co.uk/Specification/specification.html

LightWave 3D

1. PLATFORMS, PRICES, AND SUPPLIER/CREATOR

- Intel: Windows NT, 98, 2000, Pentium 266 or better, 64MB RAM Minimum; DEC: Alpha Windows NT v.3.51 or later, 64MB RAM Minimum; MAC; PowerMac Systems 8.6 or later, 128 MB RAM, Minimum
- $2,495 new; between $495–$995 for upgrade depending on current version
- NewTek: http://www.lightwave6.com/
  http://www.newtek.com

2. APPLICATIONS

- LightWave 3D is a 3D animation system offering features such as full ray tracing, motion blur, depth of field, variable lens settings, and may other special effects that allow users to create stunning images and animations
  - Animation
  - Facial Animation
  - Film Making
  - Image Editing
  - Inverse Kinematics
  - Photogrammetric 3D Model Reconstruction
  - photorealistic Animation System
  - Rendering Terrain Data
  - Surfacing Tool

3. EXAMPLES/SAMPLES

- F-14 Modeled using Lightwave:
  http://www.fxartist.com/_gallery/_personal/F-14s/SideCU.htm
- Lightwave World Gallery:
  http://www.lightwaveworld.com/gallery.html
- Hypervoxels:
  http://www.octura.com/3d/HV.htm
- Gallery Index for Newtek LightWave 3D:
  http://www.newtek.com/products/lightwave/gallery/gallery.html
- LightWave 3D User Profiles:
  http://www.newtek.com/products/lightwave/profiles_main.html

4. SUPPORTED FORMATS

- Animation — AVI, QuickTime

- Imagery — Alias, BMP, Cineon, YUV, JPEG, IFF, PICT, PCX, PSD, RLA, SGI, TGA, TIFF, TIFF_LogLUV, RAD, Sun, VPB
- Objects — 3DS, OBJ, DFX, FACT
- Other — QTVR, Illustrator

5. WEB RESOURCES

- Lightsource: http://www.lightsource-3d.com/tuts_others.htm
- Lightwave Tutorials: http://www.3dlinks.com/tutorials_lightwave.cfm
- Lightwave Plug-ins: http://www.3dlinks.com/software_plugins_lightwave.cfm
- Magic Media: http://www.magic-media.com
- LightWave World: http://www.lightwaveworld.com/
- LightWave 3D Frequently Asked Questions: http://www.li.net/~rlhomme/lwfaq.html
- Yahoo!Groups — LightWave: http://www.egroups.com/group/lw3d/
- Tutorials and FAQ: http://www.newtek.com/products/lightwave/tutorials/tutorials_main.html
- Forum: http://www.newtek.com/products/lightwave/tutorials/tutorials_main.html
- Newsgroups:
  - comp.graphics.apps.lightwave
  - alt.binaries.3d.lightwave
  - z-netz.alt.lightwave

Lightworks

1. PLATFORMS, PRICES, AND SUPPLIER/CREATOR

- UNIX, Microsoft Windows, and MAC platforms
- From $25 up to $500 per user
- Lighwork Design corporate: http://www.lightwork.com/about/abpg.htm

2. APPLICATIONS

- Lightworks is a rendering engine for 3D design software applications that is a flexible, affordable solution for high quality photorealism

3. EXAMPLES/SAMPLES

- http://www.lightwork.com/galleries/aec_gallery/gaaepg.htm
- http://www.lightwork.com/galleries/graphics_gallery/gagrpg.htm
- http://www.lightwork.com/galleries/industrial_gallery/gaingp.htm
- http://www.lightwork.com/products/machineworks/prmapg.htm

4. RESOURCES

- http://www.lightwork.com/products/lightworks/prlipg.htm#Layer
- http://www.lightwork.com/products/lightworks/prliopglpg.htm
- http://www.lightwork.com/news/latestnews/nepg.htm
- http://www.lightwork.com/home.htm

Lipservice

1. PLATFORMS, PRICES, AND SUPPLIER/CREATOR

- PC
- $285
- Joe Alter, Inc.: http://www.joealter.com

2. APPLICATIONS

- LipService is a 3D facial sculpting and animation plug-in and standalone for lightwave. It was used to create a 3D animation movie "Jersey". "Jersey" has also been awarded 'Best of Imagina' from the Imagina festival

3. EXAMPLES/SAMPLES

- http://www.joealter.com/lipservice/interpolation.htm
- http://www.joealter.com/lipservice/puppeteering.htm

4. FUNCTIONS

- Modeling:
  - Objects: Line, arc, circle, polygon
  - Advanced Objects: Motion splines
  - Transformations: Nonlinear morphing, nonlinear interpolation

- Editing and Manipulations: Manipulates vertices on thousands splines, translation, inflation, neutralization, smoothing
- Rendering:
  - Lights: Attenuation
  - Materials: Texture mapping, color texturing
  - Other: Puppeteering mode to animate a face

5. WEB RESOURCES

- http://www.videosystems.com/html/2000/july/features/alter/alter.htm
- http://cgw.pennnet.com/home/
  articles.cfm?ARTICLE_ID=83525&VERSION_NUM=2&Section=Articles
- http://www.joealter.com/

LithTech Development System

1. PLATFORM, PRICES, AND SUPPLIER/CREATOR

- PC, applications can be ported to Playstation2 and X-Box
- Varies by licensing options, e-mail for more information: sales@lithtech.com
- LithTech, Inc.: www.lithtech.com, subsidiary of Monolith Productions: www.lith.com

2. APPLICATIONS

- The LithTech Development System (LTDS) is comprised of platform-independent tools and technologies, which are licensed alongside components developed for a specific platform. These tools are used by 3D programmers and game programmers to make 3D-based applications

3. EXAMPLES/SAMPLES

- Game made with first generation of LTDS — Shogo:
  Mobile Armor Division: www.shogo-mad.com, follow media link for 3D engine movies
- Game made with second generation of LTDS — No One Lives Forever: www.the-operative.com, follow technology and download links for engine, movies, screenshots, and use of the LTDS

4. FUNCTIONS

- LithTech Development System:

  - Animation (vertex and skeletal systems) and modeling system
  - Terrain module
  - Networking module
  - Command console
  - Physics and collision detection module
  - Client/Server game object methodology
  - Abstract memory management methodology

- Platform Specific Module (PC, PlayStation 2, or Xbox):

  - 3D and 2D Rendering Technology
  - Sound Technology
  - Operating System Support

- LithTech Support Services:

  - Tutorial sample applications
  - Access to LithTech technical support team
  - API, content creation, and programming reference manuals
  - 2-day training session at the LithTech offices

- Tools and Plug-ins:

  - DEdit Environment Creator
  - ModelEdit
  - FxEd Visual Effects Editor
  - World preprocessor
  - 3D Studio Max Exporter
  - Maya Exporter

5. WEB RESOURCES

- http://www.developium.com

- http://www.flipcode.com

LS-DYNA

1. PLATFORMS, PRICE, AND SUPPLIER/CREATOR

- All Platforms

- $75

- Livermore Software Technology Corporation: http://www.lstc.com/index.html

2. APPLICATIONS

- LS-DYNA predicts a car's behavior in a collision and the effects of the collision upon the car's occupants

- LS-DYNA is capable of simulating projectile penetration, blast response, and explosives. LS-DYNA's predecessor, LLNL DYNA3D, was originally written for military simulations

3. EXAMPLES/SAMPLES

- LS-POST: http://www.lstc.com/news/post.htm

- Bra analysis: http://www.arup.com/dyna/applications/other/other.htm

- LS-OPT For Unix or Linux: http://www.lstc.com/news/lsopt.htm

- LS-NIKE3D: http://www.lstc.com/prod.html

4. WEB RESOURCES

- Scientific and Engineering Research: http://cac.psu.edu/beatnic/Reports/

- LS-DYNA Version 950 Info: http://www.kbs2.com/info/V950INFO.HTM

- Technology: http://www.swri.org/3pubs/brochure/D64/AUTO/autofac.htm

LSS Vista

1. PLATFORMS, PRICES, AND SUPPLIER/CREATOR

- 32-bit Windows platforms (95, 98, 2000, and NT)

- £750/year

- McCarthy Taylor Systems, Ltd.: http://www.mccarthytaylor.com/

2. APPLICATIONS

- LSS is a powerful PC-based Digital Terrain Modeling System. LSS Vista provides fully rendered 3D views and real-time virtual tours with textured features, such as trees, hedges, fences, etc. and image draping, such as raster maps and aerial orthophotos — valuable when interpreting a site or design. In addition, this product offers many powerful volume calculation, section reporting, and plotting facilities. Plans may be digitized from an external tablet and models merged together for the creation of final design plans and views

3. EXAMPLES/SAMPLES

- LSS Products: http://www.mccarthytaylor.com/products.htm
- LSS in Action: http://www.mccarthytaylor.com/lssinaction.htm

4. FUNCTIONS

- Three dimensional views and real-time fly-bys (virtual tours). Textures may be applied to the DTM in order to represent different materials or zones and images applied to point and link features to represent such things as trees, hedges, walls, fences, and buildings
- Raster maps and aerial orthophotos may also be draped onto the DTM with the minimum of user intervention and the combined model flown or walked through in real time
- Joystick, gamepad, or keyboard control of 3D virtual tours
- Display up to seven DTMs in the same 3D view simultaneously, with full control over transparency
- Animated water "flood" level facility within the 3D view and virtual tour
- Calculation of volumes between two surveys, broken down by surface code if required, using cross sections or highly accurate complex triangular vertical prisms
- Plotting of sections through up to 50 DTMs simultaneously to any Windows-compatible printer or plotter
- Reporting and output of section data
- Digitizing of plans via a tablet, including the ability to "stream" and condition contour data
- Design of variable offset features

5. WEB RESOURCES

- http://www.mccarthytaylor.com/
- http://ctiweb.cf.ac.uk/cticbe/resguide/lss.html
- http://www.vterrain.org/Packages
- http://www.pitandquarry.com/st-compute2.html

LumeTools

1. PLATFORMS, PRICES, AND SUPPLIER/CREATOR

- LumeTools is now available in Lightwave 3D and MentalRay for Softimage versions
- Prices (http://www.dynamic-realities.com/products/lumetools/:
  - For Lightwave 5.5+ or Inspire
  - Intel $795
  - Alpha $795
  - Mac $795
  - SGI $1595
- Company:
  - Dynamic Realities: http://www.dynamic-realities.com/products/lumetools/; http://www.lume.com

2. APPLICATIONS

- LumeTools is a set of five plug-in toolsets that allow you to realistically create and surface objects and scenes. You can purchase the whole set or each individual set separately
  - LumeLandscape: http://www.dynamic-realities.com/products/lumetools/landscape/
  - LumeWater: http://www.dynamic-realities.com/products/lumetools/water/
  - LumeLight: http://www.dynamic-realities.com/products/lumetools/light/
  - LumeMatter: http://www.dynamic-realities.com/products/lumetools/matter/
  - LumeWorkbench: http://www.dynamic-realities.com/products/lumetools/workbench/
- The LumeTools collection is originally developed for the MentalRay renderer used by Softimage

3. EXAMPLES/SAMPLES

- Gallery on Lume website: http://www.lume.com/gamma/0.45/gallery.html

4. FUNCTIONS

- LumeLandscape Set:
  - landscape — A highly versatile shader that will help you to map textures to your terrain models in extremely useful and natural ways, through attributes such as slope, height, noise functions. For example, on a single piece of terrain geometry it could be used to create dusty pile-ups on plateau surfaces, exposed rock faces in steeper cliff-like areas, and water stains where the ground meets the sea. Especially useful in situations where the size and shape of an object makes handmade textures impractical

- mist — Provides both a true layered fog, along with a depth fading effect superior to Softimage's built-in. You can take advantage of Mist's plug-and-play ease to simply create a beautiful layered fog; or, for greater control, it allows for directional variations specified with texture maps, and can be applied to any enclosed volume, not just the atmosphere
- facade — Facade places virtual cardboard-cutouts in a scene, allowing you to replace complex geometry with simple 2D faces. Facade can then "rotate" the cutout so that it follows the movement of the camera, and avoids unwanted stretching, shadows, and reflections

- LumeLight Set:

  - glare — A shader which models the way the human eye scatters light, Glare gives you realistic glares and flares from any bright source — not just lights. For example, it will create glares off of shiny metals, flares from reflections on a water surface, you name it. Especially useful for bright areas where the image becomes overexposed
  - translucency — Allows you to easily create truly translucent textures — with blurred transparency and back-lighting scattering effects. Good for lamp shades, light bulbs, frosted glass, stained glass, sun-dappled tree leaves, etc.
  - glow — A material shader designed to simulate an object with internal lighting, as either an overall effect or specified with a texture map. You can create glow maps that respond to light levels and overexposures in a photographic manner
  - night — Simulates the eye's rods and cones, making colors appear desaturated in extremely dim lighting conditions (such as moonlight) while preserving colors in normal lighting
  - beam — A variation on the "volumetric light" shader, it gives a basic atmospheric effect around lights. By leaving out shadow calculations, Beam is ultra-fast, and can be applied to all the lights of a scene with a negligible increase in render time
  - illumination — A light shader which gives a more realistic falloff curve, along with increased control of the falloff

- LumeMatter Set:

  - metal — Helps to create perfect metal by modeling a metallic object's reflective properties, including color filtering of the reflected rays, and blurring of the reflected images
  - glass — An easy-to-use shader which models glass's transparent and reflective properties, including fresnel reflection and transparency shifts near the object's edges, coloration filtering of transparency rays (colored glass), and more
  - edge — Provides special edging effects for anytime you want to make a fuzzy mouse, a jagged rock, a blurry ghost, or a notched peg

- LumeWater Set:

  - ocean — Simulates realistic waves over a large body of water. These waves look great, animate, are easy to create, and are highly adjustable. The user can even request a looping animation, for which he provides the number of frames in the loop

- water — A simple but important shader, Water models the physics of the reflective, transparency, and coloration properties of water. In addition, this shader can let your objects know when they are wet or dry, and apply the texture you supply accordingly (a feature that we've used for a good number of non-water effects as well)
  - submerge — A volume shader which provides an underwater depth fading effect, in which the vertical light falloff from the water's surface is taken into account — vital to accurately create the "submerged" look
  - wet — Wet objects have a significantly different appearance than dry objects: some have more saturated colors, others acquire a specular highlight; the Wet shader facilitates the creation of this effect by automatically displaying those textures that the artist has designated as "wet," on any portion of the object that is beneath the surface of the water

- LumeWorkbench Set:
  - wrapAround — This lifesaver of a shader captures a 360 degree wraparound image of a scene, which can then be used as an environment, as a reflection map, or even as a QuickTime VR environment map. By allowing you to drastically simplify the geometry needed to render your scene, WrapAround can take a load off of your processors
  - distortion — Offers an improved model for the distorting effects of a wide-angle lens. Both barrel and pin cushion effects are possible
  - bumpCapture — Captures the surface information of a scene, and converts it into an equivalent bump map. This funky little shader creates grayscale maps of the relative depth of anything at which you point your camera — like creating your bump maps in 3D in Softimage, rather than painting them by hand in Photoshop
  - adjustments — Used to adjust the coloration of an image or series of images. Contrast, brightness, hue, saturation, etc. can be adjusted or animated, and all can be applied on a per-object basis

5. WEB RESOURCES

- Lume webpage: http://www.lume.com/

- Lightwave 3D version: http://www.lume.com/gamma/0.45/order.html#Lightwave

- MentalRay for Softimage: http://www.lume.com/gamma/0.45/order.html#mentalray

MapRender3D

1. PLATFORMS, PRICES, AND SUPPLIER/CREATOR

- Microsoft Windows 95

- $295.00 ($95.00 for MapRender3D Lite)
- Digital Wisdom: http://www.maprender3d.com
  http://www.digiwis.com

2. APPLICATIONS

- MapRender3D is a terrain modeling, rendering, and visualization software package using either a supplied world wide elevation database or widely available public domain DEM files

3. EXAMPLES/SAMPLES

- Andes Mountains: http://www.maprender3d.com/previews/andes3d.jpg
- World: http://www.geomall.co.kr/catalog/images/catalog/maprender3a.jpg
- 3D Map of Japan: http://www.maprender3d.com/previews/japan.jpg
- MHM High Contrast Style: http://www.maprender3d.com/styles/mhmhi3.jpg
- Classic Style: http://www.maprender3d.com/styles/class.jpg

4. WEB RESOURCES

- Geoplace Review: http://www.geoplace.com/bg/1999/productreview/1099qt.asp
- The Gemi Store: http://www.eomonline.com/GEMIsiteNEW2/CommonGEMI/Mappingsoftware/maprender.htm
- Geomall: http://www.geomall.co.kr/catalog/pages/maprender3d.html

Materialize 3D!

1. PLATFORM, PRICE, COMPANY

- PC
- $29.00
- INDOTEK Software Productions: http://www.indotek.com

2. APPLICATIONS

- Materialize 3D! is a 3D model converter, material/texture editor and polygon processor. It can be used for 3D Studio, AutoCAD, Direct3D and Persistence of Vision files. 3D Models are rendered automatically in a real-time 3D environment with textures and lighting. User can project textures, calculate vertex normals, reverse polygon ordering, and assign new materials

3. EXAMPLES/SAMPLES

- Due to the nature of this tool, is very difficult to find any examples. The most obvious one is the example provided by the company:http://www.indotek.com/material.html

4. FUNCTIONS

- Rendering:
    - Precise calculation of model center
    - Re-orientation of coordinate axis system
    - Scaling uniformly or on any axis
    - Edition of materials including surface, specular, emissive and texture
- Modeling:
    - Texture projection and texture coordinates
    - Normal calculation
    - Reverse order of polygon ordering, vertex normals and texture coordinates
    - Assign new material
- Viewports:
    - Render and select viewports
    - Background color and light emission color
    - Cull mode, specular, and bilinear texture filtering
    - Top, bottom, left, right front and back sides of model
- File Formats:
    - Importing file formats: M3D, X, DXF, R3D, 3DS
    - Exporting file formats: M3D, X, DXF, R3D, POV

5. WEB RESOURCES

- Viewpoint Corporation: http://www.viewpoint.com

- ZDNet: http://www.zdnet.com/downloads/stories/info/0,,000PJT,.html

Mathematica

1. PLATFORMS, PRICES, AND SUPPLIER/CREATOR

- Windows 95/98/Me/NT/2000, Mac OS, Linux, Solaris, HP-UX, IRIX, AIX, Digital Unix, LinuxPPC, AlphaLinux, and compatible systems
- Student version: $140; Full version: $1495
- Wolfram Research: http://www.wri.com/

2. APPLICATIONS

- Mathematica combines interactive calculation (both numeric and symbolic), visualization and simulation tools, and is a complete programming environment

3. EXAMPLES/SAMPLES

- Mathematica Demo: http://library.wolfram.com/demos/
- Mathematica Plot: http://www.physics.purdue.edu/pcn/doc/Mathetica/mathepage3.html

4. WEB RESOURCES

- http://www.indiana.edu/~statmath/math/mma/gettingstarted/index.html
- http://www.math.duke.edu/education/ccp/materials/linalg/mmatutor/
- Publication: http://bach.seg.kobe-u.ac.jp/mma/publist.html

MATLAB

1. PLATFORMS, PRICES, AND SUPPLIER/CREATOR

- Platforms: http://www.mathworks.com/products/matlab/requirements.shtml
- Prices: http://www.mathworks.com/store/
- The MathWorks: http://www.mathworks.com

2. APPLICATIONS

- MATLAB includes hundreds of functions (link should go to: http://www.mathworks.com/products/matlab/functions/functions.shtml) that focus on data analysis/visualization, numeric/symbolic computation, engineering and scientific graphics, modeling, simulation, prototyping, GUI design, and application development. It contains complex 2D and 3D visualization and analysis capabilities with sophisticated toolboxes

3. EXAMPLES/SAMPLES

- MathWorks demos: http://www.mathworks.com/products/demos

- Central file exchange: http://www.mathworks.com/matlabcentral/fileexchange/index.jsp

- Acoustic: http://www.cage.curtin.edu.au/mechanical/info/vibrations/index.html

- Astronomy: http://cdeagle.tripod.com/ccmatlab.html

- Data Analysis: http://www.mathworks.com/products/tech_computing/dataan.shtml

- Materials Science: http://www.csee.wvu.edu/~trapp/push_bound.htm

- Image Library: http://www.mathworks.com/company/pressroom/analysis_vis_dev.shtml

- Morphology: http://www.mathworks.com/products/image/

- Oceanography: http://www2.ocgy.ubc.ca/~rich/

- Optimization: http://www.mathworks.com/products/optimization/

- Orbital Mechanics: http://cdeagle.tripod.com/ccmatlab.html

- Parallel Processing: http://www.cs.cornell.edu/Info/People/lnt/multimatlab.html

- Spatial and Geometric Analysis: http://puddle.mit.edu/~glenn/kirill/saga.html

- Volume Visualization: http://www.mathworks.com/products/matlab/vol_vis.shtml

- Wave Simulation: http://www.cvrti.utah.edu/~quan/text/work.html

- Wavelets: http://www.mathworks.com/products/wavelet/

4. FUNCTIONS

- Modeling:
    - 3D Modeling
    - 2D and 3D data displays. Includes triangulated and gridded data
    - Volume visualization of scalar and vector data
    - Image display and file I/O
    - Interactive plot annotation
    - OpenGL software and hardware support
    - Specialized graphs — Quiver, ribbon, scatter, bar, pie, and stem plots
    - Matrix manipulation
- Rendering:

  - Aspect ratio control
  - Supports multiple light sources for colored surfaces
  - Camera based viewing and perspective control
  - Hidden surface removal
  - Texture mapping
  - Flat, Gouraud, and Phong lighting
  - Z-Buffer

- Animation:

  - Animation and sound
  - Movie Creation – Animated Sequences of plots
  - Visualize solutions to ordinary and partial differential equations using MPEG

- File Formats:

  - Importing/Exporting common file formats including: TIFF, JPEG, PNG, BMP, HDF, PCX, XLS, CSV, and VRML

5. WEB RESOURCES

- Mathtools.net: http://www.mathtools.net/

- MATLAB Central: http://www.mathworks.com/matlabcentral/

- Document: http://www.mathworks.com/access/helpdesk/help/techdoc/matlab.shtml

- Online Tutorial: http://www.glue.umd.edu/~nsw/ench250/matlab.htm

- Data Visualization Toolbox for MATLAB implementing Cleveland's Visualization algorithms: http://www.datatool.com/Dataviz_home.htm

- Indiana University Tutorials: http://www.indiana.edu/~statmath/math/matlab/

- MATLAB Digest: http://www.mathworks.com/company/digest/

- Octave (Open Source, Free MATLAB Clone): http://www.octave.org/octave.html

- GMU Online MATLAB resource center: http://bass.gmu.edu/matlab/matlab.html

- MIT Resources: http://web.mit.edu/matlab/www/home.html

MAXTRAX II

1. PLATFORMS, PRICE, AND SUPPLIER/CREATOR

- PC, Windows 95, 98, and NT
- $95.00

- Sisyphus Software: http://www.sisyphus.com

2. APPLICATIONS

- MAXTRAX II is a path trail generator tool used as a 3D Max plug-in. As the contact patch moves through the scene, MAXTraxII generates a trail behind it

- It consists of three distinct plug-ins. The first, MTrack, is the standard path-generator familiar to MAXTRAX I users. Notable improvements to this systems include an on-off and cyclic timing queue and the ability to use shapes as cross-sections along the MaxTrax path. GTrack, the second plug-in, is a geometry-based version of MTrack

3. EXAMPLES/SAMPLES

- http://www.sisyphus.com/nav/MaxTrax/maxtrax_images.html

4. FUNCTIONS

- Modeling:

  - Objects: Create moving logos, solid trails, grow shapes of all types and descriptions. In addition, mundane uses of MAXTRAX II include the traditional skid marks, as well as bandages trailing from a mummy, banners towed behind an aircraft, boat wakes, contrails, footprints, a gift box whose ribbon ties itself, hand writing, paint stripping, painting, phasor fire, a spider building a Web, and ticker tape blowing in the wind
  - Transformation: Spacing, align, translation, rotation, scaling, and cloning
  - Editing and manipulations

- Rendering:

  - Cameras: movable
  - Lights: shadow, point, and spotlights
  - Materials: texture mapping, procedural maps, ray-traced maps

- Animation:

  - Controllers: key-based, system
  - Advanced animations: particle-based trail builder, geometry-based trail builder and a procedural shockwave
  - Basic animation

- File Formats:

  - Importing and Exporting file formats: 3D Studio Max (3ds)
  - Additional file formats: MTrack, GTrack, GTDisk and RingWave

5. WEB RESOURCES

- http://www.digimation.com/asp/product

- http://www.sisyphus.com/nav/MaxTrax

- http://www.sisyphus.com/descript/tracksP.htm#MAXTRAX

Maya

1. PLATFORMS, PRICES, AND SUPPLIER/CREATOR

- Platforms: Windows NT, IRIX, and LINUX workstations
- Unlimited $16,000; Complete $7,500; student version $750/year (http://www.journeyed.com; 1800-874-9001 x316)
- Alias|Wavefront: http://www.aliaswavefront.com

2. APPLICATIONS

- Maya Complete is a sophisticated 3D modeling, rendering, animation, and paint software. All features in Maya Complete are integrated into a single environment that is optimized for maximum speed and possible workflow. It has been used for many purposes including commercials, character animation, and virtual reality
- Maya Unlimited is a software package for film and video production houses. It includes all Maya Complete's functionality, plus a suite of innovative tools for advanced modeling, digital clothing simulation, fur rendering, and integrated match moving

3. EXAMPLES/SAMPLES

- Maya Movies: http://www.aliaswavefront.com/entertainment/solutions/movies/index.html
- Pictures: http://www.aliaswavefront.com/entertainment/news_events/gallery/index.html

4. WEB RESOURCES

- HighEnd3D: http://www.highend3d.com
- Maya Users Ring: http://www.mayaring.com
- The Jackals Forge: http://www.thejackalsforge.2sxy.com
- Maya MEL scripts: http://www.animagrafx.com.au/plugins.html
- Yahoo Article about Maya: http://biz.yahoo.com/bw/010213/ca_alias_w.html
- http://www.digitalproducer.com/pages/alias_wavefront_unveils_maya_com.htm

- WorldWide Users Group Maya Forum: http://www.wwug.com/forums/maya/

MentalRay

1. PLATFORMS, PRICES, AND SUPPLIER/CREATOR

- Main Unix Platforms, Linux, Windows 2000, NT
- $1000 – $2500 per CPU (OEM by Autodesk)
- Mental Images: http://www.mentalimages.com/index.html

2. APPLICATIONS

- MentalRay is a leading high-performance, photorealistic ray tracing and scanline rendering package. With an extensive track record in feature films, MentalRay is widely acknowledged as the most advanced 3D rendering solution on the market
- Users of MentalRay include most of the leading special effects and digital film studios, game developer companies, and companies in the automotive and aerospace industries

3. EXAMPLES/SAMPLES

- Gallery on mentalimages.com: http://www.mentalimages.com/c251.html
- Gallery on SOFTIMAGE and MentalRay resources: http://softimage.ancientfuture.net/gallery.html

4. FUNCTIONS

- Modeling:
  - Works with several front-end software systems (such 3DSMax) for modeling, animation etc.
  - Simple, efficient, and full-featured hierarchical scene description language, fully text-based with optional binary vector data for increased performance
  - C language API for the entire scene description language, multilevel scene graph, multiple instancing of objects and light sources
  - Curve and surface geometry: free-form surface bases: Bezier, B-spline (including NURBS), Cardinal, and arbitrary basis matrix, Taylor; rational and non-rational
- Rendering:

- OpenGL accelerated rendering; ray tracing, used automatically and transparently where necessary for refraction, reflection, ray-traced shadows, etc.; two alternate ray tracing acceleration methods: BSP and regular grids; contour rendering: cartoon animation, fine control over contour placement, overlaps, width, color, transparency, and other user-definable criteria; incremental changes: when rendering an animation, it is sufficient to define the differences from one frame to the next, instead of redefining the entire scene for every frame; Intermediate frame data that is not changed, such as tessellations, is cached. Shadows, Volume rendering, Motion and depth blurring, Global Illumination

- Animation:
  - Works with several front-end software (such as 3DSMax) for animation, but also has its own scene description language
- File Formats:
  - There are 36 built-in image file formats with automatic content-based type and subtype recognition and conversion when reading: Wavefront RLA and RLB, Softimage PIC and Zpic, Alias image, Dassault Systèmes CATIA, SGI RGB and RGBA, JPEG, 8 TIFF, RGBA Targa Quantel/Abekas, 576x720 (PAL) and 486x720 (NTSC), portable pixmaps (PPM), 12 uncompressed texture formats for all data types, high-speed memory-mapped raw images for all data types, Microsoft BMP 32-bit uncompressed, PostScript line drawings for contours 16 user-defined pluggable image file formats

5. WEB RESOURCES

- Product Info and update download on discreet.com:
  http://www2.discreet.com/products/
  d_products2.html?prod=mentalray&cat=overview

- SOFTIMAGE and MentalRay Information, Education, and Content:
  http://softimage.ancientfuture.net/

- MentalRay Frequently Asked Questions:
  http://www.cinegrfx.com/newpages/mray-faq.html

- MentalRay news on Autodesk's home page:
  http://www3.autodesk.com/adsk/item/0,,273832-123112-126954,00.html

Merlin 3D

1. PLATFORMS, PRICES, AND SUPPLIER/CREATOR

- PC Windows 95/98/2000/ME/XP

- $595 – $795
- Merlin3D: http://www.merlin3d.com

2. APPLICATIONS

- Merlin 3D is a 3D software for modeling, texturing, scene building, animation, and rendering. It has been designed for all-purpose 3D creativity rather than just one specialized area. Merlin can be used by professionals for a variety of applications such as CAD, Digital video, game development, design, and architecture

3. EXAMPLES/SAMPLES

- http://www.merlin3d.com/products/examples.htm
- http://www.merlin3d.com/gallery/
- http://www.merlin3d.com/digitalmedia.htm

4. FUNCTIONS

- Modeling:
  - Objects: 2D/3D primitives (circle, square, sphere, box, cube, cylinder, cone, knot, torus). 3D text
  - Transformation: Real-time modifiers: stretch, scale, uniform scale, bend, taper, twist, pull, relax, and bulge
  - Surface Patches: Create and edit surfaces, ideal for terrain, anatomy, etc.
  - Polyface Editing: Edit faces, vertex, or edge
  - Multiple Levels of Undo: has 10 levels of undo/redo
  - Booleans: Create any object by adding, subtracting, or intersecting two objects together to make a new object
- Rendering:
  - Camera Tools: (Free and Target) move, pan, dolly, orbit, origin rotate, field-of-view, stare-at, zoom, region zoom
  - Lights: directed, point, projector, area, and spotlights
  - Light Properties: Adjust color, shadow on/off/type, volume lighting, projector and falloff type
  - Materials: transparent/masking surfaces, load/save/create textures
  - Radiosity and hybrid radiosity: load and save
  - Ray Trace: preview and full ray trace rendering
  - Antialiasing
  - Fog, Ground fog
- Animation:
  - Basic controls: editable spline-based animation paths, function curves, key framing, shape, deformations, materials, AVI
  - Timeline key frame editing. Real-time recording with optional NAV 3D

- Basic animation: viewpoint movable, object translation, rotation/revolution and scaling, etc.
- BasicScript language: control the object behaviors
- File Formats:

  - File formats: DWG, DXF, SAT, IGES, STEP, PRJ, OBJ, 3ds, m3d and COB
  - Image formats: Jpeg, tiff, targa, bitmap

5. WEB RESOURCES

- View tutorials: http://www.merlin3d.com/products/tutorials.htm

- Download a trial version: http://www.merlin3d.com/products/download.htm

- http://www.news-serve.net/DTP/Merlin.html

- http://www.digitalproducer.com/pages/merlin3d_debuts.htm

Mesa

1. PLATFORM, PRICE, AND DEVELOPERS

- Originally designed for Unix/X11 workstations. Now supports Amiga, Apple Macintosh, BeOS, NeXT, OS/2, MS-DOS, VMS, Windows

- Free; Open Source

- Developers:

  - Original Developer: Brian Paul: brian@mesa3d.org
  - Contributors Webpage: http://www.mesa3d.org/devel.html
  - hosted by SourceForge: http://sourceforge.net/projects/mesa3d/

2. APPLICATIONS

- Mesa is a freeware low-level 3D graphics library with an API similar to the API of OpenGL. The original purpose is to emulate OpenGL commands on platforms that don't support OpenGL. The library can be used as a direct replacement for OpenGL, either statically or dynamically linked to applications compiled with the standard OpenGL headers

3. EXAMPLES/SAMPLES

- Mesa Demos on SourceForge: http://sourceforge.net/project/showfiles.php?group_id=3&release_id=15281

- SGI sample OpenGL implementation: http://oss.sgi.com/projects/ogl-sample

4. WEB RESOURCES

- Mesa Webpage: http://www.mesa3d.org/
- Mesa: http://freshmeat.net/projects/mesa/
- Mesa User's Guide: http://www.mesa3d.org/Mesa/MesaUsersGuide.html
- Mesa Mailing Lists: http://sourceforge.net/mail/?group_id=3
- PMesa Webpage: http://pmesa.sourceforge.net/
- PMesa: http://freshmeat.net/projects/pmesa/
- OpenGL: http://www.opengl.org/
- GLX: http://www.sgi.com/software/opensource/glx/
- X Window System: http://www.x.org/
- XFree86: http://www.xfree86.org/
- Silicon Graphics, Inc. (SGI): http://www.sgi.com/

Meshwork

1. PLATFORMS, PRICES, AND SUPPLIER/CREATOR

- Mac (both classic and Mac OS X)
- $30.00 (Free download on internet)
- Codenautics: http://codenautics.com

2. APPLICATIONS

- Meshwork is a 3D triangle-mesh modeling program for MacOS. It is designed especially for making compact, efficient objects for use in 3D games or on the Web. It can also be used to produce VRML for the Web, models for POV-RAY, sprites, models for OpenGL applications, and more

3. EXAMPLES

- Click on "Made With Meshwork" on side menu at the following URL: http://codenautics.com/meshwork/index.html

4. FEATURES

- Menus:

- File Menu: new, open, import, close, save, save as, export, quit
- Edit Menu: undo, redo, cut, select all, select none, select connected, duplicate
- Vertex Menu: relax, tense, find overlaps, combine overlaps, find strays, set bone
- Transform Menu: Face front, face out, invert face, flip horizontal, flip vertically, scale (X, Y, Z dimensions), rotate (X, Y, Z dimensions), subdivide
- Create Menu: box (X,Y,Z direction), sphere, sphere2, cylinder, cone, extrude, lathe
- Camera Menu: orthographic (cavalier projection), anaglyph, center selection
- Display menu: hide selected, hide others, show all, draw edges, draw vertices, draw faces, 3D preview, poses

- Toolbar:
  - Mode tool: add vertex, connect, split, disconnect, polygon (3-20 sizes), select, center, add bone
  - Symmetry buttons: Y-Z plane symmetry, +/- Y, +/- Z symmetry
  - Grid option: constrained to regular grid, grid spacing, active/invisible
  - Coordinate displays: current coordinate, current coordinate in texture map
  - Material palette: smooth, color, texture map, mapping, axis, center, size
  - Zoom buttons: zoom in, zoom out

- Keyboard Controls:
  - Arrow keys: move vertices up, down, left, right
  - Numeric keypad: move vertices X, Y and Z directions
  - Shift key: move vertices 20 pixels/keypress
  - Control key: move vertices one pixel

- File Formats:
  - Importing Format: DXF, 3DS, 3DMF
  - Exporting Format: DXF, 3DS, 3DMF, POV-Ray, VRML

5. WEB RESOURCES

- http://codenautics.com/meshwork/index.html
- http://www.angelfire.com/ri/hepheastus/DXF.html
- Newsgroup: http://www.egroups.com/group/meshwork/

MGF (The Materials and Geometry Format)

1. PLATFORMS, PRICES, AND SUPPLIER

- PC
- The program can be freely downloaded directly from its official website

- Greg Ward: GJWard@Lbl.Gov; http://radsite.lbl.gov/mgf/

2. APPLICATIONS

- The Materials and Geometry Format (referred to henceforth as MGF) is a description language for 3D environment light simulation and rendering. The materials are physically based and rely on color, reflectance, and transmittance for good accuracy and reproducibility. The geometry is based on boundary representation using simple geometric primitives such as polygons, spheres, and cones

3. WEB RESOURCES

- Official MGF website: http://radsite.lbl.gov/mgf/, includes online manual, example objects, example scenes and downloads of the software

- http://radsite.lbl.gov/mgf/scenes.html

- http://radsite.lbl.gov/mgf/objects.html

- http://radsite.lbl.gov/mgf/compare.html

- http://radsite.lbl.gov/mgf/mgfhtml/detexamp.html#begin

MicroStation TriForma

1. PLATFORMS, PRICES, AND SUPPLIER/CREATOR

- Microsoft Windows 95/98/NT

- $$$$$

- Bentley Systems, Inc.: http://www.bentley.com

2. APPLICATIONS

- MicroStation TriForma is a modeling tool for building design and drawing production

3. EXAMPLES/SAMPLES

- http://www.bentley.com/triforma/

- http://www.bentley.com/products/triforma/3views.jpg

- http://www.bentley.com/products/triforma/triforma.gif

- http://www.bentley.com/products/triforma/build50.jpg

4. WEB RESOURCES

- http://www.bentley.com/products/triforma/
- http://www.bentley.com/products/triforma/new.htm
- http://www.bentley.com/products/triforma/about.htm
- http://www.cadonline.com/reviews/software/cad/899triform/features.htm

MICRO SYSTEM OPTIONS: 3D GRAPHIC TOOLS

1. PLATFORMS, PRICES, AND SUPPLIER/CREATOR

- PC (Windows 95, NT, and 3.1)
- $$$$
- Micro System Options: http://catalog.vbonline.com/microsystem/default.htm

2. APPLICATIONS

- 3D graphic tools 5.5 provides extensive three dimensional graphics capabilities to Visual Basic and Visual C++ developers via DLL API interfaces, VBX and OCX (aka ActiveX) controls

3. EXAMPLES/SAMPLES

- http://moreinfo.vbonline.com/vbonline/micsys/3dgrap50/download.htm

4. WEB RESOURCES

- http://moreinfo.vbonline.com/vbonline/micsys/3dgrap50/info.htm
- http://catalog.vbonline.com/items.htm

MilkShape 3D

1. PLATFORMS, PRICES, AND SUPPLIER/CREATOR

- PC
- Shareware ($20 to register for 1.x upgrades)
- Chumbalum Soft: http://www.swissquake.ch/chumbalum-soft/ms3d/

2. APPLICATIONS

- A low-polygon modeler and editing utilities, originally designed to edit Half-Life (a game developed by Valve) models; it now has the abilities to import many file types and model from different games. (For example, Quake I, II, III, Unreal, and Team Fortress.) Its primary usage is amateur game development and game modification

3. EXAMPLES/SAMPLES

- Chumbalum Soft's Gallery: http://www.swissquake.ch/chumbalum-soft/ms3d/screenshots.html

4. FUNCTIONS

- Modeling:
  - Objects: polygonal, skeletal spline
  - Transformation: translation, rotation, scaling, mirror, and align
  - Editing and manipulations of character's texture, and vertices
- Rendering:
  - Cameras: adjustable, movable
  - Lights: fixed
  - Lights' properties: ambient, diffuse, and specular
  - Materials: texture mapping, and some basic control over light reflection
- Animation:
  - Controllers: key-based
  - Basic Animation
- File Formats:
  - Importing file formats: SMD (Half-life), MDL, MD2, MD3 (Quake), NOD, BDY, MOT, 3D, OBJ, ASC, LWO, DXF, INC, WRL, 3DS, ASCII (MilkShape 3D), RAW, RIB
  - Exporting file formats: SMD, MDL, MD2, MD3, NOD, BDY, MOT, 3D, OBJ, ASC, LWO, DXF, INC, WRL, 3DS, ASCII, RAW, RIB

5. WEB RESOURCES

- Tutorial on character editing:
  http://www.planetfortress.com/tf2models/tuto/ms3d_sc/tuto_ms3d_sc3.htm
- An Art.counter-strike.net article:
  http://art.counter-strike.net/milkshape-01-01.shtml

MindsEye

1. PLATFORMS, PRICES, AND SUPPLIER/CREATOR

- Linux
- Free
- Mindseye: http://mindseye.sourceforge.net/main.html

2. APPLICATIONS

- MindsEye is a modular and extensible 3D modeling/animation package with support for NURBS surfaces, designed for Linux and Unix systems. It's designed to allow multiple scenes and to provide extensive network support

3. EXAMPLES/SAMPLES

- A 3D model being created in MindsEye App:
  http://psylab.unn.ac.ru:8102/LinuxSite/LINUX_JURNAL/May1998/article1.html
- Another 3D model being created in MindsEye App:
  http://www.sourceforge.net/dbimage.php?id=1534

4. WEB RESOURCES

- MindsEye Website: http://mindseye.sourceforge.net/main.html
- Linux Focus:
  http://psylab.unn.ac.ru:8102/LinuxSite/LINUX_JURNAL/May1998/article1.html

Mirai

1. PLATFORMS, PRICES, AND SUPPLIER/CREATOR

- PC Windows NT and SGI's Irix
- $6495.00
- IZware: http://www.nichimen.com/index.html

2. APPLICATIONS

- Mirai is a 3D animation system that is aimed at 3D game development houses, as well as companies that need a high-end character animator, "biomechanical" motion editing, advanced inverse kinematics (IK) tools. Mirai, which means "prosperous future" in Japanese, is the next evolution of Nichimen's N-World suite of real-time content creation tools, widely considered the real-time industry's most powerful content creation package — having long been used by industry-leading game developers including Sony, Square, Electronic Arts, Acclaim, and Nintendo. Mirai is also suited perfectly for other applications including film and video, visual simulation, and Web-based content creation

3. EXAMPLES/SAMPLES

- 3D Images created with Mirai: http://www.nichimen.com/mirai/gallery/index.html

4. FUNCTIONS

- Photorealistic Rendering:
  - Lambert, Phong, Cook, Blinn, flat, and volume shaders
  - Unlimited layers of diffuse, bump, opacity, specular, maps for surfaces or projection lights
  - Ambient, infinite, spot and point lights
  - Render directly to QuickTime movies, full screen images, or composite over existing image sequences
- Simulation:
  - Make any object or element a particle emitter
  - Emit points, lines, or reinstances of any object
  - Animate particle birth rate, initial speed, initial angle, deviations and life span
  - Animate particle color, size and opacity
  - Behavioral properties for particle systems-obstacle avoidance, groupmate avoidance, match velocity, follow path, and more
  - Real world physics-field and flow forces plus collision detection on rigid or deforming meshes
- Full-featured 2D paint and fast 3D paint:
  - Multiple 2D/3D paint editors simultaneously

- UV map mode shows coordinates on 2D image
- Familiar paint tools
- Customizable brushes
- Apply paint, filter, and recolor operations through any brush or shape
- Multiple resolutions up to 64-bit
- Distortion mode in both 2D and 3D
- Built-in color reduction

- Animation:

  - Standard transformation matrix and displacement animation
  - Animate or keyframe in an open viewer or over a sequence of background plates

- Skeletal Structures:

  - Full topological manipulation of joints, bones, or bodies:
  - revolutionary modeling on default or custom skeletons
  - Save multiple poses on a single skeleton
  - Cut and paste parts of skeletons, maintaining poses
  - Easily define skeletal degrees of freedom
  - Automatic mesh skinning with color coded skins and easy skin part reassignment

- Skeletal Inverse Kinematics (IK) and Forward Kinematics (FK):

  - Quaternion solutions for increased accuracy and speed
  - IK automatically enabled for any joint, even during creation
  - IK on multiple joints at the same time, even across multiple skeletons
  - Instant constraint creation with "tack" and "glue" pin objects
  - Natural IK movement through the skeleton root
  - All IK and FK moves always available; no special "modes"
  - Use IK on skeletons of any topology (biped, multipled, or custom)
  - Mirror any FK operation with symmetry around any axis
  - Full control over IK solver and bone stiffness
  - Move, axis move, scale, rotate, or position one or more joints

- Biomechanical Motion Editing:

  - Motion capture import/export: .amc, .bvh, .htr
  - Easily map skeletal motion data to Mirai's "human" skeleton
  - Blend motion capture data with artist defined keyframe motion
  - Convert motion data into poses or rotation curves
  - Generate transitions and loops based on intelligently selected events or at artist-specified frames
  - Blend multiple motions into one motion or generate discrete "transition" motions
  - Instant loop creation
  - Interactive motion scaling: scale pelvis height, hand distance and orientation, step distance and width, arm and leg rotation and extension

- Modeling:

  - Context sensitive menus show only legal commands for selected elements
  - Winged-edge data structure ensures topological consistency

- Maintains UVs, face parts, skin parts, and displacements during creation and after smoothing
- Model on vertices, edges, face, bodies, or collections of these elements on one object or across objects
- Powerful magnet operations for easy organic sculpting
- Projection, UV, and per-face texture mapping, with multiple sets of UVs per object

- File Formats:
  - 3D I/O: Obj, 3DS, VRML 2.0, DirectX, Game Exchange 2.0, HMD (Export Only)
  - 2D I/O: Mirai (.mir), .tiff, .jpg/.jpeg, .sgi, .bmp, .targa
  - Motion I/O: Acclaim, BioVision, Motion Analysis, Game Exchange 2.0
  - Movies: Quicktime 3.0

5. WEB RESOURCES

- Mirai Website: http://www.nichimen.com/mirai/index.html

- Digital Producer Article "Nichimen Graphics Launches Much Anticipated Mirai Animation System": http://www.digitalproducer.com/pages/nichimen_graphics_launches_much_.htm

- ZNet News Article: http://www3.zdnet.com/zdnn/stories/news/0,4586,388513,00.html

- A list of resources on the net: http://gamespot.com/gamespot/stories/news/0,10870,2451979,00.html

- A PC Magazine article: http://www.creativepro.com/story/news/3695.html

Model Magic 3D

1. PLATFORMS, PRICES, AND SUPPLIER/CREATOR

- Windows 95 (with Opengl32.dll); Windows 98; Windows NT

- $39.95

- Imageware Development: http://www.imagewaredev.com/

2. APPLICATIONS

- ModelMagic3D is an interactive 3D modeling package used to create OpenGL scenes rendered in real-time. It builds 2D and 3D objects from pre-defined primitives and adds text, lighting, lens flare effects, and animation

3. EXAMPLES

- Gallery: http://supershareware.co.uk/ASP/ buildframe.asp?URL=screenshot&S=&P=&ID=8642
- Gallery: http://www.imagewaredev.com/whatsnew.htm

4. RESOURCES

- New release information: http://www.imagewaredev.com/modelmagic3d.htm
- Create OpenGL scenes in real-time: http://www.northernskytech.com/ MM3DPR.html

Molecules-3D

1. PLATFORMS, PRICES, AND SUPPLIER/CREATOR

- PC
- $49.95
- Molecular Arts: http://www.molecules.com/index.shtml

2. APPLICATIONS

- Molecules-3D enables users to build and examine 3D molecular models

3. EXAMPLES/SAMPLES

- Molecules-3D: http://www.molecules.com/m3d25int.shtml
- Molecular Modeling Software: http://www.indigo.com/software/mol3d.html
- Molecules-3D Pro: http://www.compuchem.com/m3d.htm

4. WEB RESOURCES

- Software: http://www.indigo.com/software/molecular-modeling-software.html
- Images and Animations: http://www.okc.cc.ok.us/sshore/personal/chemart.htm
- Chemistry Resource Page: http://www.athabascau.ca/courses/chem/resource.html

Moray

1. PLATFORMS, PRICES, AND SUPPLIER/CREATOR

- Program is available for windows 95/98, NT 4.0, and 2000
- 159 German Marks (US$72)
- SoftTronics: http://www.stmuc.com/moray/index.html

2. APPLICATIONS

- Wire-frame modeler for Persistence of Vision Raytracer (POV-Ray, see http://www.povray.org) that allows the user to see and interactively modify the 3D model or scene they are creating. It allows the setup of an object hierarchy structure. The software can be extended by third party plug-ins so that its capabilities can be expanded

3. EXAMPLES/SAMPLES

- 3D X-Wing fighter sample: http://www.stmuc.com/moray/images/ xwingframe1.jpg
- Alex Bruch's gallery using Moray 3: http://members.nbci.com/ABruch/ povgme.htm

4. FUNCTIONS

- Modeling:
  - Primitive objects: cube, sphere, cylinder, cone, torus, disc, plane, super-ellipsoid, Bezier patches, height fields, text, translation sweep (extrusion), rotational sweep (lathe), tapering sweep, point light, spotlight, area light, camera. Blobs and triangle meshes can be imported
  - Complex objects: many users have submitted objects to the Object Library, which is available at: http://www.stmuc.com/moray/meobjs.html
  - Plug-in objects: rounded cube, rounded disc, lensflare, galaxy, grass, dome, smoke, columns, spray. All supported plug-in objects can be found on this page: http://www.stmuc.com/moray/meplugin.html
  - Transformations: scale, rotate, translate. Local coordinate system (pivot point) is supported. Transformation can be limited to specific axes and ranges. Basic inverse kinematics support
  - Editing: Bezier patch editor is included. Objects can be arranged in layers, the wire-frame color can be changed
- Rendering:
  - Camera: interactively adjustable and movable (aspect ratio, pan, zoom, orbit, track, dolly, roll). Focal blur and lens settings supported
- Animation:

- Basic keyframe animation supported via plug-in
- File Formats:
  - Import: mdl, udo, blb, raw
  - Export: pov
  - Plug-ins: dll

5. WEB RESOURCES

- Moray homepage: http://www.stmuc.com/moray/
- Persistence of Vision Tracer (POV-Ray): http://www.povray.org/
- POV-Ray Book Raytracing Worlds with POV-Ray (Uses Moray): http://www.povray.org/povzine/povzine1/raytrace.html
- FAQ for using POV-Rays in Moray: http://www.students.tut.fi/~warp/povVFAQ/morayVFAQ.html
- Review of Moray v3.2 (Japanese): http://www.stmuc.com/moray/mecgw.html

MOTIONGANG

1. PLATFORMS, PRICE, AND SUPPLIER/CREATOR

- PC
- $249.00
- Hitachi: http://www.hitachi.co.jp/index.html

2. APPLICATIONS

- MotionGang is plug-in software for LightWave3D that makes real human animation more easily. You can create human animation by specifying parameters such as motions, paths, and others from GUI menu

3. EXAMPLES/SAMPLES

- Sample movies: http://www.hitachi.co.jp/Div/omika/prdcts/m_gang_e/E_demomov.htm

4. WEB RESOURCES

- Trial version: http://www.hitachi.co.jp/Div/omika/prdcts/m_gang_e/E_trial_1.htm
- Manual: http://www.hitachi.co.jp/Div/omika/prdcts/m_gang_e/E_sousa_1.htm

- MotionGang FAQ: http://www.hitachi.co.jp/Div/omika/prdcts/m_gang_e/E_faq.htm

Motivate 3D

1. PLATFORMS, PRICES, AND SUPPLIER/CREATOR

- PC, Windows 95 and NT 4.0 environment
- $$$$$
- The Motion Factory: http://www.motion-factory.com/home.html

2. APPLICATIONS

- Motivate 3D is for developing 3D games and interactive multimedia titles. Motivate customers range from small development houses to industry giants
- Some Motivate users use Motivate to animate crowd scenes for film and television. Others use Motivate characters in visual simulations for academic, industrial, or military purposes

3. EXAMPLES/SAMPLES

- Demo Gallery: http://www.motion-factory.com/products/demos_content.html
- Interactive Content: http://www.motion-factory.com/products/demos_content.html
- Animation Clips: http://www.motion-factory.com/products/demos_clips.html

4. WEB RESOURCES

- Press releases: http://www.motion-factory.com/community/MAINPressReleases.html
- A list of press coverage: http://www.motion-factory.com/community/MAINPressCoverage.html
- A list of awards: http://www.motion-factory.com/community/MAINAwards.html

Minimal Reality (MR) Toolkit

1. PLATFORMS, PRICES, AND SUPPLIER/CREATOR

- Callable from C, C++ and FORTRAN programs on PC, HP, SGI, DEC, and IBM RS6000 workstations; some elements of MR Toolkit also run on Suns, Alphas, and other UNIX platforms
- Available at no cost to licensed academic and research institutions, subject to conditions
- Computer Graphics Research Group, Department of CS at the University of Alberta, Canada: http://web.cs.ualberta.ca/~graphics/MRToolkit.html

2. APPLICATIONS

- Virtual Reality and 3D/2D User Interface Software Tool
- It is a set of software tools for the production of virtual reality systems and other forms of 3D user interfaces
- It consists of a set of subroutine libraries, device drivers, support programs, and a language for describing geometry and behavior. MR Toolkit provides a device-independent and portable platform for the development of VR applications

3. EXAMPLES/SAMPLES

- Virtual stroll through the University of Alberta campus: http://www.cs.ualberta.ca/~graphics/cave/vizroom_pics.html
- Virtual walkthrough in Graphics lab (using MR Toolkit): http://www.cs.hku.hk/~tlchung/research.html
- Virtual Theme park: http://vr-atlantis.com/concept.html

4. WEB RESOURCES

- Documentation can be found at: ftp://ftp.cs.ualberta.ca/pub/graphics/
- Citations on MR Toolkit: http://citeseer.nj.nec.com/context/183084/82729
- Feature Article: LEA — Volume 7, No. 4: http://www.music.mcgill.ca/~mcentury/Papers/ts/ts.html

MultiGen Creator PRO

1. PLATFORMS, PRICES, AND SUPPLIER/CREATOR

- PC — Windows or IRIX
- $8,750 w/$3,150 annual support (Educational License)
- MultiGen-Paradigm: http://www.multigen-paradigm.com

2. APPLICATIONS

- Creating highly optimized, high fidelity real-time 3D content for use in visual simulation, interactive games, urban simulation, and other applications
  - Build interactively from within the world you're modeling
  - See everything as it will appear in real-time
  - Have exact control from global database organization down to a single vertex
  - Get low polygon counts, efficient organization, and exceptional visual quality
  - WSIWYG interface
  - System developed in OpenGL

3. EXAMPLES/SAMPLES

- multiGen Pro Image gallery: http://www.multigen-paradigm.com/gallery.htm

4. FUNCTIONS

- Modeling:
  - Objects: Sphere, 3D Text, spline curves, polymesh NURBs, fogging
  - Transformation: translate, scale, rotate about edge, rotate about point, put, rotate/scale to point, transformation edit — insert matrix
  - Editing and manipulations (vertex, edge, face, polygon, curves, objects): clipping, combine face, modify vertex, cut subfaces, texture mapping, deformation tools
- Rendering:
  - Cameras: adjustable, movable
  - Lights: position, color, shadow, infrared
  - Materials: double-sided, matte/shadow, texture mapping, light properties
  - Before and after rendering: antialiasing, motion blur, field rendering, fog, combustion, environment maps, perspective matching
- Animation:
  - Trajectory, pivot point, morphing, character animation, motion blur
  - Basic animation
- File Formats:
  - Importing and Exporting file formats: Alias, 3D Studio R4, 3D Studio Max, IGES, DXF, Lightwave, SoftImage, Strata Studio Pro, Wavefront

– Additional file formats are available through plug-ins

5. WEB RESOURCES

- A list of resources on the net: http://www.vis-sim.org/
- A 3D Gate article: http://www.3dgate.com/news_and_opinions/2001/010116/0116products.html

Mvox

1. PLATFORMS, PRICES, AND SUPPLIER/CREATOR

- SGI Irix 6.x
- $3,990
- Anamedic: http://www.anamedic.com/products/mvox_sgi/index.stm

2. APPLICATIONS

- Mvox is a software package for medical researchers who want to analyze medical images. Using advanced rendering algorithms and the computer graphics hardware in SGI workstations, Mvox produces eye-opening 3D visualizations

3. EXAMPLES/SAMPLES

- Dentistry example: http://www.anamedic.com/customers/dentistry/index.stm
  Surgical Simulation: http://www.anamedic.com/customers/graphics/index.stm

4. FEATURES

- Image Related:
  - Histogram; thresholding; drawing/editing; contour handling; statistical classification; marker-based rigid and non-rigid registration; marker-based slice alignment in 3D images
  - Measurements: distances; angles; volume; area; region of interest (ROI); color mapping
- 3D Related:
  - Iso-surface models; 3D model construction from 2D contours; Editing of 3D models; Interactive slicing
- File Formats:

  Image:

- Read: DICOM, TIFF, ANALYZE, SGI, BMP,
  TGA, HIPS-2, INRIMAGE, Raw, and BRIMG (native)
- Write: ANALYZE, HIPS-2, INRIMAGE, SGI,
  TGA, Raw, and BRIMG (native)

3D:

- Read: OFF, Cyberware, and FLEX (native)
- Write: Inventor 2.0, VRML 1.0, DXF,
  Alias/Wavefront OBJ, and FLEX (native)

5. WEB RESOURCES

- http://www.imm.dtu.dk/~mvox/

- http://biocomp.stanford.edu/3dreconstruction/software/mvox.html

- http://citeseer.nj.nec.com/15018.html

NATURAL SCENE DESIGNER

1. PLATFORMS, PRICES, AND SUPPLIER/CREATOR

- Window 95/98/2000/NT, Macintosh

- $89

- Company: Natural Graphics: http://www.naturalgfx.com

2. APPLICATIONS

- A 3D-rendering and animation program creating photorealistic nature scenes. It
  has advanced algorithms for creating realistic natural outdoor scene with trees,
  clouds, rocks, bushes, lakes, atmospheric effects, import 3D objects, and snow.
  Users can import real-world terrain data, or create their own artificial landscapes

3. EXAMPLES/SAMPLES

- Crater Lake: http://www.naturalgfx.com/buoy.htm

- Grand Teton: http://www.naturalgfx.com/gt.htm

- Lake: http://www.naturalgfx.com/lake.htm

- Grand Canyon: http://www.naturalgfx.com/canyon.htm

4. WEB RESOURCES

- Natural Scene Designer for Windows: http://www.naturalgfx.com/nsdwin98.htm
- Mac Addict: http://www.macaddict.com/news/reviews/1999_10_10.shtml
- Mac World: http://bondiboard.macpublishing.net/1999/01/reviews/natural.html
- Commercial Terrain Visualization Software Product Information: http://www.tec.army.mil/TD/tvd/survey/Natural_Scene_Designer.html
- Natural Scene Designer for Mac: http://naturalgfx.com/nsdpmac.htm

The NCAR Command Language and NCAR Graphics

1. INFORMATION

- The National Center for Atmospheric Research: http://www.ncar.ucar.edu
- NCAR Command Language: http://ngwww.ucar.edu/ncl/
- NCAR Graphics: http://ngwww.ucar.edu/ng/

2. APPLICATIONS

- The NCAR Command Language (NCL) is a programming language designed specifically for access to, analysis of, and visualization of data. NCL can be run in interactive mode, where each line is interpreted as it is entered at your workstation, or it can be run in batch mode as an interpreter of complete scripts. NCL is available for FREE in binary format for several UNIX systems
- NCAR Graphics is a Fortran- and C-based software package for scientific visualization. NCAR Graphics is available for FREE as open source under the GNU Public License, and pre-compiled binaries are available for several UNIX systems. NCAR Graphics, a time-tested UNIX package, consists mainly of over two dozen Fortran/C utilities for drawing contours, maps, vectors, streamlines, weather maps, surfaces, histograms, X/Y plots, annotations, and more

3. EXAMPLES/SAMPLES

- Sample images from the NCL home page: http://ngwww.ucar.edu/ncl/examples.html
- Sample images from the NCAR Graphics home page: http://ngwww.ucar.edu/ng/examples.html

4. FUNCTIONS

- NCL comes with many useful built-in functions and procedures for processing and manipulating data. There are over 400 functions and procedures that include routines for:
  - use specifically with climate and model data
  - empirical orthogonal functions, Fourier coefficients, singular value decomposition, averages, standard deviations, sin, cosine, log, min, max, etc.
  - retrieving and converting date information
  - drawing primitives (lines, filled areas, and markers), wind barbs, weather map symbols, isosurfaces, and graphical objects
  - file handling
  - 1-dimensional, 2-dimensional, and 3-dimensional interpolation, approximation, and regridding
  - facilitating computer analysis of scalar and vector global geophysical quantities (most are based on the package known as Spherepack)
  - retrieving environment variables and executing system commands

- NCL supports calling C and Fortran external routines, which makes NCL infinitely configurable

- NCAR Graphics Functions
  - A library containing over two dozen Fortran/C utilities for drawing contours, maps, vectors, streamlines, weather maps, surfaces, histograms, X/Y plots, annotations, and more
  - An ANSI/ISO standard version of GKS, with both C and FORTRAN callable entries
  - A math library containing a collection of C and Fortran interpolators and approximators for one-dimensional, two-dimensional, and three-dimensional data
  - Applications for displaying, editing, and manipulating graphical output
  - Map databases
  - Hundreds of FORTRAN and C examples
  - Demo programs
  - Compilation scripts

5. WEB RESOURCES

- NCL documentation: http://ngwww.ucar.edu/ncl/documentation.html

- NCL FAQ: http://ngwww.ucar.edu/ngdoc/ng/ug/ncl/gsun/nclfaq.html

- NCAR Graphics documentation: http://ngwww.ucar.edu/ng/documentation.html

- NCAR Graphics FAQ: http://ngwww.ucar.edu/ng/faq.html

NeMo

1. PLATFORMS, PRICES, AND SUPPLIER/CREATOR

- PC
- $489
- Virtools SA: http://www.next-url.com/index.asp

2. APPLICATIONS

- Interactive 3D authoring and development tool that allows you to apply interactive behaviors to 3D models created in industry standard modelers, and bring them to life in 3D applications for the Web or CD-ROM. This tool also allows you to attach behaviors to entities to create interactions, graphically assemble, and fine-tune those behaviors to an element that creates the foundation of your project. NeMo has been used in a variety of applications such as 3D Web applications, 3D games, 3D multimedia, interactive TV, interactive storyboarding, public exhibitions, computer-based training, and product presentation

3. EXAMPLES/SAMPLES

- Demos for NeMo Creation: http://www.next-url.com/demos/index.asp
- Showcase for Virtools Products: http://www.theswapmeet.com/

4. FUNCTIONS

- 3D Scene Layout Content:
  - Editable lights, cameras, and paths
  - Reposition and scale 3D entities
  - Scene navigation
- Behavioral Interactions For Objects:
  - Library of 300+ behavior building blocks
  - Downloadable behaviors (www.theswapmeet.com)
  - Drag/drop behaviors onto 3D entities
  - Creation of new and reusable behaviors, done by graphical combination of existing behaviors
  - Graphic object-oriented programming
- Content Complexity Management:
  - Hierarchical list of content: 3D entities, 2D/3D sprites, meshes, materials, textures, and sounds
  - Structuring of content into separate places and scenes
- Rendering/Runtime:

- Direct3D/Open GL compatible rendering engine
- 3D meshes, 2D/3D sprites, 2D primitives, background images
- Multiple material/multipass rendering, bitmap/procedural textures which includes color key transparency
- File Formats (Import/Export):
    - 3D Studio Max textured models and keyframe animations
    - Softimage textured models and keyframe animations (DirectX)
    - JPG, TIFF, BMP, PCX, DIB
    - AVI (ActiveMovie video format), WAV (wave format), MID (midi format)

5. WEB RESOURCES

- A list of resources on the net: http://www.theswapmeet.com/

- Press Release: http://www.next-url.com/news/press_20.asp

- Training Schedule: http://www.next-url.com/services/training.asp

Nendo

1. PLATFORMS, PRICES, AND SUPPLIER/CREATOR

- PC Windows 95, 98, or NT

    - Pentium or Pentium II Processor
    - 32 Mb RAM
    - Certified 24-bit Graphics Card
      Supported card list: http://www2.izware.com/nendo/cards/
- Price: $99; download from website at: https://secure.izware.com/nendo

- IZware: http://www.izware.com

2. APPLICATIONS

- Nendo is a 3D modeling and 3D painting tool designed with simplicity of use at its heart. The 3D modeler allows the artist to work in a "digital clay" environment making the modeling process intuitive to the user. The 3D painting tool is focused on speed, and a clean working environment without floating toolbars

3. EXAMPLES/SAMPLES

- Nendo gallery on the IZware site: http://www.izware.com/gallery/

- The artist explicitly states that he used Nendo to model some of the images in the top row. I assume he used Nendo for most of the models on at least this first page: http://www.somethingwonderful.com/tun/
- Igor Posavec had many entries in the Nendo gallery. He seems to like to model in Nendo, and render in 3D Max: http://www.3d-io.com/
  - Demo available at: http://nendo.izware.com/demo

4. FUNCTIONS

- Easily switch back and forth between modeling and painting
- Modeling:
  - Work with vertex, edge, face, body or free elements
  - Customizable viewing space: Camera controls, shading and lighting
- Painting:
  - Pop up menu via right mouse button avoids floating windows and toolbars
  - Color Selector by RGB or HSV
  - Eye dropper color grabbing
  - Configurable toolbox to allow user defined tool profiles
- File Formats:
  - Importing: VRML 2.0 .obj; Direct X; Game Exchange 2.0 .3ds
  - Exporting: VRML 2.0 .obj; Direct X; Game Exchange 2.0 .3ds; Monzoom 4.3

5. WEB RESOURCES

- IZware Nendo Site: http://www.izware.com/nendo/product/

NetImmerse

1. PLATFORMS, PRICES, AND SUPPLIER/CREATOR

- PC, Xbox, SDKs, PS2, Gamecube
- Pricing information: http://www.ndl.com/netimmerse/licensing.html
- Numerical Design Ltd. (NDL): http://www.ndl.com/

2. APPLICATIONS

- NetImmerse is a complete 3D gaming engine used by game developers, including developers of PlayStation 2, Xbox, and Gamecube games. It addition to providing a programming environment, artists can use it without programming to develop content

3. EXAMPLES

- Demos available for download at: http://www.ndl.com/netimmerse/demos.html
- A list of commercial games developed with NetImmerse available at: http://www.ndl.com/customers/index.html

4. FEATURES

- NetImmerse includes a C++ runtime API, plug-ins to 3DS Max and Maya, and tools to help the artist and programmer develop games
- A technical white paper at: http://www.ndl.com/whitepapers/1_theengine.html describes the features in detail
- NetImmerse includes continuous level of detail. CLOD allows the artist to model characters and objects at the highest level of detail. At runtime, it automatically scales the polygon count to maintain high-performance interactivity
- Deformable mesh technology (sometimes called skin) provides realism in animation. A deformable mesh is a single, seamless vertex mesh that is animated based on the movement of an underlying bone system
- The eight independent multitextures include projected lights, projected shadows, environment maps, gloss maps, detail maps, and fog maps. The shadow map can be re-rendered in every frame to match the moving character
- The terrain system simplifies the process of creating flight simulators
- NetImmerse includes a library which simplifies the creation of curved surfaces
- The runtime engine supports morphing vertices, particle systems, quaternion-based key frames
- NetImmerse provides plug-ins to 3DS Max, Maya and Multigen's Creator, and is compatible with havok.com's physics engine
- The included C++ toolkit allows developers to focus on what the users see on the screen

5. WEB RESOURCES

- Technical support is available at: support@ndl.com

- White papers at: http://www.ndl.com/whitepapers/index.html discuss many features
- FAQ's coming soon at: http://www.ndl.com/support/index.html

Now3D

1. PLATFORMS, PRICES, AND SUPPLIER/CREATOR

- 32-bit Windows
- Free
- Giuliano Cornacchiola: http://web.tiscalinet.it/GiulianoCornacchiola/Eng/download.htm

2. APPLICATIONS

- This is a 3D drawing tool that allows the user to quickly create complex, realistic 3D pictures. Includes movable light sources, various material properties, and various rendering options
- This tool can be used to make movies if used in conjunction with an animator. A good free one is Platypus: http://www.c-point.com/

3. EXAMPLES/SAMPLES

- 3D Now Picture Gallery: http://digilander.iol.it/giulios/Eng/Gallery.htm
- 3D Now Animation Gallery: http://digilander.iol.it/giulios/Eng/AniGallery.htm
- Room Drawing by Rock Keyman: http://digilander.iol.it/giulios/Eng/Galleries_Users.htm

4. FUNCTIONS

- Create Objects:
    - Shading/Rendering — wireframe, flat shading, Gouraud shading, quick Phong shading, and Z Phong shading
    - Include already created primitives of spheres (subdivision and perfect), torus, cube, GeoSphere (Tetra, Octal, Icosa), cone, cylinder (subdivision and perfect), plane (subdivision and perfect), and disc (subdivision and perfect)

- Add Material Properties to objects — material properties can be set for objects to determine how they reflect light. The program allows users to set ambient, specular, glossy, and reflect properties of materials. The user can also do bump mapping and map textures onto objects

- Add Lights to the scene — this program allows multiple lights to be placed throughout the scene that have the following characteristics:
    - Type — point, spot uniform, and spot cone
    - Intensity
    - Color
    - Can Shadow — whether the light can create shadows for objects

- Movable Cameras — the artist can switch back and forth between multiple camera positions and view the 3D picture from different views

- Pictures can be saved in *.jpg or *.bmp format or a format specific for this application

5. WEB RESOURCES

- HandBook — describes how to use the program: http://web.tiscalinet.it/GiulianoCornacchiola/Eng/Handbook.htm

- Tutorial — example Now3D images that can be loaded onto your computer: http://web.tiscalinet.it/GiulianoCornacchiola/Eng/tutorial.htm

NuGraf

1. PLATFORMS, PRICES, AND SUPPLIER/CREATOR

- PCs using Microsoft Windows OS
- $495
- Okino: http://www.okino.com/

2. APPLICATIONS

- The NuGraf Rendering System is a fast, powerful and comprehensive 3D rendering, scene composition, model viewing and model translation program. Key features include industry standard geometry import and export filters (with full texture mapping and shading support), real-time scene manipulation functions, 3D extruded font generation, a seamless user interface and high quality, fast "photorealistic" rendering tools

3. EXAMPLES/SAMPLES

- Citizen Cronograph Watch: http://www.okino.com/slidshow/watch2.htm
- Modern Living Room: http://www.okino.com/slidshow/room.htm
- Gallery of pictures made with NuGraf: http://www.okino.com/new/gallery/index.htm
- http://www.okino.com/mainpic.htm

4. FUNCTIONS

- Objects Manipulation:
  - Built-in Primitives: Box, cone, cylinder, disc, prism, rectangle, sphere, superquadric ellipsoid, and superquadric toroid. All have predefined texture coordinates
  - Easily creates extruded 3D TrueType Fonts. Transform object in perspective space
- Textures:
  - Unlimited texture layering per material, which can be offset and scaled individually
  - 47 Perlin and peachy 3D procedural texture functions
  - Full Alpha Channel Support
- photorealistic Rendering:
  - Multiple Rendering Formats (wireframe, color wireframe, hidden line, preview scanline, or fully scanline/ray trace rendering modes)
  - Soft-Edged or Hard-Edged shadows
  - Field scanline rendering mode (useful for NTSC video animation)
  - Background color scheme
- Formats Supported:
  - Listed at www.okino.com/conv/filefrmt.htm
  - 3D formats: 3D Studio r4, 3D Studio MAX, Apple 3DMF, Alias triangle, Detailer, DirectX DXF, IGES 5.3, Imagine, Lightscape, Lightwave, OpenFlight, OpenGL, POV 2/3, Pro/E .slp, Renderman RIB, Renderware, SAT (ACIS), Solid Edge v4 Strata StudioPro v1.75, TrueSpace 2 and 3, USGS DEM, VistaPro DEM, VRLM 1 and 2, Wavefront (+NURBS)
  - 2D formats: BMP, IFF, JPEG, PSD, SGI, RGB, PIC, TIFF, TARGA, CEL, FLC, FLI, GIF

5. WEB RESOURCES

- Brochures: http://www.okino.com/new/brochures/index.htm
- Product review by DCC Magazine: http://www.okino.com/dccreview.htm

OpenDX (Open Data Explorer)

1. PLATFORM, PRICES, AND SUPPLIER/CREATOR

- IBM RISC System6000, Sun, HP, SGI, DEC Alpha
- OpenDX is freeware
- IBM, the original developer of DX: http://www.research.ibm.com

2. APPLICATIONS

- OpenDX, formerly DX, is a general-purpose application for scientific visualization and analysis: http://www.research.ibm.com/dx/

3. EXAMPLES/SAMPLES

- http://www.research.ibm.com/dx/imageGallery/index.html
- http://www.tc.cornell.edu/DX/

4. WEB RESOURCES

- http://www.research.ibm.com/dx/docs/legacyhtml/refguide.htm
- http://www.research.ibm.com/dx/docs/legacyhtml/proguide.htm
- www.opendx.org

Open Inventor and VRML

1. PLATFORMS, PRICES, AND SUPPLIER/CREATOR

- IRIX, PC Windows and MAC, and UNIX
- N/A
- Silicon Graphics, Inc.: www.sgi.com/software/inventor/
- On PC Platform: http://www.tgs.com/index.htm?pro_div/oiv_main.htm~main

2. APPLICATION

- Open Inventor has become the de facto standard for development of cross-platform (Windows, UNIX, Linux) 3D graphics applications in C++ and Java. It is a powerful object-oriented toolkit with over 450 classes and an intuitive and easy-to-use programming interface that allows for rapid prototyping and development of graphics applications. OpenInventor also serves as the basis for the VRML (Virtual Reality Modeling Language) standard. It is built on top of OpenGL

- VRML is a Web-based 3D graphics file format. VRML brouser is an animation engine and platform. The first version of VRML, VRML 1.0, came into existence about 1994. Open Inventor ASCII file format came from Silicon Graphics, Inc. as the basis of VRML. VRML 2.0 came into existence on August 4, 1996 when the official VRML 2.0 specification was released at Siggraph 96 in New Orleans. VRML 2.0 became an international standard: VRML97. Extensible 3D (X3D) specification, which is extending VRML97, using the Extensible Markup Language (XML) is a work in progress

3. EXAMPLES/SAMPLES

- www9.informatik.uni-erlangen.de/eng/gallery/vis/med/
- www.fns.co.jp/avs/VRML/gallery/
- www.hitl.washington.edu/vrml/gallery/

4. WEB RESOURCES

- Inventor: http://www.sgi.com/Technology/Inventor/
- VRML: http://www.web3d.org/aboutus/VRML2000Keynote.ppt
- Web|3D Consortium: http://www.web3d.org

OpenGL

1. PLATFORM, PRICE, AND SUPPLIER/CREATOR

- Supported on all UNIX workstations, and shipped standard with every Windows 95/98/2000/NT and MacOS PC. Today, OpenGL runs on every major operating system including Mac OS, OS/2, UNIX, Windows 95/98, Windows 2000, Windows NT, Linux, OPENStep, and BeOS; it also works with every major windowing system, including Win32, MacOS, Presentation manager, and X-Window System. OpenGL is callable from Ada, C, C++, Fortran, Python, Perl, and Java and offers complete independence from network protocols and topologies
- Free

- Industry standard (http://www.opengl.org), originally developed by Silicon Graphics, Inc.: http://www.sgi.com/company_info/

2. APPLICATIONS

- OpenGL (Open Graphics Library) is a software interface to graphics hardware, or graphics API similar to Direct3D and PHIGS. It is the most popular low-level graphics library. The interface consists of a set of several hundred procedures and functions that allow a programmer to specify the objects and operations involved in producing graphical images. Most recent graphics tools and scientific applications are built on OpenGL. Its close competitor, Direct3D, is more popular on PCs for game programming

3. EXAMPLE/SAMPLES

- 3DFiles.com: http://www.3dfiles.com/screensavers/
- Romka Graphics: http://romka.demonews.com/index_eng.htm
- Author's sample programs: http://cs.gmu.edu/~jchen/graphics/

4. FUNCTIONS

- OpenGL provides a wide range of primitive graphics functions: from rendering a simple geometric point, line, or filled polygon, to texture mapping NURBS curved surfaces

5. WEB RESOURCES

- Everything you need: http://www.opengl.org
- A shortcut in OpenGL: http://www.cs.gmu.edu/~jchen/graphics/
- http://www.hellix.com/People/Agarny/OpenGL/
- http://www.njnet.edu.cn/info/ebook/graph/OpenGLRedBook/
- http://nehe.gamedev.net/opengl.asp

OpenGL VoLumizer

1. PLATFORM, PRICES, AND SUPPLIER/CREATOR

- IRIX, Windows NT, LINUX workstations

- Developers can purchase the CD and manuals direct from SGI or can download it for free from: http://www.sgi.com/software/volumizer/downloads.html
- SGI: http://www.sgi.com

2. APPLICATIONS

- OpenGL Volumizer is a library of C++ classes that facilitates the manipulation and display of voxel-based datasets
- OpenGL Volumizer is built upon the concept of the voxel as fundamental small-scale volumetric primitive, and the tetrahedron — a four-sided, three-dimensional solid object — as the fundamental volumetric primitive

3. EXAMPLES/SAMPLES

- Images: http://www.sgi.com/fun/gallery
- Java:http://www.sgi.com/fun/java
- Movies and animation: http://www.sgi.com/fun/movies

4. WEB RESOURCES

- http://www.sgi.com/software/volumizer
- http://www.hoise.com/vmw/articles/LV-VM-09-98-19.html

OpenWorlds

1. PLATFORM, PRICES, AND SUPPLIER/CREATOR

- Windows 95/98/2000/NT/ME/XP, SGI, Linux
- $2995–$14,995, depending on options selected
- OpenWorlds Inc.: http://www.openworlds.com/index.html

2. APPLICATIONS

- OpenWorlds is a toolkit for adding X3D and VRML functionality onto C++ applications. It is possible to build your own X3D/VRML browser as well using OpenWorlds
- OpenWorlds Horizon is an X3D browser and ActiveX control with full API and SDK interface for dropping into any Windows application

3. EXAMPLES/SAMPLES

- http://www.openworlds.com/index.html

4. FUNCTIONS

- Modeling:
  - OpenWorlds provides a set of interfaces (similar to COM interfaces) that programmers can use to add X3D or VRML functionality to C++ applications. Interfaces are instantiated and then registered in your C++ code
  - Objects: All standard X3D and VRML2.0 objects have been implemented, including cone, box, sphere, and extrusion. X3D extensions have been added to support rendering extensions such as Shadows, Reflections, Bump Maps, etc., and to support streaming. You can also implement customized nodes
  - Transformations: Scale, Rotate, and Translation transformations may be specified using the transform node. Scaling can occur along any specified axis. Extrusion support is provided via an extrusion node
  - Editing: OpenWorlds allows you to add just what you need in terms of functionality. X3D and VRML worlds themselves may be edited using a variety of commercially available software in a fashion similar to OpenInventor
- Rendering:
  - Cameras: VRML2.0 uses the viewpoint metaphor for positioning of cameras in the 3D scene. Viewpoints are added using a viewpoint node that specifies orientation, direction, position, field of view, etc. Further control of cameras available via the API
  - Lights: Spot directional lighting. (Note: Although VRML did not support shadows, OpenWorlds' X3D extensions provide real-time shadow support to VRML and X3D worlds.)
  - Materials: supports X3D and VRML nodes that specify materials in terms of the standard ambient, diffuse, specular, emissive, and shininess parameters. Full support of texture mapping is provided including movie textures. X3D extensions support projective texturing, real-time bump mapping, reflection mapping, real-time mirrors and mirrored surfaces
  - Rendering Modes: Although the set of rendering capabilities in VRML2.0 was somewhat limited, OpenWorlds supports advanced rendering extensions through X3D which can be applied to both VRML and X3D content. OpenWorlds multipass rendering support provides photorealistic capabilities such as radiosity, real-time shadows and mirrors, and environment mapping
- File Formats:
  - OpenWorlds supports both X3D and VRML files in a variety of encodings. The standard format for VRML files in common use is still .wrl. However, as the need for customization of 3D worlds grows, we should see more files with an X3D profile in XML

5. WEB RESOURCES

- http://www.openworlds.com/index.html

- http://www.web3d.org

Organica

1. PLATFORMS, PRICES, AND SUPPLIER/CREATOR

- All computer platforms. Optimized for Windows NT/95 and Macintosh PPC
- Retail Price: $299.00; Special Web price for PC platforms: $149.00
- Impulse Inc. (Las Vegas, Nevada): http://www.coolfun.com/

2. APPLICATIONS

- Organica provides a real time intuitive interface and a unique metaballs approach to the creation of 3D models. Essentially, Organica allows any combination of 25 different blob primitives to be used on the model, which will "blob" together to form complex organic shapes. In addition the blob primitives may be stretched, sheared, bent, and skewed to provide an infinite number of primitives. It also uses sophisticated Mesh Density controls to create objects with the best polygon count

3. EXAMPLES/SAMPLES

- Organica modeled images: http://freespace.virgin.net/r.jennings/organica.htm
- http://www.interlog.com/~blaq/gallery
- Virtual gallery: http://www.engsoc.carleton.ca/~mconlon/pics.htm

4. FUNCTIONS AND SUPPORTING FEATURES

- Modeling:
    - 25 Meta Block Shapes for building objects
    - Mesh Density Controls
    - Complete set of deformation tools including, Twist, Taper, Bend, Shear, Scale
    - Boolean Objects for creating holes, and gouging out shape areas
- Rendering:
    - Radiosity based preview rendering
    - Real time preview with window and camera scaling and perspective control
    - Quad View Interface with expandable single views
- Animation:
    - Full key cell animation control
    - Hierarchical grouping for animation control

        – Cloning of objects
        – Group and family modes
- File Formats:

        – Exporting file formats: DXF, 3DMF, LWO, 3DS, IOB, and native ORG

5. WEB RESOURCES

- Online resources: http://www.computeruniverse.net/products/e90005937.asp (click on "Galerie" under "Seite 1" for English text)

- 3D tutorial books: http://www.mkp.com/books_catalog/catalog.asp?ISBN=0-12260-499-7

- 3D graphic package review:
http://www.pcrev.com/cgi-bin/extlink.cgi?http://www.itreviews.co.uk/software/s26.htm;
http://www.pcrev.com/Reviews/Software/Graphics/Organica

PageDive

1. PLATFORMS, PRICES, AND SUPPLIER/CREATOR

- Windows

- Free

- Navigram: http://www.navigram.com/

2. APPLICATIONS

- PageDive is a free active-X control to experience 3D in your webpage or in other applications. Based on this view the company created template applications. These templates are fully functional 3D applications that can be easily configured for a specific customer, making the cost of creating and maintaining appealing 3D content on your site very reasonable. Incorporating 3D in a webpage is as easy as putting an image in a page

3. EXAMPLES/SAMPLES

- Gallery: http://www.pagedive.com/pd_gallery.htm

4. FUNCTIONS

- Small ActiveX Control (<500Kb)

- Built-in compression for 3D geometry, sound, textures, and scripting
- Advanced caching mechanisms
- OpenGL hardware accelerated graphics
- Supports both mouse and keyboard input
- Support for BMP, JPEG, and AVI graphics formats
- Real Surround 3D sound — with doppler effect, pitch control
- Easy integration in HTML with JavaScript
- Can be used in Word, Excel, Powerpoint, and Access
- Uses Microsoft IE Internet connection API
- Advanced hierachical model loading
- Specular highlight support
- Proportional true-type zero-bandwidth fonts
- Animated font support
- AVI as texture and/or alpha-channel
- Built-in FTP, SMTP and POP3 support
- Built-in TCP and UDP socket support
- Multiple independent lightsources (Parallel, point and spotlights)
- Fog support
- Dynamic texture-mapping

5. WEB RESOURCES

- http://www.pagedive.com/

PAINTER 3D

1. PLATFORMS, PRICES, AND SUPPLIER/CREATOR

- Power Macintosh
- $$$$
- Meta Creations: http://www.metacreations.com

2. APPLICATIONS

- Painter 3D allows you to interactively paint texture, bump, highlight, reflection, and glow properties directly on 3D models. It includes advanced brush capabilities with over 100 Natural-media brushes and image-editing effects, and advanced compositing controls with support for multiple floating selections which can be modified directly on the surface of 3D models

3. EXAMPLES/SAMPLES

- 3D Uses of Painter 3D: http://www.ruku.com/poserclothes.html

- 3D Samples: http://interneteye3d.com/Reviews2000/Prev/Painter3D/default.asp

4. WEB RESOURCES

- Tutorials For Painter 3D: http://www.tutorialfind.com/tutorials/corel/painter/3d/
References/FAQs: http://www.bryceworks.com/p3d/p3dfaq.html
Mac World Reviews: http://www.macworld.com/1998/07/reviews/4385.html

PANARD VISION

1. PLATFORMS, PRICES, AND SUPPLIER

- Intel/DOS, Intel/Windows9x/NT/2000, Intel/Linux

  - Tested on Intel and Sparc architecture. Developed in full ANSI-C, Panard Vision can be ported on every 32-bit architecture supporting IEEE floating point operations. (And with little work, on architectures not IEEE.) It uses some heavily optimized assembly routines on Intel processors

- Panard Vision is free for noncommercial use. Otherwise contact the author at:
Olivier Brunet
27, avenue Foch
95240 Cormeilles-en-Parisis, France
Email: pvision@panardvision.com

- Olivier Brunet: http://www.panardvision.com/

2. APPLICATIONS

- A fast, generic, and high-quality 3D renderer with support for the most common used rendering methods. The engine is intended to be used in everything which needs a fast high quality rendering

3. EXAMPLES/SAMPLES

- Game Creation using Panard Vision 3D Engine:
  - http://www.streetofshops.com/LizardFire
  - http://www.dobesland.com/engine.shtml
- Lizard Fire Studios:
  - Terrain Shots: http://www.streetofshops.com/LizardFire/terrainshots.html
  - Resolution: http://www.streetofshops.com/LizardFire/resolution.html
  - PVision Tutorial: http://www.streetofshops.com/LizardFire/tut_index.html
- Other Examples:
  - Terrain Engine (Example of Volumetric Fog, Dynamic Colored Lighting, Collision Detection): http://stuff3d.tripod.com/engines/terrain.htm
  - Indoor Engine (Dynamic Texture Coordinate Generation, Dynamic Colored Lighting, Volumetric Effects, Support for 3DS Meshes, Collision Detection): http://stuff3d.tripod.com/engines/indoor.htm

4. FEATURES (FUNCTIONALITIES)

- Panard Vision is a real-time 3D Engine (with SDK) available on Dos, Linux, Win32 platforms with support of cutting edge algorithms and most hardware API (d3d, gl, glide). It supports both hardware and software rendering
- Miscellaneous:
  - Supports multiple nonrecursive planar geometric mirrors
  - On the fly texture coordinates generation
  - Panard Primitives support (allows for GL like drawing of 2D and 3D primitives, supports for display lists)
  - Picking
  - Procedural textures (hardware and software)
  - Multiple colored dynamic light sources (infinite, spot, parallel, directional, point, user defined)
  - Support for animated textures
  - Fine-tunable collision detection (OBB)
  - Switchable Nodes (allows user to dynamically select a branch in the world graph, this can be used for Mesh LODs)
  - Environment Mapping
  - Static and pseudodynamic lightmaps (soft or hard)
  - Fast, precise calculus using floats
  - Extendable Object Oriented particle system
  - Multithreaded Real-time Adaptive Landscape Library
  - Full-featured math library (including quaternion)
  - Support for spline curves/surfaces
  - Support for mesh instancing, allowing for efficient memory usage
  - Support for convex polygons not only triangles
  - Simple/Extensible API
  - Support for user coded Special FX
  - Support for user file formats

– Heavily optimized assembly code for x86 architectures
– Little animation engine with hierarchy
– Panard Vision has a built in 3DStudio 4 mesh and animation reader, but other drivers may be implemented. Drivers for Quake I&II's bsp are also included
– No black box effect — every Panard Vision functions is documented/available

- Software Rasterizer:

    – Flat shading; Gouraud shading; Fake Phong shading (currently only in non RGB modes)
    – Mapping; Bump mapping; Perspective Corrected mapping
    – Bilinear Filtering
    – Fine-tunable ZBuffering (enable/disable on a material basis)
    – Full sub-pixel/texel accuracy (no flicker, no gap in textures)
    – Consistent rasterization
    – SBuffering to reduce overdraw
    – Paletized and RGB output modes
    – Automatic handling of colors in paletized modes; Fake/Fast 16 bits rendering; True RGB rendering (15, 16, 24, 32 bits)
    – Virtually every-resolution mipmapping
    – Generic PRECISE rasterizer to develop custom filling routines
    – Generic perspective span renderer to add perspective correction to custom fillers

- Visibility Engine:

    – User-definable visibility pipeline (allowing for BSP, Portals, etc.)
    – Infinite number of cameras
    – Big mesh classification using octrees, allowing for fast rejection of a whole mesh or big parts of a mesh
    – Indoor/outdoor suitable, efficient culling of out-of-screen meshes and parts of meshes
    – Advanced hierarchical culling/transformations, allowing for very efficient world rendering
    – Built-in support for portals

- Hardware:

    – Fog support
    – Support for user made hardware drivers
    – Built-in OpenGL, Direct3D (5,6 and 7 (with hardware transform and lighting)) and 3DFX drivers(Voodoo,Voodoo2, Rush, Banshee)
    – Support for all common and advanced hardware features (ZBuffer, Stencil buffer, Alpha blending, Multitexturing, etc.)
    – Customizable multitexture pipeline; Detail texturing
    – Real-time stencil-based shadows

5. WEB RESOURCES

- Discussion Forum:

    – http://www.croteam.com/Active/Forums/Croteam/SeriousEngine

- 3D Engine download:

  - http://www.programmersheaven.net/zone10/cat338
  - (Panard Vision Real-time 3D Engine 0.98 Free SDK. Requires DX5): http://www.filelibrary.com/Contents/Windows/133/23.html (Panard Vision 3D Engine SDK v0.99a Windows 95/98+ high-quality/speed full featured 3D engine free for non-commercial use Hardware acceleration support: Glide, OpenGL, Direct3D)

- The 3D Application Compatibility List:

  - http://home.t-online.de/home/ce-ge/appl.htm

- Panard Vision as Game engine:

  - http://www.flipcode.com/week99.shtml
  - http://www.flipcode.com/week70.shtml
  - http://www.cfxweb.net/jrobots/jerks/jfTools.shtml

Panorama Tools

1. PLATFORMS, PRICES, AND SUPPLIER/CREATOR

- Intel Pentium PC with Windows 95, 98, or 2000

  - Microsoft Internet Explorer 4.01 SP1, Netscape Communicator 4.0 or higher
  - Microsoft DirectX 6.0 or higher
  - 32 MB of RAM (64 MB recommended)
  - 10 MB of available hard drive space
  - 3D hardware accelerator recommended

- For non-commercial use: Free; For commercial use: $60.00

- Albatross Design Group (ADG), Inc.: http://www.albatrossdesign.com/

2. APPLICATIONS

- ADG Panorama Tools is a program which lets you generate, edit, and publish 360° interactive panoramic composition on the Web from a series of photos. No HTML or Java programming knowledge is required. ADG Panorama can be viewed through the ADG Java Viewer that eliminates a plug-in installation and provides the platform-independent use on the Internet. ADG Panorama Tools is a high quality professional program with flexibility that allows even novice digital imaging enthusiasts to move beyond traditional photos into 3D presentations on the Internet

3. EXAMPLES/SAMPLES

- Albatross Design Group: http://www.albatrossdesign.com/samples/

- Free download: http://www.albatrossdesign.com/products/panorama/

4. FUNCTIONS

- Basic Features:
  - Creates 360-degree panoramas
  - Automatically aligns images (Auto-stitching)
  - Automatically blends and corrects colors (Auto-blending and color-matching)
  - Automatically warps images into true cylindrical view
  - Customized designer user interface
  - Output images filtration
  - Vertical camera movement perspective correction
  - Automated panorama embedding into the webpage
  - 3D hardware support
- Viewing:
  - ADG Java Viewer
  - ADG Direct3D Viewer
- Additional Features (support available for registered commercial version users only):
  - 3D objects integration
  - Hot Links
  - ADG Screen Saver output capabilities

5. WEB RESOURCES

- AGFA article about ADG Panorama Tools:
  http://www.agfanet.com/en/cafe/softreview/

PARAFORM

1. PLATFORMS, PRICES, AND SUPPLIER/CREATOR

- Minimum System Requirements: Intel Pentium II/III 300 MHz or higher, Windows NT 4.0 (Service Pack 4 or later), 256 MB physical (512 recommended), 30 MB hard disk space, Open GL card with 24-bit True Color (16.7 million colors)
- Price: $19,000
- Paraform 2000 Inc.: http://www.paraform.com/index.html

2. APPLICATIONS

- Conceptual design, tooling modification and repair, vendor verification and inspection, manufacturability analysis, legacy data processing, rapid surfacing, reverse engineering, digital content creation, and animation

- This product is used by companies such as Ford, Mattel, Disney, Ericsson, Boeing, and Adidas to design products such as cars, toys, shoes, etc.

3. EXAMPLES/SAMPLES

- Paraforms list of applications: http://www.paraform.com/template.asp?pageid=2.1

- Fisher-Price: Toy designs for tots worldwide: http://www.paraform.com/template.asp?pageid=c.2.5.4

- Designing an automobile mirror: http://www.paraform.com/template.asp?pageid=2.5.2

- Technicom demo of Paraform: http://www.technicom.com/TechniCom_eWeekly/eWeekly_V1I26/Paraform.html

4. FUNCTIONS

- Automatic/manual curve network creation:

    - Automatically recognize curves, create features
    - Create cross-section, feature, boundary and theoretical intersection curves
    - Create and edit curves interactively
    - Automatic intersection of curves

- Dynamic templates:

    - Copy and re-use curve networks on multiple models
    - Dynamically fit curves and structured mesh to new shapes
    - Control key-feature anchor points

- Structured mesh creation and editing:

    - Capture desired levels of details from polymesh using unique spring mesh
    - Control layout, parameterization and fitting
    - Automatically generate springs from curves
    - Export spring mesh in STL format for downstream applications; Export spring mesh in OBJ format with colored texture

- NURBS surface creation and editing:

    - Control local/global surface fitting and parameterization
    - Edit/trim surfaces
    - View/export textures in color
    - Automatically manage continuity with continuity tools (C0, C1)
    - Evaluate surface accuracy with mapping tools
    - Extract bump and displacement maps from scanned data

- File formats:

- Geometry Import — IGES, OBJ, PLY, SAT, STL, XYZ
- Geometry Export — IGES, OBJ, PLY, SAT, STL
- Map Export — TIFF (8 bit, 16 bit, float)
- Color and Texture Export — TIFF, JPEG

5. WEB RESOURCES

- Article: http://www.businesswire.com/webbox/bw.021699/1102109.htm

- A distributor and reseller of leading CAD/CAM/DNC software: http://www.inhousesolutions.com/paraform/

- A Visual Guide to Paraform 2.0: http://www.mcadcafe.com/MCADVision/software_reviews/Paraform.html

PHIGS

Programmer's Hierarchical Interactive Graphics System

1. PLATFORMS, PRICE, AND VENDOR

- RS/6000 and others

- $695.00

- Sold by IBM; ISO graphics standard: www.iso.ch

2. APPLICATIONS

- Like GKS-3D, OpenGL, and Direct3D, PHIGS is a standard for 3D graphics API. It is the ISO standard for graphics with well constructed set of functions. However, OpenGL and Direct3D are the de facto graphics standard today, which come with more hardware and software support. PHIGS has been used for complex 3D applications in technical and commercial areas, including computer-aided design and manufacturing, industrial design, engineering analysis, and scientific visualization for a wide variety of graphics accelerators

3. EXAMPLE/SAMPLES

- http://www.cs.cmu.edu/~vaschelp/3d/Phigs/phigs.html#HDR2

- http://www.dia.uniroma3.it/~plasm/examples/exmpl1.html

4. FUNCTIONS

- Basic animation
- Basic primitives including 2D and 3D text, markers, lines and polygons
- Advanced primitives including triangle strips, quadrilateral meshes, concave and multicolor polygons, NURBS curves, and trimmed and untrimmed surfaces
- Line-online highlighting
- User-defined clipping volumes
- Antialiasing of primitives
- Lighting and shading
- Hidden-line/hidden-surface removal (HLHSR)
- Depth cueing
- Direct color
- Transparency
- Dithering
- Morphing
- Texture mapping (as a subset of PHIGS PLUS data mapping)
- Explicit traversal control (for immediate and mixed mode rendering)
- Archiving
- Support for Traditional Chinese, Hanual (Korean), and Kanji (Japanese), as well as Unicode Standard languages
- 12-bit visual support

5. WEB RESOURCES

- A list of resources: http://www.cs.cmu.edu/~vaschelp/3d/Phigs/phigs.html
- Books: http://www.3w-buecher.de/GamanWilliamA/GamanWilliamA3540975551.htm
- More Web resources: http://www.austin.ibm.com/idd500/usr/share/man/info/en_US/a_doc_lib/libs/phigsisosubs/APIExtCompat.htm

PhotoModeler Pro 4.0

1. PLATFORMS, PRICES, AND SUPPLIER/CREATOR

- PC
- $795
- Eos Systems: http://www.eossystems.com/

2. APPLICATIONS

- PhotoModeler Pro 4.0 is used to generate 3D models and measurements of existing real-world object or scenes. Applications include accident reconstruction, architecture, archaeology, forensics, animation, engineering, piping, 3D animation, and Web development. Some well-known customers include the National Park Service, Disney Studios, Sony Pictures Imageworks, Woods Hole Oceanographic Institute, California Highway Patrol, Houston Metro Police, Lockheed Martin, Ford, Exponent, and NASA

3. EXAMPLES/SAMPLES

- PhotoModeler: http://www.photomodeler.com/app01.html
- Aerial Survey of Monks Mound:
  - http://www.siue.edu/CAHOKIAMOUNDS/galleries/ Aerial_Survey_of_Monks_Mound.htm
  - http://www.3dphoto.dk/UK/home-UK.htm
  - http://www.photomeasure.com/examples.htm

4. FUNCTIONS

- Generate 3D models of objects for animations, visualization, view studies, points, lines, edges, NURBS curves, cylinders
- Produce photo-textured 3D models for realistic walk-bys
- DDE programmability
- Modeling:
  - Objects: NURBS, IGES
  - Transformation: translation, rotation, scaling
  - Post Processing: fit to line, grid, and plane
- Measurement tools: point, distance, length, area, angles, and volume
- Color: adjust the color and back ground color of the 3D objects
- Photos: change or assign a camera, control texturing, rotation, enter a text description, control inverse camera, control processing, camera station data

- Points: assign an ID name, change xyz data, freeze or optimize point data, assign materials and layers
- Surfaces: assign materials and layers, change to be double-sided
- Lines, edges, cylinders: assign or change materials and layers
- Curves: control smoothness, force the curve to be flat (on a plane), assign materials and layers
- Zoom functions: zoom to fit, zoom in, zoom out
- File formats:
  - _ Export file formats: IGES DXF, 3DS, OBJ, VRML, RAW formats
  - _ Loads any size image (up to memory size)
  - _ Unlimited size for photo-texture image in 3D viewer and export

5. WEB RESOURCES

- PhotoModeler: http://www.photomodeler.com
- PC plus Online: http://www.pcplus.co.uk/article.asp?id=24903

PLOT3D

1. PLATFORMS, PRICES, AND SUPPLIER/CREATOR

- Platforms:
  - Silicon Graphics IRIS workstation (some problems with IRIX 6.2)
  - DEC/VMS with DISSPLA graphics software
  - Generic Unix workstation with DISSPLA graphics software
  - Apollo/Unix with GMR3D graphics (old)
  - Generic Unix supercomputer with SGI workstation
- Prices:
  - $200
  - $32 for the Manual
- Company
  - Originally designed by National Aeronautics and Space Administration (NASA). National Technology Transfer Center (NTTC) is managing software distribution for NASA:
    http://www.nttc.edu/flash/html_version/
    http://www.openchannelfoundation.org

2. APPLICATIONS

- Plot3D is an interactive graphics program, which is mostly used by computational fluid dynamics solutions. It simulates fluid flow by showing the characteristics such as temperature, pressure, vortices, etc.

3. EXAMPLES/SAMPLES

- Here are some links to example outputs by Plot3d:
    - 1. http://www.rpi.edu/~thompb3/plot3d.html
    - 2. http://www.cc.gatech.edu/scivis/research/particlef15/particlef15.html

4. WEB RESOURCES

- Plot3D version 4.0 manual: http://www.fhi-berlin.mpg.de/th/balsac/pltm.0.html

PolyTrans

1. PLATFORM, PRICES, AND SUPPLIER/CREATOR

- Windows and Silicon Graphics IRIX Platforms
- $395.00–$495.00
- Okino: http://www.okino.com

2. APPLICATIONS

- PolyTrans provides a complete set of precise and high-quality import/export converters for the most popular industry standard 3D file formats
- PolyTrans has a set of perfect translators that is able to convert entire files from one format to another in a ideal manner such that the exported file can be loaded and rendered with few changes
- PolyTrans works well with importing huge DXF and IGES files in under one minute or large USGS DEM datasets for ultimate export to other rending programs such as NuGraf, 3D Studio, Maya, Lightwave, and Softimage

3. EXAMPLES/SAMPLES

- http:/www.okino.com/conv/conv.htm
- http:okino.com/mainpic.htm

4. FUNCTIONS

- Modeling:
  - Objects: mesh polygons, NURB and bicubic patches, and quadrics surface
  - Transformation: object manipulation, light/camera movement, all texture projections, pivot point, texture coordinates, bump mapping
  - Editing and manipulation: Shading and texture projection mapping parameters
- Rendering:
  - Cameras: viewing orientation and lighting
  - Lights: spot, point light sources
  - Materials: wireframe solid objects, point cloud
  - Before and after rendering: texture map, bump mapping, bitmap, convert in formation
- Animation:
  - Keyframe animation conversion: object, translate, scale, rotation. camera movement, field of view, etc.
- File Formats: (listed at www.okino.com/conv/filefrmt.htm)
  - Importing File Format: VistaPro, Wavefront, NugrafBDF, CAD 3A, Rhino03D Wavefront OBJor IGES 3D studio R4, LightWave, and doezens more
  - Export File Format: 3D Studio R4, 3D Studio MAX v1.2 and v2.x, DirectX Alias triangle, Apple 3D metafile and dozens more

5. WEB RESOURCES

- http://www.okino.com/conv/conv.htm
- http://www.okino.com/nrs/nrs.htm
- http://www.okino.com/testimon.htm
- http://www.okino.com/links.htm
- http://www.okino.com/conv/demos.htm
- http://www.okino.com/nrs/demos.htm

Poser 4

1. PLATFORM, PRICES, AND SUPPLIER/CREATOR

- PC, MAC
- $$$$
- Curious Labs: http://www.curiouslabs.com

2. APPLICATIONS

- Poser 4 is a 3D-character animation and design tool for artists and animators. Libraries of pose settings, facial expressions, hand gestures, and swappable clothing are available

3. EXAMPLES/SAMPLES

- Works enhanced by Poser: http://www.curiouslabs.com/gallery/html/artists.html
- More Poser Galleries: http://www.poserworld.com/gallery.htm

  - http://members.aol.com/beyondvr/newart.html
  - http://www.daz3d.com/pages/gallery/gallerymain.html
  - http://mail.curiouslabs.com/poser/Poser/Favorites4/_28.html
  - http://www.cyberpiggy.com/1graphics/Slavas.jpg
  - http://www.poserforum.org/gallery/ghost.jpg
  - http://www.alpc.com/3d/anmie.htm

4. WEB RESOURCES

- Poser4 30-Day Demo: http://www.curiouslabs.com/downloads/html/PoserDemoDownload.html
- 3D Model World: http://www.3dmodelworld.com/
- Poser World, a great resource for Poser fans: http://www.poserworld.com/
- http://www.curiouslabs.com/products/poser4/index.html
- http://www.micropubnews.com/pages/issues/1999/1099_rev-poser_mpn.shtml
- http://www.daz3d.com/
- http://www.micropace.com/Products/CUR/3005.htm

POVLAB

1. PLATFORM, PRICE, AND VENDOR/SUPPLIER

- PC
- Freeware
- Povlab: http://www.povlab.org

2. APPLICATION

- Povlab is a 3D modeling and rendering tool that builds 3D objects for the photo realistic Persistance of Vision Raytrace (POV-Ray)

3. EXAMPLES/SAMPLES

- http://pdelagrange.free.fr/povlab/pimage.html
- http://www.povlab.org/synthese/
- http://pdelagrange.free.fr/povlab/screenshot.html

4. WEB RESOURCES

- http://pdelagrange.free.fr/povlab/tutorial/tut_main.htm
- http://www.povray.org/

Persistence of Vision Raytracer (POV-Ray)

1. PLATFORMS, PRICES, AND SUPPLIER/CREATOR

- Windows, MS-Dos, Linux for Intel x86, Apple Macintosh, Amiga, SunOS, Generic Unix
- Freeware
- Persistence of Vision Development Team: http://www.povray.org/

2. APPLICATIONS

- Modeling 3D scenes via ray tracing. Modeling complex scenes involving such things as reflection, 3D materials, and arbitrary geometric objects such as spheres, ellipsoids, and cones accurately without the use of estimation. Accurate modeling of any scene is stressed, due to the fact that shadows, and other phenomena are built in. Actual rendering times are slow due to the fact that it ray traces, but it has a built in feature to ray trace several scenes and turn the collection into an animation. Rendering is done via a script language similar to C++. Graphical modelers have also been created for use with POV-Ray such as Moray, so that modeling intricate scenery and producing high-quality images is as easy as pointing and clicking

3. EXAMPLES/SAMPLES

- Gallery with source: http://rsj.mobilixnet.dk/3d/gallery/gallery.html
- POV-Ray's recommended links site: http://www.povray.org/links/

4. FUNCTIONS

- Modeling:
  - Objects: spline, polygonal, parametric, NURBS, geometric objects (cones, ellipsoids, cylinders, etc.), fractals
  - Transformation: translation, rotation, scaling, cloning, mirror, union, intersection, difference
  - Features: built in fog and reflection functions
- Rendering:
  - Camera: set at any given point
  - Lights: attenuation, shadow, volumetric lighting, Phong, colored
  - Materials: 3D and 2D texturing, scripting language to allow materials to be specified, created, mixed, and colored. Formula-based random textures (wood, stone, etc.). Reflective, translucent, opaque. Bump mapping
  - Before and after rendering: full view antialiasing, motion blur, fog
- Animation:
  - Controllers: procedural, mostly manual
- Scripting:
  - Control Structures: loops, conditionals, procedures
  - Mathematics: Built in C++ mathematics functions
  - Objects: Supports an object model similar to C/C++ structures, allows variables
- File Formats:
  - Importing file formats: POV, INC, TXT, INI
  - Exporting file formats: POV, INC, TXT, INI, AVI

5. WEB RESOURCES

- A collection of POV-Ray object scripts: http://www.povworld.de/objects/
- Tutorial on how to make basic scripts: http://povplace.addr.com/tips/transporttut.htm
- http://dir.yahoo.com/Computers_and_Internet/Graphics/3D/Software/POV_Ray/
- Official POV-Ray page: http://www.povray.org/

Pro-Engineer (PRO/E)

1. PLATFORMS, PRICES, AND SUPPLIER/CREATOR

- PC, Sun Workstations, and SGI Workstations
- $$$$$
- Parametric Technology Corporation: http://www.ptc.com

2. APPLICATIONS

- Pro/ENGINEER is used by engineers, architectures, manufacturers, and draftsmen for Design, development and manufacturing. It is a Computer-Aided-Design and Computer-Aided-Manufacturing (CAD/CAM) tool

3. EXAMPLES/SAMPLES

- Mechanical Design: http://eci2.ucsb.edu/~barkus/proe.html
- Robotics: http://www.cs.dartmouth.edu/~jonh/robots/fiat/proe-model/
- Design of a Lathe: http://www.haidekker.org/mae157/project2.html
- Aerospace Industry: http://www.stnet.it/proe/proe-gallery/proe-g1.htm
- Electronics Industry: http://www.stnet.it/proe/proe-gallery/proe-g4.htm
- Heavy Equipment Industry: http://www.stnet.it/proe/proe-gallery/proe-g5.htm
- Industrial Equipments: http://www.stnet.it/proe/proe-gallery/proe-g6.htm

4. WEB RESOURCES

- Pro/Engineer: http://www.seas.upenn.edu:8080/~meam100/ProE/ProEinfo.html
- Pro/ENGINEER Design Solutions: http://www.ptc.com/products/proe/overview/
- http://www.daz3d.com/

ProPak 3D

1. PLATFORMS, PRICES, AND SUPPLIER/CREATOR

- PC
- $$$$$

- Web Promotion Custom Gallery: http://www.webpromotion.com/

2. APPLICATIONS

- Website concept, design, and development tool. Rendering and animation tool that includes generating polygonal objects, curve surfaced objects, and particle systems
- Propak 3D allows you to view 40 file formats created using traditional 3D applications and to convert them to the Mendel 3D format (.MDX, .MCO)

3. EXAMPLES/SAMPLES

- http://www.webpromotion.com/sites.html
- http://www.webpromotion.com/propak.html
- http://www.webpromotion.com/stock.html
- http://www.mendel3d.com/factory.asp?lang=us

4. FILE FORMATS

- Animated manufacturing process demonstration
- 3D Machined part modeling, interactive headlines/DHTML
- Additional file formats are available through: http://www.andersonmfg.com

5. WEB RESOURCES

- http://www.webpromotion.com/vp.html
- http://www.webpromotion.com/identity.html
- http://www.webpromotion.com/portfolio.html
- http://www.ozdough.com/promote.html
- http://www.reallybig.com/reallybig.shtml
- http://www.2020tech.com/submit.html
- http://www.sunsteam.com/search/dir/Computers+and+Internet/Graphics/Animated+gifs/index.20.html

ProtoCAD

1. PLATFORMS, PRICES, AND SUPPLIER/CREATOR

- PC, MS-DOS Applications
- $$$
- Trius, Inc.: http://www.triusinc.com/pc3d.htm

2. APPLICATIONS

- A fast 3D Computer Aided Design and Rendering package with a 3D drawing and editing tool. Used to turn 2D drawings into 3D models. It is bundled with TubeCAD and IntelliCAD; software for pipe fabricators

3. EXAMPLES/SAMPLES

- http://www.advancedtubular.com/ProtoCAD3D.htm
- http://www.kroell-net.de/opt/galactic2.htm#OptExplore

4. WEB RESOURCES

- http://www.advancedtubular.com/ProtoCAD3D.htm
- http://www.triusinc.com/

pV3 (PARALLEL VISUAL3)

1. PLATFORMS, PRICES, AND SUPPLIER/CREATOR

- Client/Server: clients supported are COMPAQ ALPHA, HP, IBM RS/6000, IBM SP2, SGI, Linux, Sun, Cray and WindowsNT/2000 machines. Servers supported are COMPAQ ALPHA, HP, IBM RS/6000, SGI, Linux, Sun, and WindowsNT/2000 workstations with some special graphics hardware
- Free
- MIT, Department of Aeronautics and Astronautics: http://raphael.mit.edu/pv3/pv3.html

2. APPLICATIONS

- pV3 is a three dimensional, distributed, unsteady, unstructured, CFD visualization software system for supercomputers, parallel machines, and clusters of workstations. The software is used for co-processing multidimensional visualizations of scalar, vector, and tensor data generated in a distributed and/or parallel computing environment during runtime

3. EXAMPLES/SAMPLES

- Distribution: http://raphael.mit.edu/pv3/pv3.html
- http://hpcc.arc.nasa.gov/reports/annrep94/pv3.htm
- http://banzai.msi.umn.edu/~reudi/

4. FUNCTIONS

- Visualization:
  - Unsteady data, meshes, and structure computations. Structured and/or unstructured grid-meshes and dynamically adapted grids. Multiple scalar variables and vector fields, passive particle motions, 3D trajectory, some combinations of the above
  - 2D cutting planes and 1D line probes. Streamlines, bubble tracers, ribbons and surface tufts
  - Transformation: opaque, transparent, and highlight-displaying modes
- Data Extraction:
  - Contains all extraction tools expected of a 3D fluids visualization system: including geometric cuts, isosurfaces, streamlines, transient particle traces, and programmer defined. The data can be either interactively visualized or stored away for later examination
- Debugging:
  - Debugging tool for those used to the views created by flow visualization tools for solutions analysis. Allows reintegration and analysis of data dispersed across an array of processors
- File Formats:
  - Postscript, mpeg files. Callable from Fortran and C

5. WEB RESOURCES

- www.llp.fu-berlin.de/baum/graphics-graph-systems.html
- http://w3.pppl.gov/vde2000/abstracts.html
- http://sop.geo.umn.edu/~reudi/pv3b.html

PV-WAVE

1. PLATFORMS, PRICES, AND SUPPLIER/CREATOR

- Open VMS, Digital UNIX, HP-UX, AIX, IRIX, Solaris, RedHat Linux, Windows 95/98/NT
- $$$$
- Visual Numerics: http://www.vni.com/products/wave/

2. APPLICATIONS

- PV-Wave delivers high level 3D interactive visualization techniques. It is an array-oriented fourth-generation programming language (4GL) to build and deploy Visual Data Analysis (VDA) applications. These applications let users manipulate and visualize complex or extremely large technical datasets to detect and display patterns, trends, anomalies and other vital information

3. EXAMPLES/SAMPLES

- Example images: http://www.vni.com/products/image_library/index.html

4. WEB RESOURCES:

- Newsgroups: comp.lang.idl-pvwave
- PV-Wave homepage: http://www.vni.com/products/wave/index.html
- Brief PV-Wave guide: http://www-atm.ucdavis.edu/unxhelp/pvwave.html
- www.gwdg.de/~applsw/Software/anw_sw.produkte/pvwave.html
- www-vis.lbl.gov/software/pvwave.html

Quick3D

1. PLATFORMS, PRICES, AND SUPPLIER/CREATOR

- PC (Windows)
- Quick3D v2.0 is shareware; Quick3D v3.0: $99.95
- Quick3D Software: http://www.quick3d.org/

2. APPLICATIONS

- Quick3D is a shareware program that provides an intuitive interface for viewing, organizing, and converting 3D files. You can load a 3D file of almost any format, and manipulate it in 3-dimensional space. Quick3D also has many options for changing the way the model is displayed and rendered in real-time. Other features allow for exporting the model in various formats, as well as HTML for easy cataloging of files. Quick3D is small, memory efficient, and fast

3. EXAMPLES/SAMPLES

- http://www.quick3d.org/screenshots.shtml

4. FUNCTIONS

- Display options:
  - Solid; Wireframe; Hidden line removal; Lighting; Depth cueing
  - Bounding box; Center of geometric mass
  - Texturing; Eye Filters; Normal generator
  - HTML output; File Browser and File Info windows
  - Zoom dependent rotation sensitivity
  - Ability to import a .BMP background; .BMP image export; Copy to clipboard
  - Automatic viewport configuration; Unique "live snapshot" windows; Model scale function
  - Hands-free inertial rotation; Recently accessed file list; Pivot point toggle (center of geometric mass vs. local origin)
  - OpenGL hardware support
- Version 2.0 supports the following formats:
  - Truespace Object (.cob); Truespace Scene (.scn); GeomView (.off); 3D Studio (.3ds); Stereo CAD-3D (.3d2); AutoCAD (.dxf); Quake 1 (.mdl); Quake 2 (.md2); Power Render Pro (.pro); Visualization Toolkit (.vtk); Lightwave (.lwo); Wavefront (.obj); WorldToolKit (.nff); DirectX (.x); Quick3D Object (.q3o); Quick3D Scene (.q3s)

5. WEB RESOURCES

- download: http://www.quick3d.org/cgi-bin/my_downloader/my_downloader.cgi

- Quick3D manual: http://www.quick3d.org/manual.html

- Quick3D library: http://www.quick3d.org/library.html

QuickDraw3D

1. PLATFORM, PRICE, AND SUPPLIER/CREATOR

- Macintosh and PC (QuickDraw3D runs on top of QuickTime)
- Free
- Apple Computer, Inc.: http://www.apple.com

2. APPLICATIONS

- QuickDraw 3D is a graphics library that is implemented on top of QuickTime by Apple Computer. QuickDraw 3D creates models using a number of polyhedral primitives. You can define 3D models, apply colors and other attributes to parts of the models. Rendering is through three different types of perspective projection

3. EXAMPLES

- http://developer.apple.com/dev/techsupport/develop/bysubject/quickdraw3d.html
- http://devworld.apple.com/dev/techsupport/develop/issue24/truffles.html
- http://devworld.apple.com/dev/techsupport/develop/issue27/mcbride.html
- http://developer.apple.com/dev/techsupport/develop/issue29/thompson.html

4. WEB RESOURCES

- http://www.devworld.apple.com/techpubs/quicktime/qtdevdocs/RM/qd3dframe.htm
- http://developer.apple.com/quicktime/quicktimeintro/tools/
- http://www.byte.com/art/9606/sec11/art4.htm
- http://www.devworld.apple.com/technotes/tn/tn1109.html
- http://www.artifice.com/tips/vertex_interp.html
- http://www.amplifiedintelligence.com/QD3DFaq.html

RADIANCE

1. PLATFORMS, PRICE, AND SUPPLIER/CREATOR

- Windows 95/98/NT and Unix-based platforms

- Free
- Building Technologies Program: http://radsite.lbl.gov/radiance/HOME.html

2. APPLICATIONS

- Radiance is a rendering system that assures accurate luminance. The applications have been divided into two categories under electric lighting and day lighting. Another type of application is indirect lighting. Yet another application of Radiance is stage lighting which is a physically-based rendering

3. EXAMPLES/SAMPLES

- Daylighting using Radiance: http://radsite.lbl.gov/radiance/frameg.html
- Student projects: http://www.designlaboratory.com/computing/tools/rendering.html

4. WEB RESOURCES

- Applications: http://radsite.lbl.gov/radiance/papers/sg94.1/applicat.html#Begin
- Examples and resources: http://www.schorsch.com/kbase/resources/radiance.html
- Book: http://www.artifice.com/cgi-bin/alk?http://www.amazon.com/exec/obidos/ASIN/1558604995/artificeinc

Ray Dream Studio

1. PLATFORMS, PRICES, AND SUPPLIER/CREATOR

- PC and MAC
- $$$$
- Metacreations: http://www.metacreations.com/
  *note: it appears that the company is in the process of selling Ray Dream Studio

2. APPLICATIONS

- Ray Dream Studio is a 3D rendering, modeling, and animation tool

3. EXAMPLES/SAMPLES

- http://www.dram.org/rd/rdnewsub.html#miller

- http://www.ruku.com/morface.html
- http://www.ruku.com/3dto2d.html
- http://web.tusco.net/janspage/computerart/tutorials/Mkofatree/

4. WEB RESOURCES

- http://www.creativepro.com/software/home/861.html
- http://www.ruku.com/raydream.html
- http://www.zdnet.com/pcmag/features/software/1519/3d-r3.htm

RayGun 3

1. PLATFORM, PRICE, AND SUPPLIER/CREATOR

- PC
- N/A
- - Company: Right Hemisphere Ltd., New Zealand:
  http://www.us.righthemisphere.com/raygun30/raygun_home.htm

2. APPLICATIONS

- Raygun is a ray trace plug-in tool for 3D Studio Max

3. EXAMPLES/SAMPLES

- http://www.us.righthemisphere.com/gallery/raygun/screen_house/index.htm
- http://www.us.righthemisphere.com/gallery/raygun/giant_pictures/index.htm
- http://www.us.righthemisphere.com/gallery/raygun/cat/index.htm

4. WEB RESOURCES

- http://www.us.righthemisphere.com/raygun30/raygun_home.htm
- http://store.yahoo.com/3dcafe/raygun.html
- http://www.us.righthemisphere.com/gallery/tutorials.htm#RG

Rayshade

1. PLATFORMS, PRICE, AND DISTRIBUTOR

- Unix systems, PC, Mac, Amiga, OS2 (ported already or easily portable)
- Free to download: ftp://graphics.stanford.edu/pub/rayshade
- Craig Kolb and Rod Bogart: http://graphics.stanford.edu/~cek/rayshade

2. APPLICATIONS

- Rayshade is a 3D rendering tool for ray tracing images. It reads in a scene description file (such as an ASCII text file), renders the scene, and produces the ray-traced image. It is written in LEX, YACC, and C, and makes use of the Utah Raster Toolkit

3. EXAMPLES/SAMPLES

- Imagery with source code: http://www.cs.cmu.edu:80/afs/cs/misc/rayshade/ all_mach/omega/doc/Examples/rayimages.html
- Gallery (high-quality): http://graphics.stanford.edu/~cek/rayshade/gallery/ gallery.html
- Rayshade Pictures: http://www.mit.edu:8001/afs/sipb/user/mkgray/ht/ rayshade.html
- Rayshade Image Exhibit: http://www.fbe.unsw.edu.au/exhibits/rayshade/

4. WEB RESOURCES

- Rayshade Homepage: http://www-graphics.stanford.edu/~cek/rayshade
- Converter from Mathematica graphics to Rayshade input: ftp://ftp.inf.ethz.ch/org/ti/scs/ray/rayshade.m
- Graphics resources list (a comparative guide): http://www.go.dlr.de:8081/info/faqs/graphics/resources-list.1.html
- 2 sets of Stephen Peter's notes on Rayshade: http://www.fbe.unsw.edu.au/Learning/RayShade/Notes-on http://web.cs.uni.edu/Help/rayshade_2/contents.htm

Realax VR Studio

1. PLATFORMS, PRICES, AND SUPPLIER/CREATOR

- Windows and SGI
- 5-year site license (5 annual payments) £5,000; 5-year site license (single payment) £24,000; 1 concurrent user £1,000; 1 concurrent user maintenance £150
- Realax AG, Germany: http://www.realax.com/

2. APPLICATIONS

- It is a tool to prepare virtual reality simulations and design reviews and high quality visualizations. It offers modeling, materials, light effects, and textures as well as functionalities for animation and simulation

3. EXAMPLES/SAMPLES

- Surgery Real-time Animation: http://www.realax.com/docs/html/medical/utueb.htm
- Terrain Visualization: http://www.realax.com/docs/html/viss/uterrex.htm
- Control Room: http://www.realax.com/docs/html/science/uhalden.htm

4. WEB RESOURCES

- Home page: http://www.realax.com/docs/html/products/products.htm
- Other: http://www.chest.ac.uk/software/realax/overview.html
- Realax Member Club: e-mail to (member@realax.com)

Realflow

1. PLATFORMS, PRICES, AND SUPPLIER/CREATOR

- Intel PC (Windows 98/ME/NT) and DEC alpha (Windows NT)
- $595(Standard), $1175(Gold), and $2175(Platinum)
- Next Limit: http://www.realflow.com/

2. APPLICATIONS

- 3D modeling and simulation software that simulates different kinds of fluids by calculating the interaction between particles. It models the complex physical interaction between liquids or liquid and solid surfaces. Such things as particle collision, heat transfer, and material properties are all taken into consideration in the modeling process. Advertising industry is its strongest clientele, and it is expanding into the scientific community

3. EXAMPLES/SAMPLES

- Real Flow Fluid Dynamics Gallery: http://www.realflow.com/realflow/gallery/gallery.html

4. FUNCTIONS

- Modeling:
  - Objects: polygonal, particle clouds, curved surfaces (using fine meshes)
  - Transformation: translation, rotation, scaling
  - Editing and manipulations: (vertex, edge, mesh, polygon, curves) friction, elasticity, adhesiveness, speed, temperature, distance, heat conductivity, etc.
- Rendering:
  - Cameras: adjustable, movable
  - Lights: attenuation, shadow, volumetric lighting, Phong
  - Materials: blend, double-sided, matte/shadow, morpher, ray trace, shellac, multi/sub-object, top/bottom
  - More materials: texture mapping, procedural maps, ray-traced maps
  - Before and after rendering: antialiasing, motion blur, field rendering, combustion, perspective matching, environment mapping
- Animation:
  - Controllers: procedural, compound, system
  - Object's physical behavior: trajectory, pivot point, forward kinematics, motion blur, collision
  - Fluid Dynamics: mixture of fluids, fluid collision with hard surface
- File Formats:
  - Importing file formats: SD, .3DS, LWS, ASE, LWO, OBJ (Wavefront Object), DXF
  - Exporting file formats: SD

5. WEB RESOURCES

- ACM Siggraph on Realflow: http://helios.siggraph.org/industry/detail/126.html

- Dimensional Reality's Tutorial: http://www.dimensionalreality.com/generic.jhtml?pid=11

Realimation

1. PLATFORMS, PRICES, AND SUPPLIER/CREATOR

- Windows 95/98/NT (Intel), Windows NT (DEC Alpha), and Silicon Graphics
- STE Designer (which includes RealiStorm plug-ins) costs $995. VSG Developer Tools (including C++ API, STE and RealiStorm plug-ins) costs $9,990
- RealiMation: http://www.realimation.com/index.htm

2. APPLICATIONS

- RealiMation is a powerful toolset for visualizations, simulations, or games. RealiMation provides the data creation and scene management capabilities and also an API to take the data and deliver it on any platform

3. EXAMPLES/SAMPLES

- Gallery Index: http://www.realimation.com/showcase/showcaseframe.htm

4. WEB RESOURCES

- Technical Papers: http://www.realimation.com/overview/technical/technical_papers.htm
- An article: http://visualmagic.awn.com/html/reviews/feb98-realimation.html

Realsoft 3D

1. PLATFORMS, PRICES, AND SUPPLIER/CREATOR

- PC
- $700
- Realsoft Company: http://www.realsoft.fi

2. APPLICATIONS

- Realsoft 3D provides a full feature modeling, rendering, animation, and simulation software tool. It is used for architecture and modular design

3. EXAMPLES/SAMPLES

- http://www.realsoft.fi/gallery/images/alienbath1.jpg

- http://www.realsoft.fi/gallery/images/bulbs.jpg

- http://www.realsoft.fi/gallery/images/av.jpg

- http://www.realsoft.fi/gallery/images/demo11.jpg

4. FUNCTIONS

- Modeling:
    - Objects: NURBS curves and meshes, CSG, metaball object, rectangle, circle, curve, polygon, cone, sphere, cylinder
    - Transformation: translation, rotation, moving, scale, skew
    - Editing and modify (vertex, edge, face, objects): weld, extrude, sweep, beveling
- Rendering:
    - Cameras: adjustable, movable
    - Lights: support light sources including ambient, point, shadow, spot and distant lights
    - Materials: texture mapping. Parallel, cylinder, sphere, disk, mesh, cube and pointwise uv mapping medthods are available for mapping materials to objects. Visual shading language (VSL) allows the end users to define procedural material effects such as fire, marble or wood without writing the code. VSL objects (Constant, Texture, Noise, etc.) and VSL material properties (Transparency, Alpha, Color, etc.)
- Animation:
    - Controllers: keyframing. The program knows the transformation/deformation applied and defines key frame accordingly. The number of key frames is independent in each dimension of transformation components (translate, scale, rotation, skew)
    - Morphing: simply single point edit, then Realsoft 3D automatically defines the morphing animation
    - Skeleton control: a skeleton object control system is included for skeleton support feature such as inverse/forward kinematics, angle constraints for joints, and joint friction
    - Advanced simulation system: simulates gravity, electricity, magnetism, collisions, explosions, friction, forces caused by flow in a fluid, etc.
- File Formats:
    - IGES plug-in is an import/export module for Realsoft 3D. The plug-in allows you to save your projects directly in IGES 5.3 ASCII format. Loading of IGES files is also supported

5. WEB RESOURCES

- http://www.interneteye3d.com/Reviews2000/Oct/RealSoft3d4/default.asp

- http://www.planet3dart.com/sections.php?op=viewarticle&artid=24
- http://www.creativepro.com/software/home/1857.html
- http://www.amigaflame.co.uk/amireal.htm
- http://www.magnamana.com/imagecontest/newmainframe.htm

Reflex|DRAMA

1. PLATFORMS, PRICES, AND SUPPLIER/CREATOR

- Windows NT 4.0, Windows 2000
- $17,000
- Reflex Systems, Inc.: http://www.relfex3d.com

2. APPLICATIONS

- Reflex/DRAMA is a 3D software package, which provides tools for modeling, animating and rendering human characters.This technology is used in the VFX, gaming, entertainment, scientific/medical, and business applications fields

3. EXAMPLES/SAMPLES

- http://www.reflex3d.com/pic_center/mid_hair.html
- http://www.reflex3d.com/pic_center/face.html
- http://www.reflex3d.com/pic_center/blond.html

4. FUNCTIONS

- Modeling:
  - Objects: Reflex/DRAMA creates complex 3D human models with realistic features such as hair, bone, skin, and muscle
  - Transformation: Forward Kinematics (FK), Inverse Kinematics (IK) posing tools, and cloning
  - Editing and manipulations
- Rendering:
  - Cameras: adjustable, movable
  - Light: shadow, reflection, refraction, transparency, and color variations
  - Materials: Surface-stitching tools, hybrid scan-line, ray-traced, texture mapping, and a variety of specialized rendering parameters

- Animation:
  - Controllers: mouse-controlled, key-framed
  - Advanced animation: allows animating realistic 3D human models, with features such as skin, bone, muscle, and fat by using a comprehensive set of posing tools
  - Advanced simulation: allows use of direct simulation to create gravity, facial expression, etc.
- File Formats:
  - Importing and exporting file format: IGES, OBJ, DXF, BVH, HTR, ASF
  - Reflex/DRAMA allows data to be exchanged with other commercial tools Maya, XSI, 3D Max

5. WEB RESOURCES

- http://www.gamasutra.com/newswire/bit_blasts/20000728/index2.htm

- http://www.reflex3d.com/

- http://www.headshed.com/headline/july/reflex_2906.htm

- http://www.siggraph.org/s2000/exhibition/detail/156.html

REELMOTION

1. PLATFORMS, PRICES, AND SUPPLIER/CREATOR

- PC, MAC, Dec Alpha
- $795.00
- Motional Realms: http://www.reelmotion.com/

2. APPLICATIONS

- ReelMotion is a real-time 3D simulator that uses physics and collision detection to create realistic animations of objects and vehicles including cars, aircraft, motorcycles, helicopters, and nearly any rigid body object. With ReelMotion you can drive an object, make the object fly, make it climb any terrain, take action sequences using several of its cameras, roll it over, have it bounce, etc.

3. EXAMPLES/SAMPLES

- http://www.reelmotion.com/movies.htm
- http://www.reelmotion.com/movies2.htm

- http://ilsmacwww.ethz.ch/chris/reelmotion/

4. FUNCTIONS/FEATURES

- Modeling:
    - Simulated Objects: cars, trucks, hovercraft, including other ground vehicles, fixed-wing aircrafts, helicopters, motorcycles, bicycles, and objects of any shape
    - Transformations: translation, scaling, rotation
    - Model Customization: tire track/width/diameter, center of gravity, steering angle, engines, aerodynamics, shape — import any car body/chassis
- Animation:
    - Controller: procedural animation, mouse-based controls
    - Simulation Includes: landing gear, suspension, tire rotation, steering wheel, brake lights, propeller rotation, elevators, and helicopter rotor blades
    - Effectors: with the addition of effectors, one can create specialized moving parts
- Rendering:
    - Cameras: automatically generate camera motion; 11 preset behaviors, among them: dolly, cockpit, roam, chase, external, tv track; also simulate real world camera response with acceleration, lag, jitter and bounce
    - Physics Based Motion: mass and inertia effects, friction, springs and damping, and external forces
    - Environmental Simulation: wind and turbulence, atmospheric density, adjustable gravity, surface traction — ice to pavement
- Special Features
    - Easy to use Interface: game-like controls, drive or fly with mouse or joystick, real-time QuickDraw 3D or OpenGL display, autopilot assist for helicopters, airplanes, and motorcycles; templates for easy vehicle configuration
    - Terrain Detection: build and import your own terrain; automatically position objects on surfaces; object body interacts with terrain — objects can roll and bounce on the ground
    - Collision Detection: collide with moving or stationary objects, adjustable collision forces, including spring, damping, and friction
- File Formats:
    - Bio vision BVH, Acclaim ASF, AMC DXF object files

5. WEB RESOURCES

- ReelMotion Demo: http://www.reelmotion.com/demoapp.htm
- Third Party Review: http://www.macaddict.com/news/reviews/1999_02_11.shtml

RenderDrive

1. PLATFORMS, PRICES, AND SUPPLIER/CREATOR

- Cross platform: RenderDrive is a networked device, so it has the capability to work with any computer that supports compatible networking
- $$$$$$
- Advanced Rendering Technology: http://www.art-render.com/

2. APPLICATIONS

- RenderDrive is a networked rendering tool used to produce high quality images. With an array of custom processors, RenderDrive allows a scene-building environment to be true to real-world physical values

3. EXAMPLES/SAMPLES

- Links Gallery for RenderDrive: http://www.art-render.com/3/body.htm
- RenderDrive links on related tools: http://www.art-render.com/2a/body.htm

4. WEB RESOURCES

- A RenderDrive Review: http://www.cadserver.co.uk/common/viewer/archive/2001/Jan/25/news3.phtm
- Advanced Rendering Technology Links: http://homepages.tcp.co.uk/~john-mandy/art/

RenderMan

1. PLATFORMS, PRICE, COMPANY

- PC
- $5,000
- Pixar Animation Studios: http://www.pixar.com

2. APPLICATIONS

- Pixar's RenderMan is the highest quality renderer and has been production tested through successful use in feature films for over ten years. Pixar's RenderMan is stable, fast, and efficient for handling complex surface appearances and images. RenderMan's powerful shading language and anti-aliased motion blur allow designers to believably integrate stunning synthetic effects with live-action footage

3. EXAMPLES

- http://www.edit.ne.jp/~katsu/rms_tree.htm
- http://www.reptilelabour.com/software/renderman/images/MBAOpalTest.jpg
- http://www.pixels3d.com/tempest/jack_renderman.html
- http://www.edit.ne.jp/~katsu/image/sea_blue.jpg
- http://www.edit.ne.jp/~katsu/image/ray_f5_b.jpg

4. FUNCTIONS

- Modeling:
  - Objects: Subdivision surfaces, arbitrary output variables and post processing techniques, soft shadows, polygonal, point polygonal, patch, patch mesh, sphere, and cone...
  - Transformation: perspective, translations, rotation, scaling, skew transform
- Rendering:
  - Surface: reflects and transmits light
  - Light: Light emitted by a light source, light through a volume in space
  - Cameras: Attenuation of camera-bound light through space
  - Displacement: Geometric displacement of points on a surface
  - Deformation: Geometric transformation of a surface
  - Projection: Geometric mapping from camera to screen space
- Animation: light, surface, volume, displacement, transformation, imager, texture mapping, atmosphere, colors ...
- File Formats:
  - Importing file formats: RIB, SGI, IRIX version 6.4, SUN, Solaris 5.6, DEC, and OSF1 V4.0
  - Exporting file formats: RIB, SGI, IRIX version 6.4, SUN, Solaris 5.6, DEC, and OSF1 V4.0

5. WEB RESOURCES

- Web resource: http://www.lumis.com/renderman/
- Books: http://www.renderman.org/RMR/Books/

- Article: http://www.3dgate.com/tools/000320/0320renderman.html
- http://www.creativepro.com/story/news/11448.html

RenderPark

1. PLATFORMS, PRICE, COMPANY

- - Platforms:
  - – UNIX: SGI/Iris 6.4,SUN/Solaris, Linux
  - – GUI: X-window system + Motif toolkit
  - – 3D-graphics: OpenGL, IrisGL, Starbase
- Price: Free
- Company: Katholieke University Leuven, in Belgium:
  http://www.cs.kuleuven.ac.be/cwis/research/graphics/RENDERPARK/
  index.shtml

2. APPLICATIONS

- RenderPark is a photorealistic rendering program. RenderPark can compute a photorealistically illuminated 3D model or a high- or low-dynamic range image of the model as seen from a particular view using object space-radiance methods, ray tracing, bi-direction ray tracing. RenderPark is suited for quantitative prediction of the illumination in buildings that have not yet been built, for instance. A light source will be described by its luminous power for instance rather than just as a color

3. EXAMPLES/SAMPLES

- Examples of RenderPark:
  - – http://www.cs.kuleuven.ac.be/cwis/research/graphics/RENDERPARK/
    SCREENSHOTS/glass_caustic.jpg
  - – http://www.cs.kuleuven.ac.be/cwis/research/graphics/RENDERPARK/
    SCREENSHOTS/hospital1.jpg
  - – http://www.cs.kuleuven.ac.be/cwis/research/graphics/RENDERPARK/
    SCREENSHOTS/hospital2.jpg
- Galleries of RenderPark tools:
  - – http://astronomy.swin.edu.au/pbourke/rendering/renderpark/

4. FUNCTIONS

- Modeling:
  - Objects: patch, space-radiance, clustering, pixel driven radiance
  - Transformation: translation, rotation, scaling, spacing
  - Radiosity: Galerkin radiosity, stochastic Jacobi radiosity, photon map construction, random walk radiosity, etc.
- Rendering:
  - Cameras: adjustable, rotate, translated, moveable
  - Materials: multi/sub-objects, mapping, ray tracing, ray casting, batch
- Animation: light, surface, volume, transformation, imager, texture, mapping, atmosphere, luminous colors ...
- File Formats:
  - Importing file formats: MGF, VRML'97, PPM, TIFF
  - Exporting file formats: MGF, POV (experimental), RIB (experimental)
  - Additional file formats: available through plug-in

5. WEB RESOURCES:

- Website: http://threedom.sourceforge.net/about.html

- http://sal.kachinatech.com/E/0/RENDERPARK.html

RenderWare

1. PLATFORM, PRICES, AND SUPPLIER/CREATOR

- PC, PlayStation2, Dreamcast, Macintosh

- Order form: http://www.renderware.com/rwgames/orderform.html

- Criterion Software: http://www.csl.com

2. APPLICATIONS

- RenderWare3 is a high performance 3D game development toolkit. RenderWare3 has powerful and rich rendering features, including multiple cameras, colored lights, perspective-correctness, tiling, masked and lit textures, flat or Gouraud shading, and much more. It uses an object-based approach to give developers easy access to its underlying power. Offering nearly 700 API calls, RenderWare3 can provide users with complete control over their 3D world. Game development companies such as Interplay and Ubisoft have chosen RenderWare as their development tools

3. EXAMPLES/SAMPLES

- Games Developed using RenderWare: http://www.renderware.com/licensees.html

4. FUNCTIONS

- Modeling:
  - Most RenderWare3 developers use professional modeling tools such as 3DS Max and Maya to construct the game artwork. RenderWare3 offers extensive tools for importing geometry and animation from these packages
- Rendering:
  - RenderWare's PowerPipe is a modular, extensible, and open architecture
  - RenderWare3 is based upon a unique architecture that allows objects to be extended or the rendering pipeline to be overloaded at a very fine level of granularity. This powerful "plug-in" mechanism allows developers to have a very high level of flexibility. They can either use the reference implementation, or decide to replace it using advanced plug-ins that will be either developed by the vendor or third parties. Alternatively, should developers want to ensure that RenderWare3 meets their specific needs, they can also easily develop their own powerful custom plug-ins that could, at a later date, be sold to other RenderWare3 developers
- Animation:
  - RenderWare3 imports animations directly from leading modeling packages such as 3DS Max, Maya, Softimage, and Lightwave
- File Formats:
  - RenderWare3 imports worlds/objects/animations directly from leading modeling packages such as 3DS Max, Maya, Softimage and Lightwave. A RenderWare importer converts and optimizes (compiles) the worlds from these modeling packages into a format that the RenderWare World Manager can handle efficiently. All source code for plug-in exporters is provided with the SDK to enable developers to customize and extend these tools

5. WEB RESOURCES

- RenderWare 3 overview: http://www.renderware.com/rwgames/overview_set.html
- RenderWare tutorial: http://www.grovers.com/objects/rw.html
- RenderWare developers' site: http://developer.renderware.com/
- RenderWare forum: http://www.rwmodeler.com/disc1_frm.htm

Renoir

1. PLATFORMS, PRICES, AND SUPPLIER/CREATOR

- IBM PC computers under Windows-95, Windows-NT (A minimal required configuration is IBM PC/AT Pentium or compatible, 90Mhz, 32Mb RAM, 1 Gb HD, SVGA, PD (mouse))

- Unix workstations (SGI, HP, IBM, SUN, Titan) or SGI workstation under OS IRIX 5.3

- Pricing: $$$$

- Integra.: http://www.integra.co.jp/eng/products/renoir/index.htm

2. APPLICATIONS

- Renoir is software intended for 3D reconstruction of the shape and color attributes of architectural objects from photoimages

3. EXAMPLES/SAMPLES

- To learn about the science of reconstructing 3D models from photos, please visit: http://www.integra.co.jp/eng/products/renoir/functional.htm

- Reconstruction of Exterior Objects: http://www.integra.co.jp/eng/products/renoir/exterior.htm

- Reconstruction of Interior Objects: http://www.integra.co.jp/eng/products/renoir/interior.htm

- Photo-montage Examples: http://www.integra.co.jp/eng/products/renoir/photomontage.htm

4. WEB RESOURCES

- Homepage: http://www.integra.co.jp/eng/products/renoir/index.htm

- More resources: http://www.integra.co.jp/eng/products/renoir/functional.htm

- Evaluation Download link: (Renoir demo for free evaluation can be downloaded here)
    - via http: http://www.integra.co.jp/eng/products/renoir/r410i_dm.zip
    - via ftp: ftp://ftp.integra.co.jp/pub/products/renoir/r410i_dm.zip

Rhinoceros 3D

1. PLATFORMS, PRICES, AND SUPPLIER/CREATOR

- Windows 95/98/ME/NT4/Windows 2000/Windows XP
- $795 ($195 for educational purposes; $995 educational lab license)
- Robert McNeel and Associates: http://www.rhino3d.com; http://www.mcneel.com

2. APPLICATIONS

- Rhino can create, edit, analyze, and translate NURBS curves, surfaces, and solids in Windows. Rhino has limited support for polygon meshes. There are no limits on complexity, degree, or size. It can be used for: CAD, CAM, rapid prototyping, 3D Digitizing, graphic design
- Rhino combines the accuracy of traditional CAD with the flexibility of spline-based modeling technology, to create objects that are smooth NURBS curves and surfaces rather than line segments or polygon meshes. Rhino uses trimmed free-form NURBS surfaces to accurately represent curved shapes, including curved shapes with holes in them. Rhino also integrates solids (surfaces joined together at their edges) and surface modeling so that solids can be exploded into surfaces, edited, and then joined back together again. Any combination of curves, surfaces, and solids can be trimmed

3. EXAMPLES

- http://www.rhino3d.com/gallery.htm
- http://www.rhino3d.com/tutorials.htm

4. FEATURES

- Create curves: point, line, polyline, polyline on mesh, free-form curve, circle, arc, ellipse, rectangle, polygon, helix, spiral, conic, TrueType text, point interpolation, control points (vertices), sketch
- Create curves from other objects: extend, fillet, chamfer, offset, blend, from two views, cross section profiles, intersection, contour, section, border, silhouette, extract isopram (which Rhino means a line drawn on the surface), projection, pullback, sketch, wireframe, detach trim, 2D drawings, flatten developable surfaces, extract points
- Edit curves: control points, edit points, handlebars, smooth, fair, change degree, add/remove knots, add kinks, rebuild, refit, match, simplify, change weight, make periodic, adjust end bulge, adjust seam

- Create surfaces: from three or four points, from three or four curves, from planar curves, from network of curves, rectangle, deformable plane, extrude, ribbon, rule, loft, developable, sweep along a path, sweep along two rail curves, revolve, rail revolve, blend, patch, drape, point grid, heightfield, fillet, chamfer, offset, TrueType text
- Edit surfaces: control points, handlebars, change degree, add/remove knots, match, extend, merge, join, untrim, split surface by isoparms, rebuild, shrink, make periodic, Boolean (union, difference, intersection), unroll developable surfaces
- Create solids: box, sphere, cylinder, tube, pipe, cone, truncated cone, ellipsoid, torus, extrude planar curve, extrude surface, cap planar holes, join surfaces, TrueType text
- Edit solids: fillet edges, extract surface, Booleans (union, difference, intersection)
- Create meshes: from NURBS surfaces, from closed polyline, mesh face, plane, box, cylinder, cone, and sphere
- Edit meshes: explode, join, weld, unify normals, apply to surface, reduce polygons
- Edit tools: cut, copy, paste, delete, delete duplicates, move, rotate, mirror, scale, stretch, align, array, join, trim, split, explode, extend, fillet, chamfer, offset, twist, bend, taper, shear, orient, orient planar object on curve, flow along curve, smooth, project, object properties
- Annotations: arrows, dots, dimensions (horizontal, vertical, aligned, rotated, radial, diameter, angle), text blocks, leaders, hidden line removal
- Analysis: point, length, distance, angle, radius, bounding box, normal direction, area, area centroid, area moments, volume, volume centroid, volume moments, curvature graph, surface curvature, geometric continuity, deviation, naked edges, nearest point, surface analysis (draft angle, zebra stripe, environment map, Gaussian curvature, mean curvature, and minimum or maximum radius of curvature), hydrostatics
- Rendering: shade, shade (OpenGL), shade selected objects, render (with textures, bumps, highlights, transparency, spotlights, and shadows, and customizable resolution), render preview (OpenGL), render preview selected objects, turntable, export for many renderers including BMRT (ray trace and radiosity) and POV (ray trace)
- User interface: extremely fast 3D graphics, unlimited viewports, shaded working views, perspective working views, coordinate read-out, named views, popup recently-used commands, customizable popup commands, synchronize views, configurable middle mouse button, customizable icons and user workspace, customizable popup toolbar, extensive explorer-like online help, electronic updates, newsgroup support, and a 650-page color manual
- Construction aids: unlimited undo and redo, undo and redo multiple, exact numeric input, object snaps, grid snaps, ortho, planar, named construction planes, next and previous construction planes, orient construction plane on curve, layers, layer filtering, background bitmaps, object hide/show, show selected objects, swap hidden objects, object lock/unlock, unlock selected objects, control and edit points on/off, and points off for selected objects

- File formats supported: DWG/DXF(AutoCAD 2000/2000i/2002, 14, 13, and 12), STEP, CSV (export properties and hydrostatics), IGES (Alias, Ashlar Vellum, AutoFORM, AutoShip, Breault, CADCEUS, CAMSoft, CATIA, Cosmos, Delcam, FastSurf, FastSHIP, Intergrity Ware, Inventor, IronCAD, LUSAS, Maya, MAX 3.0, MasterCAM, ME30, Mechanical Desktop, Microstation, NuGraf, OptiCAD, Pro/E, SDRC I-DEAS, Softimage, Solid Edge, SolidWorks, SUM 4, SURFCAM, TeKSoft, Unigraphics), SAT (ACIS, export only), X_T (Parasolid, export only), 3DS, LWO, STL, OBJ, AI, RIB, POV, UDO, VRML, BMP, TGA, JPG
    - File management: Notes, templates, merge files, export selected objects, save small, incremental save, bitmap file preview, Rhino file preview
    - Plug-ins: Rhino supports plug-ins, currently available plug-ins at: www.rhino3d.com/plugins.htm with free SDK for developers at: www.rhino3d.com/download.htm
- 3D digitizing support: MicroScribe 3D and Faro Space Arm

5. WEB RESOURCES

- Newsgroups:

    - news://news.mcneel.com/rhino
    - news://news.mcneel.com/rhino.plug-ins

- Free downloadable Evaluation version, fully functional except saves only 25 times:

    - http://www.rhino3d.com/download.htm

Room Designer

1. PLATFORMS, PRICES, AND SUPPLIER/CREATOR

- PC

- Custom software (price unknown)

- Virtue 3D: http://www.virtue3d.com

2. APPLICATIONS

- A 3D modeling and rendering tool that uses a WYSIWYG interface to design room, that lets customers rearrange furniture, pick furniture's color, and paint the walls. It has obvious application in hardware, construction, and home renovation industries

3. EXAMPLES/SAMPLES

- Virtue 3D's product demo: http://www.virtue3d.com/roomdesigner/index.html

4. FUNCTIONS

- Modeling:
    - Objects: polygonal
    - Transformation: translation, rotation, scaling, and spacing
    - Editing and manipulations: color, choice among preprogrammed objects
- Rendering:
    - Cameras: adjustable, movable
    - Lights: ambient lighting only
    - Materials: texture mapping
    - Environment settings: environment maps, perspective matching
- File Formats:
    - Importing file formats: streamed proprietary data over the Web

5. WEB RESOURCES

- A comparison between Room Designer and other 3D software: http://www.techexchange.com/thelibrary/resources/VirtualFitChart.html

ROSS — Reconstruction of Serial Sections

1. PLATFORMS, PRICES, AND SUPPLIER/CREATOR

- PC, Silicon Graphics Workstation

- Free, but have to meet the NASA requirements

- NASA / Kevin Montgomery: http://biocomp.arc.nasa.gov/.index.html

2. APPLICATIONS

- ROSS (Reconstruction of Serial Sections) is a software package for performing serial-section reconstruction and visualization in 3D. Typically, it is used for reconstruction biological tissue, biological cells, tissues, or organs

3. EXAMPLES/SAMPLES

- Gallery from NASA: http://biocomp.arc.nasa.gov/pics/gallery/

- Reconstruction from CAT/MRI: http://biocomp.arc.nasa.gov/reconstructions/.index.html
- Reconstructed using IMOD and Rendering using Sidefx: http://anusf.anu.edu.au/anusf_visualization/viz_showcase/shaun_sandow/3drecon.html

4. WEB RESOURCES

- NASA Government: http://biocomp.arc.nasa.gov/ross/.index.html
- Technology Opportunity: http://ctoserver.arc.nasa.gov/techopps/ross3dnew.html
- NASA Government: http://biocomp.arc.nasa.gov/ross/
- Kevin Montgomery's PhD dissertation: http://www-biocomp.stanford.edu/kevin/dissertation/

RXscene

1. PLATFORMS, PRICES, AND SUPPLIER/CREATOR

- Windows and SGI
- $$$$
- Realax: http://www.realax.com/; http://www.realax.com/docs/html/products/urxsc.htm

2. APPLICATIONS

- RXscene is a modeler and scene editor with an intuitive user interface.The modeler includes a wide assortment of versatile functions, for example, extruding, revolving, volume sweeping, polygon and vertex alignments, and billboards allowing the user to quickly build complex 3D worlds

3. EXAMPLES/SAMPLES

- http://www.opendmu.de/
- http://www.realax.com/docs/index.htm
- http://www.realax.com/docs/html/medical/utueb.htm
- http://www.realax.com/docs/html/viss/viss.htm

4. WEB RESOURCES

- http://www.realax.com/docs/html/medical/utueb.html
- http://www.acadis.com/
- http://www.realax.com/docs/html/about/about.htm

SART

1. PLATFORMS, PRICE, AND SUPPLIER/CREATOR

- Windows and Unix operation systems
- Free, distributed under General Public Licence
- Miroslav Silovic: http://petra.zesoi.fer.hr/~silovic/sart/

2. APPLICATIONS

- SART is a Guile library for ray tracing and high-complexity 3D rendering and modeling. Guile is an interpreter to the Scheme programming language that provides interfaces for multiple tools to be efficiently used within an environment. You can use SART to create and render extremely complex images (such as 3D fractals, CSGs, and splines), powerful procedural textures, and even mix rendering techniques using Z buffering, ray tracing, and radiosity where appropriate, in a single image

3. EXAMPLES/SAMPLES

- Code: http://cvs.codefactory.se/cgi-bin/cvsweb.cgi/sart/examples/ .cvsignore?cvsroot=GNOME

4. WEB RESOURCES

- SART: http://petra.zesoi.fer.hr/~silovic/sart/
- Guile interpreter to OpenGL: http://atrey.karlin.mff.cuni.cz/~0rfelyus/guileGL/
- Guile main website: http://www.gnu.org/software/guile/guile.html

Satellite Tool Kit (STK)

1. PLATFORMS, PRICES, AND SUPPLIER/CREATOR

- Windows 2000, Windows NT, Windows 98, UNIX

- Pricing based on educational, government, or commercial use, number of seats, etc.
  Additional details available at: http://www.stk.com/products/pricing.cfm

- Analytical Graphics, Inc. (AGI): http://www.stk.com

2. APPLICATIONS

- STK/VO is a 3D visualization environment that displays all scenario information from the Satellite Tool Kit (STK) software suite. STK/VO is a powerful tool that provides an intuitive view of complex mission and orbit geometries by displaying realistic 3D views of space, airborne and terrestrial assets, sensor projections, orbit trajectories and assorted visual cues and analysis aids

3. EXAMPLES/SAMPLES

- Sample output animations: http://http://www.stk.com/resources/modam.cfm

4. KEY FUNCTIONS

- Situational awareness of diverse assets:

  - Land, sea, air, and space-based systems are displayed with detailed, scalable, and articulating 3D models with all of the time-varying aspects of their position and attitude. Satellite viewing opportunities with respect to time-based position of theater and strategic assets provide a situational awareness capability that can be used in any aerospace system for operational decision-making, mission planning, modeling and simulation, and training

- "Heads-up" dynamic data display:

  - Provides dynamic data display of STK parameters within the 3D globe window. Data such as vehicle position and attitude, vector orientation, lighting conditions, link performance values, and in-view status can all be displayed at a user-defined position in the globe window, attached to the vehicle or object, or within a user-defined border of the 3D globe window. These data can be used to provide instantaneous status of system operations without having to interrupt real-time operations or simulated activities

- Attitude visualization:

  - Aerospace system designers and operators have a need to understand their system's dynamic orientation with regard to multiple coordinate frames. Reams of raw numerical data are no longer required. STK/VO provides a means to dynamically display the attitude motion of objects, including visual cues in the form of multiple frames-of-reference and directional vectors that provide an instantaneous view — as well as a time-historical view via vector traces — of the attitude dynamics

- Multiple orbit frame visualization:

- STK/VO allows users to visualize orbit paths in a variety of frames to help users visualize complex orbit dynamics or maneuvers. Orbits can be visualized simultaneously in inertial, fixed, body-body relative, or relative coordinate frames

- Celestial scene modeling:

  - STK/VO provides visual cues for celestial objects, including lighting, position and orientation of the Sun, planets and stars, celestial grid, and ecliptic and equatorial planes

- Distributed, real-time operations visualization and support:

  - As an analytical and real-time tool, STK/VO can be used to quickly study problems related to telemetry, viewing opportunities, and scheduling during planning and operations

- Scalable 3D models:

  - With hundreds of detailed, scalable 3D models included, STK/VO provides realistic visualization of user's assets

- Animation and video production:

  - STK/VO gives user the capability to create and save time-dependent viewer positions and directions and capture sequential STK/VO frames for assembly into animations and/or capture for video production

5. WEB RESOURCES

- Product description: http://www.stk.com/products/explore/products/main.htm

SCED (Constraint Based Scene Design)

1. PLATFORMS, PRICES, AND SUPPLIER/CREATOR

- Runs on almost any UNIX system with X windows release 5 or later. Also runs on a PPro running Linux

- Full distributive shareware

- Stephen Chenney, CS Department at University of Wisconsin at Madison: http://www.cs.wisc.edu/~schenney/sced/sced.html

2. APPLICATIONS

- A modeling program that makes use of geometric constraints to edit objects in a virtual world
- Used for creating 3D scenes, and then exporting them
- Uses constraints to allow for the accurate placement of objects, and provides a maintenance system for keeping these constraints satisfied as the scene is modified

3. EXAMPLES/SAMPLES

- Images: http://www.cs.wisc.edu/~schenney/sced/sced.html
- Screenshot: http://linux.davecentral.com/1179_graphed.html

4. FUNCTIONS

- Create instances of objects. Each instance of a base object class inherits some initial parameters, but then may be edited individually
- Create new base objects. New basic objects can be created through Constructive Solid Geometry (CSG) operations on simpler objects, or simply by aggregating simpler objects together. Arbitrary wire frame type-objects may also be imported as new base objects
- Transform objects to set their size, orientation, and location
- Set attributes for objects, that control how the object appears when rendered. Attributes may be generic, or a string specific to the target-rendering program
- Change or rename objects such that they are exported as something else
- Interactively manipulate the view of the scene in all its parameters
- Save and restore views of the scene
- Specify the location of a camera
- Create layers of objects, to control which objects are displayed at any time
- Create light sources of various types
- Preview a scene using your favorite renderer
- Export to the renderer of your choice
- Load files in a simple description language, suitable for modeling molecules and the like

5. WEB RESOURCES

- Documentation/Download can be found at:
  http://www.cs.wisc.edu/~schenney/sced/src/sced-1.03.tar.gz
- Tutorial: http://digilander.iol.it/2g/sced-e.htm
- Readme file: http://www.itec.uni-klu.ac.at/doc/packages/sced/
- Citations: http://citeseer.nj.nec.com/context/164767/0

SciAn (Scientific Visualization and Animation)

1. PLATFORMS, PRICES, AND SUPPLIER/CREATOR

- Silicon Graphics workstations and IBM RS/6000 workstations with the GL option
- N/A
- Supercomputer Computations Research Institute at Florida State University:
  www.csit.fsu.edu

2. APPLICATIONS

- SciAn is a scientific data visualization tool

3. EXAMPLES/SAMPLES

- Examples of contour maps and surfaces:
  http://www.cs.utah.edu/~crj/cs523/examples/contours.html
- Examples of vector field visualization using arrow fields:
  http://www.cs.utah.edu/~crj/cs523/examples/arrows

4. FUNCTIONS

- Data Types:
  - Scalar and vector fields; structured and non-structured grids; datasets can have one, two, three, or more dimensions; datasets can vary through time; time steps may be irregularly spaced; automatic interpolation between time steps if desired
- File Formats:
  - NCSA HDF scientific dataset (SDS) for fields with extensions for time-dependent data, vector data, and missing data points; neutral file format (NFF) for geometry; NetCDF with extensions for vector data; PLOT-3D formatted,

unformatted, and binary files (requires FORTRAN); simple text format for fields over structured grids; protein data bank format; additional file formats can be installed

- Visualization Techniques:
  - Isosurfaces for 3D scalar data; color meshes for 2D scalar data; line contours for 2D scalar data; Balls and sticks for 1D unstructured data such as molecules; Point clouds; numeric display; geometry display; arrows display for vector fields; bounds, axes and axis labels can be displayed; mirrored and shadowed walls

- Annotations:
  - Editable text annotations and time stamps in a variety of fonts and sizes; lines and arrows; rectangular borders, outline, solid, and beveled

- Viewing Techniques:
  - Perspective view; orthographic view; side-by-side stereo view; anaglyphic (red/cyan) stereo; stereographics crystal eyes stereo; even/odd line stereo; fully interactive rotation, translation and zoom; adjustable angle of view and near and far clipping planes; flight simulator

- Color:
  - Full color (RGB) and color map mode; complete color palette editor including periodic RGB color component functions; special colors for overflow, underflow and missing data; smooth and flat color shading

- Shading:
  - Up to eight light sources in full color (RGB) mode; smooth and flat lighting; screen door translucency; alpha blending transparency (when supported by the workstation)

- Rendering:
  - Uses workstation hardware to render images; Images can be filtered after rendering to improve video quality

- Scripting:
  - Text file script mechanism for nearly all user interface operations; Automatic logging to scripts; scripts provide automated video recording

- Video Recording:
  - Records video sequences automatically using scripts; supports Sony CVR series and Panasonic TQ-2026F videodisc recorders; supports IRIS RGB and PostScript image file formats; supports JPEG file format when linked with the appropriate public domain libraries

5. WEB RESOURCES

- SciAn User's Manual: http://www.scri.fsu.edu/~lyons/scian/manual/User-Contents.html

- SciAn Reference Manual: http://www.scri.fsu.edu/~lyons/scian/manual/Ref-Contents.html

Sculpt3D

1. PLATFORMS, PRICES, AND SUPPLIER/CREATOR

IBM Comapatible	Apple Mac	Unix
Windows NT, 98, 2000 Memory: 16 MB and above 10 MB free hard disk space 256 color display	PowerMac, Quadra, Centric or Performa, system 7.1 Memory: 8 MB and above 40–160 free hard disk space 256 color display	Unix system 2.0 above Memory: 32 MB and above 40 MB free hard disk space 256 color display

- all systems require 10 MB and more free hard drive space, CD Rom for installation and 256 color display
- $$$$
- GlassPalace: http://www.glasspalace.fi/sculpt3d

2. APPLICATION

- Sculpt 3D is a 3D modeling, rendering, and animation environment for Macintosh

3. EXAMPLE / SAMPLES

- http://www.mda1.demon.co.uk/html/links.htm
- http://www.glasspalace.fi/sculpt3d/

4. WEB RESOURCES

- http://ctiweb.cf.ac.uk/cticbe/resguide/sculpt3d.html
- http://www.glasspalace.fi/sculpt3d/
- http://ftp.uni-bremen.de/aminet/dirs/gfx_3d.html
- http://www.mda1.demon.co.uk/html/links.htm
- http://cmp.felk.cvut.cz/~pajdla/Doc/3D.formats.html

Shave and a Haircut

1. PLATFORM, PRICE, AND SUPPLIER/CREATOR

- PC
- $285
- Joe Alter, Inc: http://www.joealter.com

2. APPLICATIONS

- Shave and a Haircut is a modeling tool used for hair movement and hair styling. It has been used by major studios like Disney, DreamWorks, Sony, and Imageworks

3. EXAMPLES/SAMPLES

- http://www.joealter.com/shave/twister.htm
- http://www.joealter.com/shave/twister.htm
- http://www.joealter.com/shave/grooming.htm
- http://www.joealter.com/shave/dynamics.htm

4. FUNCTIONS

- Modeling:
  - Objects: Lines
  - Advanced Objects: Splines
  - Transformations: Grab and drag scaling, collisions
  - Editing and Manipulations: Manipulates vertices on a thousands of splines, friction; allows user to cut, droop, and volumize hair
- Rendering:
  - Lights: self-shadowing, cast-shadowing, and shadow-receiving of hair, transparency and propagated light
  - Depth cueing and radiosity of hair
  - Materials: texture mapping, color texturing
  - Before and After Rendering: motion blur, bi-directional kinematics

5. WEB RESOURCES

- http://www.videosystems.com/html/2000/july/features/shave/shavehaircut.htm
- http://www.videosystems.com/html/2000/july/features/shave/shavehaircut2.htm
- http://www.joealter.com

Shout3D

1. PLATFORMS, PRICES, AND SUPPLIER/CREATOR

- All Java-enabled platforms, including Windows, Macintosh, and Linux
- The Professional Edition of Shout3D is available for $195.00/domain/year; the Educational Edition of Shout3D is available for $95.00/domain/year; and the Trial Edition is available free of charge. All Editions can be downloaded at: http://www.shout3d.com
- Shout3D is developed by Eyematic Interfaces Inc., which is based in Los Angeles: http://wwweyematic.com/

2. APPLICATIONS

- Shout3D 2.5 is a powerful combination of Java-based playback and authoring technologies that enable any standard Web client with a Java Virtual Machine (JVM) to display interactive 3D graphics without the need for special plug-ins or downloads. Web clients with JVMs are presently found in a wide variety of information appliances, including wireless devices, handheld computers, settop boxes, PCs, and computer workstations. Developed by Eyematic, the highly optimized 3D rendering engine found at the core of Shout3D 2.5 is written in pure Java (1.1) and is fully extensible via a robust set of APIs

3. EXAMPLES/SAMPLES

- Shout3D resources and home page: http://www.shout3d.com/
- More shout3d resources and examples:
  - http://www.amazon.com/exec/obidos/tg/stores/detail/-/toys/B00000IWFB/media/0000000303/107-0182620-7756550
  - http://www.amazon.com/exec/obidos/tg/stores/detail/-/toys/B00004W1B6/media/0000000439/107-0182620-7756550
  - http://www.amazon.com/exec/obidos/tg/stores/detail/-/toys/B00000DMER/media/0000000306/107-0182620-7756550
  - http://www.shoutinteractive.com/Fashion/index.html
  - http://www.shoutinteractive.com/HolidayShop/index.html
  - http://www.2dto3dcad.com/shout3d.cfm
  - http://www.viennadc.at/en/viennadc/3dmodell.html
  - http://www.accad.ohio-state.edu/VT/FINAL/Version2/demos/VirtualTheatre2.html
  - http://www.meet3d.com
  - http://frameworkmedia.net/item.asp
  - http://hmt.vio.ne.jp/roomnavi/high/index.html
  - http://mondodonna.mondadori.com/bellezza/altro/al_tuo_servizio/look3d/tool/look3d.html

- http://www.geometrek.com/members/michael/shoutAtomic.html
- http://www.sciencemuseum.org.uk/wellcome-wing/home3dj_ie4.asp
- http://www.shout3d.com/shout3d_2.0_doc_dir/docs/demo_guide/contents.html

4. FUNCTIONS:

- Modeling:
    - Shout3D scene content (meaning 3D scenes, models and keyframed animation, as opposed to user interactivity features) can be produced in any 3D modeling and animation program that exports to the VRML (.wrl) file format. Almost all significant 3D packages provide VRML export. Shout3D's .s3d file format is an extension of VRML
- Rendering/Presentation:
    - Shout3D files will typically be read, parsed, and rendered by a mechanism known as a Core Shout3D viewer. Core Shout3D viewers are not required to provide any navigation algorithm. The Shout3D API provides mechanisms for getting user input, and for getting and setting the current viewpoint. To provide navigation capabilities, a viewer may use this API to provide the user with the ability to navigate
- Characteristics/ Interface/Toolkit:
    - Shout3D provides some ready-to-run interactivity applets. Shout3D includes a couple of important custom applets that provide user interactivity. The ExamineApplet allows users to view an object or scene from any direction. The WalkApplet allows viewers to navigate through a space, complete with collision detection, terrain following, and gravity. You can use these applets just as they are, without any programming, to provide users with these basic kinds of interactivity
- Data Transfer/Compatibility
    - Shout3D content can be produced in standard 3D modeling and animation programs, but especially in 3D Studio MAX. Shout3D scene content (meaning 3D scenes, models and keyframed animation, as opposed to user interactivity features) can be produced in any 3D modeling and animation program that exports to the VRML (.wrl) file format. Almost all significant 3D packages provide VRML export. Shout3D's .s3d file format is an extension of VRML. It supports almost all of the current VRML features (nodes), but adds some very significant new nodes to provide higher graphical and animation quality. Most of these additional nodes – not found in standard VRML – are available only when 3D scenes are exported directly to Shout3D's .s3d format with a special export utility. At present, this export utility is only available for use with 3D Studio MAX. Thus only content created with MAX (or files that have been hand-edited) can exploit the full range of Shout3D powers
- Programming and customization:
    - Shout3D interactivity can be programmed in Java or JavaScript. The primary way to create custom interactivity is by writing and compiling custom Java applets. As these are simply extensions of the basic Shout3D applet, you only

need to code the features you're adding. You can also use JavaScript, written in the HTML page to call the methods of the Shout3D Java classes. This is a quick and easy way of testing interactivity ideas, although not generally satisfactory for work intended for publication

5. INTERNET RESOURCES:

- Some other resources and information on this product can be accessed at:
  - http://www.3dmagazine.net/magazine/2000/0208/

Simply 3D

1. PLATFORMS, PRICES, AND SUPPLIER/CREATOR

- Windows 95/98/2000/NT
- $49.95
- Micrografx: http://www.micrografx.com/

2. APPLICATIONS

- Simply 3D is a powerful application for creating 3D graphics and animations for documents, presentations, and the Web. It is a simple alternative to create 3D animations and stills for less experienced users

3. EXAMPLES/SAMPLES

- http://www.3dlinks.com/gallerydisplay.cfm?sid=Simply%203D%203
- http://members.tripod.co.uk/dreamwolf/simply2.html
- http://dragonlord.htmlplanet.com/galary/
- http://www.graphiccastle.com/simply.html

4. FUNCTIONS

- Wizards:
  - Instant 3D text wizard; 2D–to–3D wizard; Output wizard; Project wizard (Creates an entire project from start to output in one continuous wizard; a one-step wizard that contains all the other wizards mentioned above.)
- Features:
  - User-friendly morphing capabilities
  - Intuitive modeling functions

- 80 deformations
- Selective ray tracing capabilities for rendered images
- Drag-and-drop animation
- Support for animated GIFs, Direct3D acceleration, and VRML (Virtual Reality Modeling Language) 2.0
- Included/Pre-Generated Objects/Settings:

    - 1,000 3D drag-and-drop objects
    - 800 professional-quality textures
    - 50 lighting setups
    - 100 animations

- Formats:

    - Animated/Still formats: BMP, AVI, FLC, GIF, IVR, JPG, S3D, TGA, TIF, and WRL

5. WEB RESOURCES

- Product Information: http://www.micrografx.com/mgxproducts/simply3d.asp

- Book by Visual Software: http://www.softwareandstuff.com/ s_graph_dsk_simply3d.html

- Reviews on Software: http://www.educate.co.uk/simply3d.htm

SIMUL8

1. PLATFORMS, PRICES, AND SUPPLIER/CREATOR

- PC Windows 95, NT

- $$$$

- SIMUL8 Corporation: http://www.SIMUL8.com

2. APPLICATIONS

- Simul8 is a simulation tool that provides planning, modeling, validation, animation, and other software tools. Its Virtual Reality (VR) mode delivers an enhanced simulation view. It enables organizations to represent the simulation in a realistic 3D environment

3. EXAMPLES/SAMPLES

- http://www.simul8.com/manufacturing/jobshop3.htm

4. WEB RESOURCES

- http://www.vtil.com/home.html
- http://www.novasim.com/index.html
- http://www.simul8.com
- http://www.tcdc.com/dsofts/software/simulat.htm
- http://www.gdl.co.uk/

SketchUp

1. PLATFORMS, PRICES, AND SUPPLIER/CREATOR

- Windows-based PCs
- $495 CD; or $475 downloaded
- @Last Software, Inc.: http://www.sketchup.com/

2. APPLICATIONS

- SketchUp is a conceptual design tool for architects, furniture designers, wood workers, game developers etc. to model in 3D on a PC. The core of SketchUp's simplicity is an interface in which the user simply draws the edges of the desired model in 3D and the software automatically "fills" the shapes to create 3D geometry

3. EXAMPLES/SAMPLES

- Gallery index for SketchUp: http://www.sketchup.com/gallery.html
- Gallery on related tools: http://www.sketchup.com/multimedia.html

4. FUNCTIONS

- Modeling:
  - Approach: 3D modeling that captures more of the feel of working with pen and paper. This makes the power and fun of computer modeling accessible to a much wider variety of users. All the user must do is draw the edges of the desired model in 3D space and the software will automatically "fill" the shapes to create 3D geometry

- Avoid overwhelming the user with the large number of commands and complex concepts that are common in other packages on the market. (3D tracking, smart snaps, intelligent user-defined components, real-time 3D intersections, color-coded clues for movement in 3D space.)
- Allow focusing more on design and less on technology. Push/Pull, as the name implies, enables the user to simply click on a shape and push or pull it to create 3D geometry
- Characteristics of the Object Based or "smart" modeling systems without the complexity or steep learning curves

- Rendering:

  - Ability to apply colors and materials to models: models can be displayed with "jitter lines" to give the design a more hand-drawn look
  - Works in real-time rendered mode
  - Support for real-time shadows

- File Formats:

  - Supports the import and export of DWG and DXF files: import a DWG site plan as a starting point for design; export to DWG to create construction documents from 3D models created in SketchUp
  - Export to 3DS file format for rendering in most professional rendering applications
  - Export to BMP, PNG, TIF, JPG, and Piranesi's Epix file formats
  - Small, easily exchangeable files: easy to share designs via email
  - Freely available File Viewer for the native SKP file format

5. WEB RESOURCES

- A list of press reviews on the net: http://www.sketchup.com/press_reviews.html
- An online article: http://www.3dcgi.com/cooltech/modeling/sketching.htm

Soft F/X

1. PLATFORMS, PRICES, AND SUPPLIER/CREATOR

- PC (Windows 95 and NT)

- N/A; to order: order@andanteinc.com

- Andante, Inc. (in Japanese only): http://www.andanteinc.com/

2. APPLICATIONS

- Entry level 3D graphics tool. Full-featured modeling, texture mapping, rendering, and animation

3. EXAMPLES/SAMPLES

- http://www.zdnet.com/pcmag/features/3d98/rev4b.html
- http://www.glasspalace.fi/softfx/index.html
- http://members.iinet.net.au/~taipan1/gg01.jpg

4. WEB RESOURCES

- http://www.gomark.com/html/Design/Softfx.html
- http://www.zdnet.com/pcmag/features/3d98/rev4.html
- http://digitalvideo.com.au/dvtweb/multimedia/softFX.htm
- http://www.zdnet.com/pcmag/feature/3d98/rev4.html
- http://www.yes.ab.psiweb.com/sfx/

Softimage 3D

1. PLATFORMS, PRICES, AND SUPPLIER/CREATOR

- Windows NT, IRIX
- $$$$$
- Softimage Inc.: http://www.softimage.com; Sosftimage is a subsidiary of Avid Technologies Inc.: http://www.avid.com

2. APPLICATIONS

- Softimage 3D is a 3D modeling, animation, and rendering tool that excels at character animation. It has been used to create special effects for "Jurassic Park", "The Matrix" and "Saving Private Ryan", and to create animations for video games for the Windows PC, Nintendo N64, and Sony Playstation
- Competing tools: 3D Studio MAX, Lightwave 3D, and Maya

3. EXAMPLES/SAMPLES

- http://www.softimage.com/default.asp?URL=/Projects/Gallery/default.htm
- http://www.liebrand.nl/li/gallery/gallery.html
- http://iquebec.ifrance.com/passager/3d/softimage/soft.html
- http://www.softimage.com/Community/Xsi/Galleries/xsi_gal.htm

- http://www.algonet.se/~magman/pics-sft.htm
- 3D Links Gallery on related tools: http://www.3dlinks.com/gallerylinks.cfm
- A full list of functions in PDF format can be downloaded from:
  http://www.softimage.com/Products/3D/datasheet/SI.3.9.pdf

4. WEB RESOURCES

- The Softimage newsgroup: comp.graphics.apps.softimage
- The mail archive: http://vizlab.beckman.uiuc.edu/softimage/mail-archive/
- Product page: http://www.softimage.com/Products/XSI/default.htm
- http://www.softimage.com/default.asp?url=/Products/3D/default.htm
- A list of resources: http://www.creativepro.com/software/home/726.html
- Books: http://www.omega23.com/books/s5/s11i06softimage3D.html
- A PC Magazine article: http://www.zdnet.com/pcmag/features/software/1519/3d-r5.htm

Softy3D

1. PLATFORMS, PRICE, AND SUPPLIER/CREATOR

- PC, Operating System Windows 95, 98, and Windows NT 4.0
- Shareware, $40.00
- 3dam-development: http://www.3dam-development.com/

2. APPLICATIONS

- Softy 3D is a 3D modeling program designed especially for organic modeling. Altough Softy 3D is only a modeling program, the possibility of exporting the generated meshes to a wide variety of 3D file formats, used by the most popular 3D programs, makes it a more opened and economical option than other similar programs, because you don't have to possess the program for which the plug-in was designed

3. EXAMPLES/SAMPLES

- http://www.softy3d.com/en/gallery.htm
- 3D Links Gallery on related tools: http://www.3dlinks.com/gallerylinks.cfm

4. FUNCTIONS

- Modeling:
  - Objects: with Softy 3D one can create complex models in a simple way. To create models there are two basic types of available objects: Softsphere and Softspline objects
  - Transformation: translation, rotation of object, rotation of view, modify radio, cloning, align (move control points), Delimit cube, and mirror
  - Editing and manipulations (polygon and sphere objects)
  - Controllers: key-based, procedural, compound system
  - Basic organic modeling
- Rendering:
  - View: rotate view, restrict to X, Y or Z axis, center view, center all views, minimize and maximize views
  - Materials: shading (flat, smooth and wire shading), smooth mesh (readjusts the size and position of the faces in the model, making it more smoothed and improving its quality), and Soft Blend (blends objects together)
  - Object Fusion: four different fusion levels (soft, less soft, less hard and hard)
- File Formats:
  - Exporting file formats: 3D Studio, LightWave, trueSpace, POV-Ray, Cinema 4D, DirectX, Wavefront object, Quickdraw 3DMF, Autocad DXF, RAW Triangles and ASCII

5. WEB RESOURCES

- Resources: http://5star.freeserve.com/Graphics/CAD-Design-Modeling/softy3d.html

SolidBuilder

1. PLATFORM, PRICES, AND SUPPLIER/CREATOR

- PC
- $2,795.00 ($349.00 Educational Version); $100 for Reference manual and Tutorial
- Eagle Point Software: http://www.eaglepoint.com/

2. APPLICATIONS

- SolidBuilder allows wireframe and solid representation of buildings for prospective buyers and housing developers

- SolidBuilder is based on the SilverScreen solid modeling graphics engine. Solid modeling makes things possible that can't be done with 3D wire frame programs

3. EXAMPLES/SAMPLES

- http://www.solidbuilder.com/enlarge.asp?i=Bighous&F=solidbuilder
- http://www.solidbuilder.com/enlarge.asp?i=logleft&f=solidbuilder

4. FEATURES

- SolidBuilder's 3D Modeler:
  - Object oriented database: the building model is organized in a hierarchy of objects, not in restrictive 2D layers. Each object has a unique name such as roof3, or floor1, (etc.)
  - User controls the sequence: convenience determines the modeling sequence. For instance, one can begin modeling down from the floor or up from the footer
  - Modeling language: the language of SolidBuilder's menus and dialog boxes comes from the building industry, not from CAD industry jargon
  - Speed and ease of use: solidBuilder has been continually reshaped by modeling real buildings. Each step has been honed to minimize the time required
  - Solid sculpting commands: the modeling of complex shapes is simplified by solid sculpting commands such as Project, Trim, Split and Join
  - Fine editing: a model of a large and complex house is a combination of many simple objects. One can delete and replace objects without affecting the surrounding objects. SolidBuilder's editing tool set applies to all objects
  - Whole house editing: editing tools for the complete building include Mirror, Stretch, and Collapse commands
  - Roof generator: SolidBuilder's automatic roof generator is unsurpassed in its versatility, speed, and ease of use
  - Complex roof generation: to aid in modeling a complex roof, the software asks for roof information that is known such as "rafter depth", eave overhang, etc. It does all the calculations
  - Walls raised to roof or dropped to footer: complex walls may be created simply by raising them to a roof or dropping them down to a footer, regardless of the complexity of roof or foundation. No calculations are needed
  - Wall opening shapes: window and door openings may be arched, raked or arc topped. Pocket doors are handled in a special manner
  - Wall openings list: the list of available openings is fully customizable and can be organized by manufacturer
  - Curved walls: curved walls are framed as several short segments of wall successively stepping around a circle
  - Stairs: stairs can be straight or curved. The number of risers is automatically calculated
  - 3D graphic verification: the modeler allows the user to verify his/her specifications. Any of the user assigned details of the model, from wall type to number of trimmers in an opening, can be exhibited by highlighting the corresponding part of the model

- Automatic model checking: the modeler automatically checks for error conditions which can happen by accident and cause difficulties, such as making a right angle wall corner not quite square
- Viewing: the model may be viewed from any direction or from inside. It may be viewed from different directions simultaneously by dividing the screen into multiple view windows
- Selective visibility: any combination of objects may be made visible or invisible. For example, the view may show only roofs or only walls. Visibility choices may be assigned a name and saved for later use
- Patterns: Patterns can be applied to the surfaces of the building. New patterns can be easily created
- Rendering: rendering options include plain wire frame, hidden-line, uniformly painted, or light source shaded with shadows. Photorealistic rendering is available with 3D Studio or other rendering software
- 3D symbols: pre-modeled 3D furnishings, fittings, windows, doors and trim may be inserted into the model from symbol libraries. SolidBuilder comes with symbol libraries including appliances, kitchen cabinets, and basic 3D windows and doors. Other symbols are available and the user can modify or create symbols in SilverScreen
- Model export and import: 3D and 2D images can be exported or imported in DXF format
- Additional functions: the user is always a keystroke away from SilverScreen, a powerful general-purpose 3D solid modeling program. Additional modeling and CAD features are available in SilverScreen

- SolidBuilder's 3D Framer:

  - 3D framing generation: a 3D model of all building framing is created automatically. The framer has been enhanced to accommodate any building method which is standard in North America
  - Each stick is a solid: each piece of wood is modeled as a true solid. This allows the use of the same modeling commands as used on other parts of the building
  - Wall Framer: walls may be flat, raked, flat and raked, stepped, and have sloping bottoms. Wall tops or bottoms may also be beveled. Options provide for changing the number and thickness of plates, openings, and other framing pieces. Plate breaks are automatically staggered. Stud, joist, and rafter spacing as well as layout points are under user control
  - Wall openings: most types of wall openings are handled automatically. The user can select the number of trimmers (jacks), floating trimmers (cut to the sill), headers, kings, and sills. Each end of an opening can be framed differently. A single header can be used for multiple openings
  - Other wall components: posts-in-walls, ledgers, and several different corner conditions are provided
  - Floor and ceiling framer: the program frames floors and ceilings of any shape with joist breaks lapped or butted. It provides optional types of channel and opening framing. Joists are regularly spaced with user specified layout points and joist direction. Options include multiple layout points, doubling alternate joists, and midspan blocking. Ceilings may be sloped
  - Roof framer: SolidBuilder frames any stick built roof. It automatically cuts birdsmouths and other rafter profile cuts. Eave and gable overhangs are framed in several styles

- Framing editor: the automatically generated framing may be edited by the user. Using commands such as Insert, Split, Project and Move, the framing may be altered in any way
- Framing production drawings: easy to read drawings of each and every framed component are generated automatically, complete with dimensions and member labels. Wall drawings also include a bottom plate view
- Rafter drawings: clear and simple drawings of rafter profiles are automatically generated
- Cutting list: the cutting list can be printed as part of the framing drawing or printed separately
- Layout table: stud and joist layouts on plates, rims, headers and other rim members are automatically generated as part of the framing drawing or printed separately
- Lumber take-off: once framed, the total lumber requirement is calculated by the software. The lumber optimizer determines the lumber required for minimum waste
- Species and grade options: the species and grade to use for each type of framing (stud, block, sill, etc.) is set by the user. It allows for more than one choice for a single board type, such as both "stud" or "#2" for studs depending upon size
- Sheathing layout and cutting: sheathing layouts may be applied to floors and roofs. SolidBuilder determines the number of full sheets needed and creates pictures of how to cut them
- Steel framing: framing take-off of steel is possible with a different setup of standards and an additional database of materials
- Cutting detail: an optional report describes how to cut the stock lumber to assure that the material is used efficiently

- SolidBuilder's Estimator: Item database:

  - Three-level database: the unlimited-capacity database is organized into three levels — Division, Subdivision, and Item. The program comes complete with over one thousand items
  - Spreadsheet view: the database is displayed in a spreadsheet format. The user can move the sheet right or left to see all fields rather than reviewing items one-by-one in a separate items screen
  - Multi-item update: any field change may be applied to a single item, multiple items or all items, by using the "Mark" feature
  - Conversion formula: each item has a formula for conversion of take-off quantity to order quantity, such as square feet to rolls
  - Cost updating conveniences: Costs may be updated by percentages, either individually or by groups
  - Mark-ups: mark-ups are set by the user, with one or two cumulative percentages
  - Import and export: the Item, Subdivision, and Division records may all be imported and exported. This allows for easily importing data from other databases into SolidBuilder. SolidBuilder data can be exported to spreadsheets and word processors. Such data can be re-imported into SolidBuilder

- SolidBuilder's Estimator: Assemblies:

- Assemblies: automatic take-offs are done by using assemblies attached to the model. Each assembly consists of a collection of database items. A simple point and click adds an item from the database to the assembly
- Search: any item in the database can be found by using the Search command
- Connection to model: assemblies are attached to the model during modeling. They can easily be altered after they are attached
- Connection to plan symbols: assembles can be attached to working drawing plan symbols and may be altered afterward
- Graphic verification: the assembly assignment can be graphically verified by highlighting the model objects to which a particular assembly is attached
- Automatic take-off: at any time in the modeling process, a take-off can be automatically performed on the whole model. The result is an estimate and a grand total
- Geometry-determined take-off: each line of the database has a geometry-determined take-off method such as "gross area" or "length"
- Geometry cross reference: an optional cross reference lists all geometry that contributes to a line total

- SolidBuilder's Estimator: Estimate:

  - 3D take-off tools: the 3D model provides instant calculations of dimension, area and volume
  - Continuous on-screen totaling: the automatically-generated "estimate" is a changeable spreadsheet, not a fixed report
  - Adding or changing items: the estimate line items may be modified, other items added from the database or items can be typed into the spreadsheet
  - Subtotals: subtotal lines are automatically inserted after every division. They show continuously-updated subtotals. The user may delete these or insert other sub-totals
  - Sorting: the estimate can be sorted by a single field or by multiple fields
  - Reports: any combination of database columns can be selected to be included in a report. These combinations can be saved for subsequent use
  - Editable cutting schedule: the complete list of cut pieces of lumber is displayed in a table which the user can modify on the screen like a spreadsheet. Each cut piece is identified by its grade, its framing member type, the building part containing it, etc. This schedule can be sorted by any of these field types and then printed. After modification, the table of cut pieces can be reoptimized to use less lumber
  - Editable openings schedule: the complete list of openings is displayed in a table which the user can modify on the screen like a spreadsheet. It can be sorted and printed. It can also be inserted as a table on a working drawing
  - Export files: export files allow easy interfacing to scheduling, purchase order and spreadsheet programs

- SolidBuilder's Working Drawings:

  - Plan linework automatically generated: plan linework is generated automatically from the model. One command produces a floor plan with double-line walls, openings, floor edges, dashed roof edges, overhead beams, etc.

– Opening symbols automatically placed: one command causes all opening symbols to be automatically placed on the plan. The symbol type is remembered from the time the opening was modeled
– Section linework automatically generated: the building's sections are generated automatically by slicing the solid model along a line drawn by the user
– Elevation linework automatically generated: SolidBuilder automatically generates elevations by making a flat 2D image of any selected view of the 3D model
– Details automatically generated: portions of 3D views may be captured as detail drawings
– Framing erection drawings: framing and building information may be automatically added to plan drawings. Labeling choices include opening framing, post location, header information and shear wall and rake wall designations
– Inserting tables: any comma separated text file, such as the openings schedule produced by the estimator, may be inserted as a graphic table on a working drawing
– Auto-dimension feature: rows of parallel dimensions may be rapidly inserted with a minimum of keystrokes
– Layers: the 2D information in the working drawings is organized into layers like those of other CAD programs
– Patterns: a library of patterns includes many that are specific to residential buildings
– Linestyles: many linestyles are supported. Others are easily made
– Parametric opening symbols: plan-view opening symbols are automatically generated to the appropriate size of the opening
– Symbol libraries: many other symbols can be added to plan, section or elevation drawings from libraries of symbols furnished with the program
– Automatic regeneration: any drawing can be partially or totally regenerated from the model, without loss of notes, dimensions or symbols. This allows changes to the model to be replicated easily in the 2D drawings
– Multiple drawings arrangement: multiple drawings can be arranged and printed or plotted on a single sheet of paper
– Border drawing: any graphic output can be automatically framed in a pre-drawn border
– Symbol generator: plan and elevation symbols can be created with the same tools used to make drawings

- Miscellaneous:

– Saving snapshots: any image on the screen may be saved for later display in Pix, Tiff, or Bmp format or in slide shows
– Output devices supported: output devices include laser, inkjet and dot matrix printers, as well as pen and electrostatic plotters. Paper sizes include all those supported by the output devices
– Graphics board: all available PC graphic boards are supported, at the users choice of colors and resolution
– Microsoft Windows: solidBuilder can be run under Windows as a DOS task. A Windows version has been available since February of 1998
– Metric Units: metric units may be used in modeling and on plans. Lumber stock sizes are in North American units

5. WEB RESOURCES

- Website: http://www.solidbuilder.com/
- Newsgroups: http://www.eaglepoint.com/BDC/info/newsgroups.htm
- Industry links: http://www.solidbuilder.com/info/links.htm
- Press Releases: http://www.solidbuilder.com/info/pressreleases.asp
- http://www.solidbuilder.com/ejmp/e34logs.htm

SolidThinking

1. PLATFORMS, PRICES, AND SUPPLIER/CREATOR

- Windows and Mac platforms
- Commercial Package: $2495; Academic Package: $295
- GESTEL: http://www.gestel.com/index_f.htm

2. APPLICATIONS

- SolidThinking is a 3D modeling and rendering environment for Windows and Mac that gives users the tools for the creation of high-quality, professional 3D surface models and the power to render them with unsurpassed photo-realism: NURBS and polygonal modeling, subdivision surfaces, construction history, full OpenGL support, the most advanced modeling tools, all industry leading rendering techniques, and data exchange with most popular CAD and animation programs

3. EXAMPLES/SAMPLES

- http://www.gestel.com/Products/solidThinking/Image_Gallery/image_gallery.htm
- http://www.gestel.it//templ/view_image2.cfm?IDimg=73
- http://www.gestel.it//templ/view_image2.cfm?IDimg=9
- http://www.gestel.it//templ/view_image2.cfm?IDimg=104
- http://www.altec.com.hk/newpage1.htm

4. FUNCTIONS

- Modeling:

- Transformations: Translate, rotate, scale, mirror replicate, matrix copy, dynamic matrix copy, polar copy, step copy, dynamic step copy, combine, uncombine
- Deformations: Twist, taper, warp, shear, bend, linear stretch, lattice, pixelmap, surfDrape
- NURBS modeling: Fully NURBS-based modeling with Construction History for the greatest flexibility and precision
- Primitives: Plane, disc, cylinder, sphere, cube, cone, toroid, prism
- Curves: High quality freeform NURBS curves of order 2 to 7, real-time adjustment of curve tangency and curvature at any given point, METAcurves, Arcs, Circles, Ellipses, Lines, Polylines, Regular polygons, Helix and spiral, Break curve at specified point, Split intersecting curves, Join, Curve Tangency Align, PathCast, Curve to Plane, EdgeExtract, Isoparm Extract, Curve Offset, Refine Curve, Rebuild and Simplify Curve, Silhouette, Section
- Surfacing Tools: C2-continuity surfaces, FillPath, Extrude, Lathe, Rule, Skin, Lofting, Pipe, Birail, Trim, Intersect, Surface Offset, Blending, 3sides, Coons, N-side modeling tool, Curve network, Round, Fillet, Surface Tangency Align modeling tool, Surfaces Refine, Simplify Surface, Fit points, PointMesh from Surface modeling tool, Text-Create 3D text
- Polygonal Modeling: Advanced polygonal modeling with support of n-side polygons. Polygonal Primitives: sphere, cylinder, torus, cube, plane and disc. Create single polygon, NURBS to poly, NURBS CVs to poly, Vertices editing, Edges editing, Faces editing, Face normal editing, Refine edges, Simplify, Fill hole, Smooth, Interactive Subdivision Surfaces

- Rendering:

  - Techniques: Wireframe, Fast hidden-line, Flat, Gouraud, and Phong shaded; Preview and Full scan-line, Preview, and Full ray trace rendering(multithreaded), Hybrid rendering for integrating radiosity with ray tracing and other rendering methods
  - Radiosity: Radiosity for simulating real light effects, Progressive simulation allowing for balanced speed and accuracy, Generation of the solution for a view-dependent illumination model for the fastest result possible, Support of industry standards for the definition of the luminous intensity distribution of a luminaire
  - Shaders: Advanced parameterized procedural shaders with high quality noise function; Shade trees for combining multiple shaders; Shader classes: color source, Reflectance Model, Transparency Source, Displacement, Texture Space, Light Source, Background, Foreground, Post-processing; Highly realistic simulation of a wide range of wood surfaces, for ease of visualizing furniture, doors, cabinets, and even parquet floors; Leather shader, giving users the ability to simulate the surface finish of a wide range of leather materials; Multilayer paints, to simulate the multiple highlight and color shift effects of multilayer paints used in the automotive industry; Anisotropic reflectance shader for woven materials, to produce physically based simulations of the anisotropic reflectance properties of woven textiles and materials, such as satin; Environment-mapped and mixed backgrounds; Environment mapping(e.g., reflection mapping); etc.

- Anti-Aliasing: Anti-aliasing shader class for applying different anti-aliasing per material; Feature following anti-aliasing for the highest-quality image output (brute-force oversampling to perform extra anti-aliasing around any areas of intensity change); enhanced analytical anti-aliasing, while using minimal processing time and resources
- Lights: Unlimited number of lights; Ambient, distant, eye, goniometric, point, projector, sky, spotlight sources; Area lights; Volumetric lighting effects; Global lighting effects using real sky conditions; Radiometric or photometric measurement; Light sources using goniometric data in lighting industry-standard formats; Perceptual tone mapping, for physically accurate re-creations of the eye's response to brightness levels
- Shadows: Shadow mapping and shadows ray casting; Soft shadows; Shadows cast by semi-transparent objects; Hybrid shadow creation, combining ray tracing and scan-line rendering for fast, efficient production of ray-traced shadows
- Reverse Engineering: Minolta Vivid 3D scanner front-end. Remotely controls (via SCSI interface) Minolta Vivid 3D scanner. Data can be imported as a point cloud or a polygonal object; Cloud from PointMesh. Creates a specified number of point clouds lying on parallel planes from a given point cloud. This command can be useful to simplify a point cloud derives from 3D scanning; Curve from Point Cloud. Creates a curve from a point cloud. Advanced MicroScribe-3D support; Sketch on planes. Using Microscribe-3D scanner, creates point clouds by "sketching" a real object. The tool samples the points derived from the Microscribe-3D digitizer

- Tools:

  - Extensible libraries of Materials and Models
  - Color palette RGB and HSL
  - Supported object formats: 3DStudio; DXF; IGES; Lightwave; Maya; Rhino3D; RIB; STL; VRML
  - Support of different IGES flavors
  - SolidWorks plug-in for importing/exporting solidThinking scene files from/to SolidWorks
  - I/O plug-in for 3DStudioMAX
  - Plug-in for a seamless integration of BMRT 2.5 (Blue Moon Rendering Tools)
  - ThinkMan, the new plug-in for a seamless integration of PhotoRealistic RenderMan into the solidThining 3D environment
  - Plug-Ins Development Kit: Documentation for developers and users that want to create their own modeling tools and plug-ins. Code samples are included

- System Requirements:

  - Windows: Windows 95/Windows 98/Windows NT 4.0/Windows 2000; Pentium II PC; Graphic accelerator card 100% OpenGL/DirectX compliant and with at least 8 MB Video RAM (16 MB or higher recommended); 64 MB RAM (128 or higher recommended); 200 MB or more of free hard disk space; Two-button Microsoft-compatible mouse; CD-ROM drive for installation; Parallel or USB port; 800x600 screen resolution (1024x768 or higher highly recommended)

– Macintosh: Mac OS 9 or Higher; G3 Power Macintosh or higher; Graphic accelerator card with at least 8 MB Video RAM (16 MB or higher recommended); 64 MB RAM (128 or higher recommended); 200 MB or more of free hard disk space; Two-button Microsoft-compatible mouse; CD-ROM drive for installation; USB port; 800x600 screen resolution (1024x768 or higher highly recommended)

5. WEB RESOURCES

- Getting started with solidThinking: http://www.gestel.com/Products/solidThinking/Support/WebHelp/start.htm

- solidThinking Tutorial: http://www.gestel.com/Products/solidThinking/Support/tutorials.htm

- http://www.gestel.it/Products/solidThinking/Overview/overview.htm

- http://www.solidThinking.com/News/Archives/st_000823.htm

- http://www.solidThinking.com/Products/solidThinking/Preview/st_info.htm

- http://www.gestel.it/Products/solidThinking/Support/faqs.htm

- http://www.gestel.it/Products/Unix_products/unix_products.htm

STAR-CD

1. PLATFORMS, PRICES, AND SUPPLIER/CREATOR

- UNIX (HP, SGI, IBM, Sun), Windows-NT or Linux on high-end Intel Pentium PCs. For larger-scale calculations, STAR-CD can be migrated seamlessly as "STAR-HPC" to any multiple-CPU machine

- N/A

- Computational Dynamics LTD: http://www.cd.co.uk/products/index.htm

2. APPLICATIONS

- STAR-CD is a powerful multipurpose computational fluid dynamics (CFD) code that can assist you through the complete design and development process

- The package includes a highly functional pre-/post-processor, PROSTAR, with its Graphical User Interface and links to other CAE systems. Also available is the automatic meshing tool that can dramatically reduce your problem setup time

3. EXAMPLES/SAMPLES

- Computational Fluid Dynamics Analysis: http://www.vrac.iastate.edu/~jtchu/cfd.html

- A 3D example: http://www.cd.co.uk/products/imgs/expanded/prostar3.html

- Electrical and Electronics application: http://www.cd.co.uk/applications/electronics.htm

- Additional examples/samples: http://www.adapco-online.com

4. FUNCTIONS

- Modeling:
  - Not only does STAR-CD provide a rich source of models for turbulence, combustion, radiation, and multiphase physics; it stands alone in offering all models on all mesh types
  - Turbulent, whirling and rotating flows, periodic flows, with and without heat transfer
  - Multiple heterogeneous and homogeneous chemical reaction
  - Free surface modeling and cavitation
  - Combustion of gaseous, liquid and solid (e.g.coal) fuels
  - Multiple rotational reference frames, for analysis of turbo-machinery problems
- Mesh:
  - It is capable of dealing with unstructured meshes and cell shapes ranging from tetrahedra and prisms to general polyhedra
  - Dynamic mesh movement
- Rendering:
  - Cameras: moveable
  - Flexible geometry handling, including mixed tetrahedral and polyhedral cells
  - Embedded refinement, for enhancing local resolution and adaptive error control
  - Arbitrary mesh block interfacing to facilitate mesh generation and optimization
- Animation:
  - The entire product is about fluid field animation
  - Dynamic mesh movement, for problems such as reciprocating engines
  - Time-dependent sliding mesh with arbitrary interfacing and cyclic boundaries
- File Formats:
  - IGES, VDA, STL, ANSYS, PATRAN, NASTRAN, and PLOT3D

5. WEB RESOURCES

- Official site: http://www.cd.co.uk/products/index.htm

- Star-CD europort: http://www.gmd.de/SCAI/europort-1/A5.HTM

- North American support: http://www.adapco.com/

- A general description: http://www.adapco.com/starcd/starcd.htm

Strata 3D Pro

1. PLATFORMS, PRICES, AND SUPPLIER/CREATOR

- Macintosh, Windows 98, 2000, and NT
- $$$$
- Strata Tools, a Division of 3D.COM: http://www.strata.com

2. APPLICATIONS

- 3D modeling, rendering, and animation for all kinds of media: print, Web-enabled applications, and interactive games. It was used for the development of MYST, the most popular interactive game of 1994

3. EXAMPLES/SAMPLES

- http://sirrus.cyan.com/Online/Myst/GameShots
- http://club.3d.com/showcase/3dmod.index.html
- http://club.3d.com/pinball/movies/index.html
- http://club.3d.com/trinarc/trinarcimages.html
- http://club.3d.com/showcase/anim.index.html
- http://www.khiba.com/3DBP/lamponly3.jpg
- http://members.tripod.com/~Coloredpencilguy/index156.html

4. WEB RESOURCES

- http://www.hwupgrade.com/skvideo/icd_driver_g200.html
- http://www.renderosity.com
- http://www.strata3d.com/support/stratalist/stratalist.html
- http://club.3d.com/messageboards/lists.cgi?id_topic=2
- http://www.strata3d.com/downloads/dnloads.html
- http://www.jolie.nl/strata3D/
- http://shop.strata.com/Product.cfm?Item=14

- http://www.architosh.com/news/2000-09/000918-strataproisout.html
- http://shop.strata.com/product.cfm?item=7

(Alias WaveFront) Studio Tools

1. PLATFORMS, PRICES, AND SUPPLIER/CREATOR

- Windows 2000/NT, HP-UX, Solaris
- $$$$$$
- Alias WaveFront: http://www.aliaswavefront.com/en/Home/homepage.html

2. APPLICATIONS

- StudioTools is the leading 3D software for industrial design, automotive styling, and technical surfacing. The StudioTools software family, which includes DesignStudio, Studio, AutoStudio, SurfaceStudio, EvalViewer, and Spider, provides designers with a comprehensive suite of tools that enables complete integration throughout the entire design process

3. EXAMPLES/SAMPLES

- Studio Tools Software:
  http://www.aliaswavefront.com/en/WhatWeDo/studio/see/see.shtml

4. WEB RESOURCES

- Yahoo Article about Studio: http://biz.yahoo.com/bw/010131/alias_wave.html
- ACADALYST Labs Reviews AliasWavefront Studio v.9.5:
  http://www.cadonline.com/reviews/software/cad/0700alias/alias.htm
- AW Studio Press Release: http://www.aliaswavefront.com/en/WhoWeAre/
  press_releases/studio/1999_01_11_design_studio_nt/

Summit 3D

1. PLATFORMS, PRICES, AND SUPPLIER/CREATOR

- PC, Windows 95 with Direct X 3.0 or greater or Windows 98 or NT 4.0 with service pack 3 or above
  - Modeling and content creation mode requires DirectX5 drivers
  - Minimum system is a Pentium 133 MHz with a fast hardware accelerated video card and 32 MB RAM. Cards with the Permedia chipset are highly recommended
- $$$$
- Summit Graphic Inc.: http://www.summit3d.com/ (the Summit software is sold by Berryvale Software: http://www.berryvalesoftware.com/summit.htm)

2. APPLICATIONS

- Summit 3D allows you to create complex virtual worlds without programming. Animation includes 3D morphs, animated materials and lights. 3D Sound is a snap in Summit.

3. EXAMPLES/SAMPLES

- Demo: http://www.summit3d.com/3dsite.htm

4. WEB RESOURCES

- Summit Benchmarks: http://www.berryvalesoftware.com/sumbench.htm
- Summit Technical Support: http://www.berryvalesoftware.com/sumdiary.htm

Superficie

1. PLATFORMS, PRICE, AND SUPPLIER/CREATOR

- Linux and UNIX
- Free
- Developed by Juan Pablo Romero: http://superficie.sourceforge.net/

2. APPLICATIONS

- Superficie (surface) is a small program that allows you to visualize 3D surfaces, and to have certain interactions with them

3. EXAMPLES/SAMPLES

- Screen Shots: http://superficie.sourceforge.net/screenshots.html

- An example as graphic editor: http://linux.davecentral.com/3592_graphed.html

4. WEB RESOURCES

- Official site: http://www.geocities.com/SiliconValley/Lab/8325/superficie/

- A place to download it: http://linux.davecentral.com/3592_graphed.html

- An introduction page: http://sal.kachinatech.com/E/1/SUPERFICIE.html

- http://mail.gnome.org/archives/gnome-announce-list/1999-December/msg00016.html

- http://linuxberg.lol.li/x11html/preview/019-007-001-011C.html

Swift 3D — 3D Vector Graphics Tool

1. PLATFORMS, PRICE, AND SUPPLIER/CREATOR

- PC Windows, MAC OS 7.5.3 or Higher

- Price $139.00

- Electric Rain: http://www.erain.com/; http://www.swift3d.com/

2. APPLICATIONS

- Swift3D is an intuitive 3D application for creating, editing, and animating 3D images. These images can be created from fonts and basic 3D primitives or imported from other popular 3D modeling programs. Swift 3D allows extensive control over the extrusion, rotation, coloring and lighting of 3D images. Swift 3D supports three levels of export — Outlines, flat shading, and gradient shading. Swift 3D is compatible with other applications such as Macromedia, Flash, and Adobe to import and export 3D images and animations. It is also a file and model converter. It is used for Web Design and many Web-based applications

3. EXAMPLES/SAMPLES

- http://www.3dlinks.com/gallerydisplay.cfm?sid=3D%20Studio%20Max
- http://www.onlinedj.com/onlinemixing/index.shtml
- http://www.greenjem.com/
- http://www.wholetruth.com/asp/truth/menu.htm

4. FUNCTIONS

- Internal Modeling:
    - Swift can create 3D text from any TrueType font with control over sizing, depth and bevels
    - Objects such as spheres, cones, and cubes can be imported into Swift during internal modeling
    - During modeling, Swift applies materials to any objects that are either imported or native
- Advanced Models:
    - Swift has the ability to handles moderately complex 3D models in the 3DS format
    - Swift also supports other intersecting models
- Animation:
    - Swift comes with pre-built drag and drop animations that can be applied for motion to new or imported images
    - Complex animation can be used through key frames and then easily converted into vector file for importing purposes
- Lighting:
    - Swift has the ability to add up to 16 spot or point lights to your scene
    - Swift can create animated lighting representation
    - Swift has ability to place lights into scene for further animation
- File Formats:
    - Imports: 3D Studio Models (3DS) – Swift recognizes the materials such as camera views, lighting, and animations. EPS images — Swift recognizes all vector artwork and automatically renders images as 3D objects. AI files — Swift recognizes all Adobe Illustrator vector drawings
    - Exports: Swift provides the ability to export your scenes to the Macromedia Flash (SWF) file format. Swift also able to bring your SWF files into Macromedia Flash for further manipulation. Swift gives to the flexibility to export EPS and AI files from Swift 3D to 2D drawing programs

5. WEB RESOURCES

- http://www.erain.com/support/Swift3D/Tutorials/default.htm
- http://www.greymatter.co.uk/gmWEB/Items/00026558.HTM

- http://www.zdnet.com/pcmag/features/software/1519/3d-r6.htm

Tecplot

1. PLATFORMS, PRICES, AND SUPPLIER/CREATOR

- Windows, Linux PCs, and UNIX workstations including those from Compaq, HP, IBM, SGI, and SUN. Effective on October 10, 2001 and subject to change

Tecplot 9.0	Single-Computer Perpetual License
Windows 9X/NT/2000/ME	$1,395
Linux	$1,395
UNIX X/Motif Workstation	$2,295

- Amtec Engineering, Inc.: http://www.amtec.com/

2. APPLICATIONS

- Tecplot is plotting software with extensive 2D and 3D capabilities for visualizing technical data from analyses, simulations and experiments. Tecplot combines general engineering plotting with advanced 3D scientific data visualization

- Tecplot is the most powerful tool for scientific and engineering data visualization. It is easy to use and compatible with Windows, Linux, and Unix. There is no major learning curve — simply load in the data and start visualizing and tailoring the plots. Tecplot is a high quality graphic tool, which allows much creativity and flexibility in presenting scientific data. Some applications include visualization of 3D surfaces and volumes, metal cutting simulation, streamlines and vector, and animation. Computational fluid dynamics (CFD) Analyzer is an add-on tool for Tecplot that has the ability to calculate a variety of flow functions, perform integrations, generate time-dependent particle paths, and perform error analysis on finite difference solutions

3. EXAMPLES/SAMPLES

- Visualization:

    - Animations, contour plots, vector plots, 3D surfaces, 3D volume visualization: http://www.amtec.com/plotgallery/
    - Metal cutting simulation tool: http://www.amtec.com/contours/issue4/thirdwave.html

- Oceanography: http://www.amtec.com/Product_pages/goring.html
- Geography: http://www.amtec.com/Product_pages/georgiou.html
- Sail boat fluid dynamics: http://www.amtec.com/Product_pages/america.html
- CFD analyzer tool: http://www.amtec.com/Product_pages/cfd_analyzer.html
- Helicopter aerodynamics: http://www.amtec.com/Product_pages/martin.html
- Biomechanics: http://www.amtec.com/Product_pages/raghavan.html
- Biology of fish: http://www.amtec.com/Product_pages/faber.html

4. FUNCTIONS

- Data Operations:

  - Create, alter, and transform data: alter your data or create new data using mathematical expressions
  - Interpolate: interpolate data from one set to another using various algorithms in 1D, 2D and 3D
  - Triangulate: triangulate data points defined in a 2D plane
  - Convert cell-centered data: use tecplot to convert cell-centered data to cell-corner (nodal) data
  - Mirror: create additional data that is a mirror image of existing data
  - Rotate: rotate data in the XY plane by any specified angle
  - Equation Files: create and store equations used for complex data creation and transformation for reuse

- Data Analysis:

  - Curve fits: use the standard curves or create your own with ADK (Tecplot add-on developer's Kit)
  - Probing and data editing: interactively probe for the values in a plot by simply clicking on the point of interest. Reposition data points interactively
  - Data labeling: display the values of a field variable or the indices of each node, at each node of a plot
  - Extracting on lines: interactively define sets of points or polylines to extract data
  - Slicing: interactively move slices through 3D volume data while displaying data on the slice plane
  - Data-blanking: mask particular sets of cells or elements from a plot based on local values of field variables, grid indices, or depth
  - Isosurface and streamtrace extraction: extract isosurfaces and streamtraces generated in 3D volume data
  - Outer-surface extraction: extract and display the surface of 3D volume finite-element data

- Annotating Plots:

  - Text: place text interactively anywhere on the plot. Set the text color, angle, size, font, background box, and justification. Embed Greek letters and mathematical symbols in text strings, superscript, and subscript any character. Create user-defined characters
  - European character set: create annotation in European language character sets with the extended ISO-Latin1 character set

- Geometries: place geometries interactively on the plot, creating polylines, rectangular boxes, circles, and ellipses. Duplicate, reposition, and resize them interactively. Fill geometries with a color. Create and modify geometries (point by point) interactively or read from a file
- Active text and geometries: associate a macro function with any text or geometry object. Use a special keystroke to select an active text or geometry to execute the macro function

- Graphical User Interface:

  - Page layout: create up to 128 plots on a single page; each plot is contained in a Tecplot Frame. Interactively lay out Frames on a page, and resize, move, and delete them. Customize all attributes of Frames such as background color, border, rulers, and headers. Snap Frames and plot objects into precise positions
  - Overlaying and superimposing Frames: manage multiple overlaying Frames
  - Set selected Frame backgrounds to be transparent
  - Frame linking: link style and positional attributes between Frames
  - Animation: create and play animations of image sequences, using Tecplot utilities, or AVI output

- Automating Tecplot:

  - Macros: create macros either by recording the actions of an interactive session or with a text editor. Use embedded interactive debugger to view and test macros
  - Quick macro panel: launch a macro by clicking a button in Tecplot's interactive, customizable, multipage Quick Macro Panel
  - Batch mode processing: run Tecplot in batch mode to process data and create plots without displaying any graphics on the screen. Run Tecplot on your computer or remotely using a nongraphical terminal
  - Layer buttons: display any combination of the plot types (contours, mesh grid, vectors, scatter symbols, data boundaries, surface shade) you want on each subdivision of the dataset
  - Frame mode buttons: change your plot in any individual Frame quickly between XY, 2D, and 3D views, with a single click of the mouse
  - Viewing: zoom in and out, translate, rotate, and resize the view interactively. Center the data, and reset the range on any axis. Continuous zoom and translate combined with most mouse tools. Keyboard and mouse shortcuts add power and efficiency
  - Rendering: image is fully rendered in true color during all operations. Optional reduction in level-of-detail for 3D motion

- Others:

  - Extending: add your own specialized functions, analyses, and data input/output to Tecplot, using the included add-on developer's kit (ADK)
  - Publish your results directly to the web: create output as an HTML file with plots in PNG, AVI, and BMP formats
  - Internet connectivity: read and write data directly to and from FTP and HTTP sites

– Cross-Platform Capability: Run Tecplot on most UNIX workstations and PCs running Windows 95/98/2000/NT/XP, and Linux. Interchange Tecplot macro files, layout files, Stylesheets, color map files, and data files, which are compatible for all platform types

5. WEB RESOURCES

- Amtec Engineering, Inc.: http://www.amtec.com

- Tecplot E-Newsletter: http://www.amtec.com/contours

- A Magazine article about Tecplot (Technical Computing Magazine): http://www.adeptscience.co.uk/

- Download Tecplot Product Demo: http://www.amtec.com/Product_pages/prod3.html

- Use Tecplot 9.0 quick tutorial: http://www.amtec.com/tutorial/index.html

- Tecplot Plot-of-the-Month Archive: http://www.amtec.com/contours/issue4/plotofthemonth.html

Terragen

1. PLATFORMS, PRICE, AND SUPPLIER/CREATOR

- PC — Windows 95/98/JT/2000

- Free for Personal, noncommercial use; download link: http://www.planetside.co.uk/terragen/download.shtml

- Planetside: http://www.planetside.co.uk/

2. APPLICATIONS

- Terragen is a work-in-progress scenery generator for Windows 95/98/NT/2000. Terragen is used to create photorealistic results for professional landscape visualization, special effects, art, and recreation

3. GALLERY/SAMPLES

- Sample images: http://www.planetside.co.uk/terragen/images.shtml

- Additional images: http://www.timster.net/terracon/

- Movies: http://www.planetside.co.uk/terragen/movies.shtml

4. FUNCTIONS

- Intuitive user interface — extremely easy to use layout, along with realistic default settings, allows the creation of good-looking scenes within seconds of starting the program. Random fractal terrain — Controllable parameters allow extremely varied terrain shapes. Can also be used to "fill in" realistic terrain on a user-defined landscape

- High detail foreground texturing — the rendering engine allows extreme close-ups of landscape details with automatic level of detail adjustment

- Terrain sculpting tools — Can be used to "paint" the shape of the landscape, to position mountains and valleys or make changes to random landscapes. Random terrain generation can be used "fill in" realistic terrain over deliberately positioned mountains and valleys

- Terrain modification tools — functions for allowing overall modification of terrain shape, such as glaciation

- Combination of terrains — two terrains can be combined together to produce a new terrain, using a number of different methods such as "highest", "lowest", height addition and subtraction, to extend the usefulness of the terrain generation system

- Terrain import/export — terragen can import and export raw heightfield information in 8-bit greyscale (and soon 16-bit). Possible uses include the construction of terrains from externally created pictures. Terragen can also save files compatible with the "Import Binary" feature in VistaPro

- Hierarchical surface color map — the surface of the landscape is divided into different components, such as grass and rock. Any component (surface) may be divided further, as far as is desired. There is huge potential for very complex, detailed landscape surfaces with this system

- Water — lakes and seas can now be rendered, complete with ripples/waves and soft reflections

- Cloud layer — a 2-dimensional cloud generator and rendering system which realistically shades the clouds to give an impression that they are actually 3-dimensional. Also, an experimental 3-dimensional cloud renderer which can in most cases provide even more realistic results

- Multihaze atmospheric model — this allows for highly realistic skies and haze, while allowing room for experimentation and artistic licence

- Volumetric lighting — shadows from the terrain and clouds can be cast into the atmospheric haze to give "sunbeams" and improve the overall lighting of the atmosphere

- Realistic sunlight penetration system — calculates the dimming and reddening of the sunlight through the atmosphere. Improves foggy scenes and gives gorgeous sunsets with ease while still permitting control over its effects

- Anisotropic lighting of atmosphere — at present, this is achieved by a convincing "glow" effect applied to clouds and haze

- "Soft" shadows — although only calculated by approximation, this effect looks almost perfect and has no rendering time overhead

5. RESOURCES

- Official Guide: http://www.planetside.co.uk/terragen/guide/

- FAQS: http://www.planetside.co.uk/terragen/guide/tg_faq.html

- Tutorial and Resources Links: http://www.terrasource.net/

Texture Lab: Tiling Tools

1. PLATFORM, PRICE, AND SUPPLIER/CREATOR

- PC

- $149

- Digimation: http://www.digimation.com/

2. APPLICATIONS

- Like the original Texture Lab: Elemental Tools, Texture Lab: Tiling Tools includes a collection of material maps for 3DS Max and consists of 3 powerful mapping types. These maps may be applied to Diffuse, Opacity, and/or Bump map channels. With them, you can create tilable patterns of just about any shape. Tiling Tools allows you to create repeatable brick, shingles, fish scales, and more in minutes. Because of the procedural nature of these plug-ins, you can quickly and easily modify any parameter to make subtle changes or drastic changes in how the material looks. In many cases, this can also be animated. Texture Lab: Tiling Tools is composed of three map plug-ins: Tiling Geometry, Tiling Lattice, and Tiling Tesselations

3. EXAMPLES/SAMPLES

- Images and screenshots for Texture Lab:
  http://www.3dmax.com/shop/ProductInfo.cfm?ID=22#Samples

- Product Demo: http://www.digimation.com/asp/
  products_demo.asp?product_id=95

- Animations with Texture Lab:
  http://www.digimation.com/asp/products_animations.asp?product_id=95

4. FUNCTIONS

- Modeling:
  - Objects: repeatable brick, shingles, fish scales, etc. can be created efficiently and quickly
  - Contains over 50 preset materials for modeling use (for example, use maps in the opacity channel to create cages and grates)
  - Maps can be used as Displacement and Environment maps

- Efficiency:
  - Utilizes very little memory and generates very fast
  - Plug-in for 3D Studio Max, so it doesn't require a lot of space

- Procedural Uses:
  - Creates repetitive patterns for tiling across an object's surface
  - Allows you to easily modify any parameter to make subtle or drastic changes to the appearance of the object
  - Allows animation

- Map Plug-ins:
  - Tiling Geometry
  - Tiling Lattice
  - Tiling Tessellations

- File Formats:
  - Plug-in for 3D Studio Max, so it is solely for that use (no import/export)

5. WEB RESOURCES

- Updates/Patches: http://www.digimation.com/asp/
  products_updates.asp?product_id=95

- Books: http://www.3dlinks.com/software_plugins_max.cfm

- Any Breaking News: http://www.digimation.com/asp/
  products_breaking.asp?product_id=95

trueSpace

1. PLATFORMS, PRICES, AND SUPPLIER/CREATOR

- Windows 95, 98, NT 4.0, or 2000
- $595-listed price; $273 — educational price
- Caligari Corporation: http://www.caligari.com/

2. APPLICATION

- trueSpace is a 3D authoring tool for modeling, surfacing, rendering, and animation. It provides many abilities similar to AutoDesk's 3D Studio Max but for one-fourth the cost. It has been used in advertisements, games, art works, and animated virtual environments

3. EXAMPLES/SAMPLES

- http://www.caligari.com/gallery/anims/Aug00/index.html
- http://www.caligari.com/gallery/onemanshow/GeoffHolman/Geoff_Holman.htm
- http://www.caligari.com/gallery/images/Aug00/index.html
- http://badgerco.cjb.net

4. WEB RESOURCES

- http://www.caligari.com/products/index.html
- http://forms.caligari.com/forms/ts4down.html

TurboCAD

1. PLATFORM, PRICES, AND SUPPLIER/CREATOR

- PC
- $$$$
- International Microcomputer Software, Inc. (IMSI): http://www.imsisoft.com/

2. APPLICATIONS

- TurboCAD is a 3D CAD package sold by International Microcomputer Software Inc. (IMSI)

3. EXAMPLES/SAMPLES

- http://www.turbocad.com/community/gallery/v7/index.cfm

4. WEB RESOURCES

- http://www.turbocad.com/

Ulead COOL 3D

1. PLATFORM, PRICES, AND SUPPLIER/CREATOR

- PC
- From $49.00
- Ulead Creative Intelligence: http://www.ulead.com/cool3d/runme.htm

2. APPLICATION

- Creating eye-catching headlines for webpages, video productions, presentation and documents

3. EXAMPLE/SAMPLES

- Unmatched creativity of Ulead COOL 3D:
  http://www.webutilities.com/products/C3D/tour/part2_2.htm
- Using Ulead COOL 3D:
  http://www.cool3d.co.il/gallery.html

4. WEB RESOURCES

- Manual: http://www.ulead.com/cool3d/c3d3manual.pdf
- Tutorials: http://www.ulead.com/learning/cool3d.htm
- Learn from example: http://www.ulead.com/cool3d/spolights.htm
- Reviews and awards: http://www.ulead.com/cool3d/reviews.htm

UnrealEd

1. PLATFORMS, PRICE, AND SUPPLIER/CREATOR

- Windows 95/98/NT

- Free with purchase of Unreal Tournament: http://www.unrealtournament.com, a computer game cost $30

- Epic Games: http://www.epicgames.com, in cooperation with Digital Extremes: http://www.digitalextremes.com

2. APPLICATIONS

- UnrealEd is the single application which is needed to modify nearly every aspect of the popular game Unreal Tournament. Using constructive solid geometry, the program's 3D editor allows one to create individual objects, animated 3D characters, and large highly-detailed "levels" (environments explored within the game). Using the proprietary language UnrealScript, one may modify the artificial intelligence driving any number of automated characters in the game, or even modify the logic defining the game's fundamental rules

3. EXAMPLES/SAMPLES

- Infiltration (http://www.planetunreal.com/infiltration/): an example of what is called a "total conversion" of the game Unreal Tournament. This team of developers has used UnrealEd to model the physical appearance and the behavior of several weapons and vehicles which are commonly used by the U.S. military. They have also created expansive, realistic environments in which one team of soldiers (i.e., people playing this game over the Internet or a LAN) will engage another in combat

- Fragball (http://www.planetunreal.com/fragball/PlayGuide.html): a conversion of Unreal Tournament which uses UnrealScript and carefully-designed maps to create a new style of game which is loosely based on football and basketball, but allows the use of weapons

- PlanetUnreal's Picture of the Day archive (http://www.planetunreal.com/images/photo/archive.asp): a regularly updated set of images of interesting objects, creatures, levels, and full conversions which have been created using UnrealEd

4. FUNCTIONS

- Modeling:
  - "Brushes" are used to add/subtract from the initially solid "world" to create an environment

- Preset 3D brushes (cube, cylinder, sphere, cone, stairway, etc.)
- Methods of creating new brushes
- Rotation, scaling, stretching
- Intersection / deintersection of existing brushes
- Invisible "Actor" objects can be placed within the world to determine where moving entities in the game will stand initially
- Lights can be specified by position, color, brightness, hue, and saturation
- Textures can be taken from large available palette or imported from PCX
- For each surface, user can specify texture map, alpha, diffuse, specular, and bump map

- Animation:

  - Character animation: used for all moving characters
  - For each character model, several "frames" of animation are stored for each type of motion (standing, running, jumping, etc.)
  - Each frame shares the same number of polygons and vertices, and the same texture map
  - The game engine "flips" through the frames for the appropriate type of motion, creating the illusion of animation
  - Generally implemented in 3D Studio Max and imported

- File Formats:

  - Unreal file formats: U, UC, U3D, 3D, US
  - Can import files from the 3DS format using a free third-party program called 3DS2UNR

5. WEB RESOURCES

- the Official Unreal Technology Site: http://unreal.epicgames.com/ — is full of information and tutorials on the Unreal engine, its file formats, level construction, etc.

- Wolf's UnrealEd Tutorials: http://unreal.gamedesign.net/utc.shtml — contains a set of online tutorials which describe how to the basic and more advanced features of UnrealEd

- Blacksway's Unreal Editing Repository: http://www.unreality.org/blacksway/ — contains news pertaining to the Unreal editing community and a number of quality tutorials

Unrealty

1. PLATFORMS, PRICES, AND SUPPLIER/CREATOR

- Windows 95/98/NT

- Editor
  - $1,899 first user
    $899 for each additional user
    $1,500 license to freely distribute scenes which you create
- Client / Viewer
  - free for download
- Unrealty: http://www.unrealty.net, produced by Perilith Industrielle: http://www.perilith.com, a division of IT Future, Inc.: http://www.it-future.com

2. APPLICATIONS

- Unrealty is software that allows you to walk around in a true, honest-to-goodness real-time virtual environment. The client program uses the same engine as the popular computer game "Unreal Tournament": http://www.unrealtournament.com from Epic Games: http://www.epicgames.com to allow the user to explore and interact with a highly detailed virtual environment. Designed in part to assist real estate agents, the editor allows one to create a "locale" complete with staircases, windows, and even pools of water. A built-in UnrealScript: http://unreal.epicgames.com/UnrealScript.htm language editor/compiler lets the scene designer define behavior patterns for moveable objects and computer-controlled entities (such as a virtual tourguide). The Unrealty editor essentially creates files which are compatible with UnrealEd, but does not create game-related features that aren't needed for a real estate simulation

3. EXAMPLES/SAMPLES

- http://www.unrealty.net/network/locale.php3?id=7&page=1 — a set of maps which represent the VISS in several stages of development. The user can float throughout the interior of the space station or view it from the outside

- http://www.unrealty.net/network/locale.php3?id=6&page=2 — a walkthrough of a virtual German bank

- http://www.vrndproject.com — this standalone program implemented using the same Unreal engine technology allows you to walk or fly through the Notre Dame cathedral and observe the monks who walk its halls

4. FUNCTIONS

- Unrealty uses UnrealEd as its modeler
- UnrealEd uses Unrealty game engine to achieve animations

5. WEB RESOURCES

- http://www.planetquake.com/polycount/resources/unreal/tutorials/UTut03.shtml
- http://www.planetunreal.com/news/index.asp?function=search&advanced=1&search=unrealty&startmonth=5&startday=20&startyear=1998&endmonth=5&endday=10&endyear=2001&order=datedesc&recordcount=0
- http://www.unrealty.net
- http://unreal.epicgames.com/

VARKON

1. PLATFORMS, PRICES, AND SUPPLIER/CREATOR

- PC, SUN, and VAX
- Free for Unix (shareware); $875.00 for other platforms
- The system was originally developed by a group at the University of Linkoping in Sweden under the leadership of Dr. Johan Kjellander now the president of Microform AB. Since then the system has been owned, marketed, and further developed by Microform AB. VARKON is a trademark registered by Microform AB in Sweden: http://www.microform.se/index.htm

2. APPLICATIONS

- VARKON is a completely open general purpose interactive modeling system but also a programming language, an object oriented database, a sculptured surface modeler, fully parametric in 2D and 3D, and a very powerful development tool. VARKON can even be used as a 2D drafting system when this is needed. The VARKON tool is not intended for the average end user but rather for those who wish to develop CAD related functionality of their own. The corner stone of the system is the integrated MBS programming language with its compiler and interactive environment. VARKON can be used as a traditional CAD-system with drafting, modeling, and visualization, but the real power of VARKON is in parametric modeling and CAD applications development. VARKON includes interactive parametric modeling in 2D or 3D but also the unique MBS programming language integrated in the graphical environment

3. EXAMPLE/SAMPLES

- 3D house design for VARKON: http://www.microform.se/scrdmp8.htm

- 3D sculptured surfaces for VARKON: http://www.microform.se/scrdmp2.htm

- 2D mechanical drafting: http://www.microform.se/scrdmp4.htm

4. FUNCTIONS

- Modeling:

  - Object: polygons, points, lines, arcs, curves
  - Transformation: shading, hidden line removal, rotation, translation, scaling
  - Manipulations: closest point, silhouette, curvatures, trimming, hidden surface removal

- Rendering:

  - Lights: Gouraud, lighting, shading
  - Materials: three-dimensional texturing, composite curves, composite trimming, texture mapping
  - Before and after rendering: anti-aliasing, shading, virtual frame-buffer

- Animation:

  - Advanced Animation

- Coordinate Systems:

  - Direction of rotation: when rotating a local coordinate system with relation to another coordinate system, as you face an axis head-on, looking down the axis from the positive to the negative direction, the direction of positive rotation is counterclockwise
  - Visualization of the coordinate system: Varkon coordinate systems are two or three dimensional Cartesian systems consisting of an X, a Y, and, if the coordinate system is three-dimensional, a Z axis. Since the Varkon system imposes no fixed set of views on the model, it does not in general make sense to say that a particular axis is in a particular orientation relative to the screen

5. WEB RESOURCES

- A list of resources on the Web: http://www.microform.se/index.htm

- Another Web resource: http://www.database.com/~lemur/vk-varkon-tutorial.html

- Yet another: http://www.ubi.pt/~dfis-wg/linux/apps/free-2/linux_cad.html

Vecta 3D MAX

1. PLATFORM, PRICES, AND SUPPLIER/CREATOR:

- PC
- Vecta 3d max plug-in version 1.1 $195; Vecta 3D Standalone $74.95
- Ideaworks3D Limited website: http://www.vecta3d.com/

2. APPLICATIONS

- Vecta3D-Max 1.1 is a plug-in for 3D Studio Max that allows you to output images and animations from virtually any 3D scene

3. EXAMPLES/SAMPLES:

- Killer Sites made with Vecta3D:
  - www.mtv2.co.uk
  - www.titoonic.dk

4. WEB RESOURCES

- http://auteurs-associes.com/~niko/flash_link.html
- www.vecta3d.com
- http://www1.buyonet.com/s/b?id=4.53.48&page=pis&pi=6002
- http://www.macromedia.com/support/flash/ts/documents/flash_websites.htm
- http://www.myholler.com/flash/books.htm
- http://www.webtools.com/story/animation/TLS20001108S0001

VectorWorks

1. PLATFORM, PRICE, AND SUPPLIER/CREATOR

- PC
- 895.00
- Nemetschek North America: http://www.nemetschek.net/

2. APPLICATIONS

- Precise 2D drafting, powerful 3D modeling, and sophisticated client presentations
- Plus built-in database and spreadsheet to track costs and materials, and flexible scripting language to automate routine drafting tasks

3. EXAMPLES/SAMPLES

- VectorWorks case studies: http://www.nemetschek.net/news/casestudies.html
- VectorWorks modeling samples: http://www.nemetschek.net/gallery/index.html

4. FUNCTIONS

- Sophisticated 2D Drafting:
  - Extensive array of menu commands and tools for sophisticated drafting. The program's precision, constant on-screen and exclusive SmartCursort—which identifies relevant parallels, intersections, snaps, and tangents to create sharp, precise 2D drawings
- Powerful 3D Modeling:
  - Easy to explore concepts as well as represent final designs in 3D. In addition to 3D Surface and wireframe modeling tools, it offers true Boolean operations
- Integrated Design Environment:
  - Store all of the drawing's information (2D plans, 3D models, and data) in a single file, making it easy to coordinate and manage changes to design. Changes made in one view are updated in all other views, saving you time and reducing the risk of errors. For example, changes to a 2D plan will automatically be reflected in the 3D model, and in any reports and schedules
- Free Libraries of "Intelligent" plug-in Objects
  - Plug-in Objects are dynamic representations of real-world objects. Simply type in a new parameter and VectorWorks will re-draw the object automatically. One plug-in door can be easily configured to represent a whole library of door symbols. The objects are "intelligent" in that they behave like the real-world objects they represent
- Easy Database and Spreadsheet Functions:
  - Easy database and spreadsheet functions makes it is simple to analyze how a change will impact a project or other "what if" scenarios, users don't need to link to an external database or spreadsheet, and software will automatically update reports
- File Formats:
  - Importing file formats: DWG/DXF (version 2.5-2000i), BMP, EPSF, JPEG, PICT, PICT As Picture, PhotoShop, PNG, QuickTime, MacPaint, Metafile, Metafile as Picture, SGI, TGA, TIFF

– Exporting file formats: DWG/DXF (version 2.5-2000i) BMP, EPSF, JPEG, PICT, PhotoShop, PNG, QuickTime, MacPaint, Metafile, SGI, TGA, TIFF, VRML (requires RenderWorks), VectorScript, MiniCAD 6, MiniCAD 7, VectorWorks 8

- Database/Worksheet Export options: Comma, Tab, Merge, DIF, SYLK

5. WEB RESOURCES

- Download: http://www.nemetschek.net/downloads/vectorworks/ vwdownloadform.html

- User group: http://www.nemetschek.net/support/usergroups.html

VEGA

1. PLATFORMS, PRICES, AND SUPPLIER/CREATOR

- Silicon Graphics IRIX, Windows NT 4.0, 98, and 2000

- Prices start at $3,000

- MultiGen-Paradigm, a subsidiary of Computer Associates: http:// www.multigen.com

2. APPLICATIONS

- Vega is a software development environment for real-time visual and audio simulation, virtual reality, and general visualization applications

- Application-specific modules (plug-ins) tightly integrated with Vega, are also available for Vega (nautical, infrared, radar, advanced lighting systems, animated humans, large area terrain databases, CAD data import, DIS)

3. EXAMPLES/SAMPLES

- http://www.multigen.com/gallery.htm

- http://www.itspatial.com/virtArlington.asp

- http://www.visidyne.com/products/cloudscape/cloudscape.htm

- http://www.crc.co.jp/CRC/rc_s.html

- http://www.multigen.com/products/vegaspecial.htm

- 3D Samples: http://magellan.co.arlington.va.us/MapCenter/3dStuff/ screenshots.htm

4. WEB RESOURCES

- General information on Vega: http://www.paradigmsim.com/vega.htm

- Overview of the Vega product line: http://www.multigen.com/products/vega1.htm

- Overview of the available plug-ins: http://www.multigen.com/products/vegamod.htm

- Online catalog: http://www.multigen.com/products/pdf_files/Vega%2072dpi.pdf

- Overview of Vega GUI, Lynx: http://www.multigen.com/products/vega1a.htm

- MPI user forums including Vega: http://www.multigen.com/cgi-bin/Ultimate.cgi

- Vega's Capabilities: http://www.paradigmsim.com/products/vegamod.htm

- Graphics News: http://www.tenlinks.com/News/pr/112700multigen.htm

VFleet

1. PLATFORM, PRICE, AND SUPPLIER/CREATOR

- UNIX

- Free

- By Pittsburgh SuperComputer Center: http://www.psc.edu/Packages/VFleet_Home/ with major support from Grand Challenge Cosmology Consortium: http://zeus.ncsa.uiuc.edu:8080/GC3_Home_Page.html

2. APPLICATIONS

- VFleet is a volume renderer. It is intended for use in computational science, in that it can handle very large datasets representing multiple variables within the same physical system

3. EXAMPLES

- Animations of simulations created with VFleet can be found at: http://www.psc.edu/general/software/packages/vfleet/package_docs/development/vfleet_pics_and_movies.html

4. FEATURES

- Load and render multiple datasets simultaneously

- Volume masking

- Optional trilinear interpolation
- Optional 3D mipmapping
- Camera control
- Scripting support

5. WEB RESOURCES

- Online user's guide available at: http://www.psc.edu/general/software/packages/vfleet/package_docs/development/vfleet1.1.html

View3D

1. PLATFORMS, PRICE, AND SUPPLIER/CREATOR

- Sun (SunOS and Solaris), HP, IBM, Digital Alpha, and SGI, and on PCs running Linux or Solaris X86, and also on Windows NT via DataFocus NuTCRACKER libraries
- $459.00
- Qualecad: http://www.qualecad.com/index.html

2. APPLICATIONS

- View3D is an OSF/Motif compliant widget that offers the application developer a powerful but easy to use way of creating interactive 3D data displays. Built on top of the OpenGL graphics standard, View3D is capable of rendering a wide range of 3D datatypes, from simple surfaces to complex geometric shapes. It is ideally suited for use as a front end for technical applications requiring 3D graphics. View3D is a tool which requires almost no knowledge of 3D graphics. Any application developer with a background in X Windows and Motif programming can create a 3D application

3. EXAMPLES/SAMPLES

- http://myweb.worldnet.net/~tomsoft/View3D/screenShot.html
- http://www.cs.duke.edu/~wys/view3d/

4. FUNCTIONS

- Modeling:

- Objects: mesh surfaces: quad meshes, triangle meshes, raster, 3D volumes, marker, facet, geometric, lines, points, polygons, and text
- Transformation: translate 3D Studio data (.3ds) and project (.prj) files into .iob format
- Editing and manipulations: vertex, vector, color, transparency, fill (wireframe, solid), axes and lights Grid, stack, booleans, scatter, visual

- Rendering:

  - Lights: multiple lights source, all with user_definable location and intensity, and may be spotlights or point lights
  - Materials: color, transparancy, texture mapping, wireframe models with hidden lines removed. It can be used in calls to XintView3DCreateMaterial() and XintView3DChangeMaterial()
  - More materials: attributes: light, shade_model, draw_mode, draw_grid. Multi_color, color_scale, range_color, color_index
  - Before and after rendering: virtual framebuffer, motion blur, field rendering, volumetric fog, fog, environment maps, Gouraud shading

- Other functions:

  - Viewer: pop, push stack
  - 3D Object: change material, change object, query material, query object

- Animation:

  - Control module, including rotation, picking, translation, zooming, selection, interactive editing and GUI
  - Animations: isolines, footprints, hole dimensions, and mechanical clearances, clipping, hierachical objects, layered deformation, copper layers, internal planes, silkscreen, solder mask, solder reflow

- File Formats:

  - Importing file formats: external MCAD, graphics application VRML
  - Exporting file formats: MCAD, VRML, IDF

5. WEB RESOURCES

- http://www.int.com/products/widget_info/view3d/doc/pick.html

- http://www.int.com/products/widget_info/view3d/view3d.htm

- http://www.pygott.demon.co.uk/prog.htm

- http://www.visualbeans.com/index.html

- http://products.ics.com/libs/view3d/datasheet.html

Vis5D

1. PLATFORMS, PRICE, SUPPLIER

- Platforms

    - Silicon Graphics workstations with IRIX 5.x or later. IBM RS/6000 workstations with AIX 3 or later. OpenGL-based 3D hardware is supported. Sun workstations with SunOS 5.x or later. HP workstations with HP-UX A.09.01 or later. PEX-based 3D hardware is supported. DEC Alpha workstations with OSF/1 V1.3 or later. IBM PC compatibles with Linux v1.2 or later. 90MHz Pentium or faster CPU recommended. Windows NT running on Intel. OS/2 running on Intel

- Free

- Supplier:

    - Space Science and Engineering Center
      University of Wisconsin-Madison
      1225 W. Dayton St.
      Madison, WI 53706
    - http://www.ssec.wisc.edu/~billh/vis5d.html

2. APPLICATIONS

- Vis5D is a scientific plotting and graphics program. Vis5D is a system for interactive visualization of large 5D gridded datasets such as those produced by numerical weather and ocean models

- Vis5D's strengths include viewing 3D volumes and animating variables over time

- Vis5D works on data in the form of a five-dimensional rectangle. The data are real numbers at each point of a "grid" or "lattice" which spans three space dimensions, one time dimension, and a dimension for enumerating multiple physical variables

- Contour line slices, colored slices, volume renderings, etc., of data in a 3D grid, then the images are rotated and animated in real time.The Vis5D system is very widely used by scientists to visualize the output of their numerical simulations of the Earth's atmosphere and oceans. Vis5d is a popular program for 3D visualization of meteorological fields

3. EXAMPLES/SAMPLES

- Sulfer dioxide with isolines of nitric acid: http://www.ssec.wisc.edu/~billh/radm.gif

- The air that we breathe: http://whyfiles.org/030air_pollution/detect2.html/

- Hurricane Andrew simulation:

    - http://gewex.meteo.mcgill.ca:8080/liu/hurricane_andrew.html

- http://www.news.wisc.edu/chancellor/yourworld/1415.html
- Vis5D datasets of UW-NMS Operational Forecasts: http://mocha.meteor.wisc.edu/vis5d-oper.html
- 3D Links Gallery Index for Vis5D: http://www.scd.ucar.edu/vg/ResearchGallery.html
- TAO project images using Vis5D: http://www.pmel.noaa.gov/tao/vis/tao-vis.html

4. FUNCTIONS

- Transformations:
  - rotating, zooming, and panning the graphics
- Visualization:

  Contours/Isosurfaces:
  - displays contour loops of any active variable on any surface
  - individual loops can be labeled
  - enables isosurfaces to be created based on scalar variable, vector component, vector magnitude or coordinate
  - allow dynamic visualization of a range of isovalues
  - isosurfaces show the 3D volume bounded by a particular isovalue

  contour and colored slices:
  - Slices allow to look at planar cross sections of data in the 3D box
  - Slices can be oriented either horizontally or vertically
  - slices depict either contour lines, colored slices, wind vectors, or wind stream lines
- Interactivity:
  - Ease of use via interactive control panel
- Animation:
  - real time animation of isosurfaces
  - real time animation of contours
  - real time animation of volumes
- Rendering:
  - volume rendering
  - alpha blending
  - system without 3D graphics hardware use mesa
  - rendering can be improved by adjusting the color and opacity mappings
  - lighting parameters
- Texture Mapping:
  - to display a 2D image over a surface in 3D. Vis5D can display images over the topography (or bottom of the 3D box when topography is turned off) such as satellite or map images

- Additional Graphics Features:
  - Wind trajectories: trace the motion of air through the 3D volume much line smoke trails in a wind tunnel. Wind trajectories can be created and displayed
  - Vectors, contour lines, streamlines
  - Clipping planes: six new clipping planes have been added in Vis5D version 5.0. This allows you to manipulate the viewing volume in a more precise manner
  - Display groups: multiple displays can be grouped together in up to 9 groups
- Data Exchange:
  - Picture or printing format: XWD (X Window Dump), RGB, GIF, PostScript, Color PostScript
  - Vis5D reads data in two file formats, both of which store data in a compressed format that vis5d can access quickly and efficiently. The formats are also unique to Vis5D so outside data must be converted, a task which is somewhat eased by several example conversion programs supplied with the package

5. WEB RESOURCES

- http://www.cdc.noaa.gov/iips/amsvis/hibbard/#1

- Scientific Data Processing and Visualization: Software Package — Vis5D
  http://sal.kachinatech.com/D/1/VIS5D.html

- http://www.arsc.edu/resources/software/Vis5D.html

- Vis5D datasets of UW-NMS Operational Forecasts:
  http://mocha.meteor.wisc.edu/vis5d-oper.html

VisAD

1. PLATFORMS, PRICE, AND SUPPLIER/CREATOR

- Platform independent because VisAD is a Java component library

- Free

- http://www.ssec.wisc.edu/~billh/visad.html: VisAD was written by programmers at the SSEC Visualization Project at the University of Wisconsin-Madison Space Science and Engineering Center, by programmers at the Unidata Program Center, by programmers at the National Center for Supercomputer Applications, and by programmers at the Australian Bureau of Meteorology

2. APPLICATIONS

- VisAD is a Java component library for interactive and collaborative visualization and analysis of numerical data. The name VisAD is an acronym for "Visualization for Algorithm Development":

  - A general mathematical data model that can be adapted to virtually any numerical data, that supports data sharing among different users, different data sources and different scientific disciplines, and that provides transparent access to data independent of storage format and location (i.e., memory, disk or remote). The data model has been adapted to netCDF, HDF-5, FITS, HDF-EOS, McIDAS, Vis5D, GIF, JPEG, TIFF, QuickTime, ASCII and many other file formats
  - A general display model that supports interactive 3D, data fusion, multiple data views, direct manipulation, collaboration, and virtual reality. The display model has been adapted to Java3D and Java2D and used in an ImmersaDesk virtual reality display
  - Data analysis and computation integrated with visualization to support computational steering and other complex interaction modes
  - Support for two distinct communities: developers who create domain- specific systems based on VisAD, and users of those domain-specific systems. VisAD is designed to support a wide variety of user interfaces, ranging from simple data browser applets to complex applications that allow groups of scientists to collaboratively develop data analysis algorithms

3. EXAMPLES/SAMPLES

- Application of VisAD in Hydrological Modeling and Simulation: http://www.siggraph.org/publications/newsletter/v34n1/contributions/Taddei.html

- An application example: http://www.siggraph.org/publications/newsletter/v32n3/columns/images/S_Visfilesfigure1.jpg

4. FUNCTIONS

- Modeling:

  - Objects: the VisAD data model was designed to support virtually any numerical data. Rather than providing a variety of specific data structures like images, grids and tables, the VisAD data model defines a set of classes that can be used to build any hierarchical numerical data structures. Data objects include metadata defined by the classes: MathType, Unit, CoordinateSystem, Set (function domain sampling), ErrorEstimate and AuditTrail, as well as missing data indicators. CoordinateSystem transforms are done implicitly as needed in Data operations
  - Transformation translation, rotation, scaling, 3D cross cursor, others can be done extensively using java style APIs
  - Editing and manipulation: can be done extensively using Java style APIs

- Rendering:

  - Cameras and lights: adjustable and movable

- General: Compiled with Java 3D and OpenGL, can use all the rendering techniques in those two packages
- ContourWidget: the ContourWidget allows for interaction regarding the isocontours
- LabeledColorWidget: the LabeledColorWidget also allows users to see and interactively manipulate the color table
- Transparency display
- Volume Rendering: using an Integer3Dset, the volume is colored according to the index
- Projection Matrix and Aspect Ratio

- Animation:

  - Simple animation: achieve animation by using a loop in Java code
  - AnimationWidget: you can use AnimationControl to set animation on and off, to set its speed and other parameters. The AnimationWidget provides the user with the comforts of a modern UI
  - Animating a surface: for example, temperature of the Earth's surface, changes over timeImage animation: animate a series of images

- File Formats:

  - netCDF, FITS
  - HDF-5 — see Section 4 of the README file for instructions for installing the HDF-5 native library — also see NCSA's description of The VisAD HDF-5 Data Adapter
  - McIDAS, McIDAS ADDE, DODS, GIF, JPEG, TIFF, Quicktime, Vis5D
  - HDF-EOS — see the README.hdfeos file for instructions for installing the HDF-EOS native libraries
  - ASCII — see the README.text file for more information
  - Biorad, F2000
  - Shape — distributed by Unidata with their MetApps system
  - VisAD (serialized VisAD data objects)

5. WEB RESOURCES

- Official site: http://www.ssec.wisc.edu/~billh/visad.html

- A mailing list: http://www.unidata.ucar.edu/staff/russ/visad/

- A place to download the package:
  http://wuarchive.wustl.edu/graphics/graphics/packages/visad/

- A white paper: http://citeseer.nj.nec.com/hibbard98visad.html

- Sun java library for VisAD:
  http://industry.java.sun.com/solutions/products/by_product/0,2348,all-1708-99,00.html

VISVIVA AUTHORING STUDIO (VAS)

1. PLATFORMS, PRICE, AND SUPPLIER/CREATOR

- PC Windows platform and Macintosh
- The student version of the software is being offered for $79.00. The list price for VAS is $800.00, with the upgrade to 2.0 listing at $350.00
- Visviva Software, Inc.: http://www.visviva.com

2. APPLICATIONS

- The Visviva Authoring Studio provides an advanced, integrated environment which offers 2D vector graphics, 3D models, hypertexts, images, animations, and artistic interfaces all under the same design hierarchy, allowing a streamlined development process to be possible. Some of the powerful component tools of the Visviva Authoring Studio include: Object Design Workbench, 3D Object Modeler, Interface Designer, Vector Graphic Editor, Hypertext Editor, Image Painter, Animation Composer, and Subject-Oriented Studio. This set of tools is geared for the creation of games, movies, cartoons, presentations, and other multimedia projects
- A set of high-powered tools for artistic 3D modeling, drawing and painting, hypertext layout, special effects creation, intriguing game interfaces, and sophisticated animations in various styles for graphic artists who are disinclined towards nuts-and-bolts programming
- The Visviva Animation Engine can simultaneously integrate 3D figure animation, frame-by-frame animation, key parameter animation, vector graphic animation, movies, animation captures, and group animations into multimedia presentations. Authoring titles created using ScriptV can run at full speed, without compiling, in high-resolution, true color displays

3. EXAMPLES/SAMPLES

- http://www.visviva.com/product/objdesign.htm
- http://www.visviva.com/product/animation.htm
- http://www.visviva.com/product/model3d.htm
- http://www.visviva.com/product/vector.htm
- http://www.visviva.com/product/hypertext.htm
- http://www.visviva.com/gallery/index.html

4. FUNCTIONS

- Object Design: Selection tool, edit objects, arrange tools, create objects, modify objects, create image, create frame, create vector, create world3d, text tool, hypertext tool, text at path, enclosed text, test interface, animation, edit function, edit scriptV source, run application, debug, build and compile, move paper, zoom tool, state chart, animation composer, edit outline, edit node tool, freehand pen tool, line pen, polygon pen, curve pen, Bezier pen, BSpline pen, brush and eraser, polygon tool, rectangle tool, centered rectangle, ellipse tool, centered ellipse, circle tool, centered circle, spiral tool, gradient fill, mesh fill

- Animation: Trackview tool

- 3D Modeling: Selection tool, scale, edit object mesh, edit parameter, 3D modeling brush, clone tool, rotate world, camera, creation tool, modify object, light, zoom and hand, test interface, animation, edit objects

- Image Painting: Rectangle marquee, elliptical marquee, center ellipse, row marquee, column marquee, freehand lasso, polygon lasso, magnetic lasso, magic wand, global wand, square marquee, round marquee, brush tool, modifier brush, clone tool, eye dropper, effects tool, flood fill tool, gradient fill, blur pixels, sharpen pixels, smudge pixels, darken pixels, lighten pixels, saturate, desaturate, cell division, animation tool, move paper, edit outline, edit node tool, freehand pen tool, line pen, polygon pen, curve pen, Bezier pen, BSpline pen, brush and eraser, polygon tool, rectangle tool, centered rectangle, ellipse tool, centered ellipse, circle tool, centered circle, spiral tool, gradient fill, mesh fill, selection tool, arrange tool, create objects, modify object, create image, create frame, create vector, create world3d, text tool, hypertext tool, text at path, enclosed text, edit objects, test interface, zoom tool, animation

- Vector Drawing: Edit outline, edit node tool, freehand pen tool, line pen, polygon pen, curve pen, Bezier pen, BSpline pen, brush and eraser, polygon tool, rectangle tool, centered rectangle, ellipse tool, centered ellipse, circle tool, centered circle, spiral tool, gradient fill, mesh fill, selection tool, arrange tool, create objects, modify object, create image, create frame, create vector, create world3d, text tool, hypertext tool, text at path, enclosed text, edit objects, test interface, zoom tool, animation, add node, delete node, split node, join node, smooth node, symmetrical node, convert to curves, convert to lines

- Hypertext Editing: WYSIWYG

- Programming: The programming language used to program in VAS is called ScriptV. This language is an object-oriented programming language, and was developed by Visviva Software Inc. The manual for using this language can be reached at the following link: http://www.visviva.com/scriptv/main.htm

5. LINKS/WEB RESOURCES

- http://www.visviva.com
- http://www8.techmall.com/techdocs/NP990218-1.html
- http://www.transframe.com
- http://www.prweb.com/releases/1999/prweb7270.htm
- http://www.visviva.com/html_pages/vas_web.html

Visual3

1. PLATFORMS, PRICE, AND SUPPLIER/CREATOR

- DEC Alpha, HP 9000, IBM RS/6000, SGI, SUN
- Freely downloadable from site
- Written by Bob Haimes, MIT: http://raphael.mit.edu/visual3/visual3.html

2. APPLICATIONS

- Creates an interactive graphics environment for 3D visualization, either as a snapshot or as an animation
  - Written in Fortran and C, using OpenGL
  - Accepts user data in real-time, generating translatable 3D images
  - Primary use is to enable user interaction with pregenerated data, for visualization of data, as in fluid flow modeling
  - Downloadable add-ons enable math formulae visualization and particle-based simulation

3. EXAMPLES/SAMPLES

- ICEM Visual3 Brochure: http://www.icemcfd.com/visual3/v3_p1.htm

4. FUNCTIONS

- Modeling:
  - Objects: Sphere, spline curves, polymesh NURBs, primitives, polygons
  - Transformation: Translate, scale, Rotate
  - Editing and manipulations (vertex, edge, face, polygon, curves, objects): clipping, combine face, modify vertex, cut subfaces
- Rendering:
  - Cameras: Moveable

      – Lights: ambient light
      – Materials: Gouraud shaded, 24-bit color
      – Before and after rendering: antialiasing, field rendering, perspective matching

- Animation:

      – Rotation, translation, dynamic surface interaction with streamlines

- File Formats:

      – Importing: native file format
      – Exporting: images may be exported to bitmap/GIF format

5. WEB RESOURCES

- Applications built with Visual3: http://www.icemcfd.com/visual3/index.html

- Articles/Information: http://citeseer.nj.nec.com/138867.html

- Tutorials: ftp://ftp.icemcfd.com/pub/visual3/

VizStream Web Kit

1. PLATFORMS, PRICES, AND SUPPLIER/CREATOR

- Windows and Internet Explorer

- The VizStream WebKit is priced according to the number of models placed on a site and how many people visit those models. The most popular packages are:

      – up to 5 models and 2,500 visits/month for $30/month
      – up to 25 models and 10,000 visits/month for $90/month
      – up to 50 models and 100,000 visits/month for $240/month

- RealityWave Inc.: http://www.realitywave.com/

2. APPLICATIONS

- The VizStream WebKit enables the user to replace the flat, 2D pictures on your website with large, complex 3D designs, quickly and easily, without redesigning anything. It is the only truly scalable streaming 3D solution that is independent of bandwidth. VizStream downloads files of any size, over any speed connection, all within minutes

3. EXAMPLES/SAMPLES

- Medical Designs, Inc.:

    − Medical Designs designs and manufactures architectural modules for the electromechanical requirements of medical procedures performed in hospitals. Medical Designs uses the Vizstream WebKit to display 3D models of their medical solutions on their website. Medical Designs also uses the VizStream WebKit as a sales tool when designing custom solutions for clients. www.gasesmedicos.com

- Structural Research and Analysis Corporation:

    − SRAC develops designer analysis software for the mechanical CAD market. Its COSMOS/ suite of products exports XGL files and is therefore compatible with RealityWave's VizStream. SRAC uses the VizStream WebKit to enable Internet collaboration and add interactive 3D models to its website. Customers can examine the models by rotating, panning, and zooming in and out of them. www.srac.com

4. FUNCTIONS

- The VizStream provides two kinds of interfaces: ActiveX Control interface and a scene graph interface. ActiveX Control interface allows an application to connect to a VizStream Server and render the three-dimensional models that are stored on that server. The scene graph interface allows the manipulation of a streamed object. The file format is XGL. A free XGL Export Kit is provided to dramatically reduce the time it takes to produce syntactically correct XGL

- ActiveX Interface:

    − Viewing Methods: display one or more models, control which 3D models are displayed in the control and how those models are displayed
    − Overlay Methods: change the displayed material of an object or patch
    − Clip Plane Methods: add one or more clip planes to the scene
    − Edge Viewing: display and remove topological edges and vertices between the patch boundaries
    − Object Locating Methods: locate objects and patches in the models
    − XGL World Property Methods: read global properties that apply to all of the objects
    − XGL Object Property Methods: read properties for the objects
    − XGL Data Methods: provide access to the custom data
    − Rendering Methods: render the 3D scene in a multistage pipeline
    − Messaging Methods: send messages to other VizStream ActiveX Controls
    − Version Updating Methods: automatically update when the application tries to use it to access content that requires a new version
    − Events: fire a variety of events

5. WEB RESOURCES

- A Magazine article: http://www.caenet.com/ezine/20000215.html#738

VolVis

1. PLATFORMS, PRICE, AND SUPPLIER/CREATOR

- UNIX
- Free
- http://www.cs.sunysb.edu/~vislab/volvis_home.html

2. APPLICATIONS

- VolVis is a volume visualization system

3. EXAMPLES/SAMPLES

- http://www.cs.utah.edu/~crj/cs523/examples/arrows
- http://www.cs.sunysb.edu/~vislab/animations/

4. WEB RESOURCES

- http://www.neuro.ki.se/neuro/volvis_man/volvis_man2.html#_animatorbut
- http://citeseer.nj.nec.com/364156.html
- http://citeseer.nj.nec.com/hladuvka00curvaturebased.html
- http://citeseer.nj.nec.com/ryall97computerhuman.html

VoxBlast

1. PLATFORMS, PRICES, AND SUPPLIER/CREATOR

- Windows, Mac OS, and UNIX platforms
- Prices:
  - Windows: Express $3,000, real-time $8,500
  - Mac: $3,000
  - UNIX: $5,000
- VayTek: http://www.vaytek.com/index.html

2. APPLICATIONS

- VoxBlast is a fully featured 3D digital imaging application for science, engineering and medicine, providing 3D Measurement, 3D Reconstruction, 3D Volume Visualization, and 3D Rendering. It accepts stacks of registered 2D images and creates 3D projections from any viewpoint using an alpha blending or surface rendering algorithm

3. EXAMPLES/SAMPLES

- Heart rendering: http://www.vaytek.com/heart1.htm

- Ultrasound rendering: http://www.vaytek.com/ultrasnd1.htm

- Other examples: http://www.vaytek.com/vox.htm

- 3D reconstruction: http://www.vaytek.com/AN13.html

- From Hippocampal organotypic culture: http://www.vaytek.com/kraig.html

4. FUNCTIONS/FEATURES

- Tools: for pseudocoloring, transparency, lighting, 2D and 3D measurements, 2D slice viewing, cropping, auto slice tracing, seed fill, movie loop generation, filters, palette editing, surface extraction, polygon rendering, reconstruction, etc.

- Measurement oriented: extract precise information from volumetric data, fractional slice interpolation, calculate volumes in 3 different ways, object counting, get true 3D distances, areas and angles on a 3D surface, generate a standard set of 2D and 3D statistics, histogram, profile and depth plots, etc.

- Two rendering engines: an alpha based renderer for transparency effects, and a polygon renderer for surface rendering, extract surfaces from volumes in VoxBlast (2 1/2D and full 3D) which can be rendered with the polygon renderer or exported to CAD programs, overlay voxel images on polygon images and vise versa

- Network: written in Motif and X11 and includes VoxNet, a Sockets-based protocol for distributing resources on a network

- Standard features: exploring 3D datasets including: viewing from any angle, transparency, pseudocolor with 16 million colors, 2 lighting models, scripting functions with a propriety scripting language (VoxTalk), 2D cutting plane at any angle, up to 4 simultaneous 2D views, clipping plane at any angle, palette editor, movie loop generation, dataset resizing and resampling, flood fill and auto segmentation, and much more

- Image Format options: BMP, IPLab, JPEG, SIGNA, TIFF gray, TIFF and LEICA Multi-Image Color, RAW 8-, 16-, and 24-bit, BIORAD, Metamorph

- Input file format: 8-, 16-, or 24-bit integer, binary, raster scan, any size header — raw, TIFF, Picture, DICOM
- Output file format: 8-bit integer, binary, no header, TIFF, BMP, Alpha blending or surface rendering algorithm, written in X11 and Motif
- Additional Features: Graphical interface, pseudocoloring, scripting functions, merges polygon and voxel data, 2 lighting models, 2D and 3D measurements, Fractional slice interpolation, Cutting plane, Real time rendering with PCI card
- Rendering: creates 3D projections of registered 2D images from any viewpoint using an alpha blending, or surface rendering algorithm and includes tools for transparency and lighting adjustment, movie generation, enhancement filters, and pseudocolor and palette editing

5. WEB RESOURCES

- Vaytek: http://www.vaytek.com/VoxBlast.html
- http://www.linear-systems.com/products/software/specifications/voxblast.htm
- Scanalytics: http://www.scanalytics.com/product/bio/voxblast.html
- Avaluations: http://www.cs.sfu.ca/~jjo/personal/mig/VoxBlast.html
- VoxBlast Quick Reference Guide: http://www.vaytek.com/VBquikref.html

VP-Sculpt

1. PLATFORMS, PRICE, AND SUPPLIER/CREATOR

- PC
- $$$$
- http://www.engr.colostate.edu/~dga/vpsculpt.html

2. APPLICATIONS

- VP-Sculpt is a software tool for editing and reshaping 3D surface models

3. EXAMPLES/SAMPLES

- http://www.visiblep.com
- http://www.lance.colostate.edu/~dga/sculpt_overview.html

4. WEB RESOURCES:

- http://www.cyberware.com
- http://www.porenstein.com/cnc_sculpture.htm
- http://www.computersculpture.com
- http://www.engr.colostate.edu/~dga/sculpt_ref_manual.html

VRCharts

1. PLATFORMS, PRICES, AND SUPPLIER/CREATOR

- Windows 95/98/NT
- N/A
- AlterVue Systems, Inc.: http://www.altervue.com

2. APPLICATIONS

- VRCharts displays charts in 3D and provides analyze numerical data analysis. It is used for a variety of applications

3. EXAMPLES/SAMPLES

- http://www.vrcharts.com/demo/demo_industry_demographic_math.html
- http://www.vrcharts.com/demo/demo_industry_business_OSversions.html
- http://www.vrcharts.com/demo/demo_industry_geographic_swanlake.html

Web Resources

- http://www.vrcharts.com/products
- http://www.vrcharts.com
- http://www.wral-tv.com/news/wral/techtalk/1998/
- http://graphics.software-directory.com/software
- http://www.gina.com/technews/tn/

MindRender Virtual Reality Explore Kit (VREK)

1. PLATFORM, PRICE, AND SUPPLIER/CREATOR

- PC
- $$$$
- Themekit: http://www.themekit.com

2. APPLICATIONS

- MindRender VREK is a software that combines real-time 3D modeling and interactive scene design. VREK as a standalone package is ideal for creating functional, interactive, and immersive environments that can be distributed using the free MindViewer

3. EXAMPLES/SAMPLES

- http://www.themekit.co.uk/t_galsd.htm

4. WEB RESOURCES

- http://www.themekit.com
- The Monthly Virtual Reality Magazine: http://www.vrnews.com

vrTool (VR Developers Toolkit)

1. PLATFORMS, PRICE, AND SUPPLIER/CREATOR

- SGI
- Free
- http://www.lincom-asg.com

2. APPLICATIONS

- VrTool is OpenInventor-based Virtual Reality toolkit to provide a rapid prototyping capability to enable VR users to quickly get their application running with the minimum amount of effort

3. EXAMPLES/SAMPLES

- http://www.lincom-asg.com/VrTool/vrtool.html#Appl

4. WEB RESOURCES:

- http://www.lincom-asg.com/VrTool/vrtool.html

VTK — the Visualization ToolKit

1. PLATFORMS, PRICES, AND SUPPLIER/CREATOR

- PC, Mac OSX, Unix, Linux platforms
- Free, open source
- Kitware, Inc.: http://www.kitware.com/

2. APPLICATIONS

- The Visualization ToolKit (VTK) is an open source software system for 3D computer graphics, image processing, and visualization. It is a higher-level, object-oriented library that facilitates the creation of visual applications
- In VTK, applications can be written directly in C++, Tcl, Java, or Python. VTK has the capability to support a wide variety of visualization algorithms including scalar, vector, tensor, texture, and volumetric methods and advanced modeling techniques like implicit modeling, polygon reduction, mesh smoothing, cutting, contouring, and Delaunay triangulation. Map Info Corporation (NASDAQ) is adding 3D features to their software powered by VTK. VTK is used in the visualization of Diffpack Solutions, which is an object-oriented software environment for scientific computing to achieve interactive simulation and visualization. VTK is also used in the simulations of acoustic fields; CNMAT (Center for New Music and Audio Technologies) at the University of California at Berkeley has developed a system for real-time simulations and visualizations using VTK. It is also used as a parallel rendering and data processing engine at the Los Alamos National Lab

3. EXAMPLES/SAMPLES

- 3D student projects using VTK at: http://www.eng.rpi.edu/~citrit/VisClass/Proj95/
- Visualization examples from a VTK workshop at the University of Groningen: http://www.rug.nl/hpc/VTK/vtk/man.html

4. FUNCTIONS

- Rendering:

  - Surface rendering (supported rendering libraries)
  - Volume rendering
  - Rendering primitives: points, lines, polygons, triangle strips, volumes
  - Properties: ambient color; diffuse color; specular color; transparency; texture mapping; shading (flat/Gouraud); backlighting on/off
  - Lights: infinite; spot
  - Cameras: parallel and perspective projection; nice methods like elevation, azimuth, zoom, reset, and automatic camera/light creation
  - Graphics model: lights illuminate the scene; cameras define viewpoint; actors specify geometry/properties; assemblies group actors into arbitrary hierarchies; mappers define geometry/link into visualization pipeline; renderers coordinate lights, cameras, actors to create image; volumes are a type of actor with their own special properties

- Visualization:

  - Data types: polygonal data (points, lines, polygons, triangle strips); images and volumes (i.e., structured point datasets); structured grids (e.g., finite difference grids); unstructured grids (e.g, finite element meshes); unstructured points; rectilinear grids
  - Cell types: poly-vertex; poly-line; triangle; triangle strip; pixel; quadrilateral; polygon; tetrahedron; voxel; hexahedron; wedge; pyramid
  - Modeling algorithms: spheres, cones, cylinders, cubes, lines, planes, etc., axes, cursors, text, outlines, implicit modeling, decimation, texture thresholding, boolean textures, glyphs, cutting, clipping (2D and 3D), probing, normal generation connectivity, triangle strip generation, 2D and 3D Delaunay triangulation (including alpha shapes), Laplacian and windowed sinc mesh smoothing
  - Annotation: 2D and 3D text; scalar bar (scalar to color index); x-y plots ? Flying axes; overlay plane drawing; attach overlay annotation to 3D positions
  - Features: uses cached, streaming pipeline so that you can operate on gigantic datasets (i.e., deals with pieces of data). This is done completely transparently. Most imaging filters are multithreaded for parallel execution; Fully integrated with 3D graphics/visualization pipeline
  - Filter types: diffusion filters; Butterworth, low-pass, high-pass filters; dilation, erosion, skeleton; convolution; difference, arithmetic, magnitude, divergence, gradient, mean distance; FFT; Fourier, Gaussian, Sobel; histogram; threshold; permutation, conversion, padding

- File Formats:

  - Data Interface (Readers/Writers treat a single dataset; Importers/Exporters treat a scene). A variety of polygonal formats including stereo-lithography, MOVIE.BYU, Cyberware, PLY, etc.
  - VTK formats for all data types; Inventor Writer, IV Exporters; 3D Studio Importer; PLOT3D; PNM; RIB (RenderMan) Exporter; SLC (Volume) Reader; TIFF Reader and Writer; VRML Exporter and Importer; Wavefront .OBJ Exporter, .OBJ Reader; BMP reader and writer; Raw image format

5. WEB RESOURCES

- User Mailing List: http://public.kitware.com/mailman/listinfo/vtkusers
- Applications: http://www.kitware.com/vtkinuse.htm
- Examples and resources: http://www.barre.nom.fr/vtk/links-examples.html
- Book: http://www.amazon.com/exec/obidos/ISBN%3D0139546944/kitwareA/104-8390323-0566366

Vue d'Esprit 3

1. PLATFORMS, PRICES, AND SUPPLIER/CREATOR

- PC (Windows 95/98/2000, or NT 4)
- $199 standard; $99 upgrade
- E-on Software: http://www.e-onsoftware.com/Products/Vue3/index.htm

2. APPLICATIONS

- Vue 3 is a high quality 3D application that has been optimized for the creation, rendering, and animation of natural scenery. It uses elaborate outdoor lighting algorithms together with advanced rendering features to produce natural looking pictures. Dynamic Motion Reaction technology brings realistic motion to the scene, with full animation capability. Objects can be linked together to create complex animated structures, materials can be animated and a timeline provides precise control over all animation properties

3. EXAMPLES/SAMPLES

- E-on Software Vue d'Esprit Gallery: http://www.e-onsoftware.com/Gallery/Gallery.phtml
- Tropic of Capricorn: http://www.digitalblasphemy.com/dbgallery/6/capricorn.shtml
- Area 3D: Duel: http://spawns.free.fr/images/duel.jpg

4. FUNCTIONS

- Motion blur
- Advanced ray tracing engine

- Automatic velocity smoothing
- Spline based object motion
- Timeline for accurate animation control
- Ten types of adjustable motion reaction
- Optimized memory management and threading
- Automatic polygon mesh splitting
- Alpha and depth channels for compositing
- Editable object pivot points
- Countless presets
- Extended Compatibility
- Supported Formats
  - 3D Import: 3DS, LWO, OBJ, DXF, RAW, DEM, TGA
  - 3D Export: 3DS, LWO, OBJ, DXF, TGA, BMP, JPEG, GIF
  - 2D Import: BMP, JPEG, GIF, TGA, DEM
  - 2D Export: BMP, JPEG, GIF, TGA
  - Animation Export: AVI, BMP, JPEG, GIF, TGA

5. WEB RESOURCES

- Vue d'Esprit users Webring: http://www.ethervizion.com/vuewebring/
- Vue d'Esprit mailing list: http://www.egroups.com/community/vuedesprit
- Vue d'Esprit community links: http://www.e-onsoftware.com/Home/Community.htm

Wilbur

1. PLATFORMS, PRICE, AND SUPPLIER/CREATOR

- PC Windows 95, 98, and NT 4.0 operating systems
- Freeware
- Copyright by Joseph R. Slayton, at: http://www.ridgenet.net/~jslayton/software.html

2. APPLICATIONS

- Wilbur is a terrain editor, allowing a user to import terrain in a number of popular file formats. Wilbur is then used to modify the height and terrain data, which is then re-exported to any file format. It is used to:
  - Create maps of the physical world, whether of the existing Earth or of notional worlds, such as those used in wargaming and role-playing
  - Analyze terrain information contained in maps
  - Edit exiting maps
  - Conversion of data from one file format to another

3. EXAMPLES/SAMPLES

- http://www.ridgenet.net/~jslayton/tutorials.pdf — A list of tutorials describing how to run sample programs

- http://www.ridgenet.net/~jslayton/wsample/index.html — These are quick examples generated by the software author

- http://www.ridgenet.net/~jslayton/cshelf/index.html — A description of how to use Wilbur to model continental shelves

- http://www.remotesensing.org/gistrans/mail/msg00079.html — Use of Wilbur in file conversion

4. FUNCTIONS

- Modeling:
  - The primary primitive used in Wilbur is the height field. From height fields, the program will calculate texture maps and surfaces based on the field data, then color the map to show both height and slope information. In addition, Wilbur can also be used to create synthetic height fields and surfaces generated by the following algorithms: Plasma, Math function, Fractional Brownian Motion, Multifractal, Hetero Terrain, Hybrid Multifractal, and Ridged Multifractal

- Rendering:
  - Wilbur models the universe using a ray tracing model, and offers a number of advanced rendering functions. To start, the user viewpoint may be altered to almost anywhere on the map, and may zoom in and out on particular points. In addition, Wilbur offers the following functions: Clipping, Scaling, Threshold/posterizing (Used to convert a smooth surface into a series of obviously discrete steps), Area Sampling, Convolution, Blur Surface, Sharpen Surface, Cosine distortion, Inverse Cosine distortion, Sphere-mapping, Fluvial Erosion, Flip Surface, Resample/Quad Resample (using the following interpolation algorithms, if requested: Nearest Neighbor, Linear, Spline Interpolation, B-Spline Approximation, Beta Spline Approximation), Rotate, Offset, Backfill, Flood fill, Differencing, draw, paint, generate seas, find lakes, icosahedral projection, phase maps, quilt maps, and slope maps. It can also utilize the

following common map projections: Albers Equal-Area Conic, Azimuthal Equidistant, Equidistant Conic, Equirectangular, Gnomonic, Hammer, Lambert Azimuthal Equal-Arca, Lambert Conformal Cone, Mercator, Miller Cylindrical, Mollweide, Orthographic, Sinusoidal, Stereographic, Van Der Grinten, Wagner IV, and Wagner VII

- Wilbur also uses a sophisticated lighting model. There is exactly one light source, and the user can specify the geometric relationship of the light to the surface, whether a particular surface is lighted, the color depth, palettes to use for lighting, light based on altitude, light intensities (including ambient lighting and gamma correction), as well as light changes due to change in altitude or latitude. In the future, the user will also be able to specify different lighting based on slope, facing, or blending

- Animation:

  - There are no facilities for animation in Wilbur; it is a terrain editor

- File Formats:

  - PGM, DXF, BIN, BRC, BR3, TXT, MAT, MDR,DTE, PCX, INC, DT1, RAW, RD4, TGA, TER, TIN, DEM, OBJ, BMP

5. WEB RESOURCES

- In addition to the resources listed here, the software, its users manuals, and tutorials for Wilbur can be downloaded at the creator's website

- http://www.cfxweb.net/files/Detailed/708.shtml — Discussion of terrain rendering using Wilbur

- http://itg.stud.hint.no/hf/advanced/advanced.html — Advanced use of height fields in Wilbur

- http://oz.irtc.org/ftp/pub/anims/1998-01-15/schnecky.txt — Use of Wilbur

WorldBuilder

1. PLATFORMS, PRICES, AND SUPPLIER/CREATOR

- PC (Windows NT or 2000)

- Standard Version: $399; Professional Version: $999; Ordering information: http://www.animatek.com/buy.htm

-

- Digital Element: http://www.digi-element.com/index.shtml; AnimaTek International: http://www.animatek.com/index_frame.htm

2. APPLICATIONS

- WorldBuilder is a high-end comprehensive solution for modeling, animating, and rendering ultra realistic, fully functional 3D landscapes for use in computer graphics, architecture, game development, and movie production. WorldBuilder is the standalone 3D landscape tool that can work as a plug-in for 3D Studio MAX, 3D Studio VIZ, LightWave 3D, or Maya NT projects. It has been used in a number of games such as Final Fantasy Tactics, Warzone 2100, and Age of Empires

3. EXAMPLES/SAMPLES

- WorldBuilder Gallery: http://www.renderosity.com/gallery.ez?Sectionid=15

- http://www.digi-element.com/Images/awb30/Igor/desert_sunset.jpg

- http://www.digi-element.com/Images/awb20/Gallery/deepforest1.jpg

- http://www.animatek.com/demos_awb20.htm#movies

- http://www.animatek.com/images_awb20.htm

- http://www.animatek.com/users_gallery.htm

- http://www.geocities.com/SiliconValley/Code/3467/awb.htm

- http://www.voodoo-u.com/jpday.html

- http://www.homepet.com/3d/wb3.html

- http://www.umr.edu/~tcaton/images/forest.jpg

- http://www.atomic-animation.com/barr.htm

- http://www.3dlinks.com/landscape3d/g01.htm

- http://www.geocities.com/SiliconValley/Program/1794/movies_AWB.htm

4. FUNCTIONS

- Modeling with animation components:
  - Import existing landscape data or create your landscape precisely as you envision
  - Hundreds of ready-to-use animatable 3D models of plants, skies, rivers and more
  - 3D plant editor with user-friendly interface
  - 3D plants, sky and rock variators — a way to create complex scenes
  - Dynamic communication technology to work together with 3DS MAX, 3DS VIZ
  - Import/export and compositing utilities for LightWave 5.x and 6.x
  - Import/export and compositing utilities for Maya NT
  - Wind wizards make animating 3D plants, clouds, and surf easy
- Rendering:

- Rendering engine supports translucent objects (a-buffered rendering)
- Translucent objects can be rendered in an arbitrary order and still give the correct results
- Performs anti-aliasing of object edges (aa-buffered rendering)
- Max Communicators supports use of a- and aa-buffering for composite rendering with Max. This allows usage of AWB for volumetric lighting and fog in Max scenes, rendering of Max objects under WorldBuilder water and more
- Support for network rendering
- File Formats:

    - Importing file formats: 3DS, DXF, LightWave (MOT, LWS, LWO), AliasWavefront OBJ, USGS, VistaPro DEM, and Archive
    - Exporting file formats: 3DS, DXF, LightWave (MOT, LWS, LWO), VRML and Archive
    - Additional file formats are available through plug-ins

5. WEB RESOURCES

- WorldBuilder Resources provided by Digital Element: http://www.digielement.com/resources.shtml

- 3DLinks List of WorldBuilder resources: http://www.3dlinks.com/landscape3d/

- Eyerender — a new site dedicated completely to WorldBuilder: http://www.eyerender.com

- http://www.animatek.com/

- http://www.animatek.com/index_frame.htm

- http://www.geocities.com/SiliconValley/Foothills/6734/incdes.htm

- AnimaTek's resources page: http://www.animatek.com/awb_news.htm

- Discussion forum: http://www.animatek.com/board/

- Technical demos: http://www.animatek.com/techdemos.htm

- Support: http://www.animatek.com/support.htm

- Tutorials: http://www.animatek.com/tutorials.htm

WorldToolKit

1. PLATFORMS, PRICES, AND SUPPLIER/CREATOR

- Windows 98, NT and 2K, Linux, and UNIX

- Windows NT: $4,200. SGI: from $4,200. SGI IRIS, Indigo, Indigo2 and Crimson: $5,000. SGI VGX, VGXT and VTX; and Sun SPARC: $7,500. SGI RE, RE2: $9,500

- Sense8 Product Line.: http://www.sense8.com/

2. APPLICATIONS

- WorldToolkit is cross-platform real-time 3D development tool. With the high-level API, you can quickly prototype, develop, and reconfigure applications. WorldToolKit R9 supports network-based distributed simulations, CAVE-like immersive display options, and interface devices including headmounted displays, trackers, and navigation controllers

3. EXAMPLES/SAMPLES

- Mars Rover (Created with WorldToolKit): http://www.sense8.com/demos/ ROVER.EXE

- Unicenter TNG (Created with WorldToolKit): http://www.sense8.com/demos/ dl.exe

4. WEB RESOURCES

- A review article from bubu.com: http://www.bubu.com/baskara/wtk.htm

- An article: http://www8.techmall.com/techdocs/TS990809-2.html

WorldUp

1. PLATFORMS, PRICE, AND SUPPLIER/CREATOR

- PC Windows 95/98/NT

- $2000.00

- Sense8: http://www.sense8.com/

2. APPLICATIONS

- A 3D modeling, rendering, and simulation tool that is good at creating various VR worlds

3. EXAMPLES/SAMPLES

- http://www.sense8.com/demos/wup_demos.html

4. WEB RESOURCES

- Download the World Up Modeler for free: ftp://ftp.sense8.com/pub/utils/WUPModeler.zip
- Download a demo version of World Up Simulation Editor: ftp://ftp.sense8.com/pub/demos/wup/wupdemo.exe
- The World Up User's Guide (PDF): http://www.sense8.com/products/userguide.pdf

Xara3D

1. PLATFORMS, PRICES, AND SUPPLIER/CREATOR

- Mac OS 7.5.3 or higher; Windows 95/98/NT/2000
- $$$ / Free Trail Version is Available
- Xara: http://www.xara.com/

2. APPLICATIONS

- Xara3D is used to create quality 3D titles and logos for use on webpages. The images that are created by using Xara3D can be exported to other applications such as Macromedia, Flash, and Photoshop

3. EXAMPLES/SAMPLES

- Xara 3D shape samples: http://www.xara.com/products/xara3d/examples/shape.asp
- Xara 3D examples: http://www.xara.com/products/xara3d/examples/animated.asp
- http://www.graphicssoft.about.com/compute/graphicssoft/cs/xara3d/

4. WEB RESOURCES

- http://www.xara.com/downloads/xara3d
- http://www.xara.com/support/
- http://www.graphicssoft.about.com/compute/graphicssoft/cs/xara3d/

- http://graphicssoft.miningco.com/compute/graphicssoft/library/weekly/ aa072899.htm
- http://www.xaraxone.com/xara3d4/tutorial.htm
- http://wdvl.internet.com/Reviews/Graphics/Xara/

XGL

1. PLATFORMS, PRICES, AND SUPPLIER/CREATOR

- UNIX
- Free
- SUN Microsystems: http://www.sun.com

2. APPLICATIONS

- XGL is a graphics library developed by SUN Microsystems. The XGL library supports a number of graphics application programming interfaces (APIs), including other graphics libraries such as GKS and PHIGS. The XGL system requires a window system to manage drawing operations sent to a display device

3. WEB RESOURCES

- Online documentation: http://docs.sun.com/ query.html?qt=XGL&dc=titl&ed=all&Ab2Lang=C;Ab2Enc=iso-8859-1
- XGL file format specification: http://www.xglspec.org/

ZBrush

1. PLATFORMS, PRICE, AND SUPPLIER/CREATOR

- Mac and PC (Operating System)
- $292.50
- Pixologic: Http://www.pixologic.com (www.ZBrush.com)

2. APPLICATION

- ZBrush, a blend of traditional and innovative tools from Pixologic lets you create complex, high quality graphics while expressing yourself quickly. It gives instance feedback — your images render in real-time. ZBrush's unique combination of 2D and 3D capabilities yields impressive results, without putting you though a long learning curve

3. EXAMPLES/ SAMPLES

- http://www.geocities.com/pixelator2000
- http://pixologic.com/gallery/gallerylo.html

4. FUNCTIONS

- Modeling: ZBrush allows users to paint not only colors, but also material and depth information, all in the same brush stroke. It also includes light and object modeling tools and can use 3D objects for inclusion in the painting. ZBrush includes primitive objects, as well as the capability to create new objects for sculpting, which can be saved or exported for use in 3D applications

- Color/Texture: ZBrush uses Pixols, rather than pixels, to retain color, material, and depth information. Pixols (pixels) handle all required calculations for 3D effects, allowing lighting and depth effects to appear as the user paints

- Light: ZBrush allows you to place virtual light in your scene. You can control the number of lights and their properties. You can modify the lights configuration during the creation process and even at the end of the creation process, ZBrush will quickly update your canvas to reflect the new lights' settings. This makes it easy to start your drawing with default lights, and keep experimenting and modifying the properties of the lights at any time, to achieve the desired look

- ZBrush Scripting: A new text-based scripting functionality which allows ZBrush actions and functions to be automated and tailored to fit the need of the user as well as allowing ZBrush to participate in an existing art production pipeline. The scripting language is easy to use and in most cases does not require any programming skills, the user can simply create a script by recording their actions and is able to replay these scripts on demand

- Note: This is not simply a "macro" recording, it is a scripting language that can further be edited by the user in order to create "smart" scripts that can produce complex sets of action in a single key press. Further more, ZScripts allow a user to keep a record of their creation process and by re-playing these scripts, the user is able to view these scripts, share these with other users as well as able to re-use theses scripts when creating other similar object/images

- ZBrush interactive tour and tutorials: ZBrush scripting is also used in creating interactive tutorials that can reduce the "learning curve" of ZBrush and to allow users to learn advance ZBrush and art techniques by simply viewing script session that have been pre-recorded by other expert artists

- 2D/3D masking: Many ZBrush operations can now be "masked" by using 3D masks (which are applied directly to a 3D object) or by using an innovative floating stencil which allows 2D and 3D operation to be masked by a planar stencil which is placed in the canvas and can be made to "warp" itself on existing canvas topography

- 3D Import/Export: 3D import/export capability in DXF and OBJ formats that allows ZBrush to work with other existing 3D packages. 3D objects created in other applications, such as Max, Maya, Lightwave, and such can be imported into ZBrush, painted on, and re-textured by retaining the assigned UV coordinates and exported back to be used in other 3D application while retaining vertex count and order — which allows for Morph targets creations). ZBrush editing is not limited to color modification (which is the case with other 3D painting applications), in ZBrush, the actual geometry can be modified and exported while retaining the vertex count and order which allows these 3D objects to be used as Morph targets or simply be included in a 3D scene/3D animation

5. WEB RESOURCES

- http://www.electrowebanimation.com/reviews/articles/zpaint/index.htm — Review of the latest ZBrush version 1.23

- http://www.zbrushcentral.com — On line forum for ZBrush users. The ZBrushCentral.com forum is a forum designed to train ZBrush artists around the world. Outfitted with ZMovie tutorials, ZBrushCentral is a place to post questions, comments, images, tools, etc.

- http://the-internet-eye.com/Reviews2001/August/ZBrush123/default.htm

- ZBrushCentral: On line help/forum: http://www.ZbrushCentral.com

Index